Chiefs, Agents & Soldiers

Chiefs, Agents & Soldiers

Conflict on the Navajo Frontier, 1868–1882

William Haas Moore

University of New Mexico Press
Albuquerque

Library of Congress Cataloging-in-Publication Data

Moore, William Haas, 1947–
Chiefs, agents, and soldiers: conflict on the Navajo frontier,
1868–1882 / William Haas Moore.—1st ed.
p.   cm.
Includes bibliographical references and index.
ISBN 0-8263-1475-9
1. Navajo Indians—History.
2. Navajo Indians—Government relations.
3. Indians of North America—Government relations—
1869–1934.
I. Title
E99.N3M687   1994
973'.04972—dc20   93-35896
CIP

To Ginny

CONTENTS

FIGURES

(following page 136)

MAPS

Preface

The history of conflict between American Indians and the United States is partially explained and greatly confused by crucial American myths. Although they tell important truths about the people who composed them, they often limit explanations to landmark events that become static symbols of catastrophe or of resolution. Unfortunately, they neglect to tell us much about times after these events. Paradoxically, in a field dominated by myth, Native American myths receive little attention.

According to the Navajos, life began in the womb of the earth in the Black World, a small universe inhabited by Mist Beings. Among the first of these supernatural spirits was the trickster, Coyote, and it was within this embryonic world that the Navajo pantheon was born. First Woman was formed when yellow and blue clouds merged in the West; she represented darkness and death. In classic duality, another god, First Man, who symbolized dawn and became known as the Life Giver, emerged in the East. After four tries, he managed to meet First Woman. Despite this fortunate union, the Black World was quickly overpopulated, and the beings living there fought among themselves.[1]

Movement was the answer. Floating upward, the beings traveled east into the Blue World, a land already inhabited by other creatures. This new universe was a place of sorrow that did not have room for everybody. After making sacrifices, the supernatural people were able to journey south and up to the Yellow World.[2]

Although not large enough to hold all the beings, the new world was larger than the areas below. It was inhabited by many spirits. Among them was Water Monster, who had a baby. First

Woman convinced Coyote to take the child, and he grabbed it, hiding it under his arm. As a result, the waters rose, and a flood followed. After four attempts, the people escaped. Once they were in the fourth world, they discovered the baby and urged Coyote to put it back. When he did as he was told, the waters receded.[3]

The beings had reached the final world and called it Glittering. Narrative concerning the Glittering World is the story of the founding of life as it now is. It includes the creation of the Four Sacred Mountains, the building of the stars and traditional hogans, as well as an explanation of death and the origins of ceremonials. It contains a tale of the separation of the sexes, which explains how male and female oppose and complement each other. It also describes the birth of the Navajo mother goddess, Changing Woman, who was born of darkness and fathered by dawn. Maturing rapidly, she conceived her twin sons. When they learned that their father was the Sun, they journeyed to see him. After passing tests, the Twins were given the power to rid the world of monsters that had been terrorizing it.[4]

At the end of this myth, which details movement and constant change, the Navajos entered history. Coming to the Southwest just prior to the Spanish, the *Diné*, as the Navajos called themselves, used traditional Native American clans to organize themselves loosely. Originally a nomadic people, they made change a way of life. Borrowing some of their myths and ceremonies from the Pueblos, they also began acquiring and raising Spanish livestock, and by the time of Mexican rule they had become a regional military power.[5]

Unfortunately, their adaptability came at a price, and Navajo society was hardly stable. Warfare had become constant. Their linguistic cousins, the Apaches, living to the south and east, stole Navajo livestock. Mexican armies, both official and unsanctioned, invaded Navajo country looking for sheep and slaves. The Utes also contributed to the slave trade by considering Navajo women and children as commodities easily exchanged for goods in Santa Fe. And the Pueblos, viewing themselves as victims of Navajo aggression, were potential allies for any military force that wanted to inflict damage upon the Diné.[6]

The Navajos resented their neighbors, but internal conflict kept the Diné from following a consistent policy that might have kept them out of war or brought them victory. The *ricos*, men who owned large flocks, favored diplomacy, but the poor, who relied on raids to enhance their wealth, insisted that conflict continue. Despite the fact that the ricos held most positions of authority, they were not able to control their humble relatives.[7]

The Americans conquered New Mexico in 1846. According to Navajo secular myth, the Diné welcomed them. Finally, they had allies in their war against the Mexicans. Much to their surprise, however, the Americans insisted that raids on settlements stop. This seemed ridiculous to the Navajos, especially since Mexican and Ute forces continued to invade their lands in search of livestock and slaves. With such provocation, poor but ambitious men continued to attack their neighbors. The United States Army retaliated, which usually led to a treaty, followed by provocation, Navajo retribution, army counterattack, and another treaty negotiated by the ricos. This process continued until the Civil War.[8]

When the South left the Union in 1861, American military units were withdrawn from New Mexico. The newly created Confederate States of America was quick to invade from Texas. Although the Confederate attack was successful at first, militia units from Colorado and New Mexico eventually defeated the invaders. Meanwhile, an army assembled in California under the command of Colonel (soon to be General) James H. Carleton marched east to free New Mexico of the rebel menace. When he arrived too late to participate in the Civil War, Carleton decided to take on the "wild" Indians of the territory, the Mescalero Apaches and the Navajos. His war against the Navajos was fought during the winter of 1863–64 by Kit Carson and the New Mexico Volunteers. By the spring of 1864, the Navajos were a defeated people, and over eight thousand of them were exiled to the Bosque Redondo Reservation along the Pecos River in eastern New Mexico.

The Bosque Redondo years (commonly referred to as the Fort Sumner years after the fort near the reservation) are the central terror of Navajo secular myth. The trip to the Bosque was filled with stories of starvation and the kidnapping of women and children into slavery. Once they arrived in eastern New Mexico, conditions did not get any better. There was not enough to eat. They tried to raise crops as directed by the army, but their attempts failed. Carleton reasonably hoped to transform a people known for adaptability, but they refused to alter their culture substantially. Finally, in 1866, leaders who were able to consolidate power in the face of horror arrived at the Bosque. Ultimately, a treaty was signed in 1868 that allowed them to return home. Despite the fact that they had ended their exile, the Navajos now had to confront American power.

Like the Spanish and the Mexicans, the American conquerors carried Christian creation accounts with them, but they also believed in a secular origin myth that explained their greed for land. In its emphasis on change and movement, it resembled the Navajo myth. According to their tale, Europe, the Old World, was overpopulated and corrupt. A few brave individuals dared to leave. Venturing across dangerous seas, they came to the New World, which was populated only by savages. Without the influence of the old ways, a new breed of individualistic and democratic person was created. This new citizen formed a society that should have led to Utopia. After time, however, the new land experienced overpopulation, and it was time for more individuals, symbolized by Daniel Boone, Davy Crockett, and Kit Carson, to move like the Navajo spirit people to other worlds. Through several generations, they kept moving—always west—into newer and more perfect worlds until the fading of the frontier in 1890. Nevertheless, America was still more perfect than the rest of the world; it became the glittering symbol of human potential.[9]

In large part, the Anglo-American origin myth adequately explained the conquest of a continent; in fact, it gained respectability as historical theory. An important addition to the myth, however, has lost its intellectual respectability because it offered justification for the poor treatment of Native Americans. As far as the myth was concerned, the Indian was a part of nature. Like the wilderness, he should be conquered. He was either a simple, ignorant savage who had to be conquered or a noble, uncomplicated savage who possessed innocence far beyond the capabilities of his white counterpart. In either case, he was destined to vanish as an archaic notion of the past, or to live on as a poor imitation of his white conquerors.[10]

So go the myths. They describe two cultures compelled to deal with modern change. Despite the fact that these myths assist in understanding that openness to change was what helped both peoples adapt to the modern world and survive in it, neither Navajo nor Anglo-American myths go beyond pivotal events. How the Navajos lived through events after their defeat, exile, and repatriation is the subject of this study.

If the vanishing Indian myth was true, the Navajos should have suffered extinction or assimilated into the greater North American population. The fact is that they survived as Navajos. They and other Indian peoples adapted to new circumstances. How, and on whose terms, Indians changed is a historical topic just beginning to be explored. The histories of many Indian nations after U.S. military victories are few. There are some volumes dealing with government policy and a few concern themselves with Indian–government relations, but much more research about the various tribes has to be done concerning the crucial times immediately following military conquest. Many questions need to be asked. For example, how many peoples suffered psychological defeat? How did the tribes react to government policy? Which groups assimilated quickly into the larger society; who stubbornly resisted change, and who adapted according to their own priorities? Which Indian nations emerged from conflict and which ones died out? The answers to these questions and others will end a rather static view of American Indian history.

In his influential work, *The Great Plains,* historian Walter Prescott Webb stated that life for Indians after their military defeat was little more than imprisonment on reservations.[11] If the Navajos are any indication, Webb was wrong. American Indian societies were complex and hardly the same, but studies of postconquest American Indian history are needed to look past the seemingly obvious. A first step in understanding is the realization that conflicts and accommodations between native peoples and their neighbors did not end with military dominance and the accumulation, on one side, of superior numbers.

This fact is especially true for Navajos. Unlike some conquered peoples, the Diné played a great role in shaping their own destiny in the post–Bosque Redondo years. Yet, their accomplishment does not hold an important place among their own national myths.[12] Neither is it emphasized by Anglo-American sources.

Once back in their homeland, the Navajos faced two basic problems in addition to obtaining enough food. The treaty had not provided them with sufficient land, and the tribe had to avoid war. To alleviate the first problem, many Navajos simply lived off the reservation. It seemed, at first, that this Navajo solution to the land problem would lead to war, but it did not. In the time immediately after the Navajos' return home, non-Navajo settlement in lands previously occupied by the Diné was made primarily by Mexican Americans who faced discrimination at the hands of federal authority and were unable to provoke a war. Also important in this regard was the basic tactic of the Navajos' holding off-reservation land. They were militant enough in their occupation to scare off would-be interlopers and moderate enough in their response to government representatives to lessen official demands. As a result, the Indians avoided war. Nevertheless, they could not avoid conflict.

Navajo hunger and poverty added to this conflict. The government did not adequately provide for the Navajos. The Indian Bureau was slow in delivering rations, and when food finally reached Fort Defiance, there was rarely enough to go around. The treaty had also promised fifteen thousand sheep, which were late in arriving and were too few to revive the Navajo economy. Many Navajos resorted to theft from their neighbors. Since raids endangered the whole tribe, the Diné had reason to continue to rely upon the chiefs. Acting as keepers of the peace, the chiefs did not have an easy job. Tradition dictated that they use persuasion as a method of control, and it was impossible to stop all raids. Nevertheless, Navajo leaders reminded their people of the Bosque Redondo and managed to keep depredations to a minimum.

Modern anthropologists, in observing isolated populations of Navajos during the twentieth century, have noted the informal structure of Navajo leadership and concluded that the chiefs were figureheads at the beck and call of agents. What these scholars have neglected is the fact that nineteenth-century Navajo leaders were useful to their people as well as powerful. The government had picked men who already had substantial followings, and recognition of these men by soldiers and agents only increased their prestige. Although the chiefs did not constitute a formal government, they met as a council and did a credible job. They seldom acted as pawns for any agent.

Nonetheless, the chiefs had to deal with agents because these representatives of the nation that had conquered the Diné administered civilian power and controlled the issue of rations and annuities. The agents had dictatorial power in theory, but they had to share it with the chiefs who were charged with persuading their people to avoid serious conflict. This was a difficult task since conflict was normal on the Navajo frontier. The chiefs, however, were usually equal to the challenge, for they proved at least as effective in controlling their own people as the United States government was in controlling its growing population in the Southwest.

Another factor in their early successes was the cooperation of the first three agents, who were practical men with military experience whose actions, if not always their words, showed that they were not interested in achieving the other goals of government policy if they interfered with maintaining the peace. They spent a great deal of time trying to get enough supplies and rations to restore the Navajo economy. They were often unsuccessful. By working with the army, however, they managed to keep the Indians from starving. These agents also ended up respecting the chiefs and winning their cooperation.

Therefore, President Grant's first Indian policy, in which army officers were utilized as agents, was successful as far as the Navajos were concerned. With the support of the military agents, the Diné had been able, without formal government, to move toward a sense of themselves as a people and as a nation. Although they were dependent on the government for food and supplies, the Navajos managed to do some of the things that nations do. They had expanded their land base by settling off the reservation, they had maintained a semblance of peace on their frontier, and they had dealt with their criminals according to their own customs.

This independence contradicted the ideals of most Americans, and it appeared to be endangered when President Grant, in a fight with Congress, gave control over Indian appointments to the Protestant denominations. The Navajos were given to the Presbyterians. The implementation of policy was left up to the agents, and the men sent by the Presbyterians to Fort Defiance were less sympathetic to the Navajos than their military counterparts. They were also less competent, more likely to act according to preconceived notions, and less inclined to learn from circumstances.

To Navajo leaders, many of these agents were threats to their power and to Navajo needs. They often engineered rebellions, many of which were successful. Where they distinguished themselves from other Native American leaders was in eventually winning their battles with agents. They managed to do so by enlisting the support of the military and several powerful traders who lived in their territory.

The officers stationed at nearby Fort Wingate had to deal with the Navajos as much as the agents at Fort Defiance. Although they removed Navajo livestock from military lands and were exposed almost daily to Navajo beggars, drunks, and prostitutes, they had come to respect the Diné and their leaders. Most of these officers had fought Indians all over the West and had concluded that the Navajos were a uniquely vital and intelligent people who wanted to improve their material condition and live at peace with their neighbors.

Mixed with this admiration of the Navajos as a peaceful people, however, was a military concern about fighting a Navajo war that worried even General Sherman. The Navajos were the largest tribe in the Southwest and the thought of fighting them was terrifying, especially since a few hundred Apaches were tying down most units in the region.

Reflecting this concern was the army's willingness to grant autonomy to the Diné. For the most part, they were willing to allow the Indians to handle their criminals in their own way. They regularly refused to move the Navajos onto the reservation and attempted to protect the Diné from settlers and prospectors. It also seemed that the chiefs were always welcome at Fort Wingate. Furthermore, when the Navajo leaders had a serious disagreement with an agent, the officers at Fort Wingate supported them. Even though this support can be seen as part of a larger conflict throughout the West between military men and civilian agents, what appears to be unique is that the chiefs sought military support and consistently provided the army with assistance.

As historians L. G. Moses and Raymond Wilson have commented, "the patterns of leadership among Indians have yet to be sufficiently explored, let alone explained." Nevertheless, there has been a tendency to lump native leaders in the nineteenth century into two categories: (1) leaders who resisted whites to the bitter end, and (2) leaders who recognized the inevitable and attempted to reach accommodation with Americans of European descent.[13] It would be difficult to fit post–Bosque Redondo Navajo leaders into either category, for the leaders themselves were a cross section of their society prior to Kit Carson's victory.

The three principal leaders, Barboncito, Ganado Mucho, and Manuelito, were all rich men prior to Kit Carson's attack, yet their methods of dealing with Anglo-Americans were different. Barboncito had long been a peace leader prior to the 1860s, and his tactic had long been accommodation. When Carleton let it be known that the Navajos must leave their homeland or be attacked, Barboncito begged the general to reconsider. Carleton, however, could not be persuaded. Characteristically, Barboncito was one of the first to surrender after Carson's invasion. But the chief had not anticipated the terror of the Bosque Redondo Reservation, and he led an escape of five hundred of his followers in the summer of 1865. Attacked by New Mexicans, Utes, and Pueblos, his freedom was perilous, but he managed to hold out for over a year and was the last of the three principal leaders to surrender.

Ganado Mucho, of Hopi and Navajo ancestry, had attempted to remain neutral and sought refuge in his lands west of the Defiance Mountains. Despite provocation, his tactic had worked prior to the winter of 1863–64. Then Carson came with orders to round up all Navajos. Ganado Mucho went to war, although the struggle proved unequal. Hiding throughout the region, he did not surrender until the spring of 1866.

Unlike his two contemporaries, Manuelito had become famous as a warrior. Distrustful of the Americans, he rarely agreed to peace. When Kit Carson's troops attacked, there was little doubt about what Manuelito would do. He went to war. Since Carson's scorched-earth tactics surprised him, his war turned into a simple struggle for survival. Nevertheless, he held out until the fall of 1866, and his passionate style of leadership continued to frighten Anglo-Americans until his death.

Actually, Manuelito was as able to accommodate the conquerors as the others were, but there was something about his mercurial personality that kept officials off balance. In the end, he became the symbol of Navajo resistance at the Bosque, although it was Barboncito who negotiated the treaty. After their return from exile, Manuelito continued to be a symbol. Although Barboncito was named head chief by the government and Manuelito shared power with Ganado Mucho after Barboncito's death,

Manuelito's unpredictable combination of defiance, accommodation, and open rebellion was the tactic adopted by his fellow leaders.

Most Navajo leaders were willing to hunt down fellow Navajos who raided. Although Manuelito and Ganado Mucho rarely inflicted fatal punishment upon their fellow tribesmen, they did what had to be done to maintain the peace. At times, they asked the army to interfere in internal Navajo affairs, but they were also instrumental in removing agents and expanding the reservation by intimidating settlers, recruiting army and mercantile allies, and reminding the military that war was a possibility. Navajo leaders operated in a baffling manner, ever impressing upon their people that they should adapt to Anglo-American rule but also demanding their rights as a people. Although they often appealed to what seemed to be a static tradition of consensus and fragmented rule, they were really invoking the larger tradition indicated in Navajo myth, namely, that change was what enabled the people to survive new worlds. Thus, they established a new tradition of central power that later consolidated the Navajos into a nation, and it generally served the common good until the scandals of Chairman Peter MacDonald.

Unfortunately, the achievements of these leaders and the Navajo people have not been documented by historians. But as historian Peter Iverson has remarked, the Navajos are among the most studied Indians in North America.[14] Nevertheless, the late nineteenth century has been largely ignored.

The Navajo histories that have been written, however, are useful for any reader wishing to begin a detailed study. Two writers, for instance, have dealt with the Bosque Redondo. Lynn R. Bailey writes of the crimes committed by the government while the Navajos were in exile. Although Bailey has the power of moral indignation behind his narrative, he is short on detail. Much more factual is Gerald Thompson's history. Through the careful use of detail, he chronicles the administrative horrors of a poorly planned and executed social experiment. Thompson also covers the reactions of Navajos.[15]

The next detailed narratives concern Navajos in the twentieth century. Lawrence C. Kelly has written a significant study of Navajo relations with the government from 1900 to 1935. Donald L. Parman has studied the Navajos during the New Deal years, and Peter Iverson has explored Navajo developments since World War II. These authors have also included excellent background chapters concerning earlier Navajo history.[16]

Works that include nineteenth-century Navajo history after the Bosque Redondo are many, although they hardly include enough information to draw a complete picture. Most of the early survey histories were written by anthropologists such as Richard Van Valkenburgh, Ruth Underhill, and Robert W. Young, and they contain useful, if isolated, details about the Navajos and their relationships with the military, their agents, and their neighbors.[17] A number of popular authors have also attempted to survey basic events. The two most prominent, John Upton Terrell and Raymond Friday Locke, draw much of their information from the general histories written by anthropologists. They provide highly readable accounts that, nevertheless, contain information that is fragmentary and out of chronological sequence.[18]

In addition, there are scholarly works in print that try to make sense of events in nineteenth-century Navajo history. Edward Spicer, in his *Cycles of Conquest*, includes a chapter on the adaptations made by Navajos in the 1800s; it contains important insights. David F. Aberle attempts to make a brief analysis of conflict among the Navajos in his classic study of Peyote religion. In *Roots of Dependency*, Richard White examines social change among the Navajo in relationship to their environment and patterns of subsistence. Garrick Bailey and Roberta Glenn Bailey, in what they call an "ethnohistory," have published a detailed history of the Navajo culture and economy.[19]

A number of books and articles also give detailed insights into more specific events, regions, and individuals. Frank Reeve, in a series of articles in the *New Mexico Historical Review*, outlines the development of Navajo relations with the United States government and surveys the conflict over land between Navajos and

Anglo-American settlers in northwestern New Mexico. Frank McNitt's *The Indian Traders* covers the lives of several men who lived among the Navajos, while Lawrence R. Murphy carefully explores the life of one of the Navajos' most controversial agents, William F. M. Arny. And David M. Brugge has written a remarkably detailed history of Navajos living in the Chaco Canyon region of New Mexico.[20]

Finally, two recent books deal with Navajos in the nineteenth century. Robert S. McPherson, in his *The Northern Navajo Frontier*, analyzes the relationships between the Navajos and their northern neighbors—both Anglo and Native American—between 1860 and 1900. In *"New Hope for the Indians,"* Norman J. Bender traces the evolution of Grant's Peace Policy among the Navajo.[21]

Nonetheless, there is no year-to-year narrative of Navajos from the time of their return from exile in 1868 until roughly the beginning of World War I. It is easy to understand why this gap exists; any attempt to fill it would take several volumes. Nevertheless, such a study would deepen our understanding of a great people. The story of the Navajo fight for survival in the face of Anglo-American expansion would not only make interesting reading; it would also serve as a source with which to reexamine the conclusions reached by scholars who have looked at the late nineteenth century with limited access to details.

This volume attempts to begin the process of examining late nineteenth-century Navajo history in detail. Beginning with the defeat and exile of the Navajos in 1864, it focuses on a period lasting from 1866, when the principal Navajo leaders—Barboncito, Ganado Mucho, and Manuelito—surrendered until the removal of the last Peace Policy agent in 1882. This was a time when the Navajos were almost constantly involved in conflict; yet, they were able to establish themselves firmly upon their reservation, hold lands not granted to them in the treaty of 1868, and develop a sense of themselves as a people. It may be argued that it was during this period that the Navajos learned enough about dealing with Anglo-Americans to avoid being overwhelmed by the large number of settlers who came with the Atlantic and Pacific Railroad in the early 1880s.

Whenever possible, this study attempts to record the voices of the Navajos and their leaders, although there is a limitation inherent in the historical process: the documents that record Navajo events were written by Anglo-American observers. Nevertheless, it is hoped that Navajo actions and words, when they appear in the documents, will convey their thoughts.

This study uses primary sources extensively, but it also attempts to synthesize the scholarly works of others, especially Brugge, McNitt, and Reeve. A number of regional and military histories are relied upon to bring the Navajo experience into focus in light of other developments in the Southwest. Books concerning the evolution of United States Indian policy also have been cited, and a number of anthropological texts have been consulted as well. Finally, for benefit of the reader who wishes to read further or to study the nature of literature about Navajos, books of a more popular and general nature have been cited whenever they make mention, no matter how briefly, of events that occur in the narrative.

It is hoped that this history will provide for a far broader understanding of the history of the Navajos, a successful people who have thrived in spite of forces that, upon surface examination, might have seemed overwhelming.

Acknowledgments

This book was originally written as a dissertation in a doctoral program in history and political science at Northern Arizona University, but the fact that there was need for a history of post–Bosque Redondo Navajos had been suggested to me years before: by my colleague at Puerco Elementary School in Sanders, Arizona, Bill Farnham; by essays from two of my students at Puerco, Delores Noble and Raymond Smith; by Dr. James Kearny at Arizona State University; and by Eugene Dennison of Tohatchi, New Mexico.

At Northern Arizona University, I was lucky to have my research and writing guided by excellent scholars. Dr. William. H. Lyon, with his deep understanding of Navajo history, was extremely helpful in my efforts to narrow my topic and in directing me to the right sources. Dr. L. G. "George" Moses also assisted in locating sources. In addition, George was excellent at editing for style, as was Dr. William Burke of the English Department. Another contributor was Dr. Dan Cothran of the Political Science Department, who insisted that the narrative needed a more coherent thesis.

My fellow graduate students at Northern Arizona University offered useful advice and information, especially Laura Graves and G. Dudley Acker. It was Dudley who helped me to understand why the United States Army in the West feared a Navajo war in the late nineteenth century. He was also generous in allowing me to borrow books from his large personal library and in doing routine research chores for me when I could not get to Flagstaff. Laura Graves, on the other hand, was able to help me with materials on Thomas Keam and share her extensive insights into Navajo and Hopi history.

ACKNOWLEDGMENTS

Unlike many writers of history, I have had to do most of my research and writing in a rural area far from research libraries. Fortunately, I have been able to rely on several of my colleagues at Chinle High School, Chinle, Arizona. Steve Pavlik shared books from his personal library, and Joanne Wood, Chinle High's librarian, helped me obtain materials through interlibrary loan. Finally, other colleagues provided useful help by reading manuscripts and providing other assistance: Kim Keller, Ardie Maddox, Lon Mason, and Bill Rees.

My special thanks also go to Miss Octavia Felin of the Gallup Public Library. She was always helpful. Other librarians, who will have to go unnamed, provided invaluable assistance at the following libraries: Navajo Community College, Tsaile, Arizona; Northern Arizona University; the University of New Mexico; Arizona State University; and the University of Arizona.

I must also thank Dr. Peter Iverson of Arizona State University for helping me get this manuscript to the University of New Mexico Press. At the Press, David Holtby has offered invaluable service for the past few years. Most importantly, he has been instrumental in tightening the narrative. He has also been encouraging.

Finally, I must thank my wife, Virginia Flores Moore, without whom I would never have even begun this project. Ginny was more than patient during those times when I hid in the little room I call my office to write. Ginny, this is for you.

Chiefs, Agents & Soldiers

1
Exile

In the fall of 1862, the California Volunteers under the command of James H. Carleton trekked across the deserts of the Southwest to free the New Mexico Territory of a Confederate menace originating in Texas. Arriving too late to eliminate the Texans, Carleton conceived of a more ambitious endeavor. Since the withdrawal of federal troops at the beginning of the Civil War, the "wild" tribes of the territory, particularly the Mescalero Apaches and the Navajos, had waged increased warfare against New Mexican settlements. He meant to restore peace.[1]

Even though war between Indians and New Mexicans had a long tradition with blame on both sides, Carleton took the predictable view that the Indians were responsible. Dissatisfied with the previous policy of negotiating treaties pledging the tribes to peace, he proposed a three-stage plan. He called for unrelenting warfare upon the tribes, their removal from traditional homelands, and a complete reform of their ways of life.[2]

Carleton chose Colonel Christopher "Kit" Carson to carry out the initial phase of his plan. Concentrating first upon the Mescaleros, Carson and his New Mexico Volunteers achieved quick victory and rapidly moved the prisoners to the site of Carleton's grand social experiment, the Bosque Redondo along the Pecos River in eastern New Mexico.[3] The next target was the more populous Navajo tribe.

Navajo leaders were aware of the threat. The leadership, however, was divided. The peace faction generally represented the powerful and wealthy ricos, who had much to lose in war, whereas the warrior group spoke for the poor and the young who made their fortunes by raiding nearby communities. Further complicating this division were the ties of family and clan. The peace

1

leaders, however, sought to head off disaster. In December of 1862, eighteen of them, including such noteworthies as Barboncito and Delgadito, journeyed to see General Carleton in Santa Fe to beg for a treaty. He rejected their appeals. Another attempt was made in April, but Carleton again rejected their supplications, telling them there would only be peace when the Navajos surrendered and moved to the Bosque Redondo. Carleton's demands were too much for even peace leaders to accept.[4]

Meanwhile, Carson made preparations for his campaign. A base was established at Fort Wingate. Troops were stationed at Ojo del Oso to protect supply lines. Carson also resettled old, abandoned Fort Defiance and renamed it Fort Canby. With preparations thus made, he began his campaign in July of 1863 by dispatching his forces from Fort Canby.[5]

Carson adopted a scorched-earth policy. Marching forcefully across the Navajo homeland, his New Mexico Volunteers, along with Ute, Hopi, Apache, and Zuni allies, found few Navajos to fight. Because their horses suffered from the harsh winter and were unable to live on native grass, Carson's men were compelled to abandon their animals, attack the Navajos on foot, and endure many forced marches. By December, morale was low.[6]

The Navajos, on the other hand, were even more desperate. Carson's volunteers spread out over the land. They burned crops, killed livestock, contaminated water supplies, and relentlessly kept the Indians on the run. Starvation was overcoming Navajo resistance.[7]

Finally, in January of 1864, Carleton ordered Carson to invade the Navajo stronghold in Canyon de Chelly. To Carson's surprise, his troops were able to march through the canyon without a single casualty. Many Navajos were forced out of hiding.[8]

This invasion proved to be the climax of the campaign. Navajos began to surrender in such large numbers that Carson, faced with more prisoners than he had expected, forbade further capitulations in March. Soon, parties of Navajos, escorted by troops, traveled to Bosque Redondo. This "Long Walk" became notorious among the Navajos. They would tell tales of a forced march wherein stragglers were gunned down to hurry along the caravan. Food supplies and transportation were limited, resulting in hunger and fatigue. The Navajos felt horror, and their subsequent oral histories would naturally blame the army.[9]

Despite the problems that accompanied the march to the new reservation, there were, by July, nearly six thousand Navajos resettled at the Bosque. There would be more coming shortly, and at its highest, Navajo enrollment in Carleton's experiment would surpass eight thousand.[10] Nonetheless, the general's success was short-lived, for the other aspects of his plan could not be realized.

Carleton claimed that his plans were humanitarian toward the Indians and utilitarian for whites. Whereas he removed the Indian menace and opened former Native American homelands to settlement, he also imagined that his plan to alter Indian life radically would help the aborigines advance into what he believed to be the superior ways of his own civilization. The Navajos would have to abandon their pastoral ways and become sedentary. They would learn Euro-American farming methods and congregate in settled communities. Their children were to attend schools run by Catholic priests. In such a manner, they would become independent yeomen and eventually take their place among the American citizenry.[11]

Carleton's plan failed despite his goals. Several factors led to this failure. The site of the reservation was poorly chosen. The water was brackish and so unfit for human consumption that the Indians complained that it made them sick. Army rations were new and unfamiliar to the captives. Housing was poor and firewood was nearly nonexistent. The soil was infertile.[12]

Other problems, institutional and social, begged for solution. Army and civilian Indian officials debated over who was responsible for the reservation. Two New Mexico superintendents of Indian affairs—under the Department of Interior—denied that the Bosque Redondo was a good idea and left the cost of maintaining the Indians to the army. Meanwhile, in an era in which the spoils system ran rampant, the army supply network had serious shortcomings. Shoddy, overpriced, and often useless merchandise was delivered. Tainted food was sold at exorbitant prices. Furthermore, the Navajos and Mescaleros, although they were linguistic cousins, proved to be poor neighbors and, as with many other efforts at relocation, planners had failed to account for people already residing in the area. Comanches and Kiowas, for example, menaced Navajo livestock and lives, and eastern New Mexican ranchers at first resented such a large intrusion of Indians into their region.[13]

The biggest problem, however, was that the Indians, convinced that their formers lives were wholly adequate for their needs, were not in the mood for rehabilitation. The Mescalero Apaches evacuated the reservation in 1865, and the Navajos resisted their conversion by applying considerable intellect and ingenuity.[14]

The Navajos nevertheless suffered severe psychological trauma. Navajo separation from their homeland was horrific. Disease was rampant, and medicine men claimed that the poor health of their people was the result of living beyond the tribe's Four Sacred Mountains. More immediately, people went hungry. The Navajos also experienced a desperation that led to the breakdown of morality and a reduction of their self-esteem.[15] To emphasize these terrors to the exclusion of other realities, however, underestimates Navajo cultural tenacity, which belied all rumors of their demise. The Diné, as the Navajos called themselves, displayed psychological strength and managed somewhat to conrol the effects of their exile.[16]

One indication of Navajo management of their exile was the way in which they responded to the army's wish that they become sedentary farmers. They had been marginal horticulturalists before their entrapment, but their yeomanry was supplemental to their pastoral economy. The Navajos nonetheless labored faithfully in their fields because there was a chance that crops might improve their condition. They learned some Euro-American irrigation techniques as well as how to use manufactured farm implements. They changed their dietary habits to accommodate the food supply. If the provisions proved to be inadequate, Navajos became adept in forging ration tickets and finding alternate sources of nourishment. The Navajos also learned some habits of dress from the whites, and many took advantage of their incarceration to learn new skills such as smithing.[17]

If the Navajos proved adaptable when it came to food and clothing, they nevertheless proved to be equally obstinate in resisting innovations that appeared useless. They resisted, for instance, Carleton's insistence that they live in permanent adobe structures. Navajo mores dictated that a dwelling in which some- one had died be abandoned. Thus, when the new structures proved to be no more comfortable in the winter than the traditional hogan and more difficult to abandon, they simply refused to live in them. They likewise saw no immediate gain from the removal of children from useful pursuits and insisted that the priests pay them for the privilege of teaching their children. The Diné were also reluctant to accept changes in their religious belief or their pastoral inclinations. Proselytize though they might, mission- aries met with negative results, and any Navajo who could main- tain even the smallest flock of sheep or herd of horses did so.[18]

Such resistance, if troublesome, was at least nonviolent. But not all attempts at tribal and individual autonomy were as peace- ful. Navajos often resorted to force, and this violence became progressively worse the longer they stayed at the Bosque Re- dondo. As early as the summer of 1864, Navajo raids of New Mexican ranches were reported. Although most of the raids were the work of Navajos who had not surrendered, or of other tribes, the strong suspicion existed that those on the reservation were equally as guilty. As each year passed, it became more and more obvious that the Indians, living with constant hunger, were likely to fill their stomachs by whatever means necessary.[19] By the summer of 1866, rustling from New Mexican herds was so bad that the Santa Fe *Daily New Mexican* reported:

The whole country swarms with Indians hostile and bloodthirsty. On the west side of the Rio Grande the people are harassed by Navajos who have remained in their own country in preference to joining those of their tribe at the reservation, and who hold out in defiance of General Carleton's threats and coaxings. On the eastern side of the Rio Grande, the country is overrun by Indians from the Bosque Redondo Reservation, who have already destroyed stock and property to the amount of many thousands of dollars, and slain many of the best citizens ... Unless something is soon done to protect the people, they will take the matter into their own hands and avenge their massacred friends and relatives by killing every Navajo found outside the reservation—passport or no passport. Let this idea be carried out and we will guarantee that in short time the Navajos that are left will be content to remain inside the limits of the reservation.[20]

Despite such frontier farrago, which occasionally inspired retribution in other circumstances, the Navajos continued to do what they had to do in order to survive.

The army was aware of how difficult the Navajos were to control, and it was usually reluctant to punish them. Understanding that the garrison at nearby Fort Sumner was under strength, officers in charge often relied on mere threats of retaliation. Navajo leaders, it may be assumed, knew this and dealt with authorities from a position of limited strength. On the other hand, aware of their people's hope of going home and desirous of not antagonizing the military, they urged moderation. The efforts of Navajo leaders were successful for the most part. In fact, the Bosque Redondo experience served as a counterweight to government wishes in its promotion of tribal unity and the enhancement of the prestige of Navajo leaders who learned how to handle relations with the white man. They would use this knowledge for more than a generation to come.[21]

As with leaders of other Native American groups, Navajo headmen had originally been selected, and expected to govern, by consensus. Unlike many leaders in other tribes who suffered a loss of credibility for cooperating with white authorities, most of the Navajo leaders managed to keep their constituents loyal by adopting tactics that would serve them well. They would, for example, turn in egregious offenders and justify their actions to the Diné by appealing to the traditional Navajo belief that the few must not bring punishment upon the many. At the same time, they would plead for leniency for the guilty. They were also able to use the threat of army retaliation as a method of gaining obedience. Meanwhile, they continued to urge that the tribe's most pressing concern—that they be allowed to go home—be granted.[22]

The world had become a dangerous place for the Navajos and their worldview. That the tribe happened to blunt most government programs for Navajo "improvement" into the early twentieth century cannot be attributed solely to blind luck, lack of desire for Navajo land, or the incompetence of government officials. Much of the credit must go to the Navajos themselves and their leaders. These "chiefs" were often severely restrained by demands for consensus; yet they acted in behalf of a highly adaptive society determined to survive.

American officials awarded authority to Navajos already in possession of some power. Determining leadership at the Bosque Redondo nonetheless proved difficult prior to the summer of 1866. Federal policy was based upon the idea that the government dealt with only a few Indian leaders who would bargain for the tribe. But at the beginning of the experiment, there were few leaders with enough stature to command respect. Barboncito, known for his tough diplomacy, might have been an early spokesman for the Diné. Shortly after his somewhat early surrender, however, he became disillusioned with Carleton's utopia and fled eastern New Mexico. Herrero had only a limited following. As a result, the responsibility of government recognition fell upon Delgadito, who had originally been identified as an "Enemy Navajo," one of a band of people long noted for their cooperation with Spanish, Mexican, and American representatives. Although he had briefly helped in the fight against the Americans, some doubt remained about his limited resistance during the Kit Carson campaign. He had been instrumental in arranging for the early surrender of himself and several other ricos, a surrender that was suspected of aiding in Carson's victory.[23] His position, therefore, was vulnerable. Bosque Redondo politics, however, would soon fall under the command of more forceful diplomats and warriors who were tardy in their surrender.

Navajo oral histories, as recorded in Ruth Roessel's *Navajo Stories of the Long Walk*, often indicate that Manuelito was the principal leader at the Bosque Redondo.[24] Actually, he was not, according to documents left by military and civilian officials. The fact that he is remembered as such, however, is significant, for this broad-shouldered, dashing figure symbolized the way the Navajo people remembered their resistance. Born in 1818, he had become an important war leader at an early age. Although he had amassed considerable wealth and, at times, had given in to the pleas of the peace faction, he remained a persistent foe of accommodation with the Diné's enemies.[25]

When Kit Carson's militia struck, Manuelito was determined to fight. Under Carson's style of warfare, his resistance was reduced to fleeing the invaders and keeping his forces together. He was successful in avoiding Carson. He retreated to the Grand Canyon, but some of his followers soon deserted him. Constantly on the move and attacked by Ute, Hopi, and New Mexican raiding parties, he hid in such diverse places as the Zuni Mountains; Black Mountain, to the west in Arizona; and the Escudillo Mountains, among the Coyotero Apaches. His resistance proved futile and, finally, in September of 1866, he surrendered: tired, hungry, and deserted by most of his followers.[26]

Ganado Mucho, like Manuelito, had also retreated to the Grand Canyon and lived among the Coyoteros, but he was a different kind of leader. Of both Hopi and Navajo ancestry, Ganado Mucho was a cautious man who was inclined toward diplomacy. He was, after all, a wealthy man with large herds of cattle and sheep. His tranquility was, nonetheless, severely disturbed by the unwise actions of the American military in the late 1850s.[27]

It would have been unremarkable had Ganado Mucho gone to war, but he did not, even when his fellow leaders did. During the 1859–61 war, he remained at home in his territory west of the Defiance Mountains and maintained neutrality. His policy proved to be successful. When private New Mexican expeditions marched into Navajo territory in 1862, in search of livestock and slaves, he still managed to avoid conflict. Kit Carson's invasion the following year was a different matter, however. Carson's orders called for the capture of *all* Navajos. Already filled with distrust of Anglo-Americans, Ganado Mucho rejected the capitulation of his fellow ricos and retreated. But by the spring of 1866, harassed by Pueblo, New Mexican, and Ute raiders, he had had enough. Ganado Mucho surrendered and was escorted to the Bosque Redondo. Although his arrival at the reservation with his large herds had some of the trappings of a majestic spectacle, it was marked with tragedy, for two of his daughters had been taken as slaves en route.[28]

Barboncito, who lived in Canyon de Chelly, had long been known as a peace leader, but he reluctantly turned warrior in 1860. With Carson's invasion, he was among the first to surrender, but he rapidly experienced a change of heart. Finding his confinement unbearable, he escaped with five hundred others on the night of June 14, 1865. He was hunted by New Mexican militia units, but he avoided capture.[29]

Despite the elation he might have felt after the outbreak, freedom proved hazardous. Utes were merciless in their attacks. New Mexicans crisscrossed Navajo haunts, eager to collect spoils and slaves from their old enemies. Pueblo Indians harassed Navajos without hesitation. Finally, in November of 1866, Barboncito returned to the Bosque.[30]

By the time Barboncito, Manuelito, and Ganado Mucho had reached the reservation, the Bosque Redondo had become an administrative nightmare. Because of its expense, Carleton's experiment had already come under considerable scrutiny. Investigations by various federal officials had become commonplace, especially after the Sand Creek Massacre of Cheyennes in 1864. One of the most famous of these investigations was a special joint congressional committee headed by Senator James R. Doolittle of Wisconsin. It was not, however, solely concerned with Navajos.

Accompanied by Theodore H. Dodd, civilian agent to the Navajos, the Doolittle Commission briefly examined the reservation in June of 1865, just days after Barboncito's escape. Then it moved on to Santa Fe, where hearings were held. Among the witnesses was Herrero, who testified to the cruelty of the enlisted men at Fort Sumner. Most non-Navajos giving testimony appeared to agree with General Carleton's policies, but Senator Doolittle sensed that the situation at the Bosque Redondo was critical. He documented several abuses. Once back in Washington, the committee recommended that the Interior Department conduct an investigation of its own.[31]

Special Indian Agent Julian K. Graves was appointed to conduct the follow-up. Heading out from Westport, Missouri, in November of 1865 with Agent Dodd and a train of supply wagons destined for the Bosque, Graves moved on alone when the wagons were stalled in a blizzard. Arriving in late December with bad news—there would be no additional food—his initial exposure to the reservation could not have been less promising. His reaction to the site was nonetheless favorable. Critical of some Indian Bureau personnel and the lack of supplies, Graves was impressed by the immensity of Carleton's project and recommended that the reservation be expanded.[32]

Graves was, however, made aware of Navajo opposition to their continued stay at the Bosque Redondo. At a council with fifty or sixty headmen, he listened to their complaints, and their message was strong and clear: they wanted to go home. As one spokesman said, they were like an eagle tied to the ground, wanting freedom and constantly looking to the sky. These leaders complained that the reservation was unhealthy and that they were doomed if they remained. Even though they pledged they would raid no more, Graves belittled their concerns. He told the council that within a few years life would be so good at Bosque that they would never dream of returning to their homeland.[33]

In opposition to Graves's optimism were many problems. There was large-scale antipathy toward Carleton's experiment. Called "Fair Carletonia" by New Mexico politicians and newspaper editors, the reservation was not self-supporting. It depended upon food supplies that were rarely adequate. Most importantly, the

Navajos were bristling with dissatisfaction. In all too human terms, they wanted to return home where they could feel more whole as individuals, and they were ready to provide their own solutions. It was obvious that the small garrison at Fort Sumner could do little if the Navajos decided to take matters into their own hands.[34]

One method by which the Navajos could take control of their own destinies was to leave the Bosque Redondo and take their chances in the hostile outside world. By the early summer of 1866, there were 6,915 Navajos left at the Bosque, down from an enrollment of 8,491 a year before. Part of this decline was accounted for by deaths, particularly from a measles epidemic, and a low birthrate, but much of it was due to desertion. The problem of Navajos leaving was exacerbated by the fact that there was not enough food. Recognizing this fact, the military allowed Indians to leave with passports to hunt. Many on leave never returned. Others left without passports.[35]

As desertions continued, it became clear that the Bosque was too large for the army to police. Standing as an example of General Carleton's poor planning was the reality that the Bosque Redondo lay right in the path of the infamous Comanchero trade. It was based upon booty collected by Comanches and Kiowas in Texas, which was sold for food, alcohol, guns, and ammunition to southeastern New Mexican traders. Navajo flocks and herds were important temptations for Comanches and Kiowas heading out of the Lone Star State to make their bargains. As a result, raids were frequent.[36]

The task of policing the Navajos and protecting them from unwelcome intruders fell in large part to the Navajos themselves. The traditional structure within which Navajo leaders had worked had been eliminated; leaders now had to operate within the sanction of government authority.[37] This alteration, however, did not amount to a substantial change because Navajo culture was adaptable.

It was thus that Barboncito, Manuelito, and Ganado Mucho were propelled into leadership. These men found themselves

11

faced with a difficult situation. The Navajos could not afford to be malleable wards. This fact was dramatically illustrated just weeks after Ganado Mucho's surrender.

More than one hundred Comanches attacked the Navajo horse herds. They killed the herders, one of whom was Ganado Mucho's son, and stole two hundred head. Soldiers managed to locate their trail, pursued them, and eventually engaged them in combat on July 14. The battle, however, was indecisive. The Comanches fled east, and the soldiers could not keep up. The commander of Fort Sumner, Captain William McCleave, placed picket posts to the east to protect Navajo property and lives, but even McCleave doubted the effectiveness of this defense.[38]

A year later, this spectacle would move Ganado Mucho to rare eloquence. Stricken by personal tragedy, he addressed New Mexican Superintendent of Indian Affairs A. Baldwin Norton in bitter irony. He pointed out that the Navajos had come to the Bosque because they had been promised safety. But what had they gained when their enemies were better armed than they and the army could not protect them?[39] Ganado Mucho's immediate instincts remained in character despite his caustic remarks, made after twelve months of rumination. He apparently did not organize resistance or plan an escape; instead, he reluctantly cooperated.[40]

Upon Manuelito's arrival, he also seemed accommodating. He saw the short supplies at the fort and volunteered to lead hunting expeditions, although Comanche and New Mexican war parties made the task dangerous. It was on one of these outings that Manuelito discovered errant Navajos with stolen New Mexican stock at Mesa de Leon, some twenty miles north of Fort Sumner. Manuelito attacked the rustlers and captured two of his tribesmen and eight horses. He turned his prisoners and the horses over to Mescalero Apache Agent Lorenzo Labadie at Agua Negra.[41] Manuelito's policing of his own people might have encouraged authorities, but there was enough of the unreformed individual in his behavior to mark him as less than a collaborator. Indeed, his militancy inspired fear in white officials.

Barboncito arrived at Fort Sumner late in 1866. If his surrender brought relief to the military, the ancient diplomat took no note-worthy action during his first few months at the Bosque.[42] More dramatic events were stirring.

Raids by Navajos became more frequent. New Mexicans complained that the Bosque Redondo contributed to these depredations because the hostiles could retreat to their homeland, trade their spoils for different stock, turn themselves in at Fort Wingate, and obtain military escort to the Bosque Redondo, where they would be safe from citizen retaliation.[43]

Whether or not Navajos practiced such complicated subterfuge mattered little, for the forces in New Mexico opposing the Bosque Redondo, hearing rumors that General Carleton was on his way out, were mobilizing. Territorial Secretary William F. M. Arny and New Mexico's territorial delgate in Washington, J. Francisco Chavez, relayed concerns from their constituents expressing the opinion that the Navajos should be repatriated.[44] In addition, the government transferred budgetary responsibility for the Bosque over to the Indian Bureau. The Indian Bureau claimed that it could not afford to support the Navajos. The army would have to continue its funding of the experiment; such reluctant resolve led to a desire by the War Department to alter its Navajo policy.[45]

The Navajos, in the meantime, continued their desperate struggle to survive at the Bosque, planting crops as directed but refusing to sit idly and starve. Raids continued, especially after Carleton was removed from command and replaced by the less determined General George W. Getty. The new commander of Fort Sumner, Colonel George Sykes, set up more pickets to keep the Navajos from leaving, but this precaution was ineffective.[46]

When several citizens were killed sixty miles west of Fort Sumner near Mesa de Leon, Sykes sent out an expedition under the command of Captain Elisha W. Tarlton. Tarlton's reconnaissance was unsuccessful. It seemed inevitable that conflict would occur between the Navajos and the army. Yet while tension continued to build, the Diné also had to occupy themselves with the Comanches, signs of whom were observed almost every day.[47]

In July of 1867, what could have been a major provocation occurred. On July 8, Agent Dodd was informed by two Navajos that they knew of a canyon twenty-five miles south of the fort where outlaws among their own people were hiding stolen horses. Dodd went to see Captain Tarlton, temporary post commandant, with his two informants in tow. Tarlton sent out a detachment of twenty-one men commanded by Second Lieutenant Henry Bragg, whose orders were to exercise caution and return with the horses. Under the guidance of the Navajo informers, Bragg marched his soldiers to a site near the canyon and waited until morning.[48]

Arriving in the canyon at daylight, Bragg, along with a Mexican interpreter, attempted to explain his purpose to the Indians. Once Bragg felt that he had conveyed his meaning, the soldiers rounded up approximately one hundred head by nine o'clock. The interpreter stated that the stock was probably not stolen. Bragg, however, had his orders. He directed Sergeant Terrell and four others to begin driving the horses toward the fort.[49]

On the way back, Navajos, thinking that the soldiers had stolen their property, stampeded the herd. Sergeant Terrell took his greatly outnumbered party back to the fort. Bragg, unaware of what was happening, managed by noon to collect some fifty additional horses. Then he proceeded to the fort. Five miles from his destination, Bragg was also confronted with the same Indian trick, although he was less quick than Sergeant Terrell in understanding the situation. He sent Sergeant Myers and two men after the horses. They were fired on. When Bragg heard the shots, he charged, determined that his force of eighteen men was greatly outnumbered by over two hundred Navajos, and wisely and rapidly retreated to the fort.[50]

The officers inside Fort Sumner were poorly prepared to equal Bragg's wisdom. Captain Tarlton had been drinking heavily with Lieutenant Charles Porter. When Sergeant Terrell reported the first encounter with the Navajos, Tarlton ordered Porter to investigate with twenty men. In later testimony, Porter would state that he had requested an interpreter and Tarlton had said that one was not necessary; Tarlton would claim that a translator was unavailable. Nonetheless, Porter found two hundred Navajos blocking his path. They gestured violently at the soldiers. Porter tried to speak to them in Spanish, but they would not answer. Sensing danger, the lieutenant began to move his small unit to more strategic ground. Tragically, events took a turn for the worse.[51]

An old Navajo mounted on a white horse entered the hostile group motioning wildly. None of the soldiers knew what he was trying to do, but they assumed he was a chief. Bitter Water, a Navajo nonparticipant who witnessed the fray, would later testify that the elderly Indian was not a chief, but the owner of some of the horses who wanted to ask Porter why his stock was being taken. Someone, probably Lieutenant Porter in his drunken confusion, fired in the old man's direction. Then the Navajos opened fire. The soldiers beat a disorderly retreat, chased by the Navajos, until they topped the hill overlooking Fort Sumner. Five soldiers had been killed. Several others, including Porter, had been wounded.[52]

The spectacle of United States troops running from a column of Indians undoubtedly shocked the soldiers at the fort, but it also alarmed Navajo leaders. One of the headmen, Narbono, observed diplomatically that it was like a quarrel between brothers. Manuelito took more dramatic action. When Lieutenant Robert McDonald, an officer respected by many Navajos, decided that further violence could be prevented by talking to the hostiles, Manuelito grabbed his horse and attempted to stop him from going. Once he decided that McDonald would go anyway, Manuelito and several other Navajos joined the lieutenant's party.[53]

McDonald's detachment wasted no time in heading south to meet the hostiles. Major Tarlton and Delgadito rode along, but neither proved to be of much use, the former because of his drunkenness and the latter because of his reputation as a white man's Indian. When the group reached the Pecos, the angry Navajos were on the other side and obviously prepared for a confrontation. They had provided what protection they could for their women and children and had drawn up for battle. Manuelito and McDonald, however, were determined to make peace. Leaving the soldiers and their Navajo allies behind, the two men crossed the river. They told the hostiles, who turned out to be mostly young men, that the army had not intended to steal their horses. It had simply wanted to inspect them to determine whether or not they had been stolen. With Manuelito, the most respected Navajo warrior, by McDonald's side, the angry young men were soon pacified. A situation that could have resulted in the loss of hundreds of lives had been diffused.[54]

When the bodies of the four soldiers left on the field (a fifth man had died after reaching the fort) were recovered, a good portion of their clothing was missing, and their bodies were covered with wounds. The garrison was profoundly aware, in the sobering aftermath, of what could have happened. There was resentment among the soldiers. Realizing this, Navajo leaders began to exercise diplomacy. On July 12, three hundred headmen, probably every Navajo with political clout, met with Agent Dodd. They apologized for the actions of a few. They also explained that the trouble had arisen because of a misunderstanding. The conference broke up amicably, and Agent Dodd was convinced that there would be no further trouble. Meanwhile, the Navajo participants in the battle began slipping away from the reservation.[55] Whether or not they did so at the insistence of their leaders is not known, but the calmness of the Navajos prevented further trouble. In the history of Indian–white relations, wars had been caused by less serious matters.

When the army investigating officer, Lieutenant Colonel John W. Davidson, reached Fort Sumner in August, the situation remained peaceful if tense. Davidson found that the incident had resulted from the indiscreet behavior of Major Tarlton and the incompetence of his officers, with the exception of Lieutenant McDonald. Davidson further recommended that General Getty be reprimanded for leaving the fort under the command of such inappropriate officers. No Navajos were punished.[56]

The fact that the incident had been settled in the Navajos' favor might have convinced an ordinary citizen removed from the scene that the tribe had received an excellent lesson in American democracy. They had killed five American soldiers, but American justice had determined that they were not at fault. The Navajos, however, did not see it that way. They were still prisoners. They wanted to go home. More violence seemed inevitable.

New Mexican Superintendent of Indian Affairs Norton visited the Diné shortly after the clash. Although he found that they harbored no resentment, he was informed that their basic desires had not changed. Ganado Mucho complained bitterly about the inability of the Navajos to protect themselves from Comanche raids. Most of the talking that day, however, was done by Herrero. The Comanches had informed him that the Bosque Redondo belonged to them, and he believed it. After all, they were always in the vicinity. He also protested that his people lived with constant hunger and requested that the Navajos be allowed to go home. Once there, they would subject themselves to United States authority and never complain, even if they did go hungry.[57]

In August, General Getty held a talk with selected Navajo leaders: Manuelito, Ganado Mucho, Barboncito, Narbono, Delgadito, and fifteen others. Agent Dodd also attended with interpreter Jesus Arviso, a Mexican captive who had long lived with the Navajos. Getty opened the meeting by saying that he regretted the recent battle. Then the Navajos had their say. Their message was again clear.[58]

Delgadito spoke first. Probably speaking more to his fellow tribesmen than to the officers, he attempted to account for his long accommodation with the army. Then, in speaking of his repeatedly unsuccessful attempts to plant crops, he admitted that he was homesick. Next, Barboncito voiced his complaints. The Bosque Redondo had impoverished his people; even he, a leader, possessed only his body. The land was no good for crops.

He pleaded for the Navajos' exile to end. He requested that his words be carried to the president.[59]

As the Navajos left the council, they seemed satisfied, but government officials could not relax their guard. Violence always appeared as a possibility. As the summer ended, it was clear that the crops would again fail, and rumors began to circulate that there would be a large-scale outbreak. Steps were taken to supplement the Indians' diet with Texas beef. But if the meat arrived in time to keep the Navajos from starving, little could make up for their continued loss of pride, which was intensified by a Comanche raid in September. Two women were captured, and the Navajos were too poorly armed to pursue. Then, on September 26 and 27, predictions of a Navajo outbreak came true when between 200 and 250 people led by Manuelito, Barboncito, Ganado Mucho, and Muerto de Hombre escaped from the reservation.[60]

Navajo dissatisfaction undoubtedly played a role in the escape, but the immediate reason concerned a band of Utes who had stolen a few horses. This was too much for some Navajos. They headed out in pursuit of the Utes, and they did not come back.[61]

Government officials were quick to act. Superintendent Norton wired a request to Washington for four thousand blankets to pacify the remaining Indians. His request was given quick review and granted. Meanwhile, scouting parties were sent out from military posts all over the territory. In addition, New Mexican militia units roamed at large, looking for the escapees. It was the territorial expeditions that proved to be effective. In the middle of wild speculations concerning their whereabouts, the refugees surrendered; they claimed that there were just too many Mexicans in the countryside for it to be safe.[62]

If the flight of these leaders seemed inconsistent with their growing influence and power, it only appeared so in the eyes of whites. Prevailing opinion still agreed with Chief Justice John Marshall's concept that the tribes were "domestic dependent nations." Inherent in this idea were many inaccurate assumptions. One of these was that tribal leaders were potentates who wielded unlimited authority. Another was that nationalism was a dominant phenomenon.

Neither of these assumptions fit the Navajos. The experience of being subjects in General Carleton's social experiment had moved them toward a kind of "national" identity to which they previously had not been accustomed, but it was only in its beginning. Leadership was still a highly personal and informal matter. Such factors as clan relationships, personal heroics or charisma, an ability to deal with enemies, and wealth contributed to the choice of leaders. Leadership was fluid and uncertain. Although Navajo culture held, as one of its ideals, that the actions of a few should not endanger the many, this code did not go beyond a limited group. Patriotism was, as yet, a foreign ideal. It was for this reason that at the many councils Navajo leaders often spoke about themselves and their families instead of tribal interest.[63]

In 1867, tribal unity was an experiment that might bring power to the Diné, but the outcome was not certain nor was the etiquette of mass leadership set. Thus, when the rising national leaders fled the reservation, they were not criticized by Navajos left behind. Indeed, they were praised by some for resisting their white guards, and the omen raised by their unsuccessful flight undoubtedly heightened their bargaining authority with officials increasingly concerned about the fragility of the Navajo peace.

The opinion was growing in 1867 that the Navajos could not long be held at the Bosque except by more force than could be easily mustered. With Carleton and his overwhelming will gone from the territory, few people other than those making a profit in supplying the Navajos advocated a continuation of the Bosque Redondo. Others with influence in the territory, in addition to William F. M. Arny and J. Francisco Chavez, agreed that the Navajos should be allowed to return home.[64]

The Navajos, in the meantime, refused to be passive. On November 17, a group of them attacked a wagon train transporting timber to Fort Sumner and stole the mules pulling the wagons. The offenders were not captured. In January of 1868, more than three hundred Navajos left the reservation. It seemed obvious that all of them would leave if given the means. Another Navajo war appeared probable.[65]

In the nation's capital it appeared as if the entire frontier were about to erupt into a general Indian war. Burdened with a Civil War debt and the cost of reconstructing an unrepentant South, the prospect of such warfare was not pleasant. Early in 1868, Congress created an Indian Peace Commission to attempt a nonviolent solution to the Indian problems. It was made up civilian and military officials, and its purpose was to make treaties.[66]

Agent Dodd and the soldiers at Fort Sumner, anxious to pacify their charges, were quick to inform the Diné about the commission. Important men with the power to move them from their prison would be arriving soon. The Navajos, clutching at what for them was little more than a rumor, regained hope that their problem might be solved peacefully. The desertion rate dropped dramatically during the winter months. But with the approach of spring and no news of the peace commissioners, Navajo discontent reasserted itself. They refused to plant crops, ostracized Delgadito for his collaboration, and planned a mass bolting from the reservation under the leadership of Barboncito and Manuelito.[67]

Agent Dodd, fearing the worst, arranged a trip for Manuelito, Barboncito, and several other Navajo leaders to Washington, D.C., where they spoke to President Andrew Johnson. Beset with his own problems, Johnson listened to their pleas but promised them nothing. He explained that the Peace Commission was empowered to decide their fate.[68]

The peace commissioners chosen to negotiate with the Navajos were of radically different philosophies. Samuel F. Tappan had served as a colonel in the Colorado Volunteers. A humanitarian, he came to New Mexico convinced that the Navajos had been treated wrongly, and he favored relocating them in their homeland. General William Tecumseh Sherman, on the other hand, regarded himself as a no-nonsense military man who wanted to rid the West of an Indian menace by whatever means necessary. The Navajos' wishes rested squarely with this Civil War hero.[69]

Sherman had waged war and judged it inhuman. Therefore, he was interested in the reconstruction of conquered peoples, not necessarily for their own good but for the benefit of the nation. He rejected sentiment in his considerations. Not really believing that Indians could be made into self-supporting citizens, he had determined that they should be given a chance. Contrary to Navajo desires, however, he considered moving the tribe to the Indian Territory.[70]

Countering this idea, Sherman had been critical of the Bosque Redondo Reservation. He also believed that the United States had erred in acquiring New Mexico territory. If the Navajos were sent home and given some land, what would be the loss? Furthermore, he was determined to send them somewhere. He held an open mind.[71]

As Sherman and Tappan, accompanied by General Getty, approached the reservation on May 27, Navajos eagerly rode out to meet them. The landscape was barren and dry. Emerging from makeshift mud and brush hogans and hide-covered shelters, the Diné, clothed in government-issue blankets, greeted the peace commissioners. They appeared peaceful. They were certainly hopeful, for there had been omens that indicated decisions would turn in their favor. Carleton had left New Mexico. Kit Carson, their conqueror, had died just days ago.[72] The Navajos had also performed their own ceremony, which appeared to predict the future.

Several Indians had captured a coyote for a ceremony. With the animal surrounded, Barboncito approached it, said the appropriate words, and placed a shell bead in its mouth. Then, the animal was released. The coyote walked slowly away, to the west and in the direction of home. Now they were certain that Barboncito would speak convincingly and that they would finally be going home.[73]

This magic seemed to work if the initial reactions of the commissioners were any indication. Despite government reports, they were not prepared for the realities they confronted. Tappan was overwhelmed with moral indignation.[74]

If Tappan's shock came as no surprise, the fact that General Sherman was touched by the Navajos' plight could not have been foreseen. Nonetheless, the general's reactions were less emotional than they were logical. Sherman wrote to General Grant, "I found the Bosque a mere spot of green grass in the midst of a wild desert and that the Navajos had sunk into a condition of absolute poverty and despair."[75]

Soon after their arrival, the commissioners met with Agent Dodd. Wanting the commissioners to understand Navajo dissatisfaction, he repeated Navajo complaints concerning Comanche raids, poor soil and water, and insufficient fuel, adding that the only equitable solution to the Navajo problem was to let them go home.[76]

Negotiations began the next morning at Fort Sumner. It seemed an unequal match, with the power of the United States pitted against a ragtag assemblage of defeated and demoralized Indians. Fortunately for the Navajos, their will was extremely important. It was clear to those present at the initial meeting that the Indians could not long be held at the Bosque, nor be relocated without their consent, by the few soldiers available. It was also obvious that the Navajos had wisely chosen their chief spokesman. Barboncito was a little, mustached, very dark, kind man who, in fact, might have, upon first acquaintance, seemed comical, but those who heard him speak rarely laughed.[77]

General Sherman began the conference by speaking slowly, trying to accommodate to the laborious translation. His words had to be translated from English to Spanish by James Sutherland, and then from Spanish to Navajo by Jesus Arviso. In addition to being time-consuming, the process was difficult. English and Spanish were principally noun—adjective languages, which expressed abstract thoughts concisely and took many words to make specific descriptions. Navajo, on the other hand, was a verb language that required considerable detail to convey general ideas, while the meanings of its words allowed for concrete specifics with little modification. Sherman nevertheless seemed concerned that his meaning be made clear. He asked a question that had already been answered by Dodd: Why had the Navajos failed to become self-supporting farmers?[78]

Barboncito's reply did not immediately answer the general. He simply that stated that life had not been good for his people at the Bosque Redondo. It was not natural that they lived there, and their numbers had decreased. He spoke of home:

> When the Navajos were first created, 4 mountains and 4 rivers were pointed to us, inside of which we should live, that was to be our country and was given to us by the First Woman of the Navajo Tribe. It was told to us by our forefathers that we were never to move east of the Rio Grande or west of the San Juan rivers and I think that our coming here has been the cause of so much death among us and our animals. That our God when he was created (the woman I spoke of) gave us this piece of land and created it especially for us and gave us the whitest of corn and the best of horses and sheep.[79]

Conveniently not mentioning that he had twice attempted to escape, he claimed that the Navajos had done everything they had been told with no good results. The land was not productive. They had diligently planted crops; they had received no yield. That was why they had refused to plant this year.[80]

Barboncito added that he did not feel that the Bosque Redondo was intended for the Diné. He let Tappan and Sherman know that the Navajos knew how to farm, knowledge that had proved useless. Furthermore, Navajo livestock had died in alarming numbers.[81]

Barboncito then told the commissioners that many Navajos had once been wealthy and now they had nothing. He motioned to his fellow leaders. He said that he had once been rich, but now he could not rest when he went to sleep at night. The Bosque seemed to breed death. Crops would not grow. Fuel was scarce.

Comanches were a constant source of trouble. All people in the area, Mexicans and Indians, seemed to be against them.[82]

He then concluded:

> If we are taken back to our own country, we will call you our father and mother. If you should only tie a goat there, we would all live off of it, all of the same opinion. I am speaking for the whole tribe, for their animals, from the horse to the dog, also the unborn. All that you have heard now is the truth and is the opinion of the whole tribe. It appears to me that the General commands the whole thing as a god. I hope therefore he will do all he can for my people. This hope goes in at my feet and out at my mouth. I am speaking to you now as if I was speaking to a spirit, and wish you to tell me when you are going to take us to our own country.[83]

General Sherman was impressed by Barboncito's speech, but the general had a number of considerations to ponder. If left at Bosque Redondo, the Navajos would drift away, possibly causing a war. The tribe was visibly more united and more desperate than before, and they were a large group that could cause the military many problems. To improve their condition on the present reservation would be expensive. Additionally, Tappan was sympathetic to the Indians. Commissioner of Indian Affairs Nathaniel G. Taylor had suggested that any removal to the Indian Territory must be with the Indians' consent. Ulysses S. Grant, Sherman's commander, had held similar views, despite his opinion that the Diné would ultimately come into conflict with prospectors in their homeland. Indian leaders had been tricked into giving up their tribes' lands before, but Barboncito was resolute, and the Navajos probably would not support him if he changed his mind. Sherman, nevertheless, suggested moving the Navajos to the Indian Territory.[84]

Barboncito put to rest any other idea than a homecoming for the Navajos. How could they, he asked, be expected to trust promises that the Indian Territory was fertile? They had been told that they would improve their lot by coming to the Bosque Redondo. No, they preferred to go home. Sherman seemed to acquiesce to their demands. That night the Diné chose four more representatives.[85]

The following morning, Sherman met with Navajo leaders in the field behind the hospital. As the general approached, he was besieged by Navajo women begging to return home. Nervously, he lit a cigar and demanded a translation. Clearly affected, he asked if they were all in agreement with the leaders about going home. Their reply seemed unanimous. Once the meeting began, Sherman and Tappan accepted Navajo requests. The remainder of the negotiations was spent in agreeing upon the boundaries of the new reservation and the terms of the treaty. Sherman had told them on the first day of bargaining that they would not be allowed to occupy all of their former haunts. The Navajos would only be allowed a portion of their traditional territory. He pointed at spots on maps while the Navajos mentioned scattered locations, not all of which could be found on the general's maps.[86] Misunderstanding the proposed size of the reservation was inevitable, but Sherman was probably deceitful.

In his opening arguments, Barboncito stated that he wanted the tribe to have plenty of room. He said:

> When the Navajos go back to their own country I want to put them in different places, it would not do to put them all together as they are here, if separated they would be more industrious ... You spoke to me yesterday about putting us on a reservation with a boundary line. I do not think it right to confine us to a certain part, we want to have the privilege of going outside to hunt and trade.[87]

Sherman ignored Barboncito's first plea and granted his second request.

The general said that the Navajos could leave the reservation to hunt or trade in New Mexican towns, but he reiterated his position that they could not reside off the reservation. Barboncito seemed satisfied, but he might have misunderstood. To the Navajos, who rarely conceived of land in terms of title, granting them permission to hunt may have seemed like giving them the right to live there. Furthermore, as a pastoral people who migrated with their flocks from winter to summer grazing lands—a movement that often coincided with optimal hunting—the idea of going somewhere just to hunt was probably foreign.[88]

Next, Barboncito raised a complex issue—slavery. The United States had just fought the Civil War over this question. But in New Mexico involuntary servitude still existed, as it had for centuries. Beyond the obvious similarities, however, slavery in New Mexico was different. Slaves in New Mexico were not strictly considered chattel, nor was a slave's condition solely determined by race. Neither was servitude hereditary. Both New Mexicans and Navajos practiced a form of slavery based on the taking of captives and their eventual assimilation into the community.[89]

Even though slavery might have seemed somewhat more benign in the Southwest than it had been in the American South, cruel practices abounded on both sides. The problem was exacerbated by the fact that most of the captives were children, a reality that caused grief to New Mexican and Navajo parents. By 1868 the Diné had fared far worse than their enemies. When Americans had taken control of New Mexico in 1846, the Navajos had been known for holding large numbers of Mexican captives. Even so, the Spanish who preceded the Mexicans had initiated the practice. The number of Navajo captives had grown under American rule since the tribesmen were gradually losing ground to their enemies. By 1862 the estimated number of Navajo captives held by New Mexicans ranged between fifteen hundred and three thousand.[90]

When Barboncito spoke of slavery, it was not the first time that Navajo leaders had raised the issue. The army had reacted to Navajo requests and searched for Navajo captives, but the results had been poor. Now, speaking through Jesus Arviso, a Mexican captive of the Navajos who had acquired some prestige as a Navajo, Barboncito requested that the Diné be permitted to leave the reservation to search for lost relatives. General Sherman was not hard to convince: he told Barboncito that all United States laws against forced captivity would be enforced, and he granted the chief's request. Barboncito seemed satisfied; yet the problem of captives on both sides would last into the twentieth century.[91]

The next morning, Saturday, May 30, Sherman presented a treaty that followed a standardized format for Indian agreements. Article II described the location of the reservation legally.[92] It is doubtful that the Indians understood, but Sherman, in an attempt to explain things less technically, stated:

> We have marked off a reservation for you, including the Canon de Chelly, and part of the valley of the San Juan, it is about (100) one hundred miles square. It runs as far south as Canon Bonito, and includes the Chusca mountain, but not the Mesa Calabesa [sic] you spoke of; that is the reservation we suggest to you, it also includes the Ceresa [Carrizo] mountains, and the bend of the San Juan, not the upper waters.[93]

The reservation, once surveyed, was approximately half of what the general indicated. It did not include all of the Canyon de Chelly country because it left out the adjoining Chinle Valley. The location of the "bend" referred to by Sherman was not certain, although the surveyors would fix it at the Hogback. The homes of many Navajos were cut off by the boundaries. To the south a good deal of the Navajos' traditional winter grazing lands had been excluded by a provision allowing for a railroad. He failed to inform the Indians that a railroad was even being considered, much less that Article IX of the treaty pledged them not to interfere with its construction. Nor did he inform them that the railroad company would receive grants of land in territory that they had traditionally regarded as their own.[94]

Navajo leaders could not have known about the railroad provision, but they certainly knew that their land base would be smaller. Barboncito nevertheless made no objections. No one knows why. One assumption could be that he was bargaining from a position of weakness and that any treaty allowing the Navajos to go home was, no matter how limiting, the best of all possible evils. This makes sense, considering the fact that his constituents were of a single mind in their desire to return home. Getting there without an agreement would be dangerous and hardly a certainty.

Another explanation, however, exists that does not contradict the first and credits the Navajo leaders for being competent negotiators. The hunting provision, misunderstood as it was, gave the Navajos an excuse to occupy off-reservation lands. A statement made by Sherman at the negotiations, but not included in the treaty, also seemed to give the Navajos another opening:

> Any Navajo can now settle in this Territory and he will get a piece of land not occupied, but he will be subject to the laws of the country. . . . any Navajo could go wherever he pleased in this territory and settle with his family but if he did he would be subject to the laws of the Territory as a citizen.[95]

Although Sherman later explained that he only meant that a Navajo could settle on vacant lands as any other citizen and thereby forfeit his tribal rights, he did not mention the procedures the Indians should follow to file a claim.[96] The Navajos did not understand the concept of title. Nonetheless, they knew how to use land and hold it. That might have been their intention all along: to go home, occupy land, and do anything short of war to keep it. After four years at the Bosque Redondo, the Navajos had no legitimate reason to trust government officials. It was logical for them to look at government promises as future bargaining chips in a game in which the assurances inevitably would be broken and the ante raised.

Regardless of whether the Navajos understood the size of their reservation, the fact remained that they received far less land per capita than any tribe that signed a treaty in 1868. This occurred, in part, because of a belief that the Diné, as a pastoral people, had advanced to a point where they could be easily expected to transform themselves into farmers who needed less land than Indians who relied upon hunting and gathering as their chief means of support. They were pronounced ready to become horticulturalists, and a provision was included within the treaty that called for the individual allotment of lands on the reservation to be divided into 160-acre plots.[97]

The other provisions of the treaty were summarily explained. They would have to turn their criminals over to government authorities. They would also be required to send their children to schools that the government would build at the impossible ratio of one to every thirty pupils. An agent would be assigned to live among them. Annuity goods would be paid to them for a period of ten years, at a rate of no more than five dollars per Indian except to those engaged in mechanical or agricultural pursuits—they would get ten dollars. The government promised to buy the Navajos fifteen thousand sheep and goats to replenish their herds. Finally, it agreed to aid in their relocation.[98]

They were going home! An abiding dream had come true— almost. The next day was a Sunday, by the standards of the times not a day on which to do business. The hours must have seemed long. To a people who took so much pride in ceremonies, who placed so much trust in ritual, even the marking of a white man's treaty was a necessary prerequisite before they could truly believe that their nightmare had ended.

Monday, June 1, 1868, was a cloudy day. With an appropriate sense of spectable, most of the Navajos waited outside the council room while twenty-nine leaders met with the commissioners inside. Sherman asked the leaders if they all approved of the treaty; they said that they did. Then, according to Manuelito, Sherman told them to do right so that they could look other people in the face. He ended the tension in the room by saying, "My children, I will send you back to your homes."[99]

Beginning with Barboncito, the Navajo leaders put their marks upon the treaty. The crowd outside waited, their patience wearing thin, until the headmen emerged, followed by Sherman, who was besieged. Navajos begged him to send them home. They embraced him. He allowed himself to relax. Smiling, he told them to return slowly.[100]

But Sherman acted quickly. He issued orders the same day to General Getty for their return. He also commanded the moving of Fort Wingate to a more western location, to better serve and control the returning exiles. In assuming that the Navajo relocation would proceed smoothly and without incident, Sherman erred, but he could have done little else. The Navajos were more than willing to endure the hardships of inadequate preparation. It is doubtful that they could have been held much longer.[101]

Five days later, on June 6, events seemed to conspire against the treaty. A detachment under Lieutenant John W. Jordan approached Twelve Mile Creek and discovered four white men face down in the water. Each body held Navajo arrows; three showed evidence of torture.[102]

General Sherman was still in New Mexico, and the incident angered him. General Benjamin S. Roberts, now in command of Fort Sumner, reacted quickly by calling for Barboncito, Delgadito, and Manuelito. Sherman, he implied, would not accept their good faith unless the offenders were turned in. The Navajo leaders reacted quickly. Questioning their people closely, they discovered who the criminals were. The renegades had left the reservation, but the chiefs turned their names over to Roberts. Resistance to this action among the Navajos was minimal; they wanted no interference from a few malcontents. A detachment was sent out under the command of Lieutenant Deane Monahan that caught up with the offenders before dawn twenty miles south of Las Vegas near Apache Springs. The Navajos were asleep when the soldiers arrived. Monahan issued orders that they be surrounded, but Juh Sanchez, the leader, awoke in time to foil the plan. Sanchez fired at the soldiers, and a battle ensued. The Navajos, however, were outgunned. Forced into a ravine, and with Sanchez mortally wounded, and two of their number killed, the outlaws surrendered soon after daylight.[103]

Thus, the Navajo leaders proved their good faith. The Navajo exile was about to end. The hardship had been extreme. Many had died, and the birthrate had dropped. They had once been the "Lords of the Earth." Now, they were impoverished. They had suffered severe trauma, but they had avoided psychological defeat. Like the recently defeated South, they refused to change their ethos substantially, although they now recognized limits to their power. Like the newly freed slaves, whose enthusiasm was soon to be dashed, they testified to the hopeful striving of the human character and the unwillingness to surrender to the human condition.

2
The Return Home

On June 18, 1868, the Navajos began their exodus. Escorted by troops under the command of Major Charles J. Whiting, the procession of approximately 7,300 Navajos stretched for ten miles. Fifty-six army wagons attempted to carry the old and infirm, but most of the Indians had to walk and carry their meager possessions on their backs. They also drove the remainder of their once substantial herds: 940 sheep, 1,025 goats, and 1,550 horses—less than an animal per person. As the Navajos traveled through San Carlos and Tijeras canyons, through Albuquerque, and roughly along the present route of Interstate 40, army rations were soon in short supply. The Navajos spread out over the countryside in search of available sources of nutrition such as prairie dogs, rabbits, and yucca stocks.[1]

As the procession moved along at a maddeningly slow pace, amid the sounds of creaking wagons and saddles, the bleating and neighing of livestock, human cries and shouts, and the steady shuffling of feet, Navajos knew, despite their longing for the old ways, that they were not returning to the past. Through stubborn resistance, they had won a battle for autonomy, but they were entering an unpredictable time in which familiar practices would have to be abandoned. For instance, warfare had to stop. Manuelito recognized this. After signing the treaty, according to one oral tradition, he put his weapons symbolically aside and addressed the Diné:

> I have no use for these; I don't want to use these further because I see there is no hope in the future for us as long as we keep this up. As long as we're fighting and raising trouble, we're just doing harm to our people. I have found this out, so we might as well just forget about it and lead a peaceful life for the welfare of the People.[2]

Manuelito's call for peace, however, was rhetorical, for if the Navajos were to survive in their native land, they would have to continue their resistance through both personal and group action.

While their journey homeward moved along, the individual stories of the travelers seemed to foretell the future and reflect their bittersweet happiness. A twelve-year-old girl who would later be known as Hosteen Allemigo's Older Wife, for example, had been taken captive during the trip to the Bosque Redondo. General Sherman had said that the Navajos could look for their relations, and the girl's father, taking the general at his word, raced ahead of the caravan to Albuquerque. He found his daughter with a family living south of the town and tried to buy her with jewelry he had been hoarding. His offer was refused, but he patiently waited. When the Navajos reached Albuquerque on July 5, he was able to offer two horses in addition to his initial price. The girl was allowed to return to her family.[3]

It would be more than a generation before the problem of slavery went away. The Santa Fe *Daily New Mexican*, only a month later, would declare that Navajo slavery was misunderstood; the Navajos, it stated, were "a savage and barbarous people." To return children accustomed to a more civilized life with New Mexican families would be cruel. The little girl's father was indeed lucky. But it was time for a little Navajo luck. At Albuquerque, the Rio Grande was flooded, and rafts had to be built to ferry the women and children, wagons, and the weaker livestock. Still, the Navajos struggled forward.[4]

As the procession took on a looser formation, smaller groups were formed. Within one of these was a husband and wife with a sick baby, malnourished because her mother could not nurse her. Attempting to comfort the child, the mother kept dropping behind. The father, worried that they might lose the safety of the group, grew impatient, and when the child uttered what appeared to be a death cry, he insisted that the baby, in her cradleboard, be hung from a tree and left behind. He attempted to drag his wife along, but when she heard another sound from the child, she rushed back to the tree. Angry and certain that the baby would die anyway, the father was hurrying to regain his position in the group when he noticed a broken cactus stem. Out of it dripped a milky substance. Desperate, he hurried back to his wife, fed the liquid to the baby, and she revived. He gathered more cactus stems and rushed his family along.[5]

Miraculous events such as this one did not seem extraordinary to the Navajos. To them, their victory at the Bosque Redondo had been a miracle and their return home a spiritual event. When the Navajos first saw Mount Taylor, one of their Four Sacred Mountains, they were overcome with emotion. Many fell to the ground, and even the soldiers were touched by their heartfelt ecstasy. One group, when it camped at the foot of this natural shrine, feasted on prairie dogs which, if not their usual fare for celebration, may have resembled a wondrous, ceremonial meal.[6]

This sense of wonder, soon to be enshrined in legend, was, however, tempered by blunt reality. Even though Delgadito and about four hundred followers left the trail and headed for their former homes in the Cebolleta region, the rest of the Navajos headed for Fort Wingate. The journey had been peaceful. Only one Navajo had been caught stealing along the way, and Barboncito had forced him to walk with his hands tied to a wagon. Jicarilla Apaches conducted raids, mistakenly hoping that the Navajos would be blamed. Even the territory's leading newspaper admitted to the tribe's good conduct and congratulated the army on how well it was handling the repatriation. One observer declared that an equal number of marching soldiers would have caused far more damage.[7]

The Navajos began arriving at Fort Wingate on July 23. The original Fort Wingate, named for Captain Benjamin Wingate, a hero of the Battle of Valverde, had been located at San Rafael near the present site of Grants, New Mexico. The garrison at the old fort had been moved at the direction of General Sherman to Ojo del Oso. Due to the quickness of the Navajo return, Fort

Wingate was not prepared to handle the influx of almost seven thousand people. The troops were housed in log barracks. No provision had been made for housing the Navajos.[8]

General Sherman had assumed that the Diné would be able to plant crops that summer, but his calculations were overly optimistic. The Navajos had long since lost their supply of seeds to Kit Carson's militiamen, and the growing season in their portion of the Southwest was rarely long enough to accommodate planting in July or August. Thus, the Navajos were left to their own devices. The cautious majority, waiting for the sheep promised in the treaty, camped in the vicinity of Fort Wingate, dependent upon army supplies and gathering from the countryside what they could to supplement their diets: wild tubers, berries, and seeds; rabbits, squirrels, and deer. Fortunately, there was a good crop of piñon nuts that year. The more venturesome Navajos, however, returned to their former homes as soon as possible.[9]

The land to which the Navajos returned has usually left nonnative observers in awe. It is roughly encircled by the cardinal points of the Navajo universe, the Four Sacred Mountains: Mount Taylor, in New Mexico; Hesperous Peak, in western Colorado; Mount Blanca, near Alamosa, Colorado; and the San Francisco Peaks, in Arizona. Navajoland is located at the southern end of the Colorado Plateau and noted for its variety: high forested mountains, tablelands covered with piñon and juniper, and tracts of wasteland. As novelist Frank Waters has observed, the one unifying feature is rock. This phenomenon has led many to conclude that Navajoland is a place of mystery. Yet it is a territory of ecological fragility. Seen by non-Indians as both beautiful and ugly, it has been perceived as invigorating to the human spirit but, paradoxically, a land of isolation. It is a domain of big skies. In the Navajo country, the climate can be cold and snowy in the winter, dry and dusty in the spring, the summer warm and rainy except during droughts, and the fall pleasant but prone to early frosts. For all of its harshness, it is a spectacular land, and it is easy to understand why the Navajos loved it.[10]

The Navajo Reservation Today
in Relation to Surrounding States

It was soon evident that the Navajos were not settling only on treaty lands. Manuelito located his family east of the treaty line near Tohatchi. Ganado Mucho moved with his followers back to the Rio Pueblo Colorado Valley, near the present settlement of Ganado and west of the boundary. Others occupied lands as far west as the Hopi country and the Coconino Basin; they took control of lands to the east of the line in western New Mexico as far north as the San Juan River and as far south as Fort Wingate and Ramah. Navajos also resettled along the Puerco and Little Colorado rivers south of the reservation. Isolated Navajo settlements were located near Cebolleta and Cubero at Cañoncito and near Alamosa.[11]

Despite the fact that the Navajos were using more land than allowed in the treaty, they could not reoccupy all of their former territory. Some of the Navajos' land had been settled in their absence by Mexican-American herders, who grazed their flocks east of the reservation. Roman Antonio Baca, a former Navajo slaver, had set up the village of San Mateo on the northwest side of Mount Taylor, in 1864. Southeast of the reservation, a ranch had been established on the slopes of the Zuni Mountains by Paulo Candelaria and his brother-in-law, José María Marez. Similarly, people the Navajos considered interlopers settled along the San Juan and Puerco rivers. The military reservation at the new Fort Wingate also took away valuable acreage and, in 1869, the hamlet named San Rafael was founded on the old site of Fort Wingate. There was still land to the east available for Navajo use. In recognition of this, the surveyor general of New Mexico, John A. Clark, urged the United States Land Office, on July 17, 1868, to survey lands in western New Mexico, for white settlement would rapidly fill up the area.[12] Although the government ignored his predictions, his assessment presaged a lengthy conflict.

The Navajos had more immediate problems. Their territory was not the paradise that their memories had told them it was. Living off the land proved precarious, and their former homes had undergone the ravages of Kit Carson's campaign. Their fields

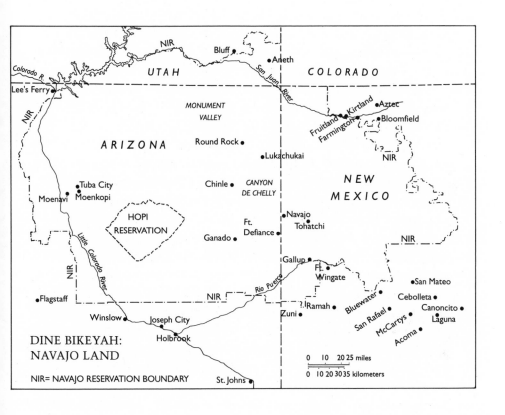

DINE BIKEYAH:
NAVAJO LAND

NIR= NAVAJO RESERVATION BOUNDARY

were trampled and covered with overgrowth. Their hogans were either burned or collapsing. Their corrals had fallen. The peach trees in Canyon de Chelly had been burned to stumps. Without enough sheep to revive their economy and lacking sufficient horses for adequate transportation, the temptation to rebuild their livelihood by raiding their neighbors was great, especially since they had little of value to trade. Fortunately, some returned to Fort Wingate to receive rations. Others accepted assistance from Navajos who had not gone to the Bosque.[13]

Agent Dodd estimated that there were seven hundred Navajos who had not surrendered, but in 1865 New Mexico Indian Commissioner Michael Steck had claimed that five thousand had never surrendered. Part of the discrepancy between the two figures can be explained by the guesswork involved in making a census. For example, in 1870, Special Indian Agent William F. M. Arny would claim that there were 14,349 Navajos. Even allowing for natural population increase, Arny's figures would indicate that half of the tribe had avoided capture. The true number, however, probably fell somewhat short of the figures of Steck and Arny and considerably more than those of Dodd. One writer has concluded that the number who never surrendered was between fifteen hundred and two thousand.[14]

Some of those who had not surrendered had fled west past the Hopi villages to the Coconino Basin, the San Francisco Peaks, and the Grand Canyon. Others retreated south to the Little Colorado and the White Mountain Apache country. Another group settled to the east in the Alamo region, at the lower end of Alamosa Creek. The best-known refugees, however, belonged to bands living to the north and under the leadership of Hoskaninni.[15]

At any rate, the help offered by these renegades was limited. At Fort Wingate, rations were running low, and Navajos were slipping away to occupy lands off the reservation. Agent Dodd, however, could not get a survey, the lack of which made it impossible to keep the Navajos where they were supposed to be. He also was in dire need of Spanish interpreters to enable him to communicate with the Navajos.[16] Despite these limitations, Dodd worked energetically.

Following orders issued by Sherman, Dodd found a site for the agent at old, abandoned Fort Defiance. He picked the fort because of nearby timber and the availability of grazing lands. Nonetheless, locating the agency at Fort Defiance presented many problems. At the southern end of the reservation, the fort was not centrally placed, and the nine hours it took to travel from Fort Wingate to the agency made immediate military intervention impossible. In addition, the buildings at the agency, which Dodd decided to refurbish, had deteriorated badly.[17]

Adding to these problems were other events that occupied the agent's mind. As much as they had promised peace, the Navajos were compelled by circumstances into wreaking violence against their old enemies. The Diné were hungry, and some of them stole food on the hoof. Shortly after their return, Navajos stole livestock from Pueblo Indians living north of Santa Fe. They also took horses from John Watts at Fort Bascom, New Mexico, and mules from Anglo-American settlers at Bluewater. The flocks of New Mexican herdsmen were temptations difficult to resist. The New Mexicans were not entirely guiltless, however, because a party of these sheepherders had made a raid through Navajo and Ute country just prior to the exiles' return, and they also grazed their flocks on reservation land. They complained of Navajo theft when the Indians insisted that they leave. In addition, they were occupying off-reservation lands that the Navajos considered their own. When the Indians believed their efforts would be successful, they drove the intruders away.[18] Despite the hostility that these two peoples felt for each other, this new conflict was not yet war. Rather, it fit into a larger pattern of southwestern violence and theft in which rustling an occasional unbranded cow or sheep was an accepted, if not legal, practice. Fighting over the control of land was also normal as was witnessed that year in the struggle on the plains of eastern New Mexico between Mexican-American sheepmen and Texas cattlemen. Yet there was a crucial difference. The Navajos were Indians. Indians rarely won struggles over land.

Of more concern for the Navajos was conflict with the Utes, who lived in northwestern New Mexico, southwestern Colorado, and southeastern Utah. The Navajos and Utes had been traditional enemies. During the Kit Carson campaign, the Utes had been the Navajos' most ferocious foes. As a result, the Diné harbored resentment toward their neighbors. The two tribes, in fact, seemed on the verge of war. As soon as the Navajos arrived at Fort Wingate, Ute parties scouted their camps. The Diné offered to make peace. The Utes refused and conducted raids, in which they managed to capture several women and children as well as a number of horses and some ammunition. The Utes also kidnapped a man whom they castrated and released. Both Agent Dodd and Ute Agent William F. M. Arny tried to restore the peace, but some Navajos had lost their patience and attacked the Utes, many of whom had not participated in recent outrages.[19]

Dodd was so worried about the Ute problem that he requested military protection for his charges, but he was refused. He had little time, however, to worry about the inability of the army to make a show of force. In attempting to make the old buildings at Fort Defiance livable, he had to concern himself with preparing the Navajos for the next year's planting. He requested permission to buy 4,000 bushels of seed wheat and 1,400 bushels of seed corn as well as 400 dozen hoes, 250 dozen wool cards, and 150 dozen large axes. More immediately, he wanted more rations for the Navajos at Fort Wingate, a request that would never be adequately answered by the Indian Bureau. Dodd begged the army for what little it could spare. Frustrated, he plugged away at his job, calling for a gathering of the Diné on November 1. The 7,111 people who assembled were a majority of the tribe. He was able to use the opportunity to explain the necessity of the Diné remaining at peace with their neighbors and to urge them to be patient about the government's delay in delivering the promised sheep.[20]

Dodd was a tired and overworked man. On January 16, 1869,

just before the dependent Navajos and the agent were moved to Fort Defiance, he died of a stroke. Henry Wood Dodd, his brother, served temporarily until a new agent could arrive. Dodd's successor, Major J. Carry French, who had briefly been an agent to the Utes at the Abiquiu Agency, arrived at Fort Defiance on February 20, 1869. He was immediately confronted with many difficulties. Conflict between the Navajos and Utes continued, and confrontations with settlers became progressively more serious. French was quick to complain that the agency had been run "rather loosely."[21] This initial reaction may have been a result of his misunderstanding of the Navajo power structure.

To the extent that the government had made any plans at all to control the Navajos, it had contemplated the use of Navajo leaders. Barboncito had been made head chief by General Sherman. Ganado Mucho was designated subchief for the western Navajos, and Manuelito was appointed subchief in the east. Herrero, Delgadito, Armijo, Largo, Chicquito, Muerto de Hambre, Hombre, Narbono, and Narbono Segundo were recognized as headmen of known bands, and all of these men together were used as a council that met at the agent's request. Agents would come to recognize other leaders as well. Regardless of the false assumptions that the leaders had authoritarian power and could easily execute orders from the agent, intelligent agents soon learned that the real Navajo power structure was less formal. The leaders had gained some power because of government recognition, but their authority was hardly supreme. Many leaders, such as Hoskaninni, held power without government approval, and the exercise of control over the Navajos by authorized headmen occurred as often through the use of diplomacy as through command.[22]

Major French, despite his misunderstanding, was somewhat sympathetic to the Navajos' plight. He saw the situation as chaotic and, indeed, it was. His first day on the job, he received communications telling him of trouble. A John Ryan had written to inform him that two Navajos had been killed by Mexican Americans near El Rito. The letter writer blamed the Mexicans, complaining that the murderers had taken three mules and three horses from the victims. French also learned that Navajos were taking and killing cattle belonging to private supply trains. Accusations would soon be circulating that Navajos had killed two Tecolote men, Luis Aragón and Juan Gutiérrez, during a raid on February 20, at Sierra de la Cruz, sixty miles from Fort Bascom.[23]

A month later, matters took a turn for the worse. A smallpox epidemic had broken out, and French was endeavoring to get Navajos to come into the agency for vaccinations. Parties of Navajos had ventured out to steal horses and mules at Jemez and to bring retribution upon their old Bosque Redondo enemies, the Comanches. Most stolen horses and mules, according to French, were being traded in New Mexican towns. Nevertheless, he had already returned several horses and mules to their owners and was certain that no stolen animals had entered the reservation. He was concerned about unknown numbers of Navajos "roving about the country" and off the reservation, but he was satisfied that most of these people would return if the sheep and goats promised in the treaty would be provided.[24]

French attempted to restrain the Navajos by whatever means available. One restraint upon the Diné was Barboncito. The great orator who had obtained their release from exile was sick and not able to be of much assistance. Back from Canyon de Chelly because his presence was required at Fort Defiance, the old man was reduced to delivering oratories to impatient young men. He reminded them of the Bosque Redondo. When he was able, he rode out over the country with the same message, but his advice was undoubtedly rejected by some young men in the way that such counsel is often spurned by the inexperienced. Barboncito was even accused of being a white man's Indian, but his efforts were not all in vain. Most of the Navajos showed remarkable restraint.[25]

The Utes severely tested Navajo restraint. Earlier, Navajos had stolen Ute horses. They subsequently traded the animals for sheep, and violence continued. Both peoples still held captives from the other side, and the Utes had their own perspective.

Pushed into smaller and smaller reservations because gold had been discovered in southwestern Colorado, the two bands of Southern Utes—Wiminuche and Capote—now observed that their old enemies, whom they had helped the whites defeat, had been given lands in the San Juan country. They regarded the Diné's reoccupation of the area as a threat to their territorial integrity.[26]

Nevertheless, the Diné living along the San Juan River were easy prey. The early post-Bosque Navajos were poorly armed and tended to live isolated from one another. The Diné farming along the San Juan were under constant Ute harassment by early summer. Major French declared that the Navajos seriously wanted to end hostilities, but the fighting continued. On September 30, Navajos farming approximately a hundred miles from Fort Defiance were in a hogan eating when they were fired upon by Capote Utes. A woman not participating in the meal was killed in her sleep. The Navajos rushed out of their hogans to get their weapons. One man managed to grab a gun, only to be mortally wounded before he could get off a shot. Other Navajos managed to knock a Ute off his horse and kill one of the stolen mares before the attackers could get away with ten horses and a considerable number of sheep.[27]

Four relatives of the slain Navajos unsuccessfully pursued the raiders. Other Navajos talked with Corones, a Ute leader, and were able to identify the specific lodges guilty of the crime. The Ute agent Lieutenant J. B. Hanson, however, failed to act. Navajo leaders, despite provocation, urged restraint. To show their good faith, they were very cooperative when a Wiminuche chief appeared at Fort Defiance in December. He claimed that Navajos had stolen nine horses. The headmen went out and found seven of the animals, but the Capote matter would trouble Navajos for years.[28]

Concurrently, Navajos were coming into serious conflict with their neighbors. Due to a government issue of seeds, the Indians had been able to plant crops, but the yield, if any, was months away. The summer would be a lean one. It would also be dangerous for off-reservation Navajos who were quickly regarded as nuisances by New Mexicans and their territorial government. In late May or early June, Navajos stole three animals from Roman Baca of San Mateo because he would not release Navajo slaves, and a man named Gonzales accused them of running off his sheep. French suggested that Gonzales's livestock had been stolen by White Mountain Apaches who had disguised themselves as Navajos, but he admitted that Navajos living south of the reservation—a group the chiefs could not control—had been "behaving very badly," stealing mules, horses, burros, and cattle. He feared that further incidents might provoke serious confrontations.[29]

Major French was correct. On June 26, a party of Navajos attacked the Thomas Luna ranch sixteen miles west of Belen and attempted to drive off three thousand sheep, although they were only able to escape with about three hundred. The next day, Luna, his brother Juan, José María Baca, and five or six other men headed out after the raiders. After a day and a night, the party caught up with the Indians in the Datil Mountains at nine in the morning and recaptured the sheep. Hurrying home, the Lunas soon discovered that the Navajos did not give up easily. They had reinforced their numbers from a nearby camp and rushed ahead to set up an ambush. As the Lunas dismounted to lead their horses through a narrow pass, they were attacked. The two Lunas and Baca were killed. The remaining men rallied and barricaded themselves. The battle continued until nightfall, when the Navajos pulled away, driving most of the sheep before them. The ranchmen, with their horses dead, struggled home to tell their tales. At the same time, a supply wagon was attacked by Navajos near Fort Craig, and its eight mules were stolen. A few days later, Navajos were allegedly selling the tobacco bags of the Lunas and Baca in Cubero.[30]

Fear took hold in New Mexico. Acting Territorial Governor Herman H. Heath urged New Mexicans to arm themselves against the Navajos and even offered to supply citizens with weapons. When two well-armed Navajos appeared in Santa Fe on July 10 to do some trading, they were arrested by Sheriff José D. Sena for suspicious behavior and turned over to New Mexico Super-intendent of Indian Affairs J. M. Gallegos, who advised the sheriff to keep them in jail until the army could return them to the reservation.[31]

Indian scares had a history of leading to war. A little over a year after the signing of the treaty, neither Superintendent Gallegos nor General Getty relished the possibility. Apaches, relatively small in number, were tying down the undermanned army, and civil violence was also requiring military action. The thought of having to do battle with over eight thousand Navajos was frightening. Both men acted to contain the situation and reassure the public. Gallegos wrote to the commander of Fort Wingate on July 13 to urge that no passes be issued for Navajos to leave the reservation, and he had his letter published. Getty sent a more specific order to Fort Wingate. He demanded that the Navajos not be allowed to leave the "well defined limits" of the reservation without a military guard.[32]

There were, however, several problems involved with Galle-gos's request and Getty's order. First of all, neither man had dealt directly with the large number of Navajos living off the reservation. It was impossible for the small garrison at Fort Wingate to force them to live where the treaty said they should. Secondly, the boundary was still being surveyed. Nobody was quite sure where it was. Illustrative of this geographic confusion was the fact that Navajo agents believed that Fort Defiance was in New Mexico rather than in Arizona.[33] Finally, the raids could not be stopped by mere letters, and they continued.

On July 23, forty Navajos were reported east of the Sandia Mountains where they allegedly drove off between ten thousand and twelve thousand sheep. If this example of Navajo plunder seemed exaggerated, stories of Navajo depredations continued to come into Santa Fe from Bernalillo, Barranco, Chama, Abi-quiu, and Capia. On occasion, the radiers had been chased by groups of citizens, but the perpetrators always seemed to escape.[34]

Territorial Governor Robert B. Mitchell had had enough. Frus-trated that New Mexico had no law that allowed him to call out the militia, he issued a proclamation that held out the possibility of war. He declared that any Navajos found off the reservation, unless they were under military escort, would be regarded as common enemies of the territory. Citizens were authorized to take appropriate action.[35] Wanting to avoid war, federal officials began to counteract the proclamation's negative effects, and they soon found out what military men in the field had known all along, that the Navajos were not the only ones committing crimes.

Although crimes against Navajos were not as well documented as their own depredations, it was obvious that citizens of New Mexico had taken advantage of their former enemies. For example, two more Navajos had been killed at El Rito on May 1, one of them the son of a headman, Armijo. That summer, a woman and a child of Delgadito's band had been killed on Matthew McCarty's ranch fifteen miles west of Cubero, on Acoma Pueblo land.[36]

It was ironic that Delgadito's followers should have been singled out. Delgadito's people had had a history of cooperation with Spanish, Mexican, and American officials prior to the Bosque Redondo. It had come as a surprise to them that General Carleton wanted to imprison them also. Once in exile, they had faced discrimination at the hands of other Navajos, and Delgadito had requested permission from General Sherman for his people to live apart from the rest of the Diné. The general's comment about Navajos settling off the reservation, if they would agree to subject themselves to the same laws as other inhabitants, had been directed to these "Enemy Navajos," a name given to them by their own people. Upon their return to the Cebolleta region, they had been relatively peaceful, although there were some desperate acts made by hungry people. Nine sheep and several sacks of corn had been stolen from Cubero, but the situation seemed calm.[37]

This fragile tranquility, however, was shattered by Governor Mitchell's proclamation. Sometime in late August, a Mexican American visited Navajos who lived seven miles west of Cubero. He offered to trade a number of sheep in exchange for a horse and two mules. The Navajos agreed to the deal and, on August 29, two of them took the horse, mules, and an extra horse, on which they planned to return, and left with the man. Once away from the Navajos' home, the trader was joined by another individual. These two, Manuel Sucero and Manuel Chaves y Gonzales, killed the Navajos and stole their livestock. Not long afterward, a party of townspeople came out to the Navajo settlement and drove the Indians away, in the process taking a rifle, ten dollars in silver, and several bows and arrows. Representing only a small percentage of the Cubero community, these raiders believed that they were acting under the governor's proclamation. Fourteen of the evicted Navajos reported their troubles to Delgadito. Despite his previous differences with other Navajo leaders, he gained the support of Barboncito, Ganado Mucho, Muerto de Hombre, and Herrero in his call for justice.[38]

The commander of Fort Wingate, Major A. W. Evans, had investigated much of the rustling and violence. He had gone to Cubero to investigate the murder of the Lunas and Baca. By talking to residents of the town, he determined that the Navajos perpetrating this act had been renegades living with Apaches and that rumors of the killers selling the tobacco bags of the dead in Cubero were false. In conjunction with Major French, he had investigated the second El Rito murders and recovered most of what had been stolen. In addition, he had arrested the principal men involved in the McCarty affair, but they had managed to escape. Later, however, one of these men ventured into Fort Wingate. He was a rancher named Miller, who claimed that he had been provoked by Navajos who had stolen his cattle. Evans released the rancher, but not before confiscating his horse as a guarantee for the return of what had been stolen. The Navajos did not insist upon death for murderers. A payment to the relatives of victims had been the custom. Therefore, if the Navajos were not completely satisfied with Evans's actions, they at least found them acceptable.[39]

While carrying out his duties, Major Evans had become empathetic toward the Diné. On August 8, he wrote a letter that outlined his views to the acting assistant adjutant general, district of New Mexico. He and Major French had reported General Getty's order to the chiefs. Evans wrote that he was convinced that they all had agreed to obey the order, in spirit if not to the letter. Evans added that there were bad men among the Navajos, who would undoubtedly conduct raids in the future. Nevertheless, the vast majority of the tribe was peaceful, regardless of where they resided. Evans thought that about half of the tribe lived off the reservation, especially in areas south of Fort Defiance, along the San Juan, and east of the border in western New Mexico. These people believed that General Sherman had given them permission to live where they were. Evans was concerned about regarding so many people as hostile.[40]

He had granted people with crops in the fields the permission to remain where they were until the harvest. Most notable among these was Mariano's band, living thirty miles west of Fort Wingate. He did not believe that off-reservation Navajos caused much conflict. He blamed New Mexicans. If the Navajos had committed crimes, New Mexicans were not interested in finding the guilty, but merely in retaliating against the first Navajos they saw. Now, Evans added, the governor's proclamation had given them an excuse to raid. Perhaps in response to Evans's views, General Getty journeyed west to talk with the Navajo leaders. He explained to them the necessity of keeping their people on the reservation, and they diplomatically professed friendship toward the government. But Evans was not convinced that it was possible for them to stay only on the reservation. He proposed a de facto reservation line that ran through the summit of Mount Taylor and swerved west to keep San Mateo off the reservation.[41]

Evans's idea was not taken seriously, but General Sherman shared his suspicions of New Mexicans. If so much as a single sheep were stolen, New Mexicans, according to the general, would demand that the army do police investigations that were not within its area of expertise.[42] Even though Sherman would never adequately explain his promises to the Navajos that they could live off the reservation, he was prepared to take any precautions he could to prevent a war. All that was necessary was that word of New Mexican perfidy reach him. Now promoted to general-in-chief by President Ulysses S. Grant, Sherman sent word to Major J. M. Schofield, commander of the department of Missouri, that he wanted the repeal of Mitchell's proclamation. General Getty and the new New Mexico Superintendent of Indian Affairs, William Clinton, prevailed upon the new governor, William A. Pile, a Grant appointee, to ignore Mitchell's order, and the State Department formally instructed Pile to annul his predecessor's action.[43]

Over and above these directives, Sherman took other action. Clinton was informed that $150,000.00 had been authorized for the relocation of the Navajos. Only $8,394.24 had been spent, and $101,605.76 remained for the purchase of fifteen thousand head of sheep and goats, five hundred head of cattle, and one million pounds of corn. With the addition of other funds appropriated by Congress, Clinton was told that he had about $278,000.00 to spend on the Navajos. The military was very anxious that the money be spent. General Sherman decided that $33,000.00 of this amount was under his control; he desired that it be spent to feed the Navajos. To assure that this would be done properly, orders were issued that an army officer be present at the distribution of goods.[44]

Sherman's action helped to prevent further raiding by the Diné and their New Mexican neighbors. The Navajos' first months home had been troublesome. Of necessity, many of them raided their neighbors and occupied lands that were not theirs, according to the treaty. In doing so, they demonstrated that they had not given up the militancy that had brought them to war in the first place. There was, however, a change. Their militancy was now tempered with a realization that there was a limit to how much they could get away with. Their chiefs symbolized this fundamental change by working to control the excesses of their own people while calling for justice against the abuses of their New Mexican neighbors.

51

New Mexican objection to the Bosque Redondo had been in the best perceived interests of people who lived along the Pecos River, but as can be seen from the renewed conflict once the Diné returned home, not all New Mexicans wanted them in their homeland. Settlers living on the Navajo frontier tried to provoke a war by influencing the territorial governor to issue a proclamation. This document was no less reasonable than declarations elsewhere, but it was unsuccessful in its intended outcome for two reasons: (1) Navajo militancy convinced the army that war was probable; and (2) the citizens who wanted war were loosely "Indians'" themselves, that is, people of mixed European and Native American ancestry who were subject to discrimination on the part of federal officials. Governor Mitchell had been appointed to office by the president, but, as a politician, he attempted to satisfy the demands of his constituents. In doing so, he neglected the basic racial biases of federal authority.

Meanwhile, the army had come to empathize with the Navajos as well as to fear them. Major Evans was typical of the commanders of Fort Wingate who would follow him; they seemed to appreciate the gestures of friendship offered by Navajo leaders and believed that the Indians could be controlled better if they were allowed to support themselves, even if by doing so they did not strictly go along with the terms of the treaty.

Finally, Agents Dodd and French cared little for government demands that the Navajos become farmers or live strictly on the reservation. They were mostly concerned with keeping their charges out of war. Of more long-term benefit was the appointment of a new agent who would even more actively work for Navajo interests. His name was Frank Tracy Bennett.

3
Frank Tracy Bennett

aptain Frank Tracy Bennett, the new agent from Ohio, had a distinguished Civil War record. Bennett had enlisted as an infantry private and advanced through the ranks; he was a first lieutenant by the end of the war. Rewarded also with brevet (honorary) promotions for "gallant and meritorious service" at Hoover's Gap, Tennessee, and Chickamauga, Georgia, Bennett resigned his commission soon after the war, but he was back in the army two months later and quickly promoted to captain. Left without an assignment in April of 1869, he was moved to Fort Wingate in anticipation of his nomination as Navajo agent under newly elected President U. S. Grant's plan to assign the tribes to military men.[1]

Bennett arrived at Fort Defiance on August 26, looked the agency over, and pronounced it "very dismal." His quarters were crude, poorly furnished, and leaky. He found his job frustrating because the supply network of the Indian Bureau was inefficient and the chiefs appeared to have little power. Bennett, however, was a practical man who learned on the job. He grew to trust Navajo leaders, and within a few months of his arrival, he became an advocate for the Diné, more concerned with solving their material problems than in bringing about any change in their way of life. Soft-spoken and jovial, he soon earned the respect of the Navajos, who called him "Big Belly."[2]

At first, Bennett observed that the Navajos were "fat and in good condition," but he quickly realized that the Navajo economy was in a shambles. In part, this catastrophe was the result of government planners refusing to recognize that the environmental limitations of the Far West severely hampered planting. General Sherman, for instance, had hoped that the Diné would become sedentary yeomen. The Navajos, however, knew some of the limitations imposed by their geography. Navajo farming, before the invention of barbed wire, was based upon a harmony between horticultural and pastoral economies. Navajos planted during the spring and moved their livestock, which would otherwise eat young plants, to higher elevations as soon as crops appeared, leaving them untended until harvest time. With balance between rodents and predators undisturbed, they had little fear of rodent infestation.[3]

Under such circumstances, the major danger to a harvest was unseasonable weather. Navajos had traditionally offset the effects of drought by planting more than they needed and relying on goats to provide food in case of crop failure. Sheep were not often killed, for Navajo wool products had long been items of barter. Even before the Anglo-Americans took an interest in Navajo arts, there had been a market for Navajo crafts throughout the Native American and Mexican-American trading network. A Navajo blanket, for example, had been found on a Cheyenne corpse at the site of the Sand Creek Massacre in 1864.[4]

For the Navajos, 1869 was a difficult year. Their herds were small and their supply of seeds inadequate. A freak snow and hail storm had hit the area in June. Most of the crops were destroyed. Bennett blamed the Indians for not saving what was left of the harvest.[5] Not understanding that the Navajos were away from the fields, he also failed to comprehend fully the importance his charges placed upon rebuilding their meager herds but, in time, he would alter his opinions. For the moment, he had more pressing matters to consider.

There was increased violence. Bennett had talked to the chiefs and was convinced that Navajos, especially those living off the reservation, were harassed by Mexican Americans and Utes. Rather than blaming the Indians for living in unapproved areas, he demanded that they be protected. He complained that since their return from the Bosque twelve Navajos had been killed compared to only two Mexicans. His figures were incorrect, for if all of the reports of Navajo depredations were true, four Mexican Americans had been killed; yet there was a great deal to what he said. In early September, an incident occurred that seemed to justify his conclusions. Two Navajos, ostensibly headed to Comanche country to trade, were killed at Canyon Juan Tafoya near Cebolleta and robbed of a mule and five horses. Navajos demanded justice, but Bennett felt that they were quite magnanimous; all they wanted was the return of stolen property. In reality, it was unlikely that the Navajos were going to trade with Comanches; they had probably intended to raid their old enemies. Regardless, there was no excuse, in the agent's view, for these criminal acts. He believed that Mexican Americans were attempting to provoke a war.[6]

Perhaps it was Bennett's opinions that originally attracted Navajo leaders to him. They also might have appreciated him because he did not insist that the Diné live solely upon the reservation. Whatever the reason, Bennett received their support. Forced by necessity to prevent war, the leaders knew that they had to go out in search of stolen livestock and return what they could; but bringing this about was not an easy task, especially in a time when the Navajos' sense of their nation and of their responsibilities was still inchoate. Taking action might foster resentment among fellow tribesmen unless the tribe could get something in return. In this respect, a dedicated agent whom the people believed was acting on their behalf was helpful. Wrongdoers could be told that they must stop, for their deeds were hurting the agent's effort on behalf of the larger group. Finally, the chiefs needed to do more than just recover stolen property; they also had to show that they were correcting injustices against their people.

With this in mind, Barboncito, Delgadito, and Narbono requested permission in late September to go to Canyon Juan Tafoya to recover stolen livestock. Bennett wrote to Clinton to endorse their request, adding that with minor exceptions the Navajos were behaving peacefully.[7] Nonetheless, as a military man, he was appalled by the Navajo leaders' lack of command. The distribution of annuity goods was coming up, and he made plans to bolster their power.

The day of the distribution, October 2, was also an opportunity to count the Diné. The chiefs informed Bennett that not all of their people could make it. Some were sick; others had to stay home to take care of livestock. Nonetheless, 6,954 people appeared that day, and Bennett had the others appear on October 18. During these two days, 8,481 Navajos were issued goods. Bennett was certain that some of the Indians had drawn two issues, but he believed that the number counted adequately reflected the population. To improve upon the chiefs' authority, Bennett asked them to designate ninety-four subordinate leaders. He issued these men coats, pants, and other goods and informed them that he and the chiefs had appointed them "captains" to exert control over the tribe. If they failed, they would be removed, and others would be given the extra annuities. He predicted that they would "do a great deal of good."[8]

Bennett's general behavior was working a change in some attitudes. Manuelito, who had previously avoided agents, appeared on October 3, to return four stolen horses and a mule. Yet the great warrior did not apprehend the rustlers. This was to become a method of operation for Navajo leaders, and Bennett raised no objections. His decision made the jobs of the chiefs easier, but he was unable to accomplish all that he wanted. His request for passes for the chiefs had been denied.[9] The agent, however, did not lose much face because an opportunity to build up goodwill presented itself.

In November, the promised livestock finally arrived. Purchased in La Cueva, New Mexico, the animals had been driven to Fort Defiance and were a little thin, but the sheep were tough, little Spanish *churros* who managed to survive and multiply under the extreme care provided by their new owners. The distribution of the animals, 2 per person, took five days, and 8,121 people appeared for the distribution of 14,000 sheep and 1,000 goats. It was fifteen months after the signing of the treaty, and the number of animals given out was short of what the Indians required. But the event was filled with wonder and hope. Bennett remarked that he had never seen so much gratitude.[10]

He saw an immediate reward for his efforts. Ganado Mucho, Narbono, Manuelito, and Agua Grande heard that livestock stolen at Rio Arriba was being brought onto the reservation. Acting quickly, they chased after the rustlers. Finding the thieves' camp, the chiefs approached and the criminals fled. They did not attempt pursuit. They rounded up eight horses and turned them over to Bennett. They told him that probably there had been more animals and they had been eaten. The agent accepted their explanation and waited for someone to claim the horses.[11]

Bennett, however, could not wait in peace. Representatives of Zuni Pueblo, located southeast of the Navajos, visited Fort Defiance, met with Bennett, reported Navajo depredations, and demanded that justice be done. The agent gathered the available chiefs and held a council. The Navajos and Zunis had been enemies for a long time. The Zunis had probably gotten the worst of it, but the Navajos also had a grievance that they detailed at the meeting. In 1863, the Navajo leaders explained, the Zunis had held one hundred Navajos as prisoners. Tired of feeding them any longer, the Zuni chiefs marched the captives, almost naked, into the pueblo square and told them to run for it. With the exits blocked, the Navajos ran desperately through the narrow corridors of the village, only to be clubbed to death. At the council, the Zuni representatives, forced to sit through a recitation of their crime, demanded less than expected. Even though there had been many depredations, they agreed to concentrate on only one, the recent robbery and murder of one of their tribesmen. Navajo leaders proposed that the stolen goods be replaced, and the Zunis accepted their offer. In an orgy of goodwill, the Navajos removed articles of clothing and gave them away. The Zunis left in peace.[12] Bennett, ignoring the fact that no murderer had been apprehended, was pleased with the outcome, but the agreement was only a truce.

Truces seemed to be the order of the day, for permanent peace was beyond the capacity of the Navajo leaders. On November 17, the Santa Fe *Daily New Mexican* reported that either Navajos or Utes had raided Rio Oso and taken nineteen horses. A few days later, Indians attempted the theft of twelve thousand sheep in Doña Ana County. A posse led by Tuburio Madrid caught up with the Indians, killing three in battle. The sheep and a stolen horse were recovered, as was a shepherd boy who had been taken captive and stabbed three times. The tribe of the raiders was not identified, but it was difficult to conceive of any tribe other than the Navajos that could absorb the stolen sheep.[13]

Concurrently, three or four parties of Navajos had raided Paiutes. One of the raiders had been killed, but not many people, according to Bennett, complained about his death. He concluded that most Navajos believed that "he got what he deserved." The agent was pleased with the chiefs for discouraging raids. With information provided by them, he had been able to reason with several groups of would-be raiders and convince them of the error of their ways.[14]

Bennett, nonetheless, warned Superintendent William Clinton that the government needed to do more. The Navajos would steal before they would starve. He urged more government aid:

> In my opinion the majority of the Navajos (with the exception of a few young men) are as quiet, peaceably disposed, and as industrious as any Indians on the face of the Globe, and that the chiefs, and nearly all, are using great exertions to have everything peaceable and quiet, and all stealing stopped, and just at present is the time that they need all the encouragement possible.[15]

Bennett, of course, was pointing out the central dilemma that he faced. The government wanted to pacify the Navajos, but it was unwilling to satisfy their basic needs.

The government hoped that the Navajos would become self-supporting, but it failed to provide them with adequate means for rebuilding their economy on a smaller land base. It was a policy equation that used the wrong arithmetic. If the Navajos were to revive their economy, they had to use more land than the government had given them. At the same time, they had to pacify Anglo-Americans. Navajo leaders were able to blunt reactions to the most outrageous forms of Navajo self-help. Even so, their pre-national political structure prevented them from becoming out-and-out government apologists. The Bosque Redondo had not defeated the Navajos psychologically. In late 1869, they were a dynamic people who, with an expanding population, were intent upon reviving their economy. To do this, they needed land and livestock. They demanded leaders who justified most of what they did or minimized the results of punishable acts.

Similarly, Navajo leaders expected their agent to defend the tribe's position. By the end of 1869, the Diné resided off the reservation wherever they could. Although they had been blocked somewhat to the east and south, they had moved west and north and attempted to hold what lands they could to the east. They had established a Navajo frontier. Bennett recognized this when he, unlike his predecessors, refused to pay lip service to the idea that the Navajos could survive solely on the reservation. He knew that forcing all Navajos to live on the reservation was impossible, but his decision to leave the Indians where they were was open to criticism. He may have understood that this problem would require years of patience, but in the interim, he decided to emphasize the positive.

In December, Bennett called the chiefs together in council. He told them that he wanted the raiding to stop. The leaders replied that they would do all that they could. If they heard of a raid, they would organize parties to halt it, using force if necessary. They added that they were at peace with all of their neighbors, and Bennett endorsed their fiction.[16]

Ironically, an incident occurred in the same month that belied this optimism. Several Cañoncito Navajos traveled to Fort Defiance in November. When they returned, they found the body of a woman where normally she had chopped wood. One Navajo, José Castillo, was informed that two Mexican Americans had attacked her and taken her little girl into captivity.[17] The slavery issue would not go away in spite of laws against involuntary servitude.

This fact was emphasized early in 1870, when Bennett arranged for Barboncito and other leaders to visit Santa Fe. Traveling under military escort, the chiefs were treated well by New Mexicans along the way and impressed by their treatment in the territory's capital. Nevertheless, when they met with Clinton, they complained about slavery and took Clinton to homes in Santa Fe where six Navajo women were held captive. The superintendent pledged to investigate the matter, but nothing was done. Despite this unsatisfactory conclusion, Clinton urged the chiefs to stop Navajo raids, and they pledged to do their best.[18]

In the meantime, Bennett hired Thomas and William Keam as Spanish interpreters. Thomas Keam had been born in Cornwall County, England, and served in the English mercantile marine. While docked in San Francisco, he abandoned seamanship and enlisted in Carleton's California Volunteers. Once in New Mexico, he served with Kit Carson in the New Mexico Volunteers. Keam was promoted to the rank of second lieutenant during the Navajo war. After the Navajos' return from exile, he was back in their country looking for work, along with his brother who had joined him. Bennett soon tried to get Thomas on the payroll as a clerk, a job that he already did.[19]

In late January of 1870, Bennett sent William Keam and Lieutenant S. Ford, special Indian agent, on a trip through Cebolleta, Albuquerque, and Santa Fe in search of captive Navajo children. They had no luck. Many Navajos had located their children but, short of kidnapping, there was little else they could do if those holding them were unwilling to release them. Ford and Keam were told that the children did not want to leave. Bennett, who refused to accept these rationalizations, did not believe that the Indians could receive justice in New Mexico's courts.[20]

Bennett was angry with New Mexicans. He thought they were too quick to label Navajo raids as insidious because they too were rustlers and Navajos were forced to fight them to get their property back. He was certain that no one had voluntarily returned any stolen property to a Navajo since he had been agent. He wrote:

> I could work here to much better advantage, if the good and law abiding Mexicans were to show the same spirit in returning stolen property and furnishing the bad men as the good men of the Navajo tribe have shown toward them. The Chiefs are continually asking me to do all possible for them, and express their dissatisfaction that nothing has been done in regard to returning stolen property to them.[21]

Bennett was so enraged that he was even willing to blame some Navajo crimes on Mexican Americans.

Manuel Antonio Jaramillo, a freighter, had an ox stolen from him while delivering goods to Fort Wingate. Such thefts were not rare, but it was the agent's opinion that freighters headed into Navajo country should be less careless. He urged that supply trains not be allowed in the area unless they were made up of at least eight wagons. The chiefs, however, had a more practical solution. They delegated a few Navajos under the charge of Delgadito to escort the wagons.[22]

The chiefs continued to act on the agent's behalf. When Indians from Acoma Pueblo showed up at the agency claiming that Navajos had stolen four horses and ten head of cattle, the headmen located the horses but not the cattle. Delgadito took the Acomas with him to reclaim the horses, but the situation was not easily solved. The Pueblo agent wanted payment for the cattle.[23]

Bennett agreed to pay for the cattle, but he insisted that an affidavit be filed in Santa Fe. Despite the fact that he offered to endorse the claim, he earned the wrath of Captain Evans at Fort Wingate for not handling the matter more expeditiously.[24] He wrote Bennett:

> Pray who is to make the Affidavit to which you refer? And if it should be made by a Pueblo Indian who knows so much about Affidavits—and then should go to Santa Fe, and then to Fort Defiance, and then be favorably endorsed by you . . . WHAT NEXT? And about how soon do you think payment would be made?[25]

61

Evans believed that Bennett should give the Acomas ten head of cattle out of the agency herd, but he had other items to raise with the agent. He had been told that Navajo outlaws were contemplating three different raids: one to Canyon Juan Tafoya, another along the Rio Grande, and a third east of the Rio Grande.[26]

Bennett replied that anyone could file an affidavit. He claimed that he was only following policy. In reply to Evans's contention that Navajo raids were about to happen, Bennett insisted that the chiefs were ignorant of any violation of law. The Acomas went home without their cattle.[27]

As the Acoma matter indicated, there was a growing tension between Bennett and the military. The army, however, did not disagree with the strategy of avoiding war and downplaying raiding. Like Bennett, officers preferred to emphasize how peaceful most Navajos were. In fact, raids were still frequent. Navajo flocks were increasing more rapidly than they could have done by reproduction.[28] But Bennett and the army disagreed about how to handle the problem. Bennett relied on the chiefs to return what had been stolen. Army officers, at this point in time, wanted offenders punished.

Bennett and the army agreed on the reason for the raids. The Navajos were a poor people. As representatives of a government that wanted peace, the agent and his military counterparts were concerned about the inefficiency of the Indian Bureau in supplying Navajo needs. In late February and early March, Bennett had to put off the issue of annuity goods for lack of supplies. When he did call in the Navajos on March 16, he did not have enough seed wheat and had to restrict the issue to those who seemed most enthusiastic. Many of the farm implements supplied by the government were inappropriate. The hoes, for example, were too small, and he could not get the government to send bigger ones. Bennett heard a rumor that the Navajos were selling their annuities for sheep. He denied it, but the rumors were probably true. In May, Bennett was finally able to issue seed corn and reported that all able-bodied Navajos were working in their fields. During this time, the Diné went hungry. The army provided emergency rations.[29]

Raids, however, continued. In early March, Bennett mentioned in a letter to Clinton that the number of claims for stolen stock was growing. In April, he was embarrassed by a theft of sixty cattle from the agency corrals. Bennett cut off beef rations at Fort Defiance, but he was certain that the chiefs were curbing most thefts. In an important way they were. Pressure upon the eastern Navajos had lessened somewhat because New Mexican settlement in the area had slowed. It seemed, moreover, that perceptions were changing. The chiefs were turning in more livestock, and Bennett insisted that the majority of Navajos were peaceful. This rudimentary public-relations effort seemed to work. In May, New Mexico Governor William A. Pile praised the Navajos because no white man had been killed by Navajos in the previous six months.[30]

Whatever satisfaction Pile's acclamation may have brought, Bennett had little time to reflect. About May 3, three Navajos went to Zuni to trade. The day after they returned, Bennett observed two drunks. When he ordered the men to go to their hogans, they went peacefully, but the agent was worried about the consequences of alcohol on the reservation. He had heard that a white trader in Zuni was bartering for whiskey, ammunition, and powder. He sent word to Fort Wingate, but the army was aware of the situation. In March, a visitor to Fort Wingate had reported that a trader, Solomon Barth, was dealing in illegal goods. Earlier in the year, Barth had been appointed as post trader at Camp Apache and would later become one of the founders of St. Johns, Arizona.[31]

In May, troops from Fort Wingate went out four times to Cubero and Zuni in search of illegal traders. Soon, Barth's brother Morris was placed in the guardhouse at Fort Wingate on charges of selling gunpowder, lead, and whiskey to Apaches. Two others were locked up, and charges would eventually be pressed against Solomon Barth. Nevertheless, none of these men were convicted.

Bennett was angry. Navajos had purchased whiskey, and he wanted illegal merchants to be punished.[32]

As usual, Bennett had little time to concentrate on a single issue. On May 30, he started an inspection trip to Canyon de Chelly. About halfway there, he was caught in one of the worst storms in his experience, and he was forced to turn back. The ground was frozen the next three nights, and almost all Navajo crops were killed. The Navajos were, in Bennett's words, the "most sorrowful, down hearted people that I ever saw."[33]

This crop failure led to increased raiding. Not wanting to cut into their flocks for food, the Diné saw raiding as a reasonable alternative to starvation. Renewed violence caused an open dispute between Bennett and Major William Redwood Price, the new commander of Fort Wingate. Bennett visited Cebolleta, Santa Fe, and Albuquerque in June, looking for slaves, and he came back convinced that the Navajos would never get justice unless they received outside help. People in the New Mexican towns were afraid to discuss the matter. The Navajos were dissatisfied. Bennett did not blame them.[34] When he returned, he faced the anger of the military.

Major Price wrote to the acting assistant adjutant general for the department of New Mexico, William A. Kobbe, on June 11. He mentioned that he had stolen livestock in his possession, and the Navajos who returned the animals knew who had stolen them, but they refused to talk. He thought that Bennett encouraged this habit. Believing that no illegal act should go unpunished, Price asked Barboncito how the Navajos punished criminals.[35]

Barboncito could have answered that his people usually punished offenders by demanding payment from them or from their relatives. Perhaps he did, and his meaning fell victim to a poor translation. In any case, Price understood him to say that the Diné did not punish criminals. He asked the chief how he took care of raids. Barboncito replied that the process was simple. When the headmen heard of stolen property, they went out to speak with those who held it, and the thieves usually gave it up with little resistance. Bennett, Price claimed, supported this formula because he was afraid. Isolated at Fort Defiance, he did not have protection if the Navajos became hostile. Price therefore urged that the agency be moved closer to Fort Wingate.[36]

There was considerable evidence of Navajo aggression. In early July, Special Indian Agent William F. M. Arny observed three hundred Navajos in the Chaco Canyon "engaged in war practice." He spoke with Navajo leader Agua Grande, who returned a stolen horse and some mules. Bennett noted, in August, that the chiefs had turned several animals over to him: twenty sheep, eleven horses, three burros, and a mule. He was convinced that he could continue to get their support.[37] Major Price found the situation more difficult.

Groups of Navajos had stolen livestock in Laguna and Los Lunas. Manuelito heard of the raids and sent word to Bennett that he had recovered some of the stock. Bennett requested military assistance. Price ordered Captain S. B. W. Young into the field. Young's detachment of fifty men proceeded to a valley about twenty-five miles from the fort. Setting up camp, Young sent word to Manuelito, who was seven miles away, that he had come to see him. Soon after dark, interpreter Jesus Arviso and three Navajos brought in thirty-two sheep, three horses, and two burros.[38]

Young sent word to Manuelito asking him to discuss the theft. A messenger returned with word that Manuelito had left for home, stating that he had no further business with Young. The captain spoke to Arviso and determined that Manuelito knew who the thieves were but would not surrender them. As Young returned to the fort, he believed that he was retreating and that hostile Navajos thought he was afraid of them. Arriving at Fort Wingate on August 25, he asked Bennett if the thieves should be punished. Bennett's reply was that he did not think so since the Indians had apologized to him and Manuelito.[39] Young angrily wrote:

The principle of paying high rewards to these Indians for returning stock that they have stolen and allowing the thieves to go scot-free, if carried out properly for the fiscal year will no doubt obviate the necessity of an appropriation from Congress next year and thereby save one hundred and sixty eight thousand (168,000) dollars to the Public Treasury, and at the same time make the Navajo Nation a self-sustaining institution.[40]

Captain Young was narrow in his assessment of Manuelito's actions; the Navajo leader had used force against his own people to recover stolen property at about this time, a significant escalation in his own efforts against the raiders.[41] Major Price, on the other hand, was confronted with angry citizens.

Fifty armed men appeared at Fort Wingate under the leadership of the Los Lunas probate judge Antonico Lunas. They claimed that 462 sheep, 1 horse, and 2 burros had been stolen from them on August 7. They had formed a company and followed the tracks of the rustlers to the edge of the reservation. They identified the thirty-two sheep, the burros, and one of the horses returned by Manuelito as their own. They also recognized two remaining horses as belonging to a man who lived across the river from them. Price handed over the animals. But the group was still angry and ready to fight. He doubted that the rustlers' apology to the agent and Manuelito would satisfy them. He sent Lunas to meet with Bennett.[42] Whatever came of this conversation is not known, but Price was embarrassed. He wrote Bennett:

I consider such a policy very unjust to the Military authorities and to the citizens of this Territory and unhumane [sic] towards the Indians, it is an encouragement to them to steal which if pursued, will lead to war with them and the killing and destruction of property of many of them, who are good and desire to live in peace.[43]

Not much came of this disagreement. Conflict, however, continued.

In August, Navajos stole four mules from Anastacio Sandoval in Chaparita. In late September, the chiefs turned in sixty-seven head of stolen sheep. In early October, Special Agent Arny, still on tour, came across a group of Cañoncito Navajos who had just completed a successful raid on the Coyotero Apaches. Arny noted that they had captured eleven children whom they refused to surrender.[44]

Not all news was bad for the authorities. In September, for instance, the Utes, claiming that the whites would eventually take all Indian lands, urged the Navajos to go to war. After talking it over among themselves, the Diné rejected the offer. They had too much hostility toward the Utes, and the Navajos did not see much point in waging war.[45]

More significantly, the Diné and the Mormons were about to make significant progress toward peace. The two groups had been fighting an off-again, on-again guerrilla war for years. What brought the two peoples into contact was a complex combination of Mormon theological doctrine and perceptions of American social and political circumstances. According to their founding prophet, Joseph Smith, Native Americans were Lamanites, descendants of lost Israelites who had gone bad after having the good fortune of witnessing a visit from Jesus. Mormons believed that it was their responsibility to bring these children of God back into the fold. Their current leader, Brigham Young, was convinced that the Mormons had not seen the end of persecution by their fellow Americans. His people had been driven out of many locations, and he was certain that the Latter Day Saints, as they called themselves, would have to move to another land. This insight led to Young's decision, in 1872, that northern Mexico offered opportunity. Young believed that his people must establish a line of settlements stretching south toward the border. In this manner, he hoped to lessen the hardships that might be suffered on a migration.[46]

Mormons had moved south quickly after settling the Salt Lake Basin in 1847. By the 1850s, the faithful were approaching Navajo borders in southern Utah. They made their first excursion into Navajo territory in 1854 and another the following year. One of the major characters in the development of the West, Jacob Hamblin, soon stepped into the picture. He was a tall, soft-spoken man who claimed to have received a message from on-high that promised a Native American would never kill him as long as he never caused an Indian to shed blood. Honest and fearless and a devout Mormon with eight wives, one of them a Paiute, Hamblin was dedicated to his mission.[47]

When rumors reached the Mormons, in 1858, that a civilized tribe of Indians, the Hopis, existed to the south, Hamblin was ordered to investigate. The Hopis received him in friendship, but they rejected his religion. He returned the following year. In 1860, Hamblin tried to return to the Hopi villages, but one of his party was killed by a group of Navajos. Forced to return to southern Utah, he was back among the Hopi a year later. As the Navajos became involved in hostilities with Americans, however, many of them retreated north, and life on the Mormon–Navajo frontier became perilous, especially after Kit Carson's campaign. Beginning in 1863, Navajo and Ute raids into southern Utah were frequent. By 1866, Brigham Young told his followers on the frontier to live in fewer and less scattered communities and to barricade their corrals. With the help of Paiutes, the Latter Day Saints were able to make raids tougher to accomplish, but the Navajos still represented a nuisance that cost the settlers a considerable amount of money. In 1869, Mormon militia attempted twice to capture offending Indians by invading Navajo country with little success.[48]

Mormon leaders sent several appeals, but no action resulted. Officials in New Mexico lacked the resources to stop Navajo raids. In late 1869, however, a letter from Mormon elder Erastus Snow reached Superintendent Clinton. Clinton forwarded the letter to Bennett, who called a council in early 1870. According to Bennett, the chiefs were anxious to settle the issue. They admitted that many of their people had gone into Mormon country, but they had been told that these groups had gone hunting. Now, they agreed, they would try to bring this raiding to a halt.[49] The Navajo leaders, of course, could not keep their promise. Many of the Diné who were raiding Utah had not been to the Bosque Redondo and were not under government control, and most Navajos regarded the Mormons as a separate people from the Americans. It would take time for the leaders to get the word out that Mormons were also included in their pledge not to fight Americans.

A month later, Navajo raiders stole several horses from Charles Pulsipher at Hebron, Utah. In February, Major Evans reported that he had heard of a group of men planning to raid the Mormons. Periodic rustling forays occurred throughout the spring and summer, but these were few in comparison to what the Mormons believed would happen during the late fall and early winter.[50]

Brigham Young faced a dilemma. With ever-increasing immigration to his colony, his people needed more land. The Navajos were forming an effective barrier against their southern expansion. Military force had not been effective, and he could not be sure of government support if a war developed. Therefore, in the spring, he traveled to Kanab with his counselor, George A. Smith, and with Snow to meet with Hamblin.[51]

Meanwhile, Hamblin had determined that trouble with the Navajos had to be settled peacefully. He made up his mind to talk with them as soon as circumstances permitted.[52] He expressed these thoughts to President Young and tried to make his point forcefully:

> I told him that I desired to visit the Navajoes [sic], and have a talk with them; that there had been a number of raiders killed, and I never saw a Navajoe's bones on the ground, the flesh having been eaten by wolves and vultures . . . that I always abhorred the shedding of blood, and desired to obtain peace in some better way.[53]

Young agreed with Hamblin.

Hamblin's opportunity to go to the Navajos presented itself in the person of the explorer Major John Wesley Powell, who had asked Brigham Young to provide him with a guide to the canyon country. Powell, who was in charge of an expedition attempting to map the West, had experienced some trouble during his Colorado River expedition the previous year with a group of Paiutes, and he needed to assure his expedition's safety when it explored the Colorado River and its canyons. President Young recommended Hamblin. The two men met in September, visited the Paiutes, crossed the Colorado at what would be the site of Lee's Ferry, and were in the Hopi villages by October.[54]

As Powell, Hamblin, a Hopi interpreter, and Mormon pioneer Ammon M. Tenney left Oraibi, they noticed that they were being followed by two Navajo riders. The Navajos kept their distance from the white men, but they came to the rescue just as the small party was about to be ambushed by two other Navajos. The ambushers were disarmed. The Hamblin party arrived at Fort Defiance on November 1. Some six thousand of the Diné had gathered for a distribution of annuities. Captain Bennett welcomed Hamblin and arranged for a council.[55]

Even though the council was held on November 5, there were several days of informal talks and a brief meeting on November 4 with Barboncito. Powell, who had lost an arm at Shiloh, spoke, falsely giving the impression that he was a government representative. He praised the Mormons and added that they paid taxes which, in part, bought the Navajos' annuity goods. He reminded the chiefs that the government would send soldiers if the raiding did not stop.[56] Then Hamblin spoke:

> What shall I tell my people, the Mormons, when I return home? That we may live in peace, live as friends, and trade with one another? Or shall we look for you to come prowling around our weak settlements, like wolves in the night? I hope we may live in peace in time to come. I have now gray hairs on my head, and from my boyhood I have been on the frontiers doing all I could to preserve peace between white men and Indians. I despise this killing, this shedding of blood. I hope you will stop this and come and visit and trade with our people. We would like to hear what you have got to say before we go home.[57]

Barboncito was diplomatic.

He emphasized that many of the raiders had not been to the Bosque and were rarely at Fort Defiance. He pointed out that the Mormons had killed several Diné. He added that the Navajos were often blamed for Paiute raids. But he agreed that there should be peace. Barboncito walked up to Hamblin, put his arms around the fifty-one-year-old frontier veteran, and said, "My friend and brother, I will do all that I can to bring about what you have advised. We will not give all of our answer now. Many of the Navajos are here. We will talk to them tonight."[58]

Barboncito spoke to a number of Navajos that night. None of the white men understood what he was saying, but they all agreed that it was a well-presented speech. They noticed many Navajos nodding in agreement. Nevertheless, not all were convinced. The next day, several men rode around on Mormon horses and gestured for the visitors to get them back if they could. Despite this provocation, the talks went on. Hamblin agreed to let the Navajos have the animals they possessed as long as they agreed to stop the raids. Barboncito was remarkably honest in replying that he would try, that the chiefs would return stolen property when they found it, but that they could not guarantee the conduct of all their people. This satisfied Hamblin, and an agreement was reached.[59]

Bennett wrote a letter and gave it to Hamblin. In it, he expressed his belief that the Navajo leaders would do their best to keep the agreement. Bennett claimed that the chiefs would go any place to stop raids, using force if necessary. Barboncito was true to his word. Powell traveled to Fort Wingate to catch a stagecoach east, and Hamblin returned to the Hopi villages. Barboncito met him there with several headmen who had not been at Fort Defiance. The talks went peacefully. Later in the year, Barboncito visited northern renegades to urge them to remain at peace. When Hamblin made it home to Kanab, there were eighty Navajos waiting there to trade. To show his goodwill, he traded fifty of the church's tithing horses for Navajo blankets. The Indians went away satisfied.[60]

If the relative peace that resulted from the agreement with the Mormons represented the best of Barboncito and Bennett's diplomacy, there were events to finish out the year that re-

71

minded them that Navajo affairs were still in crisis. On November 25, Acoma rustlers stole two horses from Barboncito. Busy with other matters, he had Bennett issue passes for two of his followers to go to Acoma. Upon their arrival, Barboncito's men were informed by the governor of Acoma that he had apprehended the thief, but he did not have the horses. The rustler had gone to Los Lunas and traded the mounts for an inferior horse, a pistol, a carbine, twenty yards of manta, twenty yards of calico, some chile, flour, sugar, and a box of matches. Not knowing what to do, Barboncito's representatives returned to inquire about the appropriate action. Barboncito requested that Major Price send a detachment to Los Lunas to pick up his property. Instead, the military expedition went back to Acoma, picked up what the rustler had received in trade, and headed for Fort Wingate. During the return, three soldiers deserted and took the horse, the pistol, and the chile with them. When Barboncito learned what had occurred, he was angry, and Bennett protested vehemently.[61]

Navajo raids continued. In December, Juan Sedillo and Federico Lopez were attacked by twelve Navajos thirty-five miles from Albuquerque. William Werner of Rio Grande wrote Clinton that everybody who was out on the road could attest to the fact that Navajos were in the vicinity of Rio Abajo and that the mountains east of Albuquerque were "full" of the tribesmen.[62]

Bennett's time in office had been dramatic. Soon after his arrival at Fort Defiance, he expressed the belief that the chiefs lacked authority. Not understanding Navajo power structures, he acted to help the chiefs by bringing other headmen into his system of administration—an act that helped, despite the fact that it was made upon the wrong assumptions, for the men "given" power already had it. It was not long, however, before the chiefs were proving him wrong by displaying their own authority, although not in a way that was immediately recognized by most of the officers at Fort Wingate. But Bennett understood that they were attempting to police their own people in their own way, and he adopted a policy that would eventually be copied by the army because the Navajo proved to be good at controlling themselves. Unfortunately, Navajo leaders operated only as part-time enforcers, and they could not stop all of the raids.

Bennett tried to encourage their efforts. He more or less ignored government policy and did not insist that Navajos live on the reservation. Nevertheless, raids increased, and Bennett tried to protect his charges from adverse reaction by blaming the Utes and New Mexicans. He also reminded his superiors that Navajos had their own grievances. Those living off the reservation were constantly harassed, and most Navajo captives held in New Mexican settlements had not been returned.

Navajos seemed to respond to their agent. He was well liked and achieved a reputation among the Diné as a fair man. It was perhaps for this reason that Manuelito began to cooperate. The warrior appeared to be much more militant, both in policing his own people and in responding to American authority. Occasionally resorting to violence to control the eastern Diné, he used subterfuge to deal with Captain Young, who demanded that he act according to American law.

Although conflict continued, non-Navajo deaths decreased due to Navajo restraint. Yet settlement of lands claimed by the Diné to the east of the reservation slowed because of perceptions of Navajo militancy. This same contradictory message seemed to enable the Navajos to settle with the Mormons, who felt the wrath of federal authority and attempted to settle matters on their own. Bennett assisted both sides, and Barboncito, in the last great political act of his life, was able to influence Navajos who had not been to the Bosque Redondo.

The Navajos' struggle, however, was not over. Their old battles continued, and the government was instituting a new direction in policy. The only indication the Indians had of this change was the fact that Bennett was leaving. Although Bennett had offered unsuccessfully to resign his commission in the army to stay on as agent, he did not act dramatically when he left. On February 1, 1871, Bennett wrote to the recently appointed New Mexico superintendent of Indian affairs, Nathaniel Pope, that he had received two hundred head of cattle. The meat from these animals, he estimated, would last until February 3. He stated that the Navajo population was 8,238 and added, almost as an afterthought, that his successor, James Miller, had arrived on January 30. Bennett returned to active duty in the army.[63]

4

Grant's Peace Policy

S outhwest of Navajo country on the morning of April 29, 1871, near Camp Grant, Arizona Territory, a party of six Anglo-Americans, forty-eight Mexican Americans, and ninety-four Papagos laid in ambush. At sunrise, under the leadership of prominent Tucson citizens, William Sanders Oury and Jesus María Elias, the vigilantes swooped down upon the Indians and met with little resistance. When the battle ceased, the unofficial posse discovered that it had killed eight Apache men and one hundred women and children. Most adult males in the band, which had surrendered to Lieutenant Royal Emerson at Camp Grant, had been out hunting. Twenty-eight children were taken captive and held as slaves.[1]

As word of the "Camp Grant Massacre" spread from tribe to tribe, invoking fear and distrust, newspaper accounts attracted national attention. President Grant, for instance, called it "pure slaughter." The citizens of Tucson, on the other hand, were not so critical. Frequent Apache depredations, they felt, justified the group's action. When participants were brought to trial for murder, they were acquitted by a local jury. People who believed in justice were infuriated.[2]

Disagreement over the Camp Grant matter symbolized a longstanding debate over Indian policy between Anglo-American factions. Two of these groups represented geographical regions. Many westerners felt that they were under siege from Indian attack. Advocating a raw Manifest Destiny, they were rarely concerned with the rights of Native Americans, whom they saw as obstacles to progress. Those who bothered to justify removing this roadblock claimed that Indians did not use land in the ways that

God had intended; they were a vanishing race destined for extinction.[3]

Certain advocates of white dominance, however, were unwilling to await the fulfillment of their prophecies; they wanted to help extinction along and advocated war. Others, unwilling to call for extermination, were against all but the most limited and undesirable reservations and believed that violent action was the only language that the aborigines understood. Failing to comprehend the grief that their beliefs would cause among the natives, militant westerners watched constantly to determine if Indian lands were desirable, relying on a sympathetic local press to advertise such developments.[4]

These ideas contrasted sharply with those of reformers, largely in the East, who wanted to protect Indians and bring them into the mainstream of American civilization. Provoked in part by incidents such as the Camp Grant Massacre, these reformers saw the Civil War as their original stimulus. As a moral crusade against slavery, the war had released reform energies within the country. Once the slaves had been freed, a good number of idealists looked for a new issue with which to concern themselves. Several of these moralists, closely identified with Protestantism, turned to solving the issue of what to do with Native Americans. Distrustful of the military and westerners, they sought a way to bring a peace to the frontier that would allow for the advance of American civilization and justice for the natives.[5]

This impulse to help the Indian was hardly new to the American republic, but it became the focus of much attention and renewed vigor toward the end of the 1860s. The work of the Doolittle Commission and the Peace Commission represented the beginnings of the movement as well as the stimulation of further activity. When President Grant was preparing to take office in 1869, he was visited by a group of Quakers. The Friends urged Grant to adopt a policy based upon Christianity and peace. They also encouraged him to appoint Christian men as agents. Grant's answer has become famous. "Gentlemen," he said, "your advice is good. I accept it. Now give me the names of some

Friends for Indian agents and I will appoint them. If you can make Quakers out of the Indians it will take the fight out of them. Let us have peace."[6]

The president added an important caveat by stating that any Indians who did not accept the new policy would fall victim to a "severe war policy." His warning was lost, however, in the general clamor about peace with the Indians. Grant appointed eighteen Quakers to posts on the plains, but he filled the remainder of the positions with army officers. He named as his first commissioner of Indian affairs a Seneca Indian, his former aide-de-camp Ely S. Parker. Grant and Parker tried to move Indian affairs back into the hands of the military, but when a Congress eager to restore patronage defeated his attempts and outlawed the practice of filling Indian positions with military men, the president gave in to the Christian reformers and handed over the job of appointing agency personnel to Protestant religious denominations. Grant also accepted the reformers' idea of an independent, unpaid Board of Indian Commissioners to oversee the implementation of policy.[7]

With these imperfect instruments in place, Grant's Peace Policy gradually took on several objectives that promised to end the Indian wars. Native Americans were to be placed upon reservations with Christian agents, schoolteachers, missionaries, and farmers who would teach them the arts of civilization. The Indians were to be taught how to live like other Americans and to give up their former ways. Eventually, they would assimilate into American life, but in the meantime, they were to be isolated from rough frontier elements, who were forbidden to enter the reservations, and placed under the control of "good" people who would guide them.[8]

No one bothered to ask the Indians. They were to become Christians, send their children to school, and farm individual plots of land. It was understood that they would cooperate if they wanted to survive. Nonetheless, difficulties were soon apparent. The Board of Indian Commissioners was not given equal power with executive authorities, and the churches discovered that finding good Christians who were also good administrators as Indian agents was a formidable task. Nor was it always possible to eradicate violence with Christian forbearance. Some Christian agents arrived at the reservations as pacifists and left some time later as hardened advocates of war. Finally, some westerners were rabidly opposed to peace with the Indians.[9] In short, the Peace Policy was not much more effective, and not very different in its goals, from Carleton's experiment with the Navajos.

By 1871, Navajos ironically had developed ways to check frontier pressures and probably saw the Peace Policy as a threat. Their leaders had managed to win the goodwill of government agents and the military, and they had accomplished with their loose political structure what might have seemed impossible, a relatively effective control of their most troublesome people. The Diné had also been able to command the respect of their neighbors by their large population, their reputations as warriors, their raids, and their obvious willingness to protect what was theirs.

Their willingness to use force on occasion had been demonstrated when, as early as 1869, Navajos drove New Mexican herds off land they believed to be their own. Such protectiveness continued into the 1870s, when, at times, the Diné proved to be touchy about even casual intruders. For example, James G. H. Colter, who founded Colter, Arizona, to the south of present-day Springerville in 1872, had his first Indian trouble on the Navajo Reservation. Colter and a number of his employees were transporting several wagons of supplies across Navajo lands. Their presence was soon detected by 150 Navajos. Some of the hired hands informed Colter that they thought it best to fire at the Indians before they had a chance to respond. Colter commented that the odds were against them and that it would be a good idea to avoid a fight. He decided to negotiate. In the long, tortuous talk that followed between men who knew little of each other's language, Colter conveyed his meaning to the Navajos. He offered half of a wagonload of foodstuffs as a "toll" across the reservation and was delighted when the Indians accepted his offer. As soon as the Navajos left, Colter and his men drove their teams all night and into the next day until the animals were exhausted and they were well beyond the realm of the Navajos.[10]

Such Navajo actions tended to instill a healthy respect among their neighbors that partially explained the limited nature of Anglo-American and Mexican-American retaliation for Navajo raids. In addition, the army had become an effective force in policing non-Navajo aggressors. Laws against slavery and peonage had removed one of the causes for New Mexican attacks, as had Navajo insistence that the laws be enforced. Finally, the Diné had not yet felt the full brunt of the advancing Anglo-Americans. The Navajos, in short, seemed to have established themselves as a permanent strand within the fabric of the Southwest and had accomplished a rough parity with their neighbors. It appeared that no Indian tribe needed less of the reformers' protection.

The Navajos, nevertheless, were assigned to the Presbyterians who, like many Protestant churches at the time, already had a loose administrative structure to accept their new responsibilities. Their Board of Foreign Missions added Indian missionary and educational work to its duties. Finding agents for the nine agencies given them did not appear difficult at first. Indeed, they were confident in the initial years of the Peace Policy. To accomplish this formidable task, the Board hoped to find young men and women who could teach and minister to the health of their wards. These soldiers for Christ were expected to be married, to provide a good example to their wards, and to discourage the temptation to cohabit with natives.[11]

The first individuals to represent the Presbyterians and the Peace Policy to the Navajos were not agents, but missionaries and teachers. The first missionary to arrive was James Madison Roberts, a recent graduate of the Western Theological Seminary of Allegheny, Pennsylvania. Newly married, Reverend Roberts arrived at Fort Defiance on January 15, 1869, just in time to preside at Dodd's funeral. The chiefs, ever observant of new arrivals at the agency, questioned Roberts about his intentions, and he declared that he had come to provide for the education of Navajo children as stipulated in the treaty. Although Navajo leaders promised to aid his efforts, the school was not successful. Few children enrolled, and hungry Navajos stole his chickens, broke into his kitchen, and milked his cows. Despite these setbacks, Roberts petitioned Agent French for one hundred acres to be used as a farm school. When French and the Indian Bureau dodged the issue, he was disappointed. Dependent on Presbyterian donations for his living expenses, he hoped to be appointed as agency teacher and declared that Navajo children would not be truly educated until they were confined to a boarding school.[12]

Roberts was disappointed again when the new teacher, Miss Charity Ann Gaston of Knoxville, Illinois, arrived on October 12, 1869. She was a tall, angular woman who had done some teaching in the Indian Territory among the Choctaws. She was given the salary of six hundred dollars per year that Roberts had hoped for. If Miss Gaston was ever enthusiastic about her new position, her hopes were dashed upon viewing the school, a crumbling adobe structure that would double as her living quarters. Nevertheless, school began in November, and she saw a rise in enrollment from thirty-five to forty students. Gaston taught the English alphabet and arithmetic, as well as sewing and knitting to the girls. She found the students easy to control and intelligent, but she also reported some difficulties.[13]

Although attendance had at first averaged twenty-two, it dropped and eventually proved extraordinarily uneven, as high as thirty-three and as low as three. This phenomenon seemed to have resulted from a concern on the part of the Navajos that what the teacher was conveying to the children was a sort of magic. Parents were reluctant to submit normal children to such potential evil and often sent slaves and unhealthy offspring to the school. Even these were not allowed to stay long enough to be sufficiently contaminated. The Diné were also hesitant to remove their children from useful pursuits such as herding sheep. Like Roberts, Miss Gaston proposed to remedy the situation by forcing the children to live full time with a family, where "they would progress more rapidly in learning the English language and civilization." Meanwhile, Roberts continued as a teacher, and Bennett recommended that an industrial school be established to teach skills that the Navajos would find more useful.[14]

Miss Gaston was able to get along with Agent Bennett, but Roberts had problems. Disgusted by the phenomenon of white men living with Navajo women—despite the fact that they had been married according to Navajo custom—Roberts insisted that a surveyor who was living with a Navajo marry her. Bennett, who respected most liaisons between Navajo women and Anglo men, disapproved because the woman in question was a "public woman." Nonetheless, Roberts performed the ceremony and earned the anger of Bennett and the Indian Bureau.[15]

Miss Gaston, however, had some personal satisfaction. John Menaul, a medical doctor and ordained minister, had been a Presbyterian missionary in West Africa. Despondent over the loss of his wife and suffering the ill effects of a tropical climate, Menaul returned to the United States to seek another mission. He arrived at the agency on November 16. His success as a missionary was no more spectacular than that of Roberts, but this little man fell in love with Gaston. The two would eventually marry.[16]

Whatever conjugal bliss John and Charity Menaul may have experienced, they could not regard their missionary efforts as successful. They felt some encouragement when, in February 1871, James H. Miller, an appointee of the Presbyterians and the new agent, arrived at Fort Defiance. Miller was a native of Huntington County, Pennsylvania. He had enlisted in the Fifty-fifth Pennsylvania Volunteers during the Civil War and achieved the rank of lieutenant after three years of service. After the war, Miller settled in Neosho, Missouri, where he acted as a real-estate salesman, an elder in the Presbyterian church, and a teacher. Although he was not an ordained minister, he was considered a conscientious and competent administrator.[17]

Miller was open-minded. Indicative of his tolerance was the fact that he allowed Thomas Keam, married to a Navajo woman, to remain in his position as translator, even though Roberts lobbied against him. Although marriages between Anglo-American and Indian women had been tolerated, if not encouraged, since colonial times, Keam's marriage in the custom of his wife's people called into question his Christianity. Miller, however, ignored criticism directed at Keam. He also agreed with the analysis of Bennett that the Diné were starving. Navajo leaders explained to the new agent that crops had been bad because of a short growing season. They appeared before Miller almost daily to request more rations. They were worried about the well-being of their people. So was Miller. In February, hungry Navajos had stolen two of the agency work oxen. He feared that they would take more if nothing was done to end their privation. He was certain that the chiefs were doing all they could to prevent trouble, but even they admitted that they could not stop hungry people from stealing food for long.[18]

The chiefs were correct. Navajos stole livestock from Piedra Lumbre, just west of Ventanas. Hungry Navajos took a horse from the agency corral, and large numbers of them appeared daily at Fort Defiance to beg for meat. The military, anxious to prevent depredations, again stepped in to prevent disaster. The relief provided by the army lasted approximately twenty days, until the civilian Indian authorities could replenish the Navajo subsidy in March with 400,000 pounds of corn and 700 head of beef.[19]

As a result of these emergency rations, the Navajos were able to survive until spring, but their struggle for land promised to be more difficult. Navajo herdsmen were engaged in a feud with the army over the grazing land at Fort Wingate, and small numbers of settlers were again moving into Navajo haunts. Mexican-American settlers drifted into the Cabezon Peak area northeast of Mount Taylor and founded the village of La Posta. Navajos living there, at what they considered their far eastern frontier, were reluctant to leave. They would struggle unsuccessfully for two generations to remain. To the south, Anglo and Mexican-American farmers began to locate along Silver Creek, a tributary of the Little Colorado, in Round Valley. To the north, the Latter

Day Saints, encouraged by the Navajo peace, occupied more of southern Utah, and in an important first step toward their colonization of Arizona, a ferry was established on a Colorado River crossing first discovered by Jacob Hamblin. The ferry's operator, John D. Lee, was a fugitive from justice for his role in the brutal Mountain Meadows Massacre of western immigrants by Mormon settlers. Regardless of the operator's reputation, the ferry enabled the Mormons to consider more serious exploration to the south.[20]

Miller was convinced that conflict was inevitable and Navajo prosperity unlikely unless the treaty's provision to divide the land into individually owned plots was implemented. He wanted to keep the Navajos on the reservation, and he attempted to withhold rations and annuities from those who lived away from it.[21] Navajo leaders tried to convince their new agent otherwise, but March proved too eventful and sad a month in which to educate him.

Miller was tormented by the belief that the Utes and the Navajos were close to war. On March 1, a band of Utes who had been living on the Navajo Reservation and trading with the Diné attempted to steal eleven Navajo horses. In the resulting fracas, one Navajo was wounded before his people could recover most of the animals. Navajos expressed concern about danger in the San Juan River Basin. Narbono, for instance, lived east of the reservation in the Chuska Valley. His people had failed to plant crops the previous year because of inadequate rainfall, and Miller was putting considerable pressure on them to move to the San Juan region. Narbono agreed to go, but he let Miller know that he was relocating reluctantly because of the Ute danger. The agent demanded military protection.[22]

Miller's demand led to an investigation in April by Captain C. A. Hartwell, who concluded that the Utes were a threat to Navajo farmers. Nevertheless, there was no protection. More immediately, Major Price visited Fort Defiance in March. He concluded that many Navajos, living at the agency and relying too much on government rations, had not attempted to grow crops the previous year. Miller did not agree. He claimed that all able-bodied Indians were working diligently in their fields. Navajos nonetheless had to pause from their endeavors to mourn, for on March 16, after an illness of eighty-seven days, Barboncito died. This eloquent little man who had done so much to bring his people home and keep them at peace had died with little recognition from Miller, who had not really known him.[23]

Despite Miller's insensitivity, the agent was aware that he needed to revamp the Navajo power structure in order to keep the peace. At a council in April, the Navajo leaders selected Herrero as Barboncito's successor. Herrero's power would gradually be eclipsed by the growing authority of Manuelito and Ganado Mucho. There may have been a struggle among the leaders, but there is no documentation on the matter. Navajos continued to cooperate with the government when it met their needs or allowed for satisfactions that offered glimpses into the past. When Major Price, for instance, organized an expedition into White Mountain Apache country to help quell a disturbance, fifteen Navajos volunteered to go along as scouts, eager for a legitimate outlet in which to practice their old arts of warfare. Not asking for any pay, the Navajos, according to Price, were very useful.[24]

Meanwhile, Miller was anxious about off-reservation Navajos. He was convinced that an Indian's place was on his reservation; yet, aware of events such as Camp Grant, he was concerned about their vulnerability to the actions of ruthless frontiersmen. Like many Indian reformers, Miller was certain that converting Native Americans to white ways of living offered them some protection. In this regard, he recommended that the chiefs, by way of example to their people, be persuaded to live in frame houses. He advised the Indian Bureau to appropriate money to build such structures. His suggestion bore no results, but it did show his concern, ethnocentric though it was. His solicitude led him to attempt to force Navajos to do things they did not desire, while endeavoring to defend the majority of the Diné from charges of depredations. In response to a request from Superintendent

Nathaniel Pope that he force all Navajos onto the reservation, he claimed that he was doing his best. For example, Miller wrote that he had convinced a band living near Cebolleta under the leadership of Castillo to move to the reservation, but "outside influences" had intervened. At a council, the chiefs had been asked to help "bring their people back," and they had diplomatically promised to do all in their power. Miller was convinced that they would do some good, for he was satisfied that most depredations were perpetrated by those who lived off the Indians' designated lands. He informed Pope, however, that some thefts accredited to the Diné were the fault of other Indians. He cited an instance of horses stolen from Cubero, an act blamed upon his charges that actually had been perpetrated by Zunis.[25]

Possibly due to this controversy, Navajos and Zunis were again engaged in conflict by May. William F. M. Arny, now the agent to the Pueblos, complained about Navajo attacks upon the Zuni and blamed them on Miller's weakness. Actually, Navajos and Zunis both had killed two of the other tribe, but Arny was forceful in claiming that Navajos were responsible for the conflict. Miller and Arny arranged a peace meeting between the leaders of the two peoples in Zuni. Miller assigned Thomas Keam to be his representative, and Arny attended the meeting himself. The Navajos again told of the abuses of the Zuni. They ended their recitation of grievances with the story of murdered hostages, and even Arny was shocked. Nevertheless, the Zunis had come prepared and told their own tales of terror. The first meeting failed to conclude with an agreement, but the parties consented to counsel again in Fort Defiance. Keam and Arny rode with the negotiators to the agency, and the conference at Miller's headquarters proved successful. Navajo leaders promised to return all the stolen property they could find.[26]

The headmen kept their promise. By the end of May, they had returned 160 sheep, 29 horses, 10 burros, and 3 mules, which had been confiscated from the Zunis and other neighbors. Also in May, Miller proved himself more likely than Bennett to use force against offenders. Major Price, with Miller's approval and with the assistance of the chiefs, invaded the Chuska Valley to recover twelve horses, eighteen sheep, and two mules. Price, true to character, insisted that the chiefs bring in the rustlers. The chiefs arrested two suspects and turned them over to Price, who had them taken to Fort Union. The chiefs promised that they would continue to turn in criminals.[27]

Miller knew that the chiefs had taken a considerable political risk. He did not want them to be vulnerable. He wrote to Superintendent Pope:

> I would regard it a great calamity not only to the citizens but to those of the Indians who are disposed to labor for a support to have these thieves released. I would therefore urgently request that you use all your influence to have the Military retain them in custody, until such time necessary for the safety of the property of citizens, as well as the good of the balance of the tribe.[28]

This issue enabled the agent to focus on a Peace Policy solution to a Navajo problem—bringing Indians under the rule of American law—and he pressed authorities to make sure that an example was made of the offenders.

Miller was aware that the military did not wish to bear the cost of maintaining the guilty Indians for long. He urged Pope that they be held for six months and that the Indian bureau pay for their imprisonment. Hearing rumors that the prisoners might be released, the agent pleaded for their continued confinement. He argued that they could be turned over to civilian authorities in Santa Fe or returned to Fort Wingate where they could be fed from Navajo rations. By the end of June, Miller was ready to testify that the arrest of the two thieves had worked wonders. There was less stealing, and the chiefs were even more eager to stop the rustling. As an example of this Navajo willingness to cooperate, Miller was proud to mention that Navajos, led by Manuelito, had killed a raider in June and that the chiefs had informed him that their people were working harder than they had since their homecoming to bring in a successful crop. Nevertheless, he felt compelled to add that their agricultural success depended upon rainfall.[29]

As the Diné waited to see if the summer would escape another drought and Miller continued to be obsessed with making an example of rustlers, Major Price decided that the mere arrest of Navajo criminals was not enough to preserve peace. When a herd of three thousand cattle destined for Arizona was driven across the southern end of Navajo country, he sent a detachment of twenty men to escort the animals. He did not want the Navajos blamed for their theft should a number of the cattle turn up missing.[30] Price wrote:

> I have done this to protect the Navajos from the imputation of stealing them [the cattle] should any be lost, and to endeavor to punish the Mexicans. I believe there is a band of outlaws at Cubero and El Rito aided and abetted by one Solomon Barth who would be guilt of any enormity not stopping short of murder. A deserter was killed for his money, near El Rito the day before I passed there, and I understand that a party of them have lately driven in 900 head of cattle stolen from Texas.[31]

Authorities were increasingly concerned about the activities of Barth and other traders who did not accept contemporary sanctions against selling guns and whiskey to Indians.

Arny, for example, had discovered a ring of traders who worked freely out of Zuni, Acoma, and Laguna. He had stumbled upon an actual sale of such contraband to Navajos and Apaches. Yet, the Pueblo agent was hard pressed to obtain a conviction. When he finally got a local jury to find an individual guilty, he was appalled to learn that the criminal was given only a one-day jail term.[32] It was within this context that Price had acted.

Despite Price's endeavor to protect the Diné's reputation, the fact remained that unescorted cattle probably would have been vulnerable to Navajo theft because the summer was dry. Sedentary agriculture may have seemed a failure to the Navajos who had tried it since the beginning days of their exile. Many were convinced that they needed to rely upon expanding their herds instead of growing crops. Miller recognized this trend, if not its implications, when he observed that his charges were selling their annuity goods in order to buy livestock. He recommended that some of the Navajo annuities be paid in sheep rather than in farm implements for which the Indians saw little use.[33] Despite this request, the agent saw such action as a temporary solution to an immediate problem and still believed that the eventual civilization of the natives lay with raising large crops.

With this long-term solution in mind, Miller toured about a third of the reservation, looking for good farming land. He was disappointed. He found that approximately one acre in fifty was arable. The agent, however, was encouraged by large stands of timber and, again calling for sheep as annuities, still insisted that Navajos live exclusively on the reservation. He continued to demand that the two arrested Navajos remain behind bars and praised the leaders for their vigilance in preventing Navajo depredations. Miller was pleased by an instance in which Navajos, fearful of being charged with theft, brought in five mules that had drifted into their camp because they did not wish to be accused of wrongdoing.[34]

Not all Navajos, however, were so cooperative. In August, the Navajo prisoners escaped, but Miller was not disheartened. He praised the majority of the Diné for being well behaved, but he was not sure this behavior would last long. Miller stated that, with the continued failure of Navajo crops, his wards would steal rather than starve. Miller's predictions proved to be true when Navajos launched attacks against Apaches at Cañada Alamosa and Mormons in southern Utah. In the latter case, seventy-nine Navajos had met with the Latter Day Saints and their chief negotiator, Apostle Erastus Snow, in a continuation of the previous year's peace talks. The meetings held at Kanab were an attempt to get northern Navajos to cooperate as their official leaders had done. At first, the negotiations went well. Snow reviewed Navajo depredations, but announced that peace was a reality and that the two peoples met as brothers. Navajo spokesmen pledged their gratitude, but after Snow left the proceedings, the Indians demanded that the people of Kanab give up seventy horses, seventeen head of cattle, and a number of other Mormon possessions. Upon receiving word of this Navajo duplicity, Snow dispatched a letter to Utah Territorial Governor George L. Woods, a Missourian out of sympathy with the Mormons. Woods ignored the letter, but the Mormons organized several militia units on their own. The Diné backed down, claiming that they had only wanted to trade for the horses.[35]

If this event seemed to presage conflict between the two peoples, another instance appeared to foretell peace. When John Wesley Powell and his men camped along the mouth of the Paria during their second exploration of the Colorado River country on October 23, they came across Jacob Hamblin returning from another visit to Hopi and Navajo country with nine Navajos, who entertained the adventurers that evening with dance and song.[36] These differences in Navajo actions were easily explained by the looseness of the Diné's political structure, especially in the north.

Even though the Navajo–Mormon truce appeared to be flimsy, there was progress toward peace on another front. Navajo resentment had been building over the killing of two of their people at Canyon Juan Tafoya three years earlier, and there had been retaliatory raids against the community. In September, Miller sent Thomas Keam, Jesus Arviso, and Narbono, who was a relative of the murdered men, to the small Mexican-American community in the hills above Cebolleta to negotiate a peace. Narbono spoke of his outrage over the murders, and the local leaders complained of Navajo thefts. A settlement, due to Keam's diplomacy, was soon reached. The Navajos agreed not to steal from the village or to graze their livestock nearby, and the citizens consented to pay the relatives of the dead men a quantity of sheep and horses.[37]

Total peace, however, seemed unattainable between the Navajos and all of their neighbors. For instance, Tom Jeffords, famous for his friendship with the Apache leader Cochise, appeared at Fort Defiance with three Apaches from Cañada Alamosa in late

October; they were under instructions from their agent to recover stock that had been stolen by a group under the leadership of Antonio. Miller called a council of the chiefs. Jeffords told them of the purpose of his visit. Delgadito agreed to go with Jeffords to recover the animals. They succeeded in locating a horse and hoped to capture the other four. When Miller heard Delgadito's report, he insisted that these thefts were committed by off-reservation Navajos. He also noted that the Diné's crops had failed and wrote that the government had better feed them or further trouble would result.[38]

Miller repeated his warning as 1871 ended. In December, Navajos stole a mare and a colt from the Zunis. To most Navajos, however, peace had become an overwhelming priority. Chicquito, a headman aware that someone would have to do something to prevent conflict, stepped in to assure that his people avoided self-destruction. He searched for the rustled livestock and quickly recovered the animals. A renewal of the feud with the Zunis was prevented, but Miller warned his superiors. The Diné's crops had been poor, and they would steal from their neighbors to achieve even the least amount of prosperity.[39]

As 1872 began, Miller was still preoccupied with feeding the Navajos. On January 1, he had no corn left in his stores and only enough cattle to last until the middle of the month. Miller requested permission to borrow surplus corn from the quartermaster at Fort Wingate. While awaiting authorization from Superintendent Pope, he ran out of food, and some Navajos were starving before the end of the month. In planning for the future, Navajo leaders, realizing that their people had to rely less on crops and more on livestock, requested that some of the annuities be paid in sheep. Miller, echoing his previous recommendations, agreed. He added that the Navajos were behaving well, but he was worried that their actions would take on criminal intent if they were not fed soon. The chiefs issued the same warning. The condition of the hungry Navajos, however, was alleviated when twenty thousand pounds of corn arrived from Fort Wingate on February 13, and Price promised another fifty thousand pounds as soon as he received a request from Pope. Once Pope's letter arrived, the problem was alleviated, but the prospect of another failed Navajo crop was to haunt Miller for the remainder of his days.[40]

Fortunately for the agent's psychological well-being, Miller temporarily relaxed his guard concerning Navajo depredations. Instead, he was able to deal with the actions of the Navajos' neighbors, which were a source of bother for the tribe. In March, for example, Navajo leaders informed Miller that citizens were grazing their animals dangerously close to the reservation. The headmen were concerned that their people would steal from these stockmen and provoke trouble. Miller, anxious to prevent violence, requested that Superintendent Pope warn the New Mexicans of the danger.[41]

The Utes were also a source of worry for Miller. New developments occurred in the unresolved case of Utes who had murdered Navajos and stolen livestock three years earlier. A horse belonging to one of the slain Navajos was discovered. The chiefs wanted the animal returned. Ute Agent John S. Armstrong could not do much, for he was forced to deal with an outbreak of violence among some of the people at his agency. Capote Utes led by Sobeta had raided Mexican-American settlements in the vicinity of Tierra Amarilla. Although no one had been killed, Armstrong was distressed over the possibility of a full-scale war. Peace efforts had failed, despite the fact that troops from Fort Wingate were in the area.[42]

Armstrong wrote to Miller, requesting Navajo assistance in bringing in the renegade Utes. Citing the general goodwill between the Diné and the military, Armstrong inquired about the possibility of Navajos forbidding the Utes to trespass on their lands. Armstrong also requested that information be sent to him of Sobeta or Ignacio's whereabouts. He further asked that Navajos look for Sobeta and urge him to go to Tierra Amarilla to prevent an unnecessary war. If war resulted, however, the Ute agent wanted at least 250 Navajos to join in the fight.[43]

Curiously, the Navajo leaders, expressing little objection to most of what the Uge agent desired, showed some reluctance to go along with Armstrong's latter request. When Miller asked the leaders in council for Navajo recruits in a possible Ute war, not many of them were enthusiastic. A few of the chiefs agreed to look for Sobeta to convince him to surrender, but only Jesus Arviso, who believed that there would be as many as five hundred volunteers, was willing to commit Navajo fighting men to a war. Arviso's claims, however, were were not tested, for the outlaw Utes soon realized the good sense of surrender. A significant Ute discontent continued, and Navajo and Mexican-American settlers along the San Juan River remained in danger.[44]

In other locations, Navajo discontent resurfaced in May after several months of relative peace. Seven Navajos returning from a trading visit to Kanab attempted to cross the Colorado at Lee's Ferry, but the water was too high. They asked John D. Lee to ferry them to the other side. He replied that he had no boat, but the Indians, noticing the *Nellie Powell* which had been left behind by John Wesley Powell's exploring party, demanded transportation. Lee offered to give them an Enfield rifle and ammunition if they would ford the river at Ute Crossing a few miles away. Rejecting his proposition, they were finally told by Lee that he would take them to the other side if they would help him build a dam on the Paria River, a nearby tributary. The Navajos agreed. Lee, however, soon tired of the Navajos, for two of them engaged in petty thievery. He agreed to carry them across just to get rid of them. Once this task was accomplished, he had to resort to force over the issue of whether or not he would use the boat to escort the Navajos' horses across what he considered dangerously swift waters. With Lee holding a rifle on the Indians, they backed down.[45]

Concurrently, Hugh McBride and nine other concerned citizens of Los Lunas, New Mexico, complained during the middle of the month that a band of the Diné were living around their village and near Bear Springs for the purpose of "stealing and plundering." According to the citizens' affidavit, the Navajos were coming into the settlements in broad daylight to steal cattle. In early May, raiders had managed to get away with eleven animals. The residents of the area demanded protection.[46] The army, aware of its low troop strength, did not offer assistance.

Meanwhile, Navajo livestock had been removed from the military reservation at Fort Wingate because the army needed the grazing land for its own animals. Miller insisted that these Indians move to the reservation. When they refused to obey his order, Miller suggested to Pope that a patrol run regularly from Fort Wingate to Cebolleta or San Mateo and back to reduce the possibility of depredations. He contended that all Navajos without passes found off the reservation should be arrested by the army and forced, as punishment, to work on the buildings being constructed at Fort Wingate.[47]

Miller was still equating Navajo crime with Indians who lived off the reservation and insisting that all Navajos live within the boundaries specified by the treaty. Yet the agent had taken an inspection trip across much of the reservation and was aware that most of the land was not suitable for large-scale agriculture. He was an honest man, and his knowledge of the land's potential was undoubtedly a controlling factor in his request for a partial payment of annuities in sheep. Nevertheless, he would not directly face the fact that the reservation was too small to support a pastoral or horticultural economy. Thus, he was confronted with an inconsistency between his beliefs and the realities of Navajo existence. Rather than alter his ideals, Miller looked for a solution that could keep the Indians on their reserve and still provide for their self-support. He saw the possible Navajo exploitation of the rich San Juan area as the answer. On June 6, Miller embarked upon a journey with Jesus Arviso, agency farmer Benjamin M. Thomas, and post trader John Ayers through the Chuska Valley to the San Juan Basin. Superintendent Pope had scheduled a sojourn to Fort Defiance, and the agent wanted to be fully informed on the Navajos' lands to the north when he arrived.[48]

In Miller's absence, an early tourist, J. H. Beadle, visited Fort Defiance, accompanied by William Burgess, a blacksmith whose acquaintance he had made at Fort Wingate. Beadle would later record his experiences in Navajoland in *The Undeveloped West or Five Years in the Territories*. Beadle's observations provided a picturesque description of the Navajos in 1872.[49] As he approached, Beadle viewed the agency as quaint. He mentioned flocks of sheep, an occasional hogan, Indian farms, and curious "squaws and children." When the author arrived, he found the twenty white employees of the agency happy to see him, disappointed that he had not brought the mail, and angry that they had not been paid. They were also concerned that the government had not been doing more to help the Navajos.[50] One of them was eloquent in his condemnation of bureaucratic apathy. He said:

> There'll be another Navajo war, and we'll have to clear. These are the best Indians on the continent, willing to work, and don't want to fight. But, damn it, they can't starve to death and right here. We've destroyed their living; run off all the game and shut 'em up here, and their crops failed two years. If we were in their place, we'd fight. They must steal, or starve, or fight, one o' the three. Ain't a man here in Government employ that's been paid a cent for twelve months. They'll give the Apaches sugar and coffee and flour because they're a murderin', and won't give these men anything because they've been peaceable for eight years, and these fellows know it too. Well, they'll be another Navajo war,—that's what they'll be.[51]

Despite the basic inaccuracies in the above statement—the Navajos, for instance, were probably the ones killing off the game in their attempt at survival—and the speaker's self-serving plea for pay, the fear of a Navajo war was very real in 1872 because the Navajo economy had failed to revive.

Beadle did not find the Navajos despondent. He found them cheerful and full of hope. He was pleased by their wit, laughter, and propensity for practical jokes and pronounced them destined for civilization, "as much like a tribe of dark Caucasians as it is possible to conceive."[52]

On June 13, Beadle was eating breakfast with agency employees when one of the Miller party arrived ahead of the others, riding the only horse left, with news of Miller's death. The others arrived on foot the following day. They had a remarkable tale to tell. At dawn on June 11, Ayers, Arviso, and Thomas had been awakened at their camp on the San Juan by the almost simultaneous whistling of an arrow and firing of a rifle. Quickly rising to their feet, they saw two Utes disappearing into the brush, driving horses ahead of them. Ayers asked Miller, who was still reclining, for a comment. Receiving no reply, Ayers shoved the agent with his feet. When there was no response, the party frantically attempted to revive Miller, only to find that a bullet had penetrated the top of his head and traveled to a point behind his right eye. With his arms and legs folded just as they had been when he had gone to sleep and a peaceful countenance on his face, they were certain that he had died instantly.[53]

There were worse fates for men and women in those days than instant death. But Miller had left behind a wife and infant son. He had been wise enough to overlook the Navajo marriage of Thomas Keam in spite of contemporary disdain for such relationships, and although he abandoned Bennett's open attitude toward off-reservation Navajos, he did not abandon the policy of putting great faith in Navajo leaders. As a Presbyterian missionary, he was a failure, but as an advocate for his charges, he had begun to succeed. Beadle, declaring that the Navajos had lost an active friend, praised the agent as "a true Christian, faithful official, and brave man."[54] Despite such tribute, Miller probably would have preferred to be remembered as a tough but fair administrator. Forced by his beliefs to follow an impossible and locally unpopular policy, he was proudest of what he thought to be the beneficial effects of the imprisonment of the two Navajo outlaws. The reduction of Navajo raids, however, had more to do with the efforts of the chiefs than with anything their agent had done.

The Diné had acted wisely. In an era when atrocities against Native Americans were all too common—at the same time and in the same region as the Camp Grant Massacre—Navajos had blunted frontier hostility. By being alternately bellicose and diplomatic, they and their leaders had bought time and ignored the Peace Policy. Failure to institute this grand social experiment may have been Miller's largest shortcoming, but the Navajos did not see it this way. Navajo leaders appreciated the fact that he could be manipulated. As a result, they had been able to control Navajo affairs. Nevertheless, Miller would not be missed, for the next white man to attempt to direct their lives was, in a way, one of them.

5
Thomas Keam and the Christians

Thomas Keam, left in charge of the agency by Miller and appointed acting agent after the Presbyterian's death, was as competent as anyone who attempted to administer Navajo affairs in the nineteenth century; yet his tenure was short and controversial. Described by historian Frank McNitt as a man equally at home in a hogan or in the office of an important official, Keam had the trust of the Navajos, the military, and some westerners.[1] During his term of office, the Navajos were as peaceful as they had ever been, but he was criticized severely. Keam was accused of keeping company with traders, men whom the reformers considered disreputable.[2] He implemented few of the Peace Policy goals. But these charges could have been made just as easily against Miller. It seemed, rather, that Keam's domestic situation was at the heart of the controversy.

In 1869, Keam had been married to a Navajo named Salt Woman. The fact that he had been married by a Navajo medicine man in the tribal basket ceremony, as opposed to Christian nuptials, added to the controversy. Many refused to recognize the legality of his wedding and the legitimacy of his two children: Tom, born in 1870, and Billy, born in 1872.[3] Keam's reaction to this lack of acceptance testified to the contradictions in his personality. Dedicated to what he considered to be justice for the Navajos, he also craved respectability among whites. Although his marriage and children had helped him to establish himself among the Navajos, he was aware that his family reduced his effectiveness in the larger arena of white political power. Caught in a situation that he was too human to reconcile, Keam eventually denied his marriage.

Nevertheless, Keam seemed to serve the Navajos well. Unlike the Christians, he appeared to have few goals for the Navajos except to keep them out of war and improve their economic condition. His approach was ideal from the perspective of the Diné, who wanted to blunt, if not control, government actions. Nonetheless, Keam was a practical man. He seemed to take office with every intention of holding it and did his best to satisfy the missionary reformers. But his day-to-day management of Navajo affairs brought him into conflict with those who insisted that government policy be taken to its inevitable conclusions.

Once in power, Keam was promptly beset by two problems: the repercussions of Miller's murder and continued Navajo raids. A frost struck on June 18. Most of the Navajo crop was destroyed; many of the wild plants upon which the Diné relied for subsistence also failed to produce fruits and seeds. In addition, the weather was particularly dry. It looked as if most of the crops still alive had little chance of survival. Fortunately, Miller's suggestion that ten thousand sheep be handed out instead of annuity goods was granted by the government that summer, and some Navajo raids were prevented. This, however, was only a partial answer, for the Navajos were reluctant to turn to their flocks for food.[4]

During June, some Navajos raided their neighbors, but Navajo leaders, who had reason to feel that they had a friend in the acting agent, added to their vigilance. Keam reported at the end of the month that the headmen had brought forty-six horses and mules into the agency, some of which had been returned to their New Mexican owners; others had been sent to the Jicarilla Apache Reservation under Manuelito's escort. He was holding twelve animals until they could be claimed by their owners.[5] The chiefs, however, wanted food in return. Keam wrote:

> The chiefs are doing all they possibly can to recover all stolen stock brought on the reservation, but tell me at the same time it is impossible to keep their people on the reservation, as most of them have nothing to eat; and stealing is resorted to by some to keep from starving.[6]

The problem of Navajo starvation, however, was not addressed, and raids continued.

Navajos raided Bluewater, New Mexico, east of the reservation. In addition, reports came in concerning Miller's murder. On July 27, Keam wrote to Superintendent Pope that a group of Navajos had journeyed north of the San Juan and met with the wives of the Utes who had killed Miller. With touching sympathy, they begged that the women be left alone. Their men had run off long ago, and they did not know where they were.[7]

Supplemental to this Navajo investigation, Major Price looked into the crime on his own by riding to Fort Defiance. Price was convinced, after talking to Jesus Arviso and John Ayers, that he could identify the murderers, alleged to be two Wiminuches in Ignacio's band. Price requested permission to hunt for the Ute chief, who was reportedly in Utah trading with the Mormons. Price's authorization, however, did not materialize. Nevertheless, the business of the army on the Navajo frontier did not come to a close. In late July, word had reached Fort Wingate that Navajo raiders had been active between Santa Fe and San Miguel. They were now headed back to the reservation, and Captain A. B. Kauffman, the temporary commander at Fort Wingate, requested that Keam apprehend the offenders.[8]

Keam was convinced that the chiefs were doing their best and expressed the opinion that the Navajos who were stealing were hungry. He added that most raiders lived off the reservation. Keam's attention, however, was momentarily distracted. General Oliver O. Howard, working as a special Indian inspector, arrived at Fort Wingate in early August with a group of Arizona Apaches returning from a trip to the nation's capital. He wanted to put an end to feuding between the tribes. The principal Navajo leaders greeted the general, but refused to talk with the Apaches. By using considerable persuasion, Howard got the representatives of the two peoples together. Once the negotiations had begun, the chiefs exchanged long lists of grievances, but they soon promised to work for better understanding between their peoples. The leaders embraced at the end of the negotiations and celebrated through the night. Howard was happy at the result. The general also appeared pleased with Keam's work and solicitous toward Navajo leaders. When Manuelito, for instance, told him of Navajos still being held slaves, he seemed very perturbed.[9]

Actually, a relatively large number of Navajo slaves, demonstrating a persistence rare among southwestern captives (including their Mexican-American counterparts under Navajo control), left their New Mexican masters in 1872, which seemed to be the year when many of them realized that they had a legal right to be free. This repatriation accounted, in part, for a large population increase among the Diné in 1872. Included among these escapees were many Navajo women who found the "civilized" life more difficult than the "savage" existence with their own people. Navajo leaders were worried, however, about other, more tightly guarded individuals who were unable to escape, and Keam reflected this concern when he recommended that the government hire an investigator to help recover Navajo captives.[10]

Keam's advice was rejected, but Howard did arrange for Keam's appointment, on August 5, as special agent for the development of Navajo resources. The following day, he gave Keam permission to form a Navajo police force. The idea was not original with Keam. Bennett had recommended such a group in 1870, and Miller renewed the suggestion a year later. Keam, however, had the advantage of not having to process his request through the inefficient bureaucracy of the Indian Bureau. Instead, he had the opportunity to deal directly with a man who had the president's ear. As a result, the agent was able to quickly assemble a force of 130 men under the direction of thirteen chiefs. Keam named the unit the Navajo Cavalry and appointed Manuelito as its leader. He also promised that his policemen would be rewarded with uniforms, pistols, rifles, ammunition, and the same pay and rations as privates in the army. Because he had failed to bring up these details with Howard, they were subject to the scrutiny of the Indian Bureau. Thus, the force went unpaid for a considerable amount of time. Nevertheless, they did a credible job, as would be demonstrated in the drastic reduction of Navajo raids.[11]

General Howard, who was regarded as a moralistic nuisance by his fellow officers, left Fort Defiance satisfied that the Navajos were in good hands. Within days, however, he would think otherwise. Just who contacted the general is the subject of some speculation, but it was probably William F. M. Arny, who had been in contact with Rev. James Roberts, who had been dismissed at the agency due to disputes with Miller. Howard sent Keam a letter stating that he had "direct information" that some of the agency employees were speaking profanities and gambling. Howard also charged that there were two employees cohabiting with Navajo women. Howard believed that such arrangements were poor examples for the Indians.[12] Thus, Keam quickly came into conflict with some of the missionaries. Agents were supposed to civilize the Indians, not join the tribe; their job was to Christianize their wards, not participate in their heathen ceremonies.

Keam's immediate response, which he mailed to Pope on August 15, was angry and directed at Arny. Concerning the profanity and gambling charges he wrote, "I judge this false information has been given by some party who from mercenary and office seeking motives, under the cloak of Christianity, seeks to injure these men."[13] Relative to the allegation of cohabiting with Navajo women, he was eloquent. He wrote to Superintendent Pope:

> There are two Employe's [sic] of this Agency living with and married to Navajo women according to the customs of the Navajoes which in no way conflicts with their morals.
> These men have families and naturally look to the women as their wives, and treat them as such, they have been with the Navajoes and in the employ of the Government from five to seven years; are esteemed and respected by all the Indians.[14]

Keam was probably aware that his exposition would not be effective with many Christians in the Indian service. His failure to include himself among the offenders seemed to indicate as much.

Keam's argument, nonetheless, was immediately effective because Superintendent Pope had at least a practical understanding of frontier conditions, including the phenomenon of white men marrying Indian women. But Army would never approve, and he was, for the moment, merely irritating. Keam had more important concerns.

While Keam had confronted these charges, his agency farmer, Benjamin M. Thomas, had been out inspecting the reservation and its productivity. It appeared that the dour predictions of the early summer were incorrect. The crop would not be a total failure. In the late summer, the reservation had received a considerable amount of rain. As a result, Navajos, particularly those living at Chinle and Lukachukai, were anticipating large crops of corn, beans, and pumpkins. This news represented the most substantial improvement in Navajo farming since the tribe had returned from the Bosque; yet there were still problems. Thomas estimated that a third of the tribe had raised enough to support itself until January 1, while another third could hold out until November 1. The rest of the Navajo Nation had little and would quickly need rations in order to stay alive for the next three or four months. Thomas also stated that the Navajos could become self-supporting if they would farm more along the San Juan River. He had inquired among the Indians to ascertain their reasons for not moving to the San Juan, and he was told that two problems had influenced their decision. On the river, they were too far removed from the source of rations at Fort Defiance, and the hostile Utes presented them with danger. Thomas recommended that a subagency be established in the area to handle the two problems.[15]

Keam agreed with Thomas's report and made plans to visit the San Juan area in late September. In the interim, he was kept busy with other matters. Keam's appointment as special agent left the agent's job open. Frank Bennett wanted to return and resign his army commission, but another man was chosen by the Presbyterians. On September 7, William F. Hall of Washington, D.C., arrived in Fort Defiance to take up the duties of Navajo agent. Although Hall had vague instructions to free Keam from the day-to-day operations of the agency so he could spend more time in developing Navajo resources on the San Juan, there was no clear-cut division of authority, and Keam remained fundamentally in charge.[16] Only two days after taking office, Hall was mimicking Keam's thoughts. He wrote that the majority of the Navajos were contented and happy, adding that the Diné were "probably as thrifty, well-behaved, industrious, and intelligent, and occasion as little trouble to the Government or the white settlers about, as any tribe of Indians in the country."[17]

Both Hall and Keam concurred in the opinion that the Navajo Cavalry, which had brought in sixty stolen animals during the first month of its existence and had been supplemented by an army patrol along the western bank of the Rio Grande, was doing an excellent job. But there was still a problem with isolated raids. Rations had run out on September 1, and the poorer Indians had difficulty in feeding themselves.[18] Conflict between these Navajos, who represented the less fortunate, and the rest of the Diné, as represented by the chiefs who dominated the police force, was developing. White officials were slow to recognize this growing tension and created political divisions of their own that had little relationship with reality.

Keam was no exception. Word reached him in early September that Navajos had stolen livestock near Fort Stanton from Apaches and a man named Miller, and he was as quick as any missionary in blaming frontiersmen. Mexicans at Los Lunas, he claimed, had provided Navajos with passes, provisions, and powder to go to the Comanche country to raid. An Anglo-American at Fort Stanton, however, convinced them that there was more than adequate plunder nearby. Apaches had just traded stolen mules for horses and had failed to leave the region. The Navajos leaped at the opportunity. The Navajo Cavalry recovered the rustled animals, which had been driven onto the reservation. Keam, nevertheless, contradicted himself. He expressed the opinion that almost all depredations were committed by Navajos who lived off the reservation, especially those who lived close to the contaminating influence of Pueblo Indian and Mexican communities: he neglected the fact that many of his chiefs, including Manuelito and Ganado Mucho, also failed to reside where the government said they should.[19]

Keam, of course, was a man of his time. His marriage to a Navajo may have put him out of step with one aspect of the prevailing morality, but he was not a man to reject all contemporary ideas. For example, his views on American Indian education fit neatly into prevailing missionary opinion concerning minority needs. Late-nineteenth-century Americans expected a great deal from their schools. Concerned with preserving their culture in light of increased immigration, freedom for blacks, and the final conquest of the Indians, Americans saw education as the primary mechanism for providing new citizens the virtues of the predominant civilization. Although the goal was assimilation, the education offered to these emerging groups was culturally insensitive and often inferior to the schooling provided to other Americans. Convinced that minorities were intellectually lacking, the reformers emphasized vocational education.[20]

Keam possibly could have fallen under the influence of General Howard, who had established a vocational school for blacks in Washington, D.C. Whatever his rationale, the special agent endorsed vocational education as a way of getting Navajos interested in sending their children to school when he judged Mrs. Menaul's efforts as unsatisfactory. As far as he was concerned, the teacher was not at fault. He blamed the failure on the inability of the students, who displayed great practical intelligence, to grasp the English language and to comprehend the need for disciplined application of ideas learned at school, ideas he judged as inappropriate to the "wildlife" that was traditional to the Diné. In conformity with Bennett, Roberts, and Miller, Keam recommended that the school be connected with a farm that would teach practical skills.[21]

Keam was aware of the poor facilities, but he did not list these as reasons for the school's failure. He seemed more concerned with convincing Navajos that an Anglo-American education would be good for their children. There was doubt, however, that Keam's approach would work. Navajo parents were capable of teaching their children to farm, and few vocational skills bore any relation to reservation life. Indeed, the one Navajo of the era who would benefit from learning Anglo-Saxon ways was the leader of the next generation, Henry "Chee" Dodge, whose education resembled more the "three r's" taught in frontier schoolhouses than the vocational training proposed by Keam.[22] The chiefs, however, approved of their special agent, and because no one as yet was forcing many children into the school, which in any case was entirely inadequate for the tribe, education had not become a serious issue.

Keam's intentions, however, were good, as was illustrated by his journey to the San Juan Basin. Arriving at the river on September 20, he located the grave of James Miller and camped nearby for the night. The next morning, he proceeded east along the stream and quickly came to the conclusion that enough corn could be raised in the vicinity to support the whole tribe for years. He chose a site, recommended that a ten-mile irrigation ditch be dug, and estimated the cost of constructing the subagency at seventy-two thousand dollars. Keam, by way of explanation of inadequate Navajo settlement of the area, accused the Wiminuche Utes of harassing Navajo farmers. Using the traditional argument that people like the Utes, who did not use land as God had intended, be evicted from territories thus poorly utilized, Keam urged that the government protect Navajos and bring about a change that would make the San Juan to the Navajos what the "Rio Grande is to the Pueblo Indians."[23]

Major Price, meanwhile, had been at Pagosa Springs, Colorado, attempting to control violence between the Utes and miners. He believed that more prospectors would drift into the San Juan region, that many of these would venture onto lands held by Navajos as well as by Utes, and that serious conflict was inevitable. Price did not believe that Navajos should be forced to evacuate their lands. The major castigated the Utes for not making good use of their lands, like the Navajos, who had a much smaller reservation. Implying that the Utes should be compelled to accept less land, Price recommended that a military post be constructed along the San Juan, in conjunction with Keam's subagency, to prevent hostilities between the Navajos and a flood of whites whom he was certain would soon arrive. He suggested that a road be built from Fort Wingate to the new post in order to secure its supply and to serve as a visible boundary to those Navajos who would leave their reservation.[24]

Superintendent Pope endorsed the concept of a subagency on the San Juan and proposed it to the commissioner of Indian affairs. The rest of the year went by peacefully. Although a few of the tribesmen were on the brink of starvation, economic conditions for most Navajos in late 1872 were better than at any time since their return home. Their flocks were increasing at a phenomenal rate. Estimates of the number of sheep ranged from 100,000 to 130,000. The attentive care with which the Indians had handled their sheep was proving beneficial, as were their raiding and trading for additional animals. Prosperity seemed attainable, and so did peace. The Navajo Cavalry was so successful that there were no further reports of depredations by the Diné in New Mexico for the rest of the year.[25] The chiefs had done their jobs well and, for the most part, in the interest of their developing nation. Despite growing resentment from some of their people, they had been able to blunt government insistence that all Navajos live on the reservation by simply preventing large-scale rustling. It seemed a small price to pay, especially in late 1872 after their people had already added substantially to their livestock.

Not all events, however, predicted a bright future. In the north portentous events continued to occur. In the fall, a team of prospectors from Prescott, Arizona, visited Navajo and Ute country along the San Juan. Once back in Prescott in December, they gave glowing reports. Gold, they claimed, could be found everywhere on the river. Praising Navajo officials Hall and Keam for their cooperation, the explorers criticized the Utes for not allowing gold seekers on their lands and predicted that large mining operations would move in from Arizona and work the country from Fort Defiance north.[26] Even though these predictions proved to be false, word of mineral wealth on Navajo lands would long endure to challenge Navajo notions of territorial autonomy.

Trouble with the Mormons also continued. In October, John Wesley Powell, who was visiting St. George, Utah, reported that the Mormons living in the southern portion of that territory were suffering from repeated Navajo raids upon their horse herds. Mormon retaliation was a possibility. The potential for further hostilities asserted itself in December, when Brigham Young sent out an exploring expedition under Bishop Lorenzo Roundy. Jacob Hamblin went along as a guide, and the party was ordered to collect information on soil, rainfall, drainage, and topography along the Little Colorado River. The clear intention was to settle.[27] How western Navajos would react to this invasion was not apparent.

What should have been obvious, however, was that change, rather than stability, was the norm on the Navajo frontier. As 1872 came to an end, the first of several administrative changes took place that did not prove to be in the Navajos' best interest. In December, Superintendent Nathaniel Pope, who had been understanding of Keam's Navajo marriage and also the object of much criticism in Arizona for not being tough enough with the Apaches, was removed from office. There was some objection to his leaving in New Mexico, where he was praised for solving disputes between Navajos and the settlers.[28] In any case, he was replaced by a man of less foresight, Colonel L. Edwin Dudley. Charity Menaul also added to the atmosphere of change when she gave up her job as teacher because John Lowrie wanted to hire a male teacher.[29] Other administrative changes soon followed.

The Presbyterian mission board would contribute to these changes. Frank McNitt has suggested that William F. M. Arny, who had influence with the board, was out to undermine Keam's policies, but McNitt's charges are circumstantial.[30] Nevertheless, little doubt exists that Keam was headed for confrontation with the missionaries. They were likely to reject "practical" men who wanted to accept some Navajo values to maintain peace. The reformers had difficulty in understanding the Navajo rejection of their efforts. The Presbyterians they had sent had been righteous and self-sacrificing; the Indians seemed to have no gratitude, and white men who took their side were immoral and not concerned with the Indians' spiritual improvement.

The Navajos, however, knew what they wanted, and it was not Protestant Christianity. Better than the missionaries at recognizing the plurality of American life, the Diné were prepared to learn from secular representatives of the civilization that had conquered them. They had, for instance, reluctantly changed their political structure in light of United States power and were also rearranging their economy to accommodate new realities.

Navajo leaders had realized that war was no longer an effective way to increase wealth. They had endeavored to put a stop to rustling from their neighbors. The period immediately after their homecoming had been a desperate time. People needed to eat and attacks had resumed, but the efforts of the chiefs had paid off by early 1873, and raids were becoming less frequent. At the same time, the chiefs' efforts were not solely responsible for this reduction of tension, for all the persuasion of the headmen would have been to no avail had not an alternative for acquiring needed goods presented itself in the form of traders.

Southwestern Indians had long traded among themselves and with the Mexican-American communities along the Rio Grande. The Navajos had been a part of this network, which continued well past their return from exile. This commerce, however, largely concerned itself with the exchange of livestock, handicraft goods, and harvested crops; it dealt infrequently with manufactured products other than such basic goods as guns and cooking utensils.[31]

White traders began to move into Navajo country soon after the tribe's return from the Pecos. Many of them, like Soloman Barth, were unscrupulous in their disregard for the law and brought their profession into disrepute. On the other hand, numerous traders slowly built up reputations for honesty among their clients. The Mormons, for example, had not missed the opportunities presented by Jacob Hamblin's peace with the Navajos, and even the notorious John D. Lee came to be known for his fairness.[32]

The Mormons, however, operated from the fringes of Navajo country, and the direct involvement of the Diné in the larger American economy would be left in the hands of more adventurous entrepreneurs. Their numbers were many, and most of them failed. Yet they continued to come, opportunists, sometimes dealing their wares out of tents, anxious to carve out a niche on a developing frontier. Business was at first slow, and the merchandise stocked by a trader was limited to such staples as coffee, sugar, salt, canned peaches, and sometimes whiskey, because transporting merchandise was difficult. Other portable goods, such as knives and cloth, were occasionally sold. As a result, early profits were not always good, but those traders who managed to stay earned a permanent and important role in the history of the Diné.[33]

The first licensed trader at the agency was Lehman Spiegelberg, who received his license in August of 1868. Other official traders would drift in and out of Navajo country during the late 1860s and 1870s.[34] It was the off-reservation merchants, however, who began to revolutionize the Navajo economy and integrate it into the larger American capitalistic system.

Ironically, the Presbyterian Indian establishment, prejudiced by reports of the activities of men like Barth, did not approve. Its leaders found it difficult to accept the fact that the traders were doing more to change the Indians than they were. The Navajos, however, were not so judgmental. Viewing the traders as convenient instruments for the attainment of the good life, the Diné, when they were not busy increasing their flocks, began to utilize the traders as part of their economy. Bringing in blankets, horses, wool, and jewelry, the Indians quickly learned which traders were honest and frequented their posts.[35]

John Lorenzo Hubbell, the best known of these individuals, became a symbol of what a good trader could accomplish. Hubbell was the son of a father who had emigrated from Salisbury, Connecticut, and a New Mexican mother who claimed aristocratic Spanish heritage. Born in the small town of Pajarito, he had learned to speak Spanish as his first language. His early formal education had also been in Spanish from a local tutor. It was not until he was twelve that his Catholic parents sent him to a Presbyterian boarding school in Santa Fe to learn English, an experience that may have stimulated in him a lifelong talent for languages.[36]

His formal learning finished at seventeen, Hubbell chose to follow in his father's pioneer footsteps. Apparently interested in experiencing a frontier that his faith in Manifest Destiny predicted would one day end, he became a vagabond, exploring the wild country to the west of the Rio Grande. Like many romantic and affluent youths of the era, he was drawn, but not entirely captured, by the rugged lives of frontiersmen and Indians. He met and befriended John D. Lee and had sufficient contact with the Hopi to learn their language. Then in Panguitch, Utah, the romance of the West proved itself all too real and frightening when the young adventurer became involved in an incident that resulted in a serious side wound and a bullet in his leg. Left alone to die, Hubbell showed himself to be a man of considerable fortitude and courage. With no food and little water, he resolutely struggled on, crossed the Colorado River, and eventually stumbled into a Paiute camp, where he was nursed back to health.[37]

Hubbell, according to his own account, wandered into Navajo country in 1871. He was employed in 1872 in a store at Fort Wingate, under the ownership of two men named Coddington and Stover. In 1873, he opened his first trading post, just off the reservation and three miles from the present site of Ganado, Arizona. In competition with another post first owned by a man named Crary and later by John "Old Man" Leonard, he would eventually buy out Leonard. Hubbell was careful in his relations with the natives and sought the friendship of Manuelito and Ganado Mucho[38]

Hubbell, a dark-haired, short, barrel-chested man known for his friendly and hospitable nature, was nicknamed "Old Mexican" by the Navajos, and shortly after his arrival, he began to keep company with other white men, traders and nontraders alike, who came to be associated with the Navajos. Among these was Louisiana-born Dan Dubois, who had lived with the Utes during the Civil War. Dubois was married to several Navajo women and carried the mail between Fort Wingate and Fort Apache. Anson Damon had also cast his fate with the Diné. Married to a Navajo, Damon had been a butcher at Fort Sumner and moved west with the tribe when they returned home. Others included agency employees such as W. W. Owens and P. H. Williams—both of hwom would later be accused of living with Navajo women—and William and Thomas Keam.[39]

These men served as advisers to the Navajos who were learning the intricacies of American politics. To the reformers, they seemed like a motley band representing the worst of frontier society—precisely the kind of men against whom they wanted to protect the Indians. Thomas Keam, of course, was a likely scapegoat for those who wanted to end this influence. As a result of missionary lobbying, Keam was in danger of losing his position. But he and Agent Hall struggled through their duties as 1873 began, although Hall began to despair about the Navajo future and recommended that the tribe be moved to the Indian Territory.[40]

If relative peace at the agency was any indication, Keam was doing an excellent job. On January 1, Hall reported that the Navajos were in good health and well behaved despite the fact that he could not hand out food because he did not have the appropriate materials with which to manufacture ration tickets. He added that the agency was peaceful. There were no Navajo raids reported, and the only excitement at Fort Defiance was provided by a Navajo who brought in Agent Miller's horse after taking it from a Ute. Hall's greatest dilemma concerned whether or not to sell stolen, but unclaimed, animals brought in by the Navajo Cavalry.[41]

The peace at the agency was fragile, however. It had come as the result of continued efforts by the chiefs and six agents. It had been achieved without meeting the reformers' agenda. Changes directed from outside the agency were about to disrupt this tranquility, although few away from the scene could have predicted the result.

On April 22, Rev. John C. Lowrie, secretary of the Presbyterian Board of Foreign Missions, wrote to the secretary of interior. His words were carefully phrased, but they spelled the end of Keam's brief career as special agent.

> It is with much regret that the Board of Foreign Missions of the Presbyterian Church must request the removal of Thomas Keams [sic] from the office of Sub. Agent of the Navajo Agency. This request is made from no unkind feeling toward Mr. Keams personally, but from the conviction that the interests of the Navajo Indians will be much benefited by the appointment of a Sub. Agent who is more in sympathy with efforts to promote the educational and moral interests of the Indians, and whose example will encourage all such efforts.[42]

In more simple terms, Keam was removed because of his marriage and because the Presbyterian Indian establishment did not believe that he truly wanted to carry out their aims. Lowrie suggested that J. L. Gould of Santa Fe, a friend of Superintendent Dudley who had served at the Cimarron Agency, be Keam's replacement.[43]

Lowrie's request was granted, but the administrative change amounted to little because Gould stuck to Keam's policies. Superintendent Dudley contradicted Gould, despite their friendship. He claimed that no Indians were better prepared than the Navajos for accepting Christian doctrine, implying that the lack of conversions was the result of not enough effort. He also believed that Navajo crime was a thing of the past and recommended that Manuelito's police force be discontinued. Commissioner of Indian Affairs Edward P. Smith, saddled with budgetary restrictions, went along with Dudley's recommendation and demanded that Navajos remain upon their reservation as an alternative course of action. Finally, on June 12, Lowrie advised that Hall be replaced with William F. M. Arny.[44]

With the appointment of Arny, the practical agents were replaced by a man who preached morality and often served his own economic interests. Army would attempt to revolutionize Navajo affairs by preaching Christianity while trying to cheat the Indians of their lands. Fortunately, the Diné had acquired many allies. Major William Redwood Price, who had once been a critic of Navajo leaders, was now willing to blame the Utes for Navajo problems. Price also maneuvered to protect the Diné from mining interests along the San Juan. His attitude represented a commitment from an army already determined to avoid another Navajo war. In addition, the traders, in a very short time, had become economic revolutionaries for Navajos who were starved for products produced by the larger society. They were willing to help the chiefs, who were trying to understand Anglo-American society, undermine any agent who disputed their authority, for the Presbyterians, who preached Indian isolation and paternalism toward their wards, were essentially anticapitalist when it came to Native Americans.

Learning from his experiences with the government and from his friends who were traders, Thomas Keam would reevaluate his circumstances, establish himself as a trader, and continue to influence Navajo affairs. His advice was often sought by Navajo leaders, who were about to face a challenge made by the new agent.

6
William F. M. Arny

W hen William F. M. Arny, bearded and looking righteous, arrived at Fort Defiance on August 12, 1873,
Agent Hall refused to let him take charge until he
received instructions from Santa Fe. Arny was furious at Hall's
delaying tactic. He wrote to the commissioner of Indian affairs
to have the matter resolved.[1] Meanwhile, Hall declared in a letter
to Dudley, "I deem it my duty to retain possession of this Agency
until I am instructed to relinquish it to my successor by you."[2]

As he waited for nearly three weeks to take office, Arny could
look back upon a life that had been busy and dramatic. Raised
in Georgetown, a suburb of Washington, D.C., Arny had left
home at age eighteen. He moved to Bethany in western Virginia
and later to Bloomington, Illinois, where he became involved in
church politics, education, and real-estate speculation. Barely
surviving a scandal—he was accused of fathering an illegitimate
child—Arny drifted into the abolitionist movement, joined the
Republican Party, and served as chairman of the National Kansas
Committee. With the zeal of a new convert, he relocated in
Kansas and was an important leader of the antislavery campaign
in the "bloody" territory.[3]

When Abraham Lincoln took office in 1861, however, Arny
was restless and, considering himself a success in his advocacy
for the black race, he sought to repeat his efforts with Native
Americans. Arny represented a faction in the Republican Party
that Lincoln could not ignore. Thus, in 1861, he was appointed
agent to the Utes and the Jicarilla Apaches. Once in New Mexico
Territory, Arny served the government in several capacities: as
territorial secretary, as acting governor, and in a second term as
Ute agent, special Indian agent, and agent to the Pueblos.[4]

Arny's career was filled with strife. He was openly critical of Carleton and the Bosque Redondo. He feuded with Bishop Juan Bautista Lamy of Santa Fe over the undue influence of Catholic priests over the Pueblos. Finally, in his dedication to changing the ways in which Indians lived, he openly fought with his wards when they refused to cooperate. During such disputes, Arny was stubborn and often offended the Indians. When the Utes declined to go along with one of his schemes, for instance, he called them "human beasts."[5]

Arny's tirades against stubborn natives rarely inspired cooperation, but the Navajos' new agent was not an introspective man. He never doubted the effectiveness of his methods or the worth of his plans. Neither did his failtures seem to harm him politically. Arny, although he had a gift for making enemies, had powerful friends in the territory, including Thomas Tucker, the co-owner of the Santa Fe *Daily New Mexican*. He also had a talent for publicizing himself, the best illustration of which was the time he appeared at a function in Abraham Lincoln's White House dressed as a mountain man in a buckskin coat and leggings.[6]

Arny took to a job with an initial outburst of activity. Delayed by Hall's ploy, he was agitated because he was anxious to implement plans for the Navajos, which he had formulated over several years of interested observation. Arny endorsed Grant's Peace Policy, and in his fidelity to most of its aspects he far surpassed the agents who had preceded him. But he was also more stubborn and less inhibited by reality.

Arny believed that the Navajos were more suited to his brand of civilization than the Utes, a people he considered barbarous, and the Pueblos, whom he thought contaminated by Catholics. The Diné had achieved a pastoral culture. Arny believed that with guidance from Protestant Christians they could be transformed into sedentary agriculturalists. Possessing no faith in the Navajos to bring this about themselves, he believed that only God's men could do God's work. The Indians had to be isolated from frontier elements, confined to their reserve, and controlled by a police force of their own people. The Indians would send their children to a school staffed by Navajos he would train. The children would learn to read and write, and their mothers would be taught to sew and weave. Their fathers would be taught the latest farming techniques.[7]

Even though Arny's goals concerning Navajo education were essentially the same as the agents who preceded him, he was different because he was reluctant to compromise. As a representative of civilization, he knew what was best for the uncivilized. Previous agents had allowed the Navajos to develop a kind of nationalism by conceding power to the chiefs. The major concern had been to expand the Navajo economy and keep the tribe at peace. Implied, but never stated, in their policies was the possibility that the Diné would eventually fit into the American mainstream somewhat on their own terms, through a process of adjusting to government demands. Arny, on the other hand, bluntly insisted that the Indians be subservient. Carleton had attempted such a rapid cultural transformation at the Bosque Redondo and had failed. Arny, who had opposed Carleton's experiment on the grounds that the site was poor and that there were too many Mexican Americans nearby to contaminate the Navajos, did not condemn the general's basic approach.[8]

Arny was not a deep thinker; instead, he was a moralist with rigid definitions of right and wrong. What he saw at Fort Defiance offended his sense of order, and when he took control of the agency on September 1 he did so with a vengeance. Within a week, he was demanding permission to fire most of the agency employees. He wanted Jesus Arviso fired because "he is a Mexican, an immoral man, has a wife at Cubero and lives with *two* Navajo women (sisters) by both of whom he has children, he is addicted to gambling, and exerts bad influence over the Indians." Chief herder W. W. Owens was castigated for being a single man "with improper intimacy with Indian women." Anson Damon, the agency butcher, was also charged with immoral conduct with Navajo women as was another employee, Perry H. Williams. By the end of the month, Arny recommended that two more employees, Charles Hardison and William Clark, be fired for having Navajo wives.[9]

Arny wanted to replace these "squaw men," as he called them, with Christian family men who would provide a proper influence for the Indians. Thomas and William Keam were angered at the agent's action. So was John Lorenzo Hubbell. They accused Arny of lying, of firing experienced employees and replacing them with amateurs, and of being poorly qualified himself. Arny countered their arguments by claiming that the Keam brothers had libeled new agency employees by accusing them of defrauding the Navajos. He also stated that they were guilty of encouraging the Diné to continue their old ways. Unfortunately for the agent, the fact that he wanted to hire his son in some capacity seemed to prove the Keams's point.[10]

Arny's housecleaning at the agency was approved in Washington. A more careful man might have consolidated his power and enjoyed his victory. Arny, however, took further actions that would eventually make his position on the reservation weak. Thomas Keam requested a license to trade on the reservation in September. In his application, Keam stated that his brother William would be the clerk at his trading post. Lehman Spiegelberg and Herman Ilfeld, prosperous Santa Fe merchants, guaranteed a five thousand dollar bond. All seemed to be in order, but Arny blocked Keam's petition on the grounds that William Keam was not a citizen and that neither of the brothers was "a proper person."[11]

In addition, Arny suspended the issuance of rations because the Indians seemed to be well fed.[12] Failing to understand that only a portion of the Navajos could survive without government subsistence, he blundered terribly. The new agent also angered critics when he opposed plans that had been supported by all of his predecessors. The day before Arny took office, Special Navajo Agent J. L. Gould, who had just returned from an inspection of the Navajo San Juan lands, submitted a report to Superintendent Dudley. He came to the same conclusion as many before him:

The lands along the San Juan River were far superior to anything else the tribe possessed. Gould believed that the Indians, if they could develop the region's agricultural capacity, would be entirely self-supporting. He reported that the Navajos, who had largely avoided the area to prevent a war with the Utes, were willing to reoccupy the land and volunteer their labor to construct a subagency and an aqueduct for irrigation. Gould recommended that the government take up the Navajos on their offer.[13]

Not revealing his own plans, Arny rejected Gould's recommendation and defended his decision by using an economic argument sure to cater to the desires of Washington officials who were anxious about a budget-conscious Congress. Arny, possibly realizing that Keam had estimated the cost of building a subagency at $72,000, claimed that he could construct what Gould wanted for $57,500. Nevertheless, he concluded that the subagency was not needed. He also confused the issue to make it appear as if Gould were proposing that the Fort Defiance Agency be moved. If that were the case, he argued, the old agency buildings could be refurbished at a considerably smaller cost of $20,000.[14]

Gould was so frustrated by Arny's ability to confuse matters that he resigned. Before the end of September, Dudley visited the agency to meet with Navajo leaders. They told the superintendent that they wanted more land. In response, Arny replied that the headmen were correct. He advised Dudley that a tract of land, which extended six miles south from the current reservation boundary, be given to the Navajos. The addition to the reservation would enable him to eliminate a "house" located on the tract that freely sold liquor to the Indians.[15]

In early September, the order disbanding the Navajo Cavalry came into effect. Arny did as he was directed, but he praised the police force for being effective in eliminating raids. He doubted that the chiefs would be able to control their people, as police work was too time-consuming, so he asked permission to form a new police force.[16]

Arny, meanwhile, continued to act antagonistically. He so angered the Indians that they began to call him "Tarantula." When the agent left for Santa Fe on September 29, with a wagonload of corn ostensibly to feed his horses on the way, several of the chiefs were upset. Arny had stopped handing out rations, and he was leaving the agency with their supplies. They complained to Gould, who was waiting for his resignation to be accepted. Gould relayed their objections to Superintendent Dudley. He added that Arny had hired a Navajo servant and paid him with government funds. Arny replied quickly to Gould's charges. Explaining why he had taken the corn, he contended that he had paid his servant out of personal funds and accused Gould of keeping a servant himself at government expense.[17]

Although the outcome of his feud with Gould was inconclusive, Arny soon granted Gould's request for leave on October 13, pending approval of his resignation and thereby eliminated his antagonist. Despite this momentary deliverance, Arny was forced to give in to Navajo demands for rations when the year's harvest proved to be less than expected. Yet Navajo leaders were not easily satisfied. They told the agent that they did not believe more rations would arrive on time to get them through the winter. Arny attempted to reassure the chiefs, but he wrote to Dudley that he did not expect the agency's corn to last past December 15. He also worried that the Diné would resort to theft to alleviate their hunger.[18]

Despite his effort to pacify the Navajos by filling their stomachs, Arny inspired little devotion within the tribe. In talks with the headmen, he told them that the Navajos would have to alter their way of life. They would be required, as specified in the treaty, to divide their lands into 160-acre plots and to live in one place all year.[19] The agent ignored environmental factors. The acreage he was proposing was not large enough to support the Navajo flocks, and much of the land that he wanted to divide was incapable of supporting full-time horticulture.

Arny further demanded that all Navajos live on the reservation. He again ignored realities. The Indians already residing on the reserve had laid claim to the land. Those who lived off the reservation did so because they had traditionally occupied the area prior to the conquest or because lands on the reservation had already been taken. Arny overlooked these facts and preached to the Indians about ideals. If the Navajos were to survive the Anglo-American conquest of the West and become civilized, they had to get out of the way of settlement and begin to act like other Americans.[20] The Navajos had ignored demands like this before, but Arny had a talent for nagging persistence that did not allow for passive resistance.

In late October, for instance, Arny called Ganado Mucho into Fort Defiance. Arny believed that he was in control of fifteen hundred to two thousand people, who ranged all the way from his home near present-day Ganado up into Utah, and wanted him to bring all of them onto the treaty lands. The chief also had been trading with Apaches and Mormons. The agent wanted him to stop. Ganado Mucho quickly agreed to Arny's demands. When Arny learned that the chief had made the same promise to Miller, he prepared himself for the Navajo leader's evasion by planning to eliminate all rations and annuities to his people until Ganado Mucho complied with his wishes.[21]

Arny was also concerned about Navajos living east of the reservation, in the vicinity of Cubero and Cebolleta. He claimed that these groups served as informants to other Indians who wished to raid the Mexican-American settlements in the area and that they, themselves, engaged in livestock rustling. Arny argued that these Navajos, numbering in the hundreds, never came to the reservation except to collect annuity goods. During his first two months in office, Arny had sent several messages to them to come to Fort Defiance, but he had met with no success. He proposed withholding annuities from them to force their cooperation. Aware of the fact that these Indians had fooled previous agents by mixing in with the crowd on distribution day, Arny hoped to spot them with the help of Delgadito.[22]

Still, Arny believed that he had achieved some success. In late October, he met with approximately two thousand off-reservation Navajos and informed them that the government required them to live on treaty lands. They promised that they would move, and many began arriving in early November. Even Arny, however, was not totally faithful to the treaty. One headman, Chicquito, requested permission to live south of the reservation, promising to report to the agent with all of his people every day that rations or annuities were issued. Arny granted his appeal and used it as an opportunity to ask again for the tract south of the agency.[23] It is doubtful that Arny understood that the land in question had been set aside for a transcontinental railroad. But the agent had little time to ponder such details.

Nevertheless, he demanded that his wards strictly comply with the treaty. When Cebolleta Navajos, for example, continued to ignore his directives to come to the reservation, Arny complained that they were trespassing on Laguna Pueblo land and demanded military action. Meanwhile, Manuelito was causing the agent grief. In October, Arny had granted leave for the Navajo leader to go to Santa Fe. On November 20, Arny reported Manuelito three weeks overdue in returning to the agency. He also complained that the chief had moved his people even farther off the reservation, to a point in the mountains west of San Mateo. Arny's distress was heightened when one of Manuelito's followers was wounded by a New Mexican herder while trying to steal sheep. The criminal, Barbas Pardas, was said to be hiding at Manuelito's headquarters, and the chief would not hand him over.[24]

Arny felt that he could not tolerate such behavior and again demanded that force be used to move all Navajos onto the reservation. He was angry when the army failed to give its attention to the matter. Nonetheless, the agent rushed to implement his plans. He held two councils with most of the headmen in December. Manuelito attended neither. At the first, he explained that they all must live on the reservation and reside permanently on 160-acre plots. At the other meeting, Arny added that they needed to petition the government for more land and to send a delegation to Washington to argue their case.[25]

The headmen appeared cooperative, but nature interfered with the agent's satisfaction. It snowed heavily in December and early

January. Arny estimated that eighteen thousand sheep died in the cold. Isolated Navajo families were stranded without food, and Arny was compelled to go out and deliver supplies. Then just when he believed the freezing weather was going to last awhile, substantial rains flooded the area. Arny warned that unless more supplies were sent to feed the Navajos following these natural disasters, the Indians would steal to survive.[26]

Bad news also came to the agency from another front. Ganado Mucho rode into Fort Defiance in early January after crossing the Defiance Mountains, which were heavily banked with snow. He informed Arny that some northwestern Navajos had been attacked in Utah. Early reports indicated that three of them had been killed and that they had killed an Anglo-American.[27]

Navajos living far to the west and north of the reservation were little understood in 1874. Despite Arny's belief that they were under Ganado Mucho's control, these Indians were independent and, in some ways, much different from other members of the tribe. Many of the Diné living in these regions had never surrendered to the government and had not relied upon it for support. They tended to be more mobile, for the distances between their winter and summer grazing areas were greater. They also had more contact with the Utes and Mormons; and explorer John Wesley Powell, who called these Indians "the great Freebooters of the Plateau Province—enemies of other tribes and white men," had warned after an 1873 inspection of the Ute country that these Navajos could cause a war.[28]

In response to Powell's observation, Commissioner Edward P. Smith warned Arny that trouble might occur, but the commissioner's warning came too late. It is doubtful that it would have done any good. In any case, Arny panicked. He had received reports that Utes had killed a miner in Colorado. A Ute uprising seemed likely. He had heard rumors that Manuelito might enlist his followers in the Ute cause. One of Manuelito's followers, The-Kesh-E-Begay, had died in another confrontation with New Mexican sheepmen, and Arny feared that the chief might go to war to avenge his death.[29] The agent was displeased that Ganado

CHAPTER 6

Mucho had failed to control his people and was distressed that the Navajos involved in the Utah incident lived off the reservation. Nevertheless, once some of the details of the event became clear, he took the Navajos' side.

Four young Navajos had gone into Utah to trade for horses with Utes at Fish Lake. On their way home they intended to travel through Grass Valley, on the east fork of the Sevier River. Suddenly, according to the Navajo who survived, a snowstorm engulfed them. Seeking shelter, the travelers occupied a small, uninhabited cabin a hundred miles north of Lee's Ferry, which belonged to non-Mormon rancher William McCarty and his sons, Tom, Bill, and George. Since the storm lasted three days and the Indians were hungry, they slaughtered one of McCarty's calves. When McCarty learned of the Navajos' presence, he led a group of men to the cabin to evict them. They stormed inside the building without warning. Finding the remains of the calf, they killed three of the intruders—Tagla-sa-Gad, Ta-Pa-gard-Ou, and Te-Che-Chic-Chu—and left the other man for dead.[30]

McCarty told a different story. He, his sons, and a Mormon visitor named Clinger were preparing breakfast in McCarty's kitchen when four Navajos entered without knocking. McCarty ordered the trespassers to leave. They refused. Separated from their guns and unable to force the Indians out, McCarty and company were directed to leave. They retreated to the corral, all of their ammunition on belts on their persons, and there they came up with a plan that they quickly executed. Knowing that their weapons would be of no use to the Navajos, who had entered McCarty's home unarmed, they tied hay in a large bundle, set it on fire, and rolled it toward the house. The young men in the dwelling panicked. They raced out of the house and jumped on horses to flee. Two climbed on Clinger's mount, while the other two rode off on their two best ponies. The white men rushed into the house, picked up their weapons, loaded them, gunned down the two individually mounted Navajos, and gave chase to those on Clinger's horse. They killed one more man, but when nightfall came they gave up the chase.[31]

Whichever version was correct, Arny's initial reaction was to blame the Mormons. He did, however, have the presence of mind to send Ganado Mucho to investigate the matter, along with John Lorenzo Hubbell, who temporarily agreed to set aside his differences with Arny. Still believing that a white man had been killed in Utah, Arny declared that war was close at hand. On January 28, he called a council. He urged that the chiefs work for peace. They agreed. Manuelito, however, was not present, and Arny could not be certain that their promise was meaningful without the great warrior's assent.[32]

When Ganado Mucho and John Lorenzo Hubbell returned to the agency, the facts of the episode became clearer. Arny now knew that an Anglo-American had not been killed, but he and the Navajos still blamed the Mormons, who had not yet offered their version of the event. One of the Navajos, Ne-Chic-Se-Cla, had bravely made his way home. Wounded in the side, alone, hungry, and without a blanket, the young man had struggled for thirteen days. He told a story of brutal murders and claimed that all of their horses, clothing, and supplies had been stolen. His tale of pain and courage had inspired many young Navajos in the northwest to speak openly of revenge. The relatives of the slain men were demanding the payment of 192 horses and 100 head of cattle from the Mormons to compensate for their loss.[33]

On February 11, Arny called another council. Manuelito came to the meeting demanding that the New Mexicans who had killed The-Kesh-E-Begay be forced to make a payment to the dead man's relatives. Arny refused to obey the chief's command. He explained to the assembled headmen that they had to keep the peace so that their tribe could continue its good relations with the government. They made it clear that they had no intention of joining the Utes in their fight with the miners. Arny then brought up the Mormon matter. He agreed that the men who murdered the Navajo traders had been in the wrong, but he added that the murdered men should not have been off the reservation. They protested that General Sherman had given them permission to live on unoccupied lands. The agent rejected their arguments, but he suggested that they petition to see the president to have the articles of the treaty explained. They agreed. Next, he proposed a redrawing of the reservation boundaries. Although the headmen made no immediate protest, Arny's proposal was to be the center of controversy for several months.[34]

Buried within the chiefs' petition to see the president, which was dictated by Arny and transcribed by Hubbell, was a request for more land to the south of the reservation, for which the Navajos would exchange their territory in the Carrizo Mountains and along the San Juan River. Arny justified the trade by contending that war would be inevitable among the Navajos, the miners, and the Mormons unless the Indians were moved south. He declared that the Navajos would not become civilized unless they were forced upon a reservation and removed from contaminating influences such as the Mormons. It is, however, doubtful that his motives were entirely sincere. As early as 1870, he had been advertising the agricultural and mineral potential of the San Juan region in the East, and during his tenure as Ute agent, he had helped men who hoped to develop the region. Arny felt that the lands in question were just too valuable for Indians to hold, and given his background in real-estate development, he may have hoped to profit from the region's settlement by Anglo-Americans.[35]

Arny's opinions on Navajo land tenure were hardly universal, and he probably was counting on a visit by the chiefs to Washington to sell the idea. All of the post-Bosque agents had seen the San Juan region as the tribe's economic salvation. Army officers at Fort Wingate, all too willing to move the Utes out of the way of Anglo-American settlement, hoped that the Navajos would fully exploit the resources of the area. In recommending the establishment of a fort along the river as much to protect Navajo title as to guard the property of new settlers, the army seemed to have adopted a policy of pacification. The Navajos were peaceful enough. Their leaders showed moderation. It made good sense not to provoke them; after all, they were a large tribe who could do great damage if it came to war.

War, in the meantime, seemed like a very real possibility along the Navajo–Mormon frontier. The Mormons were, indeed, concerned. Although Mormon settlers in southern Utah had grown to trust some Navajos, they still harbored fears of much of the tribe. As word of the Grass Valley incident spread, rumors of an all-out war with the Diné induced many to panic. Grass Valley was evacuated, and other southern Utah communities prepared for battle. If calmer individuals urged moderation, word concerning the mood of northwestern Navajos sharpened their caution.[36]

A Hopi leader named Tuba received word from a Navajo, who owed John D. Lee a favor, that some Navajos were planning a war council. On January 15, Tuba found Lee working on his ranch near Moenavi. Heeding the Hopi's warning, Lee rode through a cold and foggy night to Lee's Ferry, from which he dispatched a rider with a note to Fort Defiance and his sons with a message to Paria and Kanab. In Kanab, they brought word to Jacob Hamblin. By telegraph, Hamblin contacted Brigham Young in Salt Lake City. The Mormon prophet was concerned. He had been planning to establish a mission at Moenkopi on Hopi land, in response to a request by Tuba, who wanted protection against Navajo raids. The Hopi chief's request had fit into Young's plan for the Latter Day Saints to set up a string of communities all the way to the Mexican border. Now, the Moenkopi settlement might have to be postponed. To put an end to any further damage to his plans, Young ordered Hamblin to make peace with the Navajos.[37]

As Hamblin left Kanab, his chances of success were small, but he felt that his people were not to blame. The McCartys were said to be troublesome, and the years to follow would prove this suspicion to be true when two of William McCarty's sons, Tom and Bill, would fall under the leadership of Robert LeRoy Parker, alias Butch Cassidy. But Hamblin's more immediate problem lay in convincing the Navajos that the McCartys were not Mormons. Failure could result in tragedy, and the Mormons could ill afford hostilities. Their plans to expand south were in danger, and the support of other Anglo-Americans was uncertain. Although he did not know it at the time, his fears that some frontier elements might side with the Navajos were substantiated four months later when the Santa Fe *Daily New Mexican*—hardly an advocate of Native American rights—held that the Mormons were in the wrong.[38]

Hamblin rode south alone. Fifteen miles out of Kanab, he was intercepted by his son with a message from Bishop Levi Stewart, urging him to return. Stewart had received word from the Paiutes that the Navajos were in no mood to negotiate.[39] Hamblin was afraid, but as he would later remember:

> I had been appointed to a mission by the highest authority of God on earth. My life was but a small moment compared with the lives of the Saints and the interests of the Kingdom of God. I determined to trust the Lord and go on. I directed my son to return to Kanab and tell Bishop Stewart that I could not make up my mind to return.[40]

At House Rock Valley, north of Lee's Ferry, Hamblin met John D. Lee. The two crossed the Colorado at Lee's establishment and traveled to Moenavi, where they found Lee's ranch house turned into a fortress by miners who were frightened by rumors of a Navajo uprising.[41]

Lee left Hamblin at Moenavi and went to prepare a defense at the ferry. Hamblin's horse was suffering from exhaustion. A non-Mormon miner, J. E. Smith, gave Hamblin one of his horses and offered his services for the peace mission, along with those of his younger brother. The three men continued their journey that night to Moenkopi, only to find that the Hopis whose assistance they had hoped to enlist had gone to a dance at Oraibi. Pressing forward the next morning, the trio moved east looking for the hostile Navajos. After a full day's ride, they rode into a Navajo camp. When Hamblin tried to talk, he was informed by one of the Indians to wait until morning, when the dead men's relatives would arrive.[42]

The following day, February 1, began peacefully. The Navajos at the camp fed the visitors a large breakfast. Just before noon, however, the relatives of the dead men arrived, and Hamblin and the Smith brothers recognized their anger. The meeting that followed was held inside a hogan. The Mormon and his companions faced twenty-four Navajos. The relatives of the slain men accused the Mormons of deception. Navajos had gone openly into Utah to trade because of Hamblin's assurances at the Fort Defiance peace talk. Now, the Mormons had murdered their relations. Invoking his honesty, Hamblin denied that his people were guilty. The older relatives demanded that the Mormons pay for lost lives with cattle and horses. Hamblin refused, contending that payment would be an admission of guilt. Next, the young men threatened the missionary's life. Ne-Chic-Se-Cla showed his wounds. J. E. Smith almost drew his revolver, but he was talked out of it by Hamblin. Eventually, tempers cooled. The Navajos agreed to spare Hamblin's life. Hamblin promised the Indians that if Hastele, a local headman away at Fort Defiance, would visit Grass Valley, he would show him the site of the murders and prove that the Mormons were guiltless. In the meantime, he guaranteed that Navajos would be allowed to trade in Utah. After eleven hours, the conference ended.[43]

Hamblin smoked cigarettes with the negotiators. The people at the camp fixed a large meal, but the missionary could not eat. A woman took pity on him and offered to fix him several items, all of which sounded unappetizing. In the end, she brought him a container of goat's milk. He drank it and went to sleep. In the morning, Hamblin rode off with the Smiths.[44] Hamblin had done little more than save his life. The Navajos of the region were not convinced that the Mormons were innocent.

The next day, the Smiths and Hamblin rode back to Moenavi. Arriving there at 8:00 P.M., Hamblin was determined to rest a few days. On February 5, more Navajos arrived and insisted upon reparations. According to some accounts, Hamblin, tired and mentally exhausted, finally gave in to their demands—a charge the missionary would deny for the rest of his life. Hamblin agreed, however, to return within twenty-five days to talk with Hastele.

The following morning, he headed home. On his way, he intercepted a band of Mormon missionaries headed for Moenkopi under the leadership of John Blyth. Hamblin warned them to send the women and children back across the Colorado. The settlers ignored his advice.[45]

Shortly after his arrival in Kanab, Hamblin was in the saddle again. In St. George, he conferred with Brigham Young, who urged him to continue his peace efforts. When it came time for Hamblin to return, he was in failing health. He attempted to borrow a wagon, but met with no luck. As a result, he mounted a horse and resumed his journey. Not long afterward, a rain and sleet storm soaked him, and by the time he reached the town of Johnson, twelve miles south of Kanab, he was barely able to stay on his horse. He received shelter from a local resident and was forced to remain half of the following day. After noon, the weather seemed to improve. Hamblin mounted his horse with difficulty and continued. Unfortunately, the storm struck again. The missionary stopped at a vacant house, built a fire, and went to sleep. The next morning, he rode to Paria, where he was joined by fellow Mormons Thomas Adair and Lehi Smithson. They continued to Moenave.[46]

Hamblin was probably late. Hastele and other friendly Navajos could not be found. Another local headman, Ketch-e-ne, claimed that the Latter Day Saints owed the relatives of the dead men 350 cattle. Ignoring this demand, Hamblin ventured on to the Hopi villages. He informed the Hopis that he had come to make peace with the Navajos. He asked them to let the Diné know that he had come for an honorable purpose. He added, with a degree of disingenuousness, that the Navajos had not met him as agreed. Nevertheless, if they would come to the scene of the crime, he would prove that his version of events was correct.[47] On March 7, Hamblin wrote a letter to Arny.

Brigham Young's ambassador apologized for not seeing Arny in person. Unluckily, he stated, there was too much snow in the mountains for him to make it to Fort Defiance. Hamblin outlined the facts as he then understood them. He guaranteed the dedication of his people to peace, but doubted that tranquility along the Navajo–Mormon frontier could be obtained under the present circumstances. He had been informed that one or two men, probably miners, had been killed between Lee's Ferry and the San Juan River. He cautioned that further violence might result if tensions were not eased. To prove his contention, he invited Arny and the chiefs to confer with him in one of the Hopi villages. If this proved to be impossible, he proposed again that three or four Navajo leaders visit Grass Valley with him when they could. He was certain that he could show them the facts. He added that his people had recently settled at Moenkopi and continued hostility would jeopardize these families.[48]

Arny replied eleven days later. While he rejected the Mormon's invitation to negotiate among the Hopis, he suggested that Hamblin come to Fort Defiance, where he was certain that peace could be arranged. Arny told Hamblin that arrangements could "be made to protect the Mormons and Miners and settlers" by defining where they could live unmolested.[49]

Arny warned, however, that war was a possibility if peace could not be negotiated. Even though the agent was conciliatory when writing to Hamblin, his statements to Superintendent Dudley were provocative. Now that he knew the Mormons were innocent of the murders, he determined that they had provoked the whole affair by moving onto Navajo lands—lands, by his own definition, off the reservation and not under Navajo title. Arny objected to a religious leader, Brigham Young, appointing an ambassador with the authority to make peace. He added that the Latter Day Saints were a bad influence upon the Diné, citing John D. Lee's role in the Mountain Meadows Massacre as an example, and claimed that Lee sold guns to the Navajos. Arny concluded that unless the Navajos and Mormons were separated, there would be a war.[50]

By April, John Blyth and his followers at Moenkopi were tired of the posturing of Hamblin and Arny. Harassed almost daily by Navajos who rode through their settlement, they wanted peace. Ira Hatch, another Mormon leader, and Blyth agreed to meet with local Navajos, only to find themselves on trial and their lives threatened. Talking their way out of the situation and being told by Navajos that Hamblin had failed to keep his appointment, Blyth and Hatch became skeptical about Hamblin's efforts. They wrote to Brigham Young to declare that their village was in danger. The Mormon president responded by sending an expedition of fifty men under the leadership of his nephew, John R. Young, which arrived just in time, for Navajos seemed on the verge of attack.[51]

Young wrote to Arny, repeating that the Mormons were not going to pay bribes to the relatives of the dead men because their people were not guilty. They were a peaceful and industrious people, but, he added, they were still willing to talk with the Navajos. The settlers at Moenkopi, anxious to keep their community alive, had recruited another Mormon, former Arizona territorial legislator Andrew S. Gibbons, as their spokesman. Young indicated that Gibbons was willing to negotiate with Arny and the chiefs. If this option was not acceptable, the Navajos could also come to Utah and meet with Mormon leaders who would prove that the Saints were innocent.[52]

Arny remained obstinate. Brighm Young, worried about the lives of his followers at Moenkopi, ordered the settlement evacuated until peace was restored. The Saints agonized over Navajo attacks upon their other frontier outposts. In May, Hamblin sent a message to several Navajo leaders, inviting them to a conference at Lee's Ferry. He offered to show them the site of the murders to prove his people's innocence. He warned, however, that Navajos crossing the Colorado River at any other place than Lee's Ferry would be considered enemies.[53]

Arny received Hamblin's communication and ignored it. It had been a severe winter. After the floods of January, heavy snows had returned, and there had been as much as two feet of snow on the ground at Fort Defiance in March. The spring melt followed, and much of the reservation had become a quagmire. He had been stuck at the agency for much of the winter, and when he had an opportunity to leave in the middle of May, he did not venture west or north to negotiate with the Mormons. Instead, he traveled to Santa Fe. Arny had some difficulty in crossing the Jemez River and the Rio Grande, which were still in flood, but he made the 240-mile trip in forty-eight hours and arrived in the territorial capital on May 19.[54]

The front page story in the *Daily New Mexican* the next day demonstrated Arny's talent for publicity and clearly outlined his views on the Grass Valley affair. He and Major William Redwood Price, commander at Fort Wingate, had recently met with the Navajos. The Diné had promised to remain at peace with all of their neighbors. But Arny left room for doubt. Many of the Indians, he explained, were poor. Due to the severe winter weather, a large number of sheep had died. Some of the Navajos had been reduced to eating their horses. Despite the indignity of this situation, the Navajos had not stolen much from their neighbors. The Mormons, however, had provoked them. War, the agent concluded, would result if something were not done.[55]

Arny then related his version of the Grass Valley incident. With Mormon help, McCarty had murdered three Navajos. According to the agent's acocunt, Arny and Price had both offered to negotiate a peace that would do justice to the dead men's relatives. The Mormons had refused their offers.[56] The newspaper article continued:

In the western region [of New Mexico Territory] miners and citizens are locating on the Pacific slopes, a portion of which the Navajoes, were encouraging the miners and citizens to locate around them. The Mormons came; they "spied out the land" and found "it good to dwell in," and in the fashion of the Mormons they got up another "Mountain Meadow" intrigue, which will result in disaster to many poor families, if the Mormons are allowed to carry out their intention. They claim that "the earth is the Lord's and the fullness thereof." They are the Lord's people and have the right to enter and take possession of the Lords [sic] heritage; in this we think they will make a mistake, as the military near them and the Indian authorities in charge, will see that justice is done to miners, gentile [non-Mormon] settlers, and the Indians, who, as we concede, some right to land given to them by the government, and who are also "the Lord's people," the high claims of the Mormons to the contrary notwithstanding.[57]

The newspaper also declared that Ganado Mucho and Aqua Grande were demanding justice.[58]

Despite the *Daily New Mexican*'s public endorsement of his policies, doubts were beginning to grow about Arny's ability to handle Navajo affairs. The chiefs were becoming restless. Thomas Keam and John Lorenzo Hubbell had friends in Santa Fe, and they lobbied against the agent whenever the opportunity arose.[59] The army also lacked confidence in Arny. Ever fearful of war, the officers at Fort Wingate had worked to establish friendly relations with the Navajos and their leaders, and Arny looked like he was about to provoke an unnecessary conflict.

Whether or not the Mormons knew enough about Arny's effectiveness as an Indian agent to distrust him, they certainly began to plan for the worst. In May, the Latter Day Saints held a church conference in St. George. Hamblin proposed that a trading post, which would also serve as a fort protecting southern Utah, be built near Lee's Ferry. Brigham Young agreed, and construction of the rock structure began in June.[60]

Arny concurrently decided that the conflict between the Navajos and the Mormons would not be settled without a government display of force. He wrote to the commander of the district of New Mexico, Colonel John I. Gregg, requesting a company of soldiers to escort him to Lee's Ferry to meet with the Mormons and the Navajos. Superintendent Dudley, however, rejected Arny's request. He informed the agent that the presence of troops might be provocative and told his superiors in Washington that Arny was not the man to restore peace. He recommended the appointment of a special agent to negotiate a settlement.[61]

While Dudley waited for the Indian Bureau to respond, Navajo leaders took action on their own. Ganado Mucho had run several errands to the northwestern Navajos on behalf of Arny, a man he did not particularly like. When he was on the Mormon frontier, he had had many opportunities to converse with northern leaders and to coax them to seek peace and calm their angry young men. Possibly because of Ganado Mucho's efforts, Hastele took Jacob Hamblin up on his offer in July.[62]

Hamblin, who had been delayed by church matters in St. George, found Hastele and several other Navajos waiting for him in Kanab. He and Ammon B. Tenney began the journey with the Indians to visit Grass Valley. At that night's camp, Hamblin retold the Mormon version of the murders. Along the way, he had telegraphed two men, Heleman Pratt and Bishop Thurber of Richfield, Utah. These men lived in the region, and Hamblin believed that they knew more than he.[63]

As the Hamblin party awaited the arrival of the Mormons' expert witnesses, there was considerable traffic in and out of Grass Valley. It appeared that the local populace was preparing for war. Nonetheless, the two men eventually joined Hamblin's expedition. That night, Pratt and Thurber told the Navajos what they knew of the murders.[64] In the morning, while the others were saddling their horses to venture over to the site of the killings, Hastele had a change of heart. He said, according to Hamblin:

> I am satisfied; I have gone far enough; I know our friends, the "Mormons," are our true friends. No other people we ever knew would have taken the trouble they have to show the truth. I believe they have good hearts. Here is Jacob; he has been traveling about to do good all winter and spring, and is going yet. When I get home I do not intend my tongue to lay idle until the Navajoes learn the particulars of this affair.[65]

The headman rode to Kanab. The rest of the party inspected the scene of the crime. Once the Navajos were satisfied that the Mormons were innocent, Hamblin and company joined Hastele in Kanab, where they determined to visit Fort Defiance. With little time to rest, Hamblin, Hastele, and Tenney set out for the Hopi villages and, eventually, the Navajo agency.[66]

When they arrived at Fort Defiance, the Mormons and Hastele did not have to negotiate with Arny. J. W. Daniels, a special Indian Bureau inspector, was there to talk with Hastele and the Mormons, and several of the chiefs were also present. Although Daniels wanted to blame the Saints, Hastele's testimony changed his mind. The Mormons and the Navajos concluded a truce.[67]

Arny's role in the matter had been provocative. It was obvious that he wanted both the Navajos and the Mormons out of the San Juan region. A war between the two would have served his purposes. A settlement had been reached because the Mormons had been ceaseless in their quest for peace and because the Navajos had used restraint. Although they had found good reason to be angry and several opportunities to resort to force, the Diné had avoided hostilities.

Their agent, however, did not recognize their achievement because it was not something that he had arranged. Meanwhile, the Diné, after almost a year of William F. M. Arny's rule, had good reason to distrust him. The Navajos had been used to agents who openly agitated for their rights. Their leaders, however, knew how to recruit allies. Men like John Lorenzo Hubbell and Thomas Keam, who did not like Arny's policies, were quite willing to assist the Navajos, and Hubbell, who transcribed the petition by the chiefs to the president, knew that Arny intended to do with the Diné's San Juan lands. Finally, the army saw the agent ignore its policies for keeping the Navajos at peace, and it witnessed his attempts to provoke a Navajo–Mormon war. Military men also gave the chiefs their assistance, for it was clear to all of these factions that the new agent was a problem they could not ignore.

In the years following the Bosque Redondo, Navajo society needed to develop "national" leaders strong enough to police their own people and to deal forcefully with the United States. Manuelito, both respected and feared by U.S. officials, probably was the most militant Navajo leader. (Courtesy National Museum of the American Indian, Smithsonian Institution, neg. no. 37814.)

A woman named Pachie posing for the camera of Ben Wittick in 1885.
(Photo by Ben Wittick, courtesy School of American Research collections in
the Museum of New Mexico, neg. no. 15946.)

Navajo medicine men were considered obstacles to progress by many of the agents. In this photograph, a medicine man poses for an unknown photographer at Fort Wingate, New Mexico, in 1885. (Courtesy Museum of New Mexico, neg. no. 44542.)

During the 1870s and 1880s the Navajos built up a good relationship with the army. One of the reasons was that many Navajos served as scouts in the Apache wars. In this photograph, we see three Navajo scouts—Pedro, Gayetenito, and Biziz—who served in the 1886 Apache campaign. (Courtesy Museum of New Mexico, neg. no. 50130.)

Largo, another Navajo scout, poses for this photo in 1886. (Courtesy Museum of New Mexico, neg. no. 50129.)

Navajos objected to conditions in many of the schools that their children attended. Black Horse, left, led a movement against the schools in the early 1890s. Later in his life, he would cooperate in efforts to educate Navajo youth. (Photo by Simeon Schwemberger, courtesy Museum of New Mexico, neg. no. 48714.)

Henry "Chee" Dodge, of Anglo and Navajo ancestry, became a rich man because he could negotiate between Anglo and Navajo traders. Dodge replaced Ganado Mucho and Manuelito as the primary Navajo leader in the 1890s. (Courtesy School of American Research collections in the Museum of New Mexico, neg. no. 15950.)

7
The Fall of Arny

In early January of 1874, several Navajos visited the ranch of the former New Mexico territorial delegate to Congress Miguel A. Otero. Days later, they told a story of murder to Manuelito. They had gone to the ranch to trade for ewes (female sheep), but when Otero's herders delivered the animals, there were many wethers (castrated male sheep) in the flock. The Navajos protested, and an altercation followed that ended when one of the herders shot a Navajo, The-Kesh-E-Begay. Otero's men fled the scene, but the Navajos waited for three days, watching over the flock. When Otero's employees returned to the site of the killing, the Indians demanded that they be given the ewes agreed upon and a payment for the life of The-Kesh-E-Begay. They received no satisfaction.[1]

Arny learned of the incident in January and used it as an excuse to warn his superiors of a Navajo war. But when Manuelito brought up the demands of The-Kesh-E-Begay's relatives on February 11, Arny denied that they had a right to make a claim. Nevertheless, as Arny attempted to clear up the chiefs' complaints prior to a May 14 meeting, he agreed to take the Navajos' side. On May 12, Arny wrote to Otero asking that he pay the relatives what they demanded. Although the agent failed to specify the Navajo demands, they had become common knowledge: 250 sheep, 1 good horse, 1 mule, 2 saddles and bridles, 1 "gun," 2 yoke of oxen, 1 log cabin, 1 wagon, 6 cows with calves, 2 steers, 2 yards of cloth, and 6 pounds of indigo.[2]

Otero had a different version of events. According to the rancher, his herders had not sold any ewes to the Navajos. Instead, two drunk Navajo men, accompanied by a woman or two, had arrived asking for a handout. His employees gave them a wether to butcher. The beggars, however, were not satisfied. They wanted two animals. Wanting no trouble, Otero's herders agreed to this demand, but the Indians would not accept even this compromise. They said they wanted ewes. The herders refused. A Navajo named Pelon drew a pistol. One of the herders tried to take the gun away. In the fracas that followed, Pelon shot off the herder's finger. Another Navajo drew his pistol, and the herders, acting in self-defense, shot him. Then the ranch hands retreated. Once they were gone, the Indians stole their provisions, clothing, and cooking utensils. A Navajo was spotted later, at Jemez Pueblo, wearing the pants of one of the herders.[3]

When Otero arrived two days later, he was not in the mood for revenge. Three Navajos, who claimed to be angry at their fellow tribesmen for starting the fight, were taking care of his flock. Otero paid them for their efforts and offered additional sums if his herders' utensils were returned. The rancher knew that Manuelito was visiting Jemez and offered to negotiate with him, but the chief sent word that he had business in Santa Fe. Otero concluded that he had done what he could. Nevertheless, he was aware that peace with the Navajos was important. He agreed to pay the Navajos if the government would reimburse him.[4]

Arny agreed to Otero's proposal, but his superiors did not concur. As a result, the problem was not solved to the satisfaction of either side, and Arny added to his list of enemies. Yet his attempted solution had been motivated by his need to win the Navajo leaders over to his proposed land swap; he needed their support to win acceptance of his land transfer. Therefore, he set out upon a strategy to court their support.

The Navajo economy was a shambles. By the end of winter, Arny estimated that thirty thousand sheep had died. Yet he made plans as early as February to restrict the distribution of food so he could use the "surplus" as payment to the chiefs. Although Frank Tracy Bennett had issued extra annuities to his captains, he and the other former agents had warned against issuing rations to headmen because rewards would be based less on need than on political cooperation. Arny, however, appeared to be less concerned with equity than with being in control.[5]

At the May 14 meeting, Arny persuaded Navajo leaders to reinstitute a Navajo police force of two hundred men under Manuelito and to pay them out of surplus annuities. The police resumed their work, and the power and prestige of the chiefs were increased.[6] Arny, on the other hand, had not added to his own authority, for Navajo leaders had put their faith in the traders, who dismissed the agent as a self-serving, religious bigot.

Despite his moves toward conciliation with the chiefs, Arny seemed unable to hide his arrogance, probably the Indians' first reason for disliking him. At the same time, the Navajos were gaining favor with officers at Fort Wingate. Several hundred Apaches in Arizona and New Mexico had effectively tied down thousands of soldiers. Under the inspiration of General George Crook, the army had attempted to break the stalemate by using Indians to fight Indians. Navajos willingly participated in the effort. Shortly after the secretary of war authorized the recruitment of Indian scouts for the Apache wars, ten Navajos enlisted at Fort Wingate. They were mostly off-reservation Indians, and they only served for the standard six-month period allowed Indian recruits. They mustered out of service in August of 1874. Nevertheless, they were the vanguard of future Navajo enlistment. Twenty-five additional Navajos signed up in July for service among the Mimbres Apaches.[7] Their devotion to duty won friends in the military for the Navajos.

Meanwhile, Arny insisted that the Diné live on 160-acre plots of land and, in a significant departure from reality, guaranteed his superiors that his wards would be self-supporting within two years. The agent also had difficulty in accepting reality concerning education. Despite his ambitious plans for schools among his wards, educating the Navajos proved to be difficult. In the spring, Arny engaged the services of "Professor" Valentine Friese. Friese was shocked by the conditions at the school. His classroom was inadequate, and there were no supplies. The teacher submitted orders for pens, pencils, slates, McGuffey's readers, chalk, erasers, and letter blocks. He offered his lessons diligently, but he was plagued with attendance problems. There were an estimated three thousand school-age Navajos. During March, Friese reported only twenty-five students. Among these, twelve were regular pupils. Arny told his teacher to give each student a ration ticket at the end of the day as a reward, but this bribe proved ineffective.[8]

Despite his failure in luring more children into school, Arny felt confident enough to hire an additional teacher, Joseph Gow, who spent his time doing clerical work since there were no students to teach. When Arny's superiors began to question his use of school funds with such limited results, he was ready with excuses. He claimed that children were not coming to school because they lived so far away. In April, Arny established a boarding facility. He hired Mrs. Catherine Stowe, a Presbyterian from Springfield, Ohio, as a matron to care for children boarding at the agency. The commissioner's office vetoed this appointment, stating that there were inadequate funds, but Arny argued that the civilization of youngsters would be held in the balance; Navajo students needed an American influence that would teach them "intellectual culture" while they were attending school. The boys needed to learn the value of physical labor, and girls to knit, sew, wash, cook, iron, and "other labors suitable to the female children." After the agent assured officials that he had sufficient funds in his own budget, Mrs. Stowe's employment was approved. Arny would declare in the fall that the "experiment" was a success, but there were few Navajo families willing to give up their children; they preferred to raise their offspring within the precepts of their own traditions.[9]

Arny, nonetheless, claimed that he viewed the Diné as abandoning custom. He believed that traditional religious and medical practices were superstitions and that Navajo medicine men were a bad influence. He hoped that their control over the lives of people could be broken by modern medicine. The agency physician had treated 2,204 Indians in the first year of Arny's tenure. The agent had investigated the effects of this treatment, and he was convinced that the doctor had proved that the medicine men were ineffective practitioners. But Arny saw the need for even better treatment. Without a hospital the physician could not be sure that patients took their medicine properly or that they were given a correct diet. Arny urged that a hospital be built for "white man's medicine" to gain credibility among his wards.[10] His request was denied.

The Navajos, meanwhile, had no intention of cooperating with the agent's goals. When he communicated with his superiors, however, Arny maintained that the Indians could be won over to his side. Never stating that the Diné had their own reasons for opposing his efforts, Arny contended that rejection of his plans was mostly the result of interference. He believed that off-reservation traders, in addition to the medicine men, were a corrupting influence upon his charges. He claimed that traders sold whiskey to the Indians, and some of them undoubtedly did. Arny also charged that they encouraged the Indians to resist his reforms. He was powerless to control these men who lived outside his jurisdiction. Most of them resided in Arizona; and because Arizona territorial officials were located far away from the reservation, they were powerless to control outlaws. To resolve this dilemma, Arny urged that "an act be passed attaching the Navajo agency and reservation to New Mexico for all judicial purposes, civil and criminal. This will aid the agent to bring to punishment bad white men who are constantly violating the law and also Indians who should be punished."[11] When his recommendation was not acted upon, Arny faced another setback in his ability to control Navajo affairs. He faced other disappointments as well.

In May, Huero, a headman who lived east of the reservation, and his followers raided the Southern Apache Reservation and stole a number of horses. Complaints were also made that Huero's people were selling whiskey to the Apaches. Attempting with no success to have the New Mexico attorney general prosecute Huero and his men, Arny visited the chief in July and convinced him to move to the reservation. Nonetheless, it took

Huero until October to make the move, and he did not stay in his new home long.[12] In spite of his optimism and a year of trying, Arny had not succeeded in moving many off-reservation Navajos onto their assigned lands.

No matter how much his plans had failed, Arny hoped for a victory that would cause all of his other projects to fall into place. If his land swap could be approved, he felt that real progress would be made. Although he had managed to obtain the chiefs' marks upon a document approving the land swap, he understood that it had little chance for congressional approval unless the chiefs made a plea in Washington. He pushed his superiors to allow a trip to the capital. Forgetting that the tribe had sent a delegation to Washington in 1868, Arny insisted that Navajos had never visited a city larger than Santa Fe. A journey east would teach them to appreciate the power of the United States. He added in his petitions that only by meeting with national leaders would the Indians ever be convinced that the treaty required them to live on the reservation.[13]

Superintendent Dudley endorsed the trip. He wrote that no group of Indians deserved such a reward more, but added that Arny should not go with them because it would be unwise for an agent to be away from his post so long. Indian Commissioner Edward P. Smith was less enthusiastic. He informed Arny that delegations were not brought to Washington merely because they wanted to come. Smith did not see any urgency. If such a luxury were granted, he suggested, Congress might not believe the Navajos needed more appropriations. Nonetheless, the commissioner concluded that if the visit could prove beneficial for peace and if the Navajos insisted, he would allow the agent to use twenty-five hundred dollars from the tribal clothing fund to take care of expenses.[14]

Arny enthusiastically accepted the commissioner's terms, but Thomas Keam, acting as a kind of agent-in-exile, plotted against Arny. It was obvious to Keam that Arny's stated purposes for the land exchange were dishonest. Arny argued that the Navajos would benefit, for the lands to the north were coveted by whites for their mineral wealth, while the tract he wanted attached to the reservation was better agricultural land. Keam felt that development of the San Juan would make the Diné self-supporting. He was appalled at the agent's gall. Despite the fact that Arny argued that the new lands would be easier to control and children living south of Fort Defiance could more easily attend school, Keam was convinced that Arny acted for selfish reasons.[15]

Keam made independent plans to be in Washington to do what he could to defeat Arny. Meanwhile, the Navajos who were to accompany Arny were not reliable as far as he was concerned. The policy, dating from the Bosque Redondo, of recognizing leaders who held power made it impossible for Arny to handpick his delegation; indeed, the agent had to make important concessions to the existing headmen to gain their consent.

Ganado Mucho, probably the most important Navajo leader, still refused to move his flocks east to the reservation. A diplomat who agreed to what the agent asked as long as he was unaffected, Ganado Mucho resented his white superior's arrogance and bungling of the Grass Valley matter. Manuelito, although cooperative on the surface, was mercurial and often as arrogant as the man the government had sent to govern him. Arny nevertheless took special care in courting his chief of police. Alone among the delegates, Manuelito was allowed to bring along his wife, Juanita, and his son, Manuelito Segundo. Arny also suffered the presence of Jesus Arviso, whom he had fired as agency interpreter a year earlier and rehired months later after the interpreter supposedly repented. The delegation, additionally consisting of Cannero Mucho, Mariano, Tierre-su-se, Cabra Negra, Cayantanita, and Narbono Primero, left Santa Fe in mid-November.[16]

Equipped with a number of craft items—saddle blankets, baskets, pottery, gloves, neckties, and a large red, white, and blue blanket—the Navajos drew crowds at stops along the way. In Denver, Arny entertained several leading citizens with his charges. A similar reception awaited them in Kansas City. In St. Louis, they held a short meeting with General Sherman. Arny then took the Navajos to Bloomington, Illinois, where he showed the Indians to his former neighbors. Finally, the delegation caught a train from Chicago for Washington, D.C.[17]

With his typical flair for publicity, Arny sent word to the Washington *Evening Star* to advertise why the delegation was coming. The newspaper announced that the Navajos wanted to exchange a section of land in the north, which was "amazingly rich in the precious metals," for "an agricultural and pastoral region" in the south. It was also stated that Arny intended that the ceded land be opened for Anglo-American settlement. The Navajos had other matters to discuss. They wanted to arrange adjustments of "some complications" in the 1868 treaty, and to demand payment for the murder of their tribesmen killed by Mormons.[18]

Unfortunately for Arny, the timing of his visit was poor. King Kalakaua and an Hawaiian delegation were in the city at the same time. The Navajos, housed in the Arlington House Hotel, had to share the publicity. Nevertheless, Arny made the best of the situation and spent the first few weeks exploring the city, visiting monuments, and viewing museum exhibitions. The agent also arranged meetings with several congressmen, the secretary of interior, and the commissioner of Indian affairs. All seemed to be going smoothly until the night before they were scheduled to meet with President Grant.[19]

Thomas Keam made a call at the Arlington House to visit the chiefs. Arny was absent, and Keam took Manuelito and several others on a tour of Washington taverns. According to historian Frank McNitt, it was during this time that Keam informed the Indians that Arny intended to give away the San Juan lands, in addition to adding lands to the south. In any case, when the Navajos returned to the hotel, they were drunk, and Arny angrily locked them in their rooms. Since his wards were in no shape for diplomacy the next day, the agent postponed their meeting with the president. The incident convinced national leaders that Arny had little control over the Navajos, and when Grant finally met with the delegation, there was no mention of the land swap.

The Navajos complained, in a general way, that they did not have enough land. They stated that they were disturbed by possible Mormon colonization of their lands and by depredations committed by miners in the San Juan region. Finally, they protested that many of their children were still captives of New Mexicans.[20]

In spite of his unsatisfactory meeting, Arny continued with his plans. When the delegation left Washington, it journeyed to New York. Convinced that Navajo blankets had enormous economic potential, the agent bought a number of spinning wheels and hired S. N. Goodale, Jr. and J. Wiedeman to install the machinery at Fort Defiance. He also engaged the services of Commissioner Smith's niece, Miss Harriet Cook, to teach Navajo women how to use the new devices. Leaving New York, Arny and the Indians toured several New England cities, including Boston and Providence, where the chiefs were put on display before church conferences. Arny announced that he had been an "intimate" friend of John Brown. He also claimed that mining lands belonging to the Navajo would be opened to settlement.[21]

On their way home, Arny and the Navajos stopped for several days at St. Louis so the agent could deliver lectures on western Indians as well as advertise the benefits of settling and investing in New Mexico. The delegation finally arrived in Santa Fe on January 30, 1875. S. N. Goodale was the first to pull into the New Mexico capital, in a stagecoach with four Navajos. Goodale introduced himself as "the master mechanic of the Navajo Nation" and praised Agent Arny for his wisdom in bringing modern machinery to primitive people. Hours later, Miss Cook reached the city. Arny made his return after dark. He was optimistic about the benefits of the trip and contended that the journey had opened up a whole new world to the Navajos.[22]

Manuelito simply said that he was happy to be home in the mountains and on the plains, where the air was "free." He had been fascinated by the East but concluded that it was far too crowded. As the weeks went by, it became obvious that the chiefs were disillusioned with their agent. They complained that too little had been accomplished by the trip, that its main purpose seemed to be publicity for Arny.[23]

Manuelito left for Fort Defiance on February 4. The Santa Fe *Daily New Mexican* made an occasion of his departure. It referred to him as the "king" of the Navajos.[24] Even though Manuelito had less than authoritarian power, the newspaper's comment was appropriate, for the chief and Ganado Mucho possessed much more strength among the Navajos and with the army than did Arny, who still hoped to control the spiritual and material lives of the Diné.

Arny and Miss Cook elected to stay in Santa Fe to attend a number of receptions. Word, however, reached the agent that things were going poorly at the agency. According to his son, William E. Arny, who had been left in charge at Fort Defiance, the winter had been harsh. Since crops had been destroyed again, rations were low and people were on the brink of starvation. William F. M. Arny claimed that Anson Damon and Daniel Dubois, Anglo-American men married to Navajo women, were spreading rumors that if the Navajos rebelled against Arny, Thomas Keam would be appointed to govern them. In addition to the potential revolt, Arny complained bitterly that Major Price had recruited Navajo scouts and taken them to the Colorado plains without his permission.[25]

Arny left Santa Fe on February 9. Once in Fort Defiance, failure confronted him, and he blamed his failure on the interference of others. Before Arny could engage his enemies, however, he was distracted by disputes with Washington officials and dissatisfied Navajos. Despite his claim of success for his Washington trip, he fell under fire for overspending. Meanwhile, Navajos were starving. Soon after returning to Fort Defiance, Arny cut rations. Angry Navajos pressured their chiefs for relief. All they could do for the moment was to complain. Arny wrote to the commissioner to request emergency appropriations. But the Indian establishment had had enough of his constant demands for funds. Attempting to bring the Navajo agency under fiscal control, Commissioner Smith told Arny that there would be no further funds until April of 1876.[26]

Ignoring the restraints put upon him, Arny angered Commissioner Smith by purchasing beef and flour, spending in excess of seven thousand dollars. Smith reprimanded him. Arny tried to explain that his purchases were needed by poor Navajos, but there was also a question about his expenditure of another seventy-five hundred dollars. Although the money had been appropriated, he seemed unable to account for the way in which it had been spent. At a council meeting on February 28, 1876, he obtained a document signed by the chiefs that stated that seventy-five hundred dollars in merchandise had been given to the chiefs to distribute among their people. This explanation was called into question when the witnesses to the document, agency farmer W. B. Truax, John Lorenzo Hubbell, and William Keam, could not recall their endorsements; however, they could remember the council meeting, and they all swore that the matter had not been discussed. Major Price believed that Arny had forged the document.[27]

At the same time that Arny's accounting procedures were being questioned, Congress disapproved his land transfer when it was discovered that part of the tract south of the reservation had already been given to the Atlantic and Pacific Railroad. Commissioner Smith suggested that land west of Fort Defiance be substituted. Since this area was unacceptable to Arny, probably because it too was rumored to be mineral rich, he spent several months looking for an alternative.[28]

The Navajos, in the meantime, had become restive. Some of the poorer Indians stole from their neighbors to feed themselves, but the practice did not become very common. Thefts also increased at the agency during the first half of the year. The trader's store was robbed. Arny requested that the army arrest the offender, but the commander at Fort Wingate refused to help. When the agent and his employees finally managed to apprehend the criminal and turn him over to the military at Fort Wingate for incarceration, he escaped a few days later. Arny blamed lax discipline among the soldiers, a complaint he would echo later when a Navajo accused of killing a Mexican American and stealing twenty dollars also escaped. When agency butcher S. Hanlon shot a Navajo, the agent was again critical of the army. Navajos surrounded the agency, demanded that Hanlon be handed over for hanging, and seemed to threaten the lives of the agency employees when Arny refused. He requested help from Fort Wingate, but the army declined to get involved. Arny was eventually able to disperse the mob. Yet it was obvious that the Diné were enraged by their agent.[29]

On May 28, Navajo leaders met in council to act formally upon this discontent. They requested that Commissioner Smith dismiss Arny. The chiefs complained that the agent had tricked them into signing invoices for a large amount of coffee, one thousand pounds of flour, and one hundred pounds of sugar, which Arny said had been given to poor Navajos during the time he had been touring the country with Ganado Mucho and Manuelito. The headmen alleged that none of these items had been delivered, and they claimed that Arny had failed to issue half of their annuity goods. They ended their petition by requesting that Thomas Keam be appointed their agent.[30]

Aware that none of the headmen spoke English, Arny correctly accused the traders of drafting the petition, but he made a serious error in assuming that the document did not represent Navajo opposition to his rule. Arny attacked the "squaw men," but he also suspected the army of plotting against him.[31] Believing that it was best to attack his critics rather than defend himself, he accused the traders and the army of corrupting the morality of Navajo women.

Navajo women had such a reputation throughout the region as being particularly beautiful and desirable that protecting their morality on Arny's terms seemed impossible.[32] The Navajos had a long tradition of intermarriage, and they were not very upset if an Anglo-American man wanted to set up a household with one of their women. Arny, however, had serious objections. The agent recommended that a law be passed that would make it a crime "for a white man to cohabit with an Indian squaw," even if he married her in the traditions of her people. Arny would make an exception for couples who married "under the laws of the United States." But even these couples should be forced to leave the reservation because "squaw men" were "retarding influences" on the Indians.[33]

According to Arny, the army was worse. He accused the officers at Fort Wingate of tolerating prostitution. His charges were undoubtedly true, but the fact that prostitution existed around Fort Wingate attested to a number of social ills that Arny's moral condemnation did not include. Fort Wingate was far from an Anglo-American settlement, and life for soldiers was boring and lonely. There were few recreational opportunities. Not many enlisted men could afford to bring their wives to the area, and there was no housing available if they could. As a result, much of their spare time was spent drinking or in the company of prostitutes, most of whom were Navajos. Prostitution was not traditional behavior among the Diné, but some poor Navajo women had taken up the trade at the Bosque Redondo, and a small number of them continued the practice after their return because they needed the money.[34]

Arny's charges, despite their truth, were politically motivated, and his solution was moralistic; he wanted the army to stop its soldiers from using Navajo women to satisfy their lusts. He also argued that the military should cease allowing Navajos to visit the post. Citing the reports of post surgeons, who had decried the high incidence of venereal diseases among the enlisted men, Arny argued that the soldiers were spreading the infections among his wards.[35]

The army was in no position to act upon Arny's charges. It had had long experience with prostitutes frequenting its posts and had found the practice impossible to stop. Closing Fort Wingate to Navajos would injure its efforts in pacification and its attempts to recruit Navajo scouts for the Apache wars. Thus, when Arny's letter to Commissioner Smith was forwarded through the secretary of war to General John Pope, commander of the department of Missouri, it seemed as if Pope would have to defend the indefensible. Instead, he went on the attack. Pope admitted that venereal diseases often made his men unfit for duty, but he implied that it was the Navajo women, and not his men, who carried the disease. He added that there would be no problem if Army would keep the women on the reservation.[36]

Army rightly could point out that he had repeatedly asked the military to force all Navajos onto the reservation, but he had been outflanked by Pope. The general's statement added to a growing consensus that Army could not control his Indians. This idea was reinforced when copies of the Navajo petition reached Reverend Lowrie and Commissioner Smith. A rumor was also circulating that Army had visited a brothel during his visit to the East.[37] It was apparent that Army would not hold office long. Nevertheless, he made another attempt to exchange the Navajo San Juan lands.

Army proposed that the Navajo tribe take two tracts of land for its far northern territory. The tract to the east was attached to the southern end of the San Juan, downstream from the river's fertile valleys. It was, Army admitted, largely desert. He concluded, however, that the Navajos had been using it for pasture and would find it useful. The western strip was located toward the northern end of the reservation. He acknowledged that there was a problem with the western addition. It came very close to Hopi lands, but he was confident that a clash of the two peoples could be avoided by moving the Hopi agency, currently located at Traut Springs, farther west. He claimed that the western tract—actually a barren area with few sources of water—was mostly arable, that two thousand Navajos occupied the land already, and that many more could make use of it. He added that few whites had settled in the region, except for traders married to Navajo women who had given him nothing but trouble. It would be good to remove them. Although he claimed that he was acting upon the chiefs' authorization, he mentioned that traders were urging the Navajos to hold onto their San Juan lands and occupy as much acreage as possible in the river basin. "In consequence of the interference and falsehoods of the 'squaw men,' " he wrote, "the Navajos claim portions of the country now occupied by white men and which is not a part of the reservation and never should be." To settle any disputes that might occur, Arny recommended that a commission be established that consisted of the governor of New Mexico; the territorial surveyor general; editor of the Santa Fe *Daily New Mexican*, W. H. Manderfield; and himself.[38]

Before Arny could do much lobbying for his proposal, Reverend Lowrie informed Commissioner Smith, on June 18, that the Presbyterian board could no longer support the agent's administration of the Diné. Lowrie claimed that the board was disappointed in the moral and educational progress that the Navajos had made under Arny. He added that the board preferred that Arny resign. If he refused, then Lowrie believed that Arny should be removed from office.[39]

In spite of Lowrie's request, Arny still hoped to hold onto power, and he called on those who owed him political favors for assistance. On July 12, Thomas B. Catron, United States Attorney for New Mexico, penned a long and rambling letter on the agent's behalf. Catron, owing his first appointment to government office to Arny's action as acting territorial governor and infamous as a land speculator, wrote that he did not act at Arny's request and defended the agent resolutely against all charges. Concerning Arny's visitation to a brothel, he claimed that the allegation had been leveled by Hank Easton, an interpreter with Arny's party. He declared that Easton was a notorious liar and that his denunciation of Arny was "in substance and intent entirely false." Having been in the East at the same time as Arny, Catron stated that he knew the truth; it had been Easton and "other persons" who had taken the Navajos to a "house of ill fame" without the agent's knowledge. When the Indians returned drunk, Arny forced Easton to return with him to the bordello to find out who had sold liquor to the Indians. Arny's visit was brief. He did not find the guilty bartender and threatened to fire Easton who, in turn, promised to slander him.[40]

Catron proclaimed that Arny was an honest man. He had improved the Indians' moral character by chasing off white men who had committed "adultery with the squaws." Arny had made remarkable progress in civilizing the Navajos. As a result of his efforts, they had acquired great skill in stock raising and horticulture. Miss Cook had taught the women to use the new loom; soon, Catron claimed, Navajo weaving would "be on an equality with the Pueblos."[41]

Most of Catron's praise, however, concerned itself with Arny's efforts to break up the liquor trade. As U.S. Attorney, he had obtained the conviction of three bootleggers, a very difficult task made possible by Arny's dogged pursuit of evidence. Catron added that Arny's continued efforts against the liquor trade were necessary to maintain peace with the Navajo, "a powerful and haughty tribe," the majority of whom supported their agent. Those who had turned against Arny, he claimed, were those who had been led astray by whiskey sellers. Without mentioning Thomas Keam, Catron referred to a "former agent," leading the opposition to Arny, who had lived in sin with a Navajo woman and had children by her. Catron also claimed that no new agent could replace Arny. His recommendation was added to by G. A. Smith, collector of internal revenue in New Mexico.[42]

With these and other letters in hand, Arny rushed to Washington. Before he left, however, twelve of the principal Navajo chiefs, including Ganado Mucho, Manuelito, and Mariano, met on July 12, with Captain George Chilson, who was temporarily in command of Fort Wingate. Settlers in western New Mexico had complained of Navajo depredations, and Chilson warned the chiefs that he would use his troops to stop these outrages. They promised to control the outlaws, and Chilson was sure of their commitment.[43]

The chiefs apparently remained close to the fort because they again presented themselves to Chilson on July 15, to complain about their agent. Accompanied by John Lorenzo Hubbell and Jesus Arviso, they asked Chilson's help in presenting their charges against Arny to the proper authorities. Then they drafted a petition addressed to the "Great Father, President of the United States." It was transcribed by Hubbell and called for Arny's removal. The chiefs complained that they had no faith in him. He had enriched himself at their expense. He had been "trifling, vacillating [sic], and unreliable." They denounced Arny for acting with "pomp and circumstance" around their people and for using "high sounding and meaningless words." The chiefs also accused him of manipulating the distribution of the Diné's annuities and rations for "the support of his personal popularity and ridiculous dignity." They further asserted that Arny had traveled all over the country while the "poor and needy" went hungry.[44]

Declaring that they needed an agent who would devote more time to meeting the needs of their people, the chiefs requested that Thomas Keam be made their agent. They said that he was the best man to represent them because he "possesses all we ask for. He has lived many years among our people, he knows us, he speaks our language, we can make known our wants to him without the danger of false interpretations of wicked and selfish interpreters." Hubbell and Arviso attested to the accuracy of the document, and Chilson swore that although he could not vouch for the accuracy of the leaders' allegations, he was certain that the criticisms of Arny were theirs. From Fort Lyon, Colorado, Major Price echoed Chilson's sentiments. The Diné had complained repeatedly that they did not trust Arny. Price contended that Thomas Keam would be the perfect agent for the Navajos because they trusted him and he could be relied upon to control them.[45]

Meanwhile, Arny had arrived in Washington, trying to win officials over to his newest land scheme and to hold onto his job. It did not take him long to discover that the nation's capital was turning a deaf ear to his intrigues. Thus, on July 22, he submitted his resignation, to take effect on December 31. Citing the letters of Catron and C. A. Smith in his defense, Arny promised to "do all in my power . . . to make the wise policy of the President a success, and show that Indians can be civilized, Christianized and made self sustaining."[46]

In spite of his resignation, Arny remained in Washington to lobby for the land swap. At the same time, his subordinates at Fort Defiance were hardly inactive. On August 8, Manuelito complained at Fort Wingate that supplies were being hauled away by agency employees. The officers at the fort were not able to act, but it was apparent that the Indians would not long tolerate Arny.[47]

On August 19, the chiefs took drastic action. They rode into Fort Defiance and told Dr. Walter Whitney, who had been left in charge, that they were taking control of the agency. Carefully avoiding deadly force, the headmen brushed Whitney aside when he objected and ordered all Navajo employees to stop work. When one of them refused, he was whipped and tied. The chiefs placed a guard at the agency buildings and over the white employees, including Arny's wife, Cicilia. They then inspected the agency, including the living quarters.[48]

In Arny's house and that of his son, the Navajos found a number of items: sixteen bolts of calico, seven gross of handkerchiefs, some denim material, four bolts of manta, several shears and butcher knives, thirteen red blankets, packages of linen thread, seventy-five pairs of children's shoes, and large quantities of tin cups. Mrs. Arny claimed that these articles were her husband's personal property, but in the harness room the Indians discovered 240 tin pails, 432 tin pans, 54 spades, 40 pounds of yarn. In another storeroom they uncovered 70 more pounds of yarn, 3,300 pounds of flour, and 54 pounds of coffee.[49]

The military was not eager to intervene. General Pope stated that the military had no jurisdiction concerning Indian agents. Nonetheless, he added that if the commander at Wingate considered the Navajo dissatisfaction to be dangerous to the peace, he should notify the commander of the district of New Mexico, Colonel John Gregg. Worried about a possible Ute outbreak, Pope urged that his officers use caution in dealing with the Navajos.[50]

Arny arrived in Santa Fe on August 23. Two letters sent by Whitney were soon in his possession. They warned him that if he returned to Fort Defiance, his life and the lives of his family would be in danger. Whitney had requested that the garrison at Fort Wingate intervene, but Captain C. A. Hartwell, temporarily in command, refused assistance until he had orders from Santa Fe. From Whitney, Arny now had his own version of events, which appeared in the Santa Fe *Daily New Mexican*. The "squaw men" had gotten the chiefs drunk and had persuaded them to take the agency by force. Lives were in danger. With this in mind, Arny submitted a second resignation on August 25, which was to take place immediately. He requested that Gregg intervene.[51]

Arny's plea left Gregg unimpressed. He telegraphed his recommendations to the headquarters of the department of Missouri. He stated that reports of "restlessness" among the Navajos

indicate trouble unless the Indian Department takes prompt measures to remedy the grievances of which they complain.

I do not anticipate a general outbreak but am apprehensive that, smarting under a sense of injustice, they will scatter in small bands over the country, committing depredations on innocent settlers.

I have instructed the Post Commander at Fort Wingate to communicate with the principal chiefs and express to them my gratification at their moderation and the hope that they will continue to exercise patience until their grievances can be placed before their Great Father in Washington.[52]

Since General Pope was on an inspection tour and unavailable, Gregg's telegram was forwarded to General Sherman, who wired the secretary of war on August 26. Sherman recommended that the secretary of interior temporarily hand control of the Navajo Agency over to the commander of Fort Wingate.[53]

The following day, the War Department relayed Sherman's request to the secretary of interior. The Interior Department quickly agreed to Sherman's recommendation, and the army ordered Major Price, whom the Navajos trusted, from Colorado back to Fort Wingate to resume his command. Meanwhile, the Navajo chiefs, responding to the officers at Wingate, released their female hostages.[54]

Captain Hartwell gathered Ganado Mucho, Manuelito, Huero,

and seventy other headmen at Fort Wingate on August 29. He read Arny's resignation to the assembled leaders, giving the Navajos some satisfaction. But Arny had asked to return to Fort Defiance to settle his remaining business and to gather his personal property. Nervous that this supplication might be rejected, Hartwell was surprised when the Indians agreed to allow their agent to return for two or three weeks. Then the chiefs were issued rations. Although the Navajos seemed to leave the fort with confidence that Arny would soon be out of their lives, the army was not so sure; the concern remained that Arny would not give up the agency easily. Colonel Gregg wired General Pope in Denver for further instructions. Pope's answer was a while in coming and had not reached Gregg on September 6, when Price arrived at Fort Wingate.[55]

Major Price left Fort Wingate on September 8. He arrived at Fort Defiance the following day, accompanied by a corporal and two privates. The Navajos offered no resistance, but Whitney refused to allow Price to take control because he had received no instructions from Arny. Price told him that he had no say in the matter and that force would be used if necessary. Whitney turned his keys over to the major, and employees were ordered to inventory government property. Price made it clear that any effort to subvert his commands would result in military supervision.[56]

General Pope, in the meantime, was unaware of General Sherman's order and suggested to Gregg that reinforcements would have to be moved in from Fort Union, New Mexico. Nevertheless, he urged caution. There were not enough troops in the territory to accomplish much by force. Pope added that troops assuming control of the Navajo Agency should limit themselves to protecting government employees and property. He concluded that the officer in charge should talk with Manuelito and warn him that depredations would surely harm his cause.[57] Ironically, with only Price and three enlisted men at Fort Defiance, it was Manuelito and his fellow leaders who protected the agency from hostile Navajos.

Whitney left Fort Defiance on September 13 and joined Arny at Bacon Springs (the present site of Coolidge, New Mexico). On September 23, Arny and Whitney reached the agency. Arny stated that he had not been instructed to turn over Fort Defiance to Price, and he did not bother to report to the major. He secluded himself in one of the buildings.[58] Price communicated with Arny the following day. He wrote:

> As the main trouble with the Indians seems to have arisen from a mis-understanding as to what was their property and what was yours, I desire to be informed at once in writing what belongs to you. I believe I can then with very little trouble find what belongs to the government.[59]

There was little that Arny could do to defend himself. He met with Price on September 25, but the two men could not agree.[60]

Arny claimed that the Navajo insurrection was the result of the intrigues of the traders and Navajo leaders, Manuelito, Delgadito, and Mariano. He declared that the chiefs wanted to control the distribution of annuity goods and rations, even though he had been the first agent to give them such power. In addition, he contended that the army had failed to do its best to stop the demoralization of the Navajos by the "squaw men" and its own enlisted personnel.[61]

Price argued that the headmen, rather than being agitated by the traders, had been provoked by their agent. Arny had tried to take away their best agricultural land and had attempted to open the possible mineral wealth of the Carrizo Mountains to prospectors. The major detailed the inadequacies of Arny's bookkeeping and the way he stored supplies, implying that the agent was dishonest in the distribution of rations and annuities. Price also expressed the opinion that Arny had not dealt with Navajo complaints. In the minds of most Navajos, Price explained, the murders in Grass Valley and on Otero's ranch had not been resolved. Arny's answer, they grumbled, had been to take a trip to Washington which, as far as they were concerned, had been for the agent's glorification.[62] Price wrote:

157

These matters are still unsettled, and I have been beseiged [*sic*] this week by all the Headmen of the tribe to endeavor to get a settlement,—the Indian method of settling is to pay something to the family of the party killed—a judicious expenditure of a few hundred dollars in sheep or horses to be given them would at any time have rendered them perfectly contented and satisfied.[63]

Although officials within the civilian Indian bureaucracy were quite willing to agree with Price and get rid of Arny because he had difficulty explaining his goals, controlling his wards, or winning the Navajos over to Christianity, few were willing, as Price was, to accept their traditions or desires.

Reverend Lowrie, for example, doubted that the Navajos had much to complain about. He wrote that Arny was an honest man who worked for the best interests of the Diné. Since no people knowingly labored against their self-interest, they must have disliked their agent because of his arrogant speaking style or because of the intrigues of white men.[64]

One of these supposed agitators was Thomas Keam. Although Keam had been given a license to trade with the Hopi on August 31, he still wanted to take charge at Fort Defiance. He had been lobbying for the job since March, but Arny's charges against him held in the mind of Lowrie, who declared that Keam was "not the kind of man a mission board could nominate." Keam's eligibility was further questioned when Thomas B. Catron pressed charges against him, his brother William, Daniel Dubois, and Anson Damon for selling liquor to Indians. Although the charges against Thomas Keam were dismissed on October 16, for lack of evidence (William Keam, Damon, and Dubois were freed of all charges on May 10, 1877), this vindication for the would-be agent came too late.[65]

Actually, even though Keam had gone to Washington to warn the chiefs, it was John Lorenzo Hubbell who spoke most for the Navajos. Reverend Lowrie's long-distance refusal to accept the legitimacy of Navajo complaints demonstrated the bankruptcy of the Peace Policy. He saw Keam simply as a "squaw man" who intrigued against Arny. In other words, he displayed an attitude—

despite his profession to be a "friend of the Indian"—that concluded that Native Americans did not know what was best for them. Arny had tried to trick the Navajos out of their most valuable lands, and he played loose with agency funds. The fact that Lowrie chose to see Keam's marital situation as the greater evil made an important comment on Presbyterian priorities.

The military's priority was to avoid war. Despite Arny's contention that the coup was engineered by the squaw men, officers at Fort Wingate claimed that the chiefs had acted because of legitimate grievances against a conniving agent. Their superiors accepted their analysis of the situation and acted accordingly, temporarily pushing civilian authority out of power to maintain order. It was evident when Major Price appeared at the agency with three soldiers and managed to take control that their decisions had been wise.

The Navajos also learned an important lesson; by getting rid of a troublesome agent, they realized that they had limited control of their own affairs and power within the Anglo-American political framework. They had accumulated it themselves by siding with the military and the traders. This fact was not lost to them. They could see that other tribes around them were losing land and power because of Anglo-American settlment. If the Navajos were to survive on their own terms, they needed to control their new agent. With this in mind, a Navajo delegation visited the Jicarilla Apaches at the Cimarron Agency in December. They interviewed Juan Julian, a Jicarilla man who had shot Agent Alexander Irvine, the man newly appointed to govern the Navajos.[66]

8
Settlers Arrive

Alexander Irvine, the new agent for the Navajos, arrived in Santa Fe on September 20, 1875, and proceeded to Forts Wingate and Defiance. He conferred with Major Price, but returned to the Jicarilla Agency in Cimarron after a few weeks, claiming that he had important business to handle. On November 11, he wrote to Price stating that he was waiting for his credentials as Navajo agent to arrive; as soon as he had them, he would relieve the major. A week later, however, Irvine informed Price that he had resigned his position because he considered the Indian bureaucracy "too vexatious."[1]

Major Price was disappointed. Despite his respect for the Navajos and their leaders, Price considered his duties at Fort Defiance to be "disagreeable and onerous." The agency had been left without beef for several weeks. He found the Indians at the agency restive. Several Navajos, according to Price, had relapsed "into their old habits of stealing and meandering." Seven horses and a mule, for instance, had been taken from W. L. Riggs, in the vicinities of Fort Wingate and Stinking Spring. Price conferred with Manuelito to arrange for the return of Riggs's animals, and he seemed agreeable when the chief brought about the return of two horses. Although he had once criticized Frank Tracy Bennett for similar practices, he made no effort to apprehend the rustlers. Price also purchased enough beef to meet the Navajos' immediate needs, and recognizing that the Indians would steal horses for food rather than slaughter sheep, he allowed a California horse trader to do business on the reservation because he felt that the ability of the Indians to obtain what they needed legally might keep them home. Despite his efforts, Price had minor difficulties that he found frustrating. Desperate Navajos repeatedly tried to steal from the agency's small supply of beef, and hungry Indians threatened his second-in-command.[2]

The major nonetheless could count on considerable Navajo support. Price was a rigid man, but the chiefs knew him as honest and competent. They also understood how he would react to conflict. The same was not true of Alexander Irvine, who had taken back his resignation almost as soon as he wrote it. When a delegation of Navajos visited the Jicarilla Apaches in December, the news they received did not inspire confidence. According to Juan Julian, a man who had shot Irvine, and other Jicarillas, Irvine was not a man familiar with handling a crisis. The Jicarillas had been angry because the meat they were given was poor, and several of them threw it back at agency employees. Both sides drew pistols, two Indians were injured, and Irvine was superficially wounded. As severe as this confrontation was, it was symptomatic of much deeper problems faced by the Jicarillas—they had lost their homeland, and the government was hard pressed to find them an alternative place to live.[3]

The Jicarilla was not the only nearby tribe losing its lands. The Southern Utes were also losing the majority of their territory due to the intrigues of mining interests.[4] Even though the Navajos were not always sympathetic to other tribes, they were perceptive enough to understand that the pressures of Anglo-American settlement that was gradually surrounding them could bring disaster. During the summer of 1875, for example, two brothers, William and Simeon Hendrickson, traveled from Animas City, Colorado, to the San Juan country to find a place to settle. Impressed by the land near the junction of the Animas and San Juan rivers, they left to make plans for settlement the following year.[5]

The Mormons also renewed their efforts to settle south of Utah. Two exploring parties were sent out in late 1875. One group, under the direction of James S. Brown, reestablished the Latter Day Saints mission at Moenkopi on December 4. They demonstrated that they were prepared to fight by erecting a stone building with twenty-inch walls on the edge of a cliff to serve as their headquarters. The other Mormon expedition, led by Daniel W. Jones, followed the Little Colorado for over one hundred miles. Jones declared that the land along the river was suitable for grazing and, in spots, adequate for raising crops. With this report in his hands, Brigham Young made plans to establish colonies along the southwestern edge of the Navajo frontier.[6]

Other people, excited by tales of mineral wealth in the Four Corners, came to lands occupied by the Navajos. The idea that the Diné possessed precious metals dated back at least to General Carleton. One of the reasons the general used for relocating the Navajos at the Bosque Redondo was that they would be an obstacle to mining development. Many New Mexicans opposed the treaty of 1868 on the same grounds. Even General Sherman, who negotiated the treaty, predicted conflict between prospectors and Navajos. After the Indians returned home, the belief persisted that their lands contained potential riches. J. H. Beadle, for instance, reported in 1872 that the officers at Fort Wingate had come to the conclusion that northern Navajo lands contained deposits of gold and silver and that Thomas Keam and others at Fort Defiance believed that the reservation was rich with diamonds. Stories were also told about John D. Lee operating a gold mine near his ferry and Hoskaninni, the northern Navajo headman, mining for silver in Monument Valley.[7]

One such tale took on the qualities of a legend. According to the story circulated throughout the Southwest, a group of twenty-one men led by a Mexican, who had been captured and raised by Apaches, had found a box canyon in the fall of 1864 filled with a fortune in gold that could simply be picked from the ground. They worked the canyon until spring. Before they could get away, all but four of the men were killed by Indians. A man named Davidson, John Brewer, a German who had the good sense to leave before the Indians attacked, and a character known only as Adams lived to perpetuate the legend. None of them were able to locate the canyon again. This failure, however, did not discourage others who were out to make a quick fortune. The more difficult it became to rediscover the gold, the more the legend grew. Although the prospectors originally believed that the gold was on Apache land, the idea that it could be found someplace else soon grew. A few decided that the canyon was near Zuni Pueblo, and many others came to the conclusion that it rested on or near the Navajo Reservation.[8]

With this growing legend of Navajo wealth came prospectors. First rushing to the mines on the Ute Reservation, by 1870 they had traveled across Navajo lands and checked their mining potential along the way. It was not long until these fortune seekers were exploring areas on the Navajo Reservation. Despite the fact that most of these expeditions went undocumented, a few representative examples have been preserved. In 1872, for instance, a group of prospectors found traces of gold in the Colorado; they borrowed John D. Lee's first ferryboat, the *Canyon Maid*, and floated downriver looking for wealth. They drifted at least as far as Marble Canyon before they smashed the boat on a rock wall. In another example, Jacob Hamblin was hired during the winter of 1875–76 to guide a group of would-be miners through northeastern Arizona, much of it Navajo land. Prospecting on Navajo land had become so widespread by 1875 that it was commonplace to observe people like John Williams, a trader near Fort Defiance, searching for precious metals in his spare time.[9]

If the Navajos learned anything from the examples of other tribes, they had to consider the growth of settlements around their reservation and the crisscrossing of their lands by prospectors as threats to their territorial integrity. They seemed to develop policies to deal with these threats. They apparently intended to halt Anglo-American expansion into their realm by occupying land and making it obvious that they would fight, as individuals and in small groups, to keep it. The Navajos gave prospectors the impression that they would resort to anything, including murder when they could get away with it, to prevent the discovery of mineral wealth within their domain, despite the fact that most rumors of rich mine fields were false.[10] These Navajo tactics would prove generally effective; nevertheless, the Diné understood that the attitudes of their agent were important if

164

they were to avoid the fates of other tribes. It was for this reason that they had traveled to learn about Alexander Irvine.

Orders were issued on November 30 relieving Major Price of duty. He was instructed to turn the agency over to Irvine, who arrived on December 5 and took control the following day. The chiefs and headmen were brought in to the agency. A council was held, and Price believed Irvine to be a "positive, truthful, and honest man" who would probably have no trouble.[11]

Irvine soon had an opportunity to prove his competence. On December 8, a visitor at Fort Defiance came with news that he had seen Navajo captives at Camp Apache. The new agent conferred with Price, who was still at the agency. At Irvine's request, Price, still in command at Fort Wingate, sent Captain J. B. Engle to Camp Apache to negotiate for the Navajos' release. Engle returned on December 30 with a Navajo girl. The Diné were happy to see her, and they seemed to accept Engle's explanation that a number of women voluntarily declined release because of their Apache children.[12]

Irvine found affairs at Fort Defiance confused, which he attributed to the fact that the Indians had ousted their former agent. Major Price, he complained, had considered the assignment temporary and had left improvements to the new agent. In spite of the confusion, Irvine at first liked the Diné. They acted in an orderly manner and were the first Indians he had observed who had ever bothered to thank him for a favor. The agent was also won over by their desire to work at wages as low as fifty cents per day, and he urged his superiors to use Navajo labor whenever practical. Irvine further admired the Indians' artistic skills, especially the skills of women who wove blankets. Unlike Arny, he encouraged them to weave in the traditional way and attempted to get rid of the machinery purchased by Arny. But the women were not the sole beneficiaries of his praise; he was impressed by the ability of the men to sew their own clothes.[13]

Irvine, however, was dissatisfied with the school. It was too small, the roof leaked, and the doors and windows were dilapidated. It had neither chairs nor desks; its furnishings consisted of four wooden benches in poor repair. These conditions, nevertheless, had not discouraged a few, persistent Navajo children. Irvine reported that there was an increase in the number of children in attendance, but he added that there were many more who needed schooling. In an attempt to explain why Navajos were not sending these pupils to school, he complained that the Indians were surrounded by "a Mexican population who are . . . inferior to them . . . in both intelligence and industry," providing them with poor examples.[14]

Irvine argued that the Navajos would eventually understand the value of education. In the meantime, he believed that the government should assist those who already appreciated what the teachers were trying to do. Navajos living in the Chuska Valley had told the agent that they would enroll their children in a school if there was a facility located close to their homes. Irvine urged that the government build a school, but his recommendation was ignored.[15]

In January, Irvine was called away to Santa Fe. During his absence, José L. Perea of Bernalillo, New Mexico, complained that a herd of his sheep had been taken by Navajos. Price investigated and found a much more complex situation. Several of Perea's hired hands and a group of Navajos had been playing a game of monte, and Perea's *mayordomo* started an argument with one of the Indians and killed him. Perea's employees fled. The Navajos came to the conclusion that they should take 450 sheep for the family of the murdered man and confiscate an additional 450 for the relatives of the man killed by Otero's men a few years before. Then they added 450 more sheep for the family of a man who had died in an accident at Fort Wingate the previous summer. Price met with Manuelito. Perea's men had admitted to Price that the murder was "brutal and barbarous," and they had tried to make a deal with the Navajos by offering them some sheep. Price told Manuelito that he owed Perea nine hundred sheep. The chief promised to bring in the herd in ten days. Two days before the deadline expired, Price was transferred to Texas. Major Osbourne, the new commander, gave Manuelito ten extra days because he was having a difficult time. Osbourne had to negotiate again with Manuelito and Perea because Manuelito misunderstood Perea's terms. But an agreement was eventually reached. Perea allowed the Navajos to keep four hundred sheep, and the rest of the herd was returned. Irvine congratulated Osbourne for his effective handling of the incident, but he had doubts about letting killers pay for human lives. He also warned the Diné against taking the law into their own hands.[16] Nevertheless, he was satisfied by the settlement. He wrote to the commissioner of Indian affairs:

> The Mexicans have needed the lesson received and now they understand that it is going to be an expensive matter to kill an Indian, and I have never heard of a Mexican having even an indictment found against him by a Grand Jury for the killing of an Indian.[17]

The chiefs seemed satisfied that Osbourne's agreement would reduce the tension on the eastern frontier.[18] Yet reasons for conflict were developing to the west of the reservation. At the beginning of 1876, two organizations, the Mormon church and a company of Boston speculators, made extensive plans to settle on the Little Colorado River. Both groups were ignorant and over optimistic about the area, especially about the river, which rapidly became known for its capriciousness.[19]

There was some concern among the Mormons about angering the Navajos. The history of Navajo–Mormon relations had not been peaceful. Western Navajos had long driven their flocks across the Little Colorado region, but they had stayed for the most part at easily defended highland locations. Since the signing of the treaty, they, along with other members of the tribe driven from the east by population pressures, had begun to relocate on the more open lands in order to increase their herds. As a result, the Diné had come to rely on the Little Colorado as an important, if seasonal, source of water. Some Navajos harbored resentment against the Latter Day Saints, and the Mormons were aware of it; but they were intent upon pushing forward with their plans. Unwilling and unable to use military force, the Mormons decided to use diplomacy to placate the Indians and to stay as far away from regions of Navajo use as possible.[20]

Arriving in small groups, approximately two hundred colonists assembled at Sunset Crossing on the Little Colorado on March 23. Then they spread out along the river in groups of fifty and established four townsites: Sunset Crossing, near present-day Winslow; Obed; Brigham City; and Allen's Camp, which they later named St. Joseph and, still later, Joseph City. The pioneers began almost immediately to build dams and to clear fields for farming. James S. Brown, acting under orders from Brigham Young, set out from the settlements across the Navajo lands to reassure the Diné that the Latter Day Saints had no intention of appropriating their lands. He failed and was often heckled by angry Indians, but the new Mormon settlements were left alone.[21]

The Boston company's expedition of forty-five men, who reached the Little Colorado in mid-April, likewise posed no threat to the Mormons. Aware of the Mountain Meadows Massacre, the New Englanders were wary of the Mormons and disappointed in the lands that they had traveled thousands of miles to settle. They journeyed farther west and left the Mormons to themselves and the hostile environment. The Saints, however, were not sure of their title to the land, for their settlements were directly in the path of the Atlantic and Pacific Railroad. Cognizant of this fact, they hoped to hold on to their land by reason of prior occupancy.[22]

The Navajos, who had occupied land south of the reservation along the Puerco River much longer than the Mormons, faced the same problem with the railroad. At a council meeting on April 6, Navajo leaders claimed that their reservation was not large enough. They asked that the reservation boundary be extended several miles to the south and that a region near Zuni Pueblo, close to present-day Ramah, be added to their domain. This latter tract was intended for Navajos who had lived at that location since the time of the Bosque. Irvine forwarded their request to Washington, where it was stalled because of previous commitments to the railroad.[23] The Diné were not surprised. They had known about the railroad land grant from their dealings with Arny. Thus, the Navajos had to resort to the same tactic as the Mormons.

Another important event occurred at the August 6 meeting. Henry "Chee" Dodge, a young man who was half-Navajo and of uncertain paternal parentage, was employed as an English-Navajo interpreter.[24] Not only did Dodge's employment make the task of interpreting easier by eliminating the necessity of using Spanish as an intermediate language; it also marked the beginning of a long career for the leader of the next generation of Navajos.

Irvine attempted to solve the Navajo land problem by getting all of the Indians to settle on the reservation, especially along the San Juan River. Thomas and William Keam visited Fort Defiance frequently, and Irvine may have been influenced by them. The agent was a bit wary of the brothers at first, but he could not get the Navajos to say anything against them. Irvine reported that Thomas Keam lived about a mile from the agency, that he no longer cohabited with a Navajo woman, and that she had gone back to her family and taken the children. Nevertheless, William Keam still lived with a Navajo woman near the Moqui (Hopi) Agency at present-day Keams Canyon. Irvine added that the brothers behaved themselves while visiting Fort Defiance and that he had no complaints against them.[25]

Whether or not the Keams had swayed his thoughts, Irvine became a strong advocate of Navajos occupying their northeastern lands. The San Juan River had been the traditional boundary between Utes and Navajos, but it is doubtful that either tribe had made extensive use of the rich country next to the river and its tributaries before 1868 because it was open to attack. In 1865, once Kit Carson had defeated the Diné, the San Juan country was almost abandoned. Nonetheless, some Navajos gradually resettled the area when the tribe returned from the Bosque, but they were still cautious about making full use of the lower elevations for fear of Ute attack. Irvine understood the Navajos' problem concerning the Utes. Navajos who planted crops in the open were in an extremely dangerous position. Those who moved their sheep down from protected highlands were more mobile, but they were still open to attack. The Utes were well armed with modern rifles. The Navajos, on the other hand, were poorly equipped with "old flint-lock muskets altered to percussion caps."[26]

Irvine tried to get the chiefs to talk to their people about moving to the region. He also agreed with the commander of the district of New Mexico, Colonel Edward Hatch, who advised that a fort should be established near the San Juan to control the Utes. Irvine added that more Navajos would settle along the river if the Navajo Agency was moved to the San Juan. He argued that the expense of relocation could be justified by the reality that the Indians would be self-supporting if enough of them established residence in the area.[27] Both suggestions were ignored, but the Navajos soon had motivations of their own to take control of their northeastern territory.

During the late spring, William Hendrickson returned with four companions and established the settlement of Farmington. Hendrickson had trouble with both Utes and Navajos who tried to run horses over his newly planted garden, but he was able to talk them out of it. More settlers followed, many of whom took out homesteads. Not all of these pioneers stayed long, but enough of them held on to convince the Navajos that they had better occupy the San Juan lowlands or lose them. Slowly, the Diné began to settle along the river, partly because their leaders were urging them and partly because they needed more land for their sheep. Whatever the immediate reasons, the Navajos found that the Anglo-American settlers served as a buffer between themselves and the Utes. In any case, the Navajos kept up a steady occupation of the area and were able to maintain a higher population than non-Indians in the region until as late as 1887.[28]

Other settlements established in 1876 appeared to complete a circle around the Diné. The Boston party, after leaving the Mormon settlements, traveled toward the San Francisco Peaks, where, at the foot of the mountains some seven miles north of current Flagstaff, they found Thomas F. McMillan, who had recently built a corral and shack. The Bostonians were a disorganized group, and most of them did not stay long. But they remained long enough to participate in a celebration. For the Fourth of July, the people at McMillan's camp stripped a pine tree of its branches and raised a flag, thus naming what was to become an important northern Arizona community. Most of the men from Boston went home or left for other locations. Nevertheless, new settlers came east from California to the area, drawn by northern Arizona's reputation as an excellent grazing region for sheep, a reputation which, in part, was due to Navajo successes.[29]

The Mormons, in the meantime, were busy establishing new communities. During the summer, they settled a mission, later called Ramah, near Zuni and adjacent to territory occupied by Navajos. Later in the year, the Saints began erecting dams at Woodruff, twenty-five miles south of St. Joseph. They moved onto the site the following year. Within the next few years, the Mormons settled at Snowflake, Round Valley, Springerville, and St. Johns. But they were not the only ones who came to the Springerville–St. Johns area; Texas cattlemen and New Mexican sheep raisers were also moving in.[30]

The Navajos were worried about this settlement of what they considered to be their territory, but Irvine was concerned about other matters. The Mormon expansion bothered him because the Presbyterians had not supplied a missionary for the agency, and he was uneasy that the Saints might fill the void. In October, Irvine had another reason to be troubled. A delegation of Utes visited the Chuska Valley to talk with Navajos about war. Since he lived nearby, Manuelito may have attended. The Navajos refused to do battle, but the Utes urged that they stockpile arms and ammunition just in case. Whether the Navajos took this suggestion to heart or not, Irvine recommended that Congress pass tougher laws against selling guns to Indians.[31]

Irvine, however, had reason to be confident concerning his wards. The total number of sheep in 1875 had been estimated at 175,000. Irvine concluded that the Navajos had increased their flocks to 400,000 in 1876. Even though such a rapid increase was unlikely, it was obvious that the Indians' attention to their flocks had been productive. During the year, the Navajos had sold at least 200,000 pounds of wool. In addition, almost every family had grown a "fair" crop of corn, and despite the fact that their wheat had been destroyed by grasshoppers, they had managed a good harvest of pumpkins, melons, and peaches.[32]

Irvine had his confidence shattered at the beginning of 1877. On January 1, over nine thousand Navajos gathered at Fort Defiance for the distribution of annuity goods. Instead of handing the goods over to the chiefs for delivery or allowing each family a number of items per family member, Irvine determined that he wanted to keep more accurate and detailed records. He demanded that each family head give his name and the number of members. The Diné refused. Irvine consequently would not allow the distribution to continue. When it appeared that the Indians might seize the goods, Irvine requested help from Fort Wingate. A sergeant and nine soldiers were sent to the agency on January 25, and the matter was quickly resolved. Most of the people cooperated reluctantly.[33]

A few of the chiefs refused. The agent attributed this to their greed. Irvine wrote that "they consider every pound of supplies and all the annuities as under their control and for their personal benefit." He was undoubtedly correct because the chiefs had been using their recently acquired power to distribute annuities and rations as a means of gaining political control and wealth. But Irvine overlooked two important phenomena. First, there was the natural reluctance of a subjugated people to give information to their conquerors. Second, there were important Navajo taboos concerning names. Each Navajo had a "war," or secret, name, which was rarely used, and a series of nicknames, likely to change over a period of time, which were used mostly to identify an individual when he was spoken of to a third party. According to Navajo custom, it was wrong to use a person's secret name and bad taste to ask him for any name.[34]

Anglo-American understanding of the Navajo point of view, however, was limited. On March 3, Congress passed legislation requiring a complete census of the tribes. When Irvine tried enforcing the new law, he found the Diné even more resistant. By the middle of July, he was ready to give up. The majority of the Navajos refused. Irvine attributed their dissent to superstition and to the fear of being laughed at by other Navajos. He argued that even if he could get his wards to cooperate, few of them had names that would distinguish one individual from another. He feared that enrollment could only be done by force, a contingency he was unwilling to resort to because the Navajos were generally prosperous and peaceful; to anger them would only cause trouble in New Mexico and Arizona, territories already plagued with more than their share of violence.[35]

Irvine might have added that there were more immediate problems for him to handle. In March, for example, he was forced to investigate the case of a captive Navajo woman living in a Mexican-American community six miles from Albuquerque. Her brother had done some detective work and found her. Then he met with her secretly; she informed him that she wanted to return home, but was not free to do so. The woman's brother reported her situation to Irvine, who inquired about her through the mail. Irvine determined that the woman was not married to the man holding her captive, but he could not obtain information concerning her status, namely, whether she was a concubine or a servant.[36]

A New Mexican official assured Irvine that the woman was free to leave, but the agent was not sure. Peonage still existed in rural New Mexico and southern Colorado. Navajos, especially women, were held without any compensation for their services except for room, board, and clothing. When free Navajos attempted to visit or to communicate with their relations, they were prevented. In some cases, the captives were told that their kinsmen just wanted them back for their labor. And some captives preferred to stay where they were. Irvine saw a dilemma that could not be solved easily. Nonetheless, he proposed that

173

the commissioner of Indian affairs recommend legislation that would establish a framework for the resolution of individual cases. According to Irvine's plan, all captive Navajos, when they were discovered, would be taken before a judge and given the opportunity to speak without duress.[37] Irvine received no response to his request.

Irvine was becoming frustrated with his job, and the lack of action from his superiors was one of the principal reasons. In April, citing the fact that some Navajos had many sheep while others had none, he advised the commissioner that it would be wise to purchase fifteen thousand sheep for the needy instead of buying clothes for the whole tribe. He pointed out that the treaty provision for support of the Navajos expired at the end of 1878; if the Indians were to be self-supporting, they needed more sheep. Although Irvine repeated his request in his annual report in September, no action was forthcoming.[38]

Irvine was also concerned about the Navajo San Juan territory. He believed that the Diné, still afraid of Ute raids, had not sufficiently occupied lands along the river. As the testimony of non-Indian settlers would soon reveal, many Navajos were relocating in the area. Yet they had not developed the region's horticultural potential, a task deemed necessary by the agent for the tribe's self-support. Irvine urged that the agency be moved to the San Juan. Understanding that Arny had estimated the cost of such a move at fifty-seven thousand dollars, Irvine argued that by using Navajo labor, he could bring it about for ten thousand dollars. He believed that such a transfer would provide his wards with enough incentive to fully exploit the region's resources. Again, his recommendation was rejected.[39]

It was not, however, just these negative responses that bothered Irvine. Matters at the agency also perturbed him. In spite of his favorable opinion of the Keams, he claimed that Anglo-American men living with Navajo women were exerting too much influence over the Navajos. His catalog of vexations went further. The chiefs were proving uncooperative. Some agency employees were not doing their jobs. A Navajo boy was released from captivity, but the agent could not find his relatives. On July 1, the pressure finally got the best of Irvine, and he resigned.[40]

Irvine would have to wait months for his replacement, but the delay was not for want of a willing applicant. Thomas Keam, perhaps sensing Irvine's frustration, had applied for the job on May 1, even before the resignation, in a letter to President Rutherford B. Hayes. Writing to Reverend Lowrie, Keam stated that he could use the trust the Navajos had in him to convince them to send their children to school. In order to get the job, Keam accumulated a number of endorsements. Alexander Irvine and the inspector general of the army, W. H. Davis, recommended him. Former agent Captain Frank Tracy Bennett wrote that Keam was trustworthy and that the chiefs wanted him in charge. Missionary Dr. John Menaul claimed that Keam was an "honest, upright man." Colonel Edward Hatch praised Keam for his temperance and the "high-minded" manner in which he ran his business affairs. F. V. Lauderdale, the doctor at Fort Wingate, added that Keam's appointment was urgent, for the Navajos were a large tribe experiencing a rapid population increase that was likely to make them a permanent factor in the West. The Navajos, Lauderdale continued, badly needed their children to be educated, and Thomas Keam was a man uniquely qualified because the Navajos trusted him to accomplish the task. Finally, ninety-eight residents of the lands bordering the reservation signed a petition, addressed to Secretary of Interior Carl Schurz, that advocated Keam's appointment.[41]

The fact that Keam was so thorough with his application may have been due to his discovery at about that time of William F. M. Arny's earlier charges against him. As a result of his new knowledge, Keam made denials. He claimed that he had never cohabited with a Navajo woman and denied ever selling liquor to Indians. Nevertheless, Keam was again opposed by Thomas B. Catron, and John Lowrie, still believing Arny's charges, refused to consider him.[42]

Thomas Keam, however, was hopeful throughout the remaining months of 1877. He took a job as interpreter at Fort Wingate and participated, along with the Navajo scouts, in an important conflict with the Apaches. Navajo scouts had spent a great deal of time in fighting Apaches during the year. In January, for example, three Navajos operating out of Fort Bayard, New Mexico, were ambushed along with nine soldiers by Chiricahua Apaches. They were able to fight their way out, and one of the Navajos, José Chaves, was decorated for bravery in action. But it was a problem with the Mimbres Apaches that most involved the Diné.[43]

In late April, San Carlos Apache Agent John Clum, acting under an Indian Bureau decision to consolidate all Western Apaches, arrived at the Mimbres Reservation at Ojo Caliente in southwestern New Mexico. With the help of Apache police, Clum was able to move the tribe to the San Carlos Reservation in Arizona by May 20. The Mimbres, however, were dissatisfied with their new home and, led by Victorio, escaped from the reservation in early September. Chased by Apache police and the army, the Mimbres were forced to abandon their exhausted mounts. They retreated to the rough country south of Fort Wingate. The Mimbres attempted to raid local ranches for horses, and, in the process, they killed twelve people.[44]

Nonetheless, the Mimbres were tired and had lost fifty-six of their own people; their leaders, Victorio, Loco, and Chivo contacted officers at Fort Wingate and informed them that they would surrender if they were not forced to return to San Carlos. On September 29, Thomas Keam was sent out with the Apache chiefs and five Navajo scouts. Keam made contact with the main body of the escapees about ninety miles south of Wingate on October 3. He met with 179 people. He informed them that his purpose was to escort them to the fort. The chiefs told Keam that most of their people would go with him, but there were a few who refused to surrender. Keam asked those men to step aside. No one did. Later, these men spoke to Keam individually and confessed that they were tired of running. On the trip to Fort Wingate, the Apaches behaved well, but they spoke frequently with Keam about how much they hated San Carlos.[45]

Captain Horace Jewett, the commander at Fort Wingate, placed the Apaches under Keam's charge and ordered them to camp a short distance from the post. They were held there while Jewett attempted to get more of them to surrender and officials debated about what to do with them. On October 11, Jewett reported that two parties had been dispatched to convince the remaining Mimbres to surrender. One of these expeditions was under the command of Mariano, the Navajo chief, and the other was headed by a scout named Juan Navajo. By October 20, approximately 233 had surrendered. In the debate concerning the Mimbres' future, most civilian officials wanted their return to San Carlos or their removal to either the Mescalero Agency or the Indian Territory. The army, on the other hand, argued for their immediate removal to Ojo Caliente because the Apaches would go there more willingly. Army officials also contended that it was important to remove the Mimbres from Navajo country as soon as possible. They might be a bad influence on the Navajos, or they could disappear by blending in with the Navajo population. The army won the argument temporarily.[46]

Ganado Mucho, meanwhile, was negotiating with the Mormons. Relations between the Navajos and the Latter Day Saints were tense. At Moenkopi, friendly Navajos had helped the Mormons protect their livestock when Paiutes threatened a raid. But James S. Brown later ran into difficulty when he moved in with a group of Navajos led by a headman called Hustelso. Brown tried to study the Navajo language, but he also learned of Navajo hostility. Three young men drew bows on him. He was threatened verbally, and his wagon was vandalized. With time, he was better treated, and he attempted unsuccessfully to explain his religion to the Indians. Once his stay was over, he traveled east with five other Mormons and met with Ganado Mucho.[47]

The old chief spoke in diplomatic words, but he also warned the Mormons. He said:

> When I heard that you had come, I quit work and came to see you. My heart is glad at this meeting with you, and that I see your wagon there, and the brush shade that your men have built. . . . We are glad that you come among us as friends, that you are making a road through our

177

country, and that you have built houses at Moencoppy [sic]. We want to
live with you in peace and let your animals eat grass in peace. But water
is scarce in this country, there is barely enough for our numerous flocks
and increasing people, and our good old men do not want your people to
build any more houses by the springs; nor do we want you to bring flocks
to eat the grass about the springs. We want to live by you as friends.[48]

Ganado Mucho also mentioned that two of his daughters were
held captive by Apaches. This was a cause of much grief to him,
but he had not left the reservation to look for them because he
loved the land and the people. Now, however, he was willing to
visit the Mormon capital for his people's sake.[49]

Arrangements were made to take a delegation of Navajos to
Salt Lake City. Beginning their journey on August 10, Brown
and the Navajos reached Salt Lake City on August 28. Brigham
Young was on his deathbed when the party arrived, and he died
the next day. The Navajos met with Daniel H. Wells, who was
temporarily in charge of the church. Before leaving for home,
they toured the sights of the city.[50]

While the Mormons and Ganado Mucho were engaged in diplomacy, Navajo relations with other neighbors were becoming
strained. In August, New Mexican ranchers east of the reservation complained that the Diné were stealing the best livestock
to build up the bloodlines of their herds.[51] More trouble came
because of disputes between Navajos and settlers in the San Juan
country.

Beginning in the spring, Anglo-American and Mexican-American settlement of the area increased rapidly. More people moved
into the Farmington region. Others homesteaded at the mouth
of Largo Canyon on the San Juan. Cattlemen moved into the
grassy mesa country and brought large herds with them.[52] The
Navajos, although they had not planted many crops, were using
the lowlands extensively for livestock grazing. They did not take
long to display their displeasure with the new arrivals.

Some Navajos told the settlers that they should leave because
the land belonged to the Diné. Many of the settlers, anxious to

keep the peace, butchered cattle and divided the meat with the Indians. This method seemed to be effective because the serving of food was associated by the Navajos with hospitality and friendship. Not all newcomers understood this, however. William Hendrickson, for example, declared, "I am convinced that they misunderstood us when we proposed settling in the country thought their own. It was their idea that we would all live together, that we would raise corn and beans and they would help us eat." Nonetheless, the main contention was land. The newcomers considered as closed to Navajo occupation the territory to the north of the San Juan River and the reservation boundary, but the Diné claimed the right of prior use. When the settlers used land that the Indians believed to be theirs, crops were trampled, herds were scattered, and threats were issued. The pioneers complained that it was impossible to erect buildings while under such harassment.[53]

It was not only the newcomers who were harassed. A Mr. Horn settled at the junction of Gallegos Canyon and the San Juan, at a site where a Navajo named Castiano had made a habit of watering his sheep each day. Horn objected to the practice because the Indian drove his animals across a portion of his land. One day, Horn drew a pistol on Castiano, who quickly jumped him, took the gun away, and struck him on the head. Horn retreated to his house, and Castiano continued to let his sheep drink. After Horn had time to cool his temper, Castiano returned the gun, but Horn was not satisfied with the Navajo's peaceful gesture. He attempted to get the army to stop Castiano from providing for his sheep.[54]

Navajo resistance also took on the form of theft, but it is unlikely that a majority of the Diné participated. As one settler, William McRae, who arrived in 1877, stated:

> We had no trouble with the owners of the sheep herds, but had considerable bother with roaming bands of young bucks, who were dubbed "Coyotes." They would steal anything they could load on a pony that they could make any use of.[55]

By the end of summer, the settlers were extremely upset at all forms of Navajo provocation.

Agent Irvine remained ignorant of the situation. He concerned himself, instead, with the liquor trade. In July, a traveler named Frank Plounteaux stopped at Fort Wingate. Observing drunk Navajos daily at the post, Plounteaux decided to investigate. He claimed in a letter to the commissioner of Indian affairs that a man named Prince, who was employed by Lieutenants C. W. Merritt and D. D. Mitchell, had sold whiskey to two Navajos. Plounteaux charged that such occurrences were frequent and that Irvine was doing nothing to stop it.[56]

Once these charges reached Irvine in late August, he sent Chee Dodge to Fort Wingate to investigate. Dodge determined that Prince was not an employee of the lieutenants; he was an English-born soldier. There was a "strong case of suspicion" against him, but the lieutenants were apparently innocent. Irvine argued that they should not even answer the accusation, for the man who made it had not stayed around long enough for them to confront him. Irvine, however, conceded that whiskey selling was a problem in every Navajo community. It was impossible for him to stop the trade because he could not apprehend or prosecute whiskey sellers who operated off the reservation. He asked for legislation that would empower him to act more resolutely, but his request was ignored.[57]

In October, Irvine had trouble with agency Navajos. Noting that the men who delivered beef to Fort Defiance for slaughter had kept the hides, the Indians claimed that the hides, as well as the meat, were theirs. They said that they needed the leather for moccasins. Irvine relayed their request to the commissioner and confessed that the Navajos might resort to force. Irvine's frustration over his inability to resolve such small issues continued. He wrote to the commissioner on October 25 and begged that a replacement be sent immediately; he desperately wanted to leave. But when the commissioner answered his request to allow the Navajos to keep cowhides by suggesting that they use buffalo hides instead, Irvine's frustration turned to anger. The agent sarcastically told his superior that Navajo country was not buffalo country and accused him of insulting his intelligence.[58]

Despite his problems, Irvine reported that the Navajo economy was generally doing well. The Indians had planted corn and wheat on all available plots except on the San Juan. They had grown large crops of melons and peaches in Canyon de Chelly. For a second time in two years, the Navajos had sold 200,000 pounds of wool. He was also pleased with the number of blankets and sheep and goat skins they had traded. He was displeased, however, that they had bargained away many of these blankets in Utah for horses. Irvine suggested that the ownership of horses be outlawed because

> they are a power for mischief, and no good ever comes of their possession of them. The horses are used for riding, not work. At first it might seem arbitrary, but it would cause the Indians to remain where they were placed, and be under better control.[59]

Irvine's proposal was probably written with the knowledge that it would never be approved, but it did represent his growing preoccupation with controlling the more unruly elements.

In November, the agent requested that ten soldiers from Fort Wingate be stationed at the agency to protect government property. He accused Manuelito of refusing to do anything to prevent the Navajos from stealing and asked permission to organize a police force of twenty-five men, who would be paid fifteen dollars per month. Unlike Arny, Irvine was unwilling to resort to illegal payments to keep police in the field. Nevertheless, he believed that Indian police were an absolute necessity for maintaining the peace.[60]

Irvine discovered that peace was very fragile late in the month, when the new residents of the San Juan region petitioned to complain about Navajo harassment. The agent investigated the matter himself. He found a few Navajos living off the reservation. They had harvested crops the previous spring along the San Juan, Animas, and La Plata rivers. In addition, he discovered Utes

181

along the La Plata. Irvine recommended that the Indians move
to their reservations in the spring. That was not soon enough
for the settlers, and they next sent a petition to President Hayes,
in which the 148 people who signed it called for the construction
of a fort at the junction of the San Juan and the Animas.[61]

Irvine, had he known of the San Juan petition, probably would
have approved, but as 1878 began he complained of the many
nagging details and situations that he faced. No funds had arrived
to pay agency employees. The mail was arriving late. He was
encouraging the Indians to live on the reservation, but the army
recruited scouts who lived away from it.[62] If given the choice,
Irvine probably would have preferred to serve the rest of his time
in office by venting his frustrations, but events of a more serious
nature prevented him from reveling in the luxury of self-pity.

In February, the San Juan settlers had a representative hand-
carry a petition directly to the headquarters of the district of
New Mexico. Hoping to press the army into action, the authors
of the document drew a dismal picture of life for residents of
the region. Asking for troops, the petition claimed that the Indians were killing their cattle, that families would be massacred
in the early spring, and that the settlements faced doom unless
assistance was forthcoming.[63]

Irvine called upon informants, and it appeared to him that
there was little danger of a Navajo attack. There were some
Navajos living off the reservation along the Animas, La Plata,
and San Juan rivers, but he had recommended in the fall that
they return to the reservation in the spring; and he was certain
that they would do so. The agent, however, was concerned about
the possibility of a Ute war. He had been informed that the Utes
were preparing to fight against the settlers along the Animas
River. They were said to be well supplied with weapons and to
be killing cattle and preserving the meat for a summer campaign.
Irvine was afraid that some Navajos would join the Utes, and
he was certain that the Utes were attempting to recruit Navajo
supporters. He had sent word to Largo, the headman in the northeast, to bring his followers onto the reservation. Finally, he rec-

ommended that the army patrol both the San Juan region and areas east of the reservation in an attempt to force the Navajos to live on their reserve.[64]

Rumors of a Ute conflict seemed all the more likely when a settler who lived on the Animas, Thomas B. Hart, reported that Navajos who had watered their flocks there for some time were leaving, in an effort to protect their animals from Utes, and not because they were complying with their agent's request. Captain Frank Tracey Bennett, who had been transferred back to Fort Wingate, spent several days at Fort Defiance talking with Navajos who had been north, and especially with Chee Dodge. Bennett reported that Navajos on the San Juan had traded with the Utes recently and none of them had heard of any Ute plans for war. Nevertheless, troops were sent to the area. The soldiers found Navajos living off the reservation and along the La Plata and San Juan rivers. The La Plata Navajos were living alongside Paiutes and Utes. The Navajos and Utes were instructed to return to their reservations. The Paiutes ran away before anybody could talk to them.[65]

With the situation in the San Juan country apparently defused, more trouble erupted to the east. A smallpox epidemic broke out in several northwestern New Mexico communities, and Irvine called in Dr. Walter Whitney from Ojo Caliente to vaccinate the Navajos. This precaution was not entirely effective, and the disease spread to the Diné.[66] But the effect of the virus was not sufficient to prevent either the Navajos or their eastern neighbors from engaging in conflict.

The first of many instances during the following year occurred in March when a Navajo threatened an employee of William Wallace who ran a trading post at Mineral Springs twelve miles west of Wingate. The Indian had also burned a stack of hay and stolen a pump. Wallace asked the military for help. Captain Bennett investigated the situation and concluded that the Navajo's action had resulted because he felt cheated by Wallace, who was not paying fair prices for wool.[67]

There were other conflicts, but what was surprising was that

Navajos who were determined to keep their lands acted moderately. Much of their attitude can be explained by the fact that their leaders had just ousted an agent, and provoking the settlers was not well advised for a people determined not to experience war, defeat, and exile. Agent Irvine, for his part, was unwilling to incite his charges. He had been honest, but his threshold of frustration was so low that he was not able to act effectively. Nevertheless, there had been no significant complaints against him, and he had treated the Diné and their leaders with respect.

Meanwhile, the army, as represented by the officers at Fort Wingate, had become almost pro-Navajo in its attempts to prevent war. All over the West, the military was critical of many civilian agents and was determined to counter some of their actions if it felt them to be unwise. With the Navajos, however, officers found themselves siding with the Indians more frequently. Their actions did not go unrecognized by the Diné. Young Navajos enlisted as scouts to assist in putting down Indian rebellion despite the fact that their people were not directly involved; undoubtedly, they joined because they needed the income, but the element of trust established between the chiefs and the army had made their actions easier.

Also building goodwill with the army was Thomas Keam. His work at Fort Wingate—his diplomacy with Victorio's followers, especially—had made him the army's choice for agent as well as that of the chiefs. Keam, however, was not able to win over the Presbyterians, although he had tried, and when the government named its new agent to replace Irvine, the appointee, John E. Pyle, was a man of lesser ability.[68]

9
Witches

John E. Pyle, the new Navajo agent, had lived in Montana prior to entering the Indian Service in 1872. Leaving his wife and family at home, Pyle came to New Mexico to assume duty at the abandoned Cimarron Agency as farmer-in-charge. Pyle was a lonely and cynical man who regarded his position as unpleasant and dangerous. Suffering from chronic diarrhea and insomnia, he accepted the Navajo job with little enthusiasm. He arrived at Fort Wingate on March 30, 1878, and was received hospitably by Captain Bennett and Alexander Irvine.[1]

Assuming command on April 1, he found the buildings at the agency uninhabitable and spent his first days taking inventory of the agency's supplies. Navajo leaders visited Fort Defiance individually to meet him. Ganado Mucho talked with Pyle three days after he arrived; the chief was not impressed. He informed the agent that he had liked Alexander Irvine immediately. Pyle, on the other hand, was too formal. The two men spent an hour talking, and Ganado Mucho seemed to change his mind when he volunteered to send messengers to inform his people that the new agent was acceptable. Manuelito, meanwhile, was out chasing rustlers. Once the chief and Pyle finally met, they did not like each other; and Pyle would later call the old warrior a beggar. The agent, however, was not completely negative about his new charges. Like many agents before him, he was impressed by the Indians' artistic and pastoral skills.[2]

Affairs at the agency ran smoothly during Pyle's first month. There were only two problems that required his attention, a bad batch of smallpox vaccine and hungry Navajos. By his third week in office, Pyle was overwhelmed by requests for corn. Navajos stated that they did not have enough to eat, but he dismissed their solicitations as lies. Despite the limited nature of his tasks, Pyle's health remained poor.[3]

Pyle spent most of his time on routine matters, filing reports and handling supplies. He requested that the agency be moved to the San Juan River. Fort Defiance was too close to the southern boundary of the reservation. There were too many lawless non-Indians whom he could not control. He added that there was not much arable land near the agency and that the buildings were dilapidated. He believed that he could relocate the agency cheaply by using Navajo labor and locally available wood. An important authorization arrived in May concerning Irvine's request for sheep for Navajos who did not have any. The Indian Bureau gave Pyle authority to buy seventy-five hundred sheep. The agent may have worried about the difficulty inherent in such a large distribution, but his principal preoccupation seemed to be his own health. Perhaps for this reason, he was impatient with Navajos who asked for help.[4]

Colonel P. T. Swaine, commander at Fort Wingate, worried about the increased incidence of Navajo drunkenness. On May 15, Swaine issued a circular that threatened the arrest and prosecution of anybody caught selling liquor to Indians.[5] Responsibility for elimination of the liquor traffic belonged with United States marshals, but they had been unable to act because of manpower shortages and increased violence elsewhere in New Mexico. Even though the army was reluctant to get involved with civilian matters, the situation was so bad as far as Swaine was concerned that he attempted extraordinary measures. Nevertheless, the army soon found out that it was no more effective in stopping the trade than civilian agencies.

There were reasons that the attempts to control the Navajo liquor trade would fail. Central to many of these causes was the fact that the rise in the visible number of inebriated Navajos indicated the existence of much deeper social problems than the mere multiplication of individuals willing to sell Indians whiskey. The Diné had endured exile and won their return home. But their homecoming, joyous as it was, had not been a simple return to the past. The Bosque Redondo experience had taught the Navajos that warfare and raiding were no longer practical. With little government assistance, Navajo leaders had managed to reduce Navajo acts of aggression toward their neighbors to simple criminal behavior. The willingness of the headmen to take such action displayed their diplomacy; the cooperation they received from most of the tribe showed the adaptability of Navajo culture.

This adaptability, however, came at a price, for other changes had to be absorbed. Localities had to give up some authority to the chiefs and to the agent. The gap between the rich and the poor grew more permanent because raiding had been removed as a legitimate means for the poor to acquire wealth. The poor, to a certain extent, were subsidized by the government, but agents who believed literally in some provisions of the treaty had claimed that government provisions were to be cut off at the end of 1878. Finally, the Navajos, especially those who lived off the reservation, saw the lands around them increasingly settled by non-Navajos. The Indians were forced to use means short of war to protect the territory they held.

These changes led to tension within Navajo society and between individuals. Before the Bosque Redondo, a great deal of this tension was released through warfare. After the treaty, individuals used alcohol as an escape, and Navajos were forced to look inward for relief, which led to the search for scapegoats to blame for their problems. Some of the Diné turned their resentment toward their leaders. As in many cultures, others blamed their malaise on witches.[6]

Witchcraft served in Navajo society as a definition of evil, and a few alienated individuals attempted its practice. As anthropologist Clyde Kluckhohn has stated, there seemed to be a correlation between Navajo fear of witches and times of tribal stress. Those suspected of this hideous practice were people at the extremes, such as the very rich, the very poor, and the old. Medicine men were also suspected because they knew how to manipulate the supernatural. About 1875, after a majority of the Diné had

187

solved immediate problems of subsistence, several witches, according to tradition, were killed. By late February of 1878, the
situation had become so critical that Alexander Irvine expressed
his concern to a number of Navajos who justified killing witches
by reminding him that Anglo-Americans had once burned them.[7]

In late May, Navajos living near the present site of Ganado,
Arizona, became upset at the suspected witchcraft of people
residing in the Canyon de Chelly area. The leader of these alleged
evildoers, according to the Navajo oral record, was a man named
Hastiin Biwosi. In the written documents of the time, he was
referred to as Hambre. Historians have assumed that he was
Muerto de Hambre, a signer of the 1868 treaty, but Muerto de
Hambre was reported to be present at a meeting in September,
three months after Biwosi's death. The individual in question
may have been another man simply named Hambre, who was
the ninth signer of the treaty, but his residences were at Ganado
and Keams Canyon. In any case, Biwosi was the leader of a group
of apparently poor Navajos who were accused of being jealous
of the prosperity of others.[8]

According to his accusers, Biwosi had sent out spies to gather
the saliva and feces of his intended victims as well as soil from
their shadows and the manure from their livestock. He buried
these items and cast spells. He also shot stones into people's
bodies. As a result, people caught colds and smallpox. Many of
the victims died, and so did horses and sheep. Once the relatives
of the victims were convinced that Biwosi was responsible, they
resolved to kill him and all of his spies. They caught at least
one of the spies, who bragged to his captors that they would all
die because spells had been cast on them. When they asked where
the items were buried, the spy told them to dig at Ganado Lake.
Afraid to touch the evil objects, the Indians asked Charles Hubbell, John Lorenzo's brother, to exhume the paraphernalia. According to oral records, Hubbell found the objects buried in the
belly of a corpse and wrapped in a copy of the treaty. This peculiar
grave supposedly signified that the treaty was no longer in effect
and that death was certain for all who had signed it. The captive

was killed near the house of Hardison, an Anglo-American married to a Navajo woman. It is also possible that another man was killed near John Lorenzo Hubbell's store.[9]

Charles Hubbell, with his brother off trading at Navajo City, New Mexico, some twenty miles north of Fort Defiance, wrote three letters to William Leonard, a trader at Fort Defiance, on May 31. Sending the first letter by Navajo courier, Hubbell wrote that there was a "big row" going on among the Diné. A "large crowd" had just left the trading post to do battle in Canyon de Chelley. Stating that one Indian had already been killed, Hubbell begged Leonard to send him his rifle as well as all the ammunition he could get. Meanwhile, the Navajo vigilantes had discovered that Biwosi was not home, but at a ceremony in nearby Cornfield. They rushed to that location and found Ganado Mucho there. When the spokesman for the group, Hash Keh Yilnaya, demanded that Biwosi be handed over to them, Ganado Mucho refused, stating that Biwosi was his clan relative. Hash Keh Yilnaya then gave a long speech condemning Biwosi. After this oration, Biwosi may have confessed. In any case, Ganado Mucho, convinced that his relative was a witch, agreed to let the party have Biwosi, and participated in his killing. Surrounding Biwosi, the angry mob threw stones at him until he was covered.[10]

Ganado Mucho hurried to protect himself from the consequences of a serious transgression, the killing of a relative. He went to Hubbell's post and excitedly appealed for military intervention. Charles Hubbell relayed the chief's message in his second letter. Ganado Mucho, he wrote, had informed him

that the Indians are arming in large numbers and that his life is in danger as well as ours and the property and he says to send soldiers immediatlly [sic] to protect himself and family and he assures us that our lives are in danger and also the store and contents. We will hold on as long as possible but that is only about two days because he says there is a big war party outfitting themselves in Canon de Chelle [sic] to come out here.[11]

Hubbell also stated that Ganado Mucho wanted him to get word to Pyle and Captain Bennett, and he ended this letter by repeating his request for ammunition.[12]

Charles Hubbell's third letter was hurriedly written, as if its author were ready to panic. He had good reason to be afraid. The Hubbell family had been frightened before. Soon after he had opened his trading post, John Lorenzo Hubbell had been tied up by a group of Navajos who were threatening to hang him. Although his brother had been rescued by Manuelito, Charles had no reason to believe that he would be so lucky. He wrote Leonard that the Indians in his region had killed Hambre. He was sure that a party of men from Canyon de Chelly would rapidly mobilize to avenge Hambre's death. He added that he would evacuate the post that night if he received information that the retaliatory group was on its way.[13]

Leonard delivered Hubbell's letters to Pyle early in the morning on June 1. Pyle forwarded them to Colonel Swaine at Fort Wingate. Believing that the trouble was caused by sectional conflict, superstition, and jealousy, Pyle requested that Swaine send troops to Hubbell's post if he judged that action was necessary to protect the lives and property of white men. Fort Wingate was understaffed. Captain Bennett had gone to Cubero, New Mexico, to defuse potential trouble between Navajos and Mexican Americans, and there were no cavalrymen on hand. Still, Swaine felt that the matter was important enough to send troops. He mounted ten infantrymen, placing them under the command of First Lieutenant G. K. McGunnigle and Second Lieutenant D. D. Mitchell, and ordered them to proceed to Hubbell's after stopping at Fort Defiance to bring Pyle along.[14]

Lieutenant McGunnigle's patrol left the fort at 7:30 P.M. with G. W. Williams acting as guide. After riding until 1:30 the following morning, the soldiers stopped to rest five hours, having traveled twenty-five miles. Then, they resumed their journey, reaching Fort Defiance at 11:00 A.M. Pyle was on hand to meet McGunnigle, and he informed the lieutenant that he did not need to rush. Word had just arrived that all was quiet at Hubbell's. McGunnigle therefore took the opportunity to rest his horses and men.[15]

At 7:00 A.M. on June 3, McGunnigle's detachment left the agency. Against his better judgment, Pyle rode along in a buckboard. The trip took approximately seven and a half hours. Charles Hubbell and the trading post's employees explained that they feared for their lives because they believed that the Indians in Canyon de Chelly would assume that they had assisted in the killings. That afternoon, Ganado Mucho and about fifty Navajos met with McGunnigle and Pyle. The lieutenant began the conference by saying that he had not come to interfere in a dispute between Navajos. He had left Fort Wingate with orders "to see that the white people were not molested." The Indians assured McGunnigle that they had no intention of harming them. They informed the lieutenant, however, that they had killed two medicine men because they had murdered their friends and relations by using supernatural powers.[16] When the Navajos were asked how they knew this, they replied

that they knew it because they (the Doctors) shot stones into their bodies and *Ganado Mucho* said that the Doctors confessed to the killing of some of his relations and that the Doctors put grass, hair, horse and sheep dung in his brothers [sic] grave. *Ganado Mucho* acknowledges to having done wrong but when the Doctor confessed to the killing of his relatives he was mad and killed them. he [sic] said he would never do so again.[17]

Ganado Mucho added that one of the men they killed had been related to him.[18]

After the chief's confession, Pyle spoke. He reprimanded the Navajos for killing people without a tribunal and told them that their superstitions were foolish. According to McGunnigle, the Indians ignored their agent. As the council ended, Pyle reminded the crowd that the troops had not been brought out to side with Ganado Mucho.[19]

The next morning, Pyle returned to Fort Defiance with Williams. McGunnigle and his troops remained in the vicinity of

Hubbell's for four days. The lieutenant found the Navajos to be peaceful. Despite McGunnigle's repeated claims that he was not concerned with protecting Ganado Mucho, the presence of troops prevented further bloodshed. A man from Canyon de Chelly informed the lieutenant that many of his neighbors had become incensed when they had heard of the killings and had begun to plan a retaliatory attack. But cooler heads prevailed, and no attack was made.[20]

McGunnigle and his mounted infantry began their return journey on June 7. When the lieutenant arrived at Fort Wingate on June 9, he reported that his detachment had traveled 160 miles round trip. The following day, Manuelito arrived at Wingate with a message he had dictated to John Lorenzo Hubbell, who was still at Navajo City. The message stated that the Navajos had tied up six medicine men accused of witchcraft and that the chief had carried the message himself to dispel Swaine's disbelief in witchcraft. Manuelito wanted troops sent to the place where they were tied, so an officer could tell the witches shooting stones into people to halt their "malpractice." Manuelito had spoken with the offending medicine men several times, and they had refused to listen, but he was convinced that they would obey soldiers and stop their evil practices. The chief was certain that many Navajos would start killing each other without military intervention. He was an enemy of the witches. He had seen them kill his cousin recently, and they had informed him that they had put a stone in his head; they had promised to kill him by the end of the summer. Despite these threats on his life, Manuelito did not want the witches killed because their deaths would start a fight that would hurt all Navajos. Stating that Swaine owed him a favor, Manuelito concluded that he would be embarrassed if the colonel did not answer his plea.[21]

Manuelito need not have worried. Colonel Swaine quickly issued orders to Lieutenant D. D. Mitchell, who left Fort Wingate on August 11, with four enlisted men. After an eight-hour march, Mitchell reached Navajo City, where he and his soldiers met John Lorenzo Hubbell, who was to act as interpreter. Manuelito was also there, and he had received word from the people who had tied up the witches. They were angry. Manuelito warned the lieutenant that they might become violent and asked him if he would be afraid. Mitchell replied that he "had not started from Fort Wingate with troops to become frightened by anything the Indians might do." Mitchell then asked the chief if he would accompany him. Manuelito answered that he had to be at Fort Wingate the next day because several Navajo scouts who owed him money were going to be paid.[22]

In the morning, Mitchell, Hubbell, and the soldiers trekked north into the Tunicha (Chuska) Mountains. After traveling for ten hours, they made camp in a little valley between two ridges. A Navajo headman unnamed in Mitchell's report came to pay a visit to the lieutenant and volunteered to ride with the troops to the place where the medicine men were being held. He, like Manuelito, warned Mitchell that the Indians were very angry at the approach of soldiers and would probably cause trouble. Mitchell told the headman that he would take care of any trouble. The soldiers broke camp at six o'clock the next morning and resumed their march. As they drew closer to their destination, more Navajos joined and rode along. This small caravan arrived at noon in a place called the Tunicha Mountain Valley where they found three Navajos tied to trees. There were ten to twelve men armed with bows and arrows guarding the prisoners.

Mitchell ordered his troops to make camp. Once this task was accomplished, the soldiers rested for two hours. During this time, approximately 150 Navajos gathered, and the lieutenant eventually called on them to form a circle because he wanted to talk with them about shooting stones into the bodies of their fellow tribesmen. Once the circle was formed, Mitchell told them to put the prisoners in the middle. After this was accomplished, he spoke to the gathering, with Hubbell translating his words.

Mitchell informed the crowd that he came as a representative of the commander of Fort Wingate. He had much to tell them about supernatural practices being used against fellow Navajos, but first he wanted them to know that the "Navajo Doctors" had sent messengers to him warning him not to come. Now the soldiers had completed their journey, and they intended to remain until some settlement was reached. Mitchell asked if anyone wanted to state his objections. When no one spoke, he said:

> The Americans no longer disbelieve in this shooting stones business and it must be stopped; this thing of certain Indians killing others in the same Tribe is an outrage and will not be tolerated longer. I am here to make these Doctors promise to stop this practice and also hear what they have to say regarding the same and if they acknowledge to having killed any Navajos.

Mitchell then asked the first prisoner in line for his comments.

The man stated that he had learned the magic spells from another Indian at the Bosque Redondo, but he had lost his medicine, and it was now impossible for him to kill anyone. He claimed that he was sorry that he had ever become involved with such evil. He had never killed a Navajo and wanted to get along with all of his people. After the first man was finished, the lieutenant asked similar questions of the other two, who answered that they were innocent. Their testimony was vigorously contested by Indians in the crowd, who claimed that they knew the last two were lying. Mitchell then resorted to a bluff. He emphatically accused the prisoners of lying and said that he knew who they were and what they looked like. If any report reached the fort that they were harming Navajos, he would have them thrown in the guardhouse. All three promised to stop practicing witchcraft, and Mitchell indicated his pleasure with their promises but demanded that they keep them. They should no longer gather sheep and horse dung or human hair.

The prisoners agreed to Mitchell's demands. Thinking that the meeting was over, he addressed the Navajos by saying that

> the Great Father in Washington was very friendly to the Navajos, that he fed them, clothed them, gave them sheep and also issued them annuity goods, and that in consideration of all this, he, the Great Father, expected

them to be at peace with one another and not be killing like a lot of dogs. If the killing continued, that the Tribe would soon be split up into factions, then other Tribes like the Utes, would come in, steal their Cattle, Sheep and Horses, and they [would] be left penniless and finally annihilated, and the Tribe become extinct.

Most of the people in the crowd seemed to agree with Mitchell, but several of them insisted that he inflict physical punishment on the prisoners to guarantee that their offenses would never be repeated. The lieutenant argued that they had learned their lesson.

Mitchell was again ready to end the talks. He had not counted, however, on the way Navajos conducted meetings, a style that relied more on consensus than on majority rule. The lieutenant also made the mistake of asking for additional comments. Several members of the crowd stated that they did not believe the prisoners' promises. Mitchell countered by saying that he had warned the witches, and if they did not stick to their word, they would be punished by the army. After consultation among themselves, the Indians requested a continuation of the discussion the next day. There were four more men they wanted Mitchell to lecture. Since they appeared anxious, he granted their request.

The lieutenant ordered the Navajos to assemble the following morning. As they were gathering, Ganado Mucho appeared with approximately one hundred followers and was greeted by many people in the crowd. While Ganado Mucho's men were unsaddling their horses, more Navajos arrived with four prisoners. Mitchell ordered these witches to the center of the circle. He repeated his speech of the day before and added that he wanted any "outfit" in their possession that was used for "throwing stones" handed over to him. One of the newly arrived prisoners went to his horse and brought back his "medicine kit." Mitchell dared him to demonstrate his powers. The man stated that he would gladly do it if the soldiers would go with him to a place where the Navajos could not see him. The crowd objected, and the lieutenant called him a liar. At this point, the man's wife stepped into the circle and astonished the audience by claiming that she had seen her husband do many evil things. He had killed her sister, his brother, and two other Navajos. She feared that he would kill her. When her spouse was asked to comment on his wife's harangue, he confessed to the murders of which she accused him and admitted to other crimes. Mitchell asked him if he intended to practice this magic any more, and he said no; he had brought his medicine along with him and would turn it over to the soldiers because of a promise he had made to his wife.

Mitchell then made each prisoner promise to stop practicing witchcraft. The old man who had confessed now added that he would make sure that the evil stopped in the northwestern portion of the reservation. Sensing an end to the spectacle, Mitchell told the crowd that if they learned of anybody making use of bad magic, they should not take matters into their own hands; they should report it to the officers at Fort Wingate. The prisoners were released, Mitchell shook hands with most of the crowd, and the soldiers left with a guide provided by Ganado Mucho. They arrived at Fort Defiance that night, June 14, at ten o'clock. The next day, Mitchell met with most of the chiefs and reported on what he had done. They thanked him for his help. Mitchell and his troops returned to Fort Wingate on the following day.

According to Navajo tradition, forty people were killed during the witchcraft scare. Isolated incidents would continue throughout the summer, but Ganado Mucho and Manuelito played important roles in containing the affair. As people became caught up in the witchcraft scare, including Ganado Mucho himself, these chiefs had two options within their culture to halt what could have become a civil war: persuasion and employment of their own force of arms. When the first proved to be ineffective, the second was not viable because it would make the situation worse. Therefore, knowing that their people did not want conflict with the army, the chiefs hoped that the soldiers, acting as outside mediators, could bring the situation to a peaceful conclusion. When the army presence resulted in success, the prestige of the two men may have been enhanced, and although Manuelito could be faulted for placing his financial gain ahead of peace, both men deserved credit for not taking sides permanently. Their actions took courage, for they believed in witchcraft and were afraid.[23]

Lieutenant Mitchell had been courageous, too. Colonel Swaine defended Mitchell's handling of the matter by stating that his experience was "that it is useless to try to convince Indians that their expectations are erroneous, and they will place little faith in us if we deny the truth of what they assert."[24] Reflecting a military tendency to accept Navajo traditions, he was also criticizing Pyle, who had tried to change the Navajos' minds.

Pyle considered the implications of the army's action in the Chuska Mountains and penned an angry letter, on June 21, to the commissioner of Indian affairs. He wrote:

> It is not impossible that persecution, revenge of real or fancied wrongs or superstition, either or all, may have had much to do with the treatment these prisoners were receiving at the hands of their tribe, but whether they had or had not I do not regard as essential in considering the question as to how far the Military or any other power, may rightfully interfere with the administration of justice, however crude and barbarous the forms may appear to our more enlightened judgement, as meted out by people to whom the the [sic] "powers that be" have given no form of civil government but who are to all intents and purposes "a law unto themselves." These prisoners are accused of procuring the death of certain of their tribe by administering pills containing fragments of glass. Does the Commanding Officer at Fort Wingate know that such is [sic] not the facts? Would the courts of the country take cognizance of the case were complaint made before the proper officers thereof! I think not, and if not, and if the military or any other power may interfere at pleasure with the rude tribunals which the Indian has, from time immemorial employed as his means of protection, where now is his protection?[25]

Pyle's argument, written, in anger, pointed out just how independent the Navajos had been in governing their internal affairs, but he would not have taken his argument further by stating that the chiefs had governed well. As far as he was concerned, they were part of the problem.

Colonel Swaine answered Pyle's complaints five days later, stating that Pyle had told Lieutenant McGunnigle while he was at Fort Defiance, that probably he would also have to intervene in a situation some fifty miles north of the agency. Swaine had taken this remark as a verbal authorization. Even though Pyle wrote to Swaine a few days later to explain that he was sure the colonel had acted with good motives in mind and that he did not want the feud to become personal, cooperation between the agent and the military came to a halt. When Swaine's reply reached Pyle in August, after traveling through offices in the War and Interior departments, Pyle was furious. He claimed that he had left no requests "to do anything or to go anywhere" and called Mitchell's expedition a "raid."[26]

This trouble over supernatural malpractice, however, was not the only violence associated with Navajos during June. According to an oral history, the Apaches had made a habit in the late 1870s of raiding Navajos north of the Little Colorado River. In June of 1878, twenty Apaches launched an attack on two Navajo communities located on the northern edge of the Painted Desert. The attackers took a number of valuable items. The Navajos, under the leadership of local headmen B'ugoettin and Natani, left in hot pursuit. When it became clear to them that they could not follow the Apaches' trail, due to the rocky nature of the country, the Navajos rushed ahead to cut off escape. The enemy did not appear. Disappointed, the Navajos rode toward their homes, only to discover that the raiders had pillaged another settlement. Convinced that the Apaches were hiding, the headmen sent out scouts to search for them. Two young men, B'ugoettin Begay and Bahe, discovered that the Apaches were hiding with their horses and their spoils in a cave with a narrow opening in Diablo Canyon, west of present-day Winslow. The Navajos rushed to the entrance, built a fire in front of the opening, and fired into the cave when the Apaches tried to escape. All of the men in the cave died.[27]

June also saw the beginning of a conflict when H. L. Mitchell moved into the country along the San Juan River in Utah. Locating himself on the north side of the river, at the mouth of

McElmo Canyon, he had trouble with Navajos almost immediately. Stubborn and rarely willing to compromise, Mitchell would not admit to the legitimacy of Navajo claims to water and grazing rights. Eighteen families joined him by the end of the year, and when the livestock industry seemed too precarious for him, Mitchell opened a trading post for Navajos while calling for their removal from the region.[28]

The authorities did not seriously consider Mitchell's demands because his community was small and the Apaches presented a much more serious difficulty. Meanwhile, Navajos fought Apaches. In July, nineteen Navajo scouts, under the command of Lieutenant Henry H. Wright and operating out of Fort Stanton, New Mexico, accompanied fifty-two men from the Ninth Cavalry on a march through the Guadalupe and Sacramento mountains in search of renegade Mescalero Apaches. This expedition fought in several skirmishes in which the Navajos proved to be effective soldiers.[29]

While Navajos working for the army were showing their heroism, their fellow tribesmen and Agent Pyle were engaged in other matters. On Sunday, June 30, Pyle was pleased with the morning. He found the agency quiet. The previous day had been difficult because so many noisy Indians had been at Fort Defiance. Now he could forget all that. For a man who missed the fellowship of Sunday services, the tranquility was compensation, but his bliss was disturbed in the afternoon by a group of Navajo gamblers betting for pistols and valuables. The agent spoke to them in an attempt to get them to stop, but they did not listen until he reached into the game, forcibly seized the cards, and threw them into the wind. The game stopped.[30]

Such victories came infrequently to Pyle. He impaired his already frail health by worrying. Early in July, for example, Pyle received orders from the commissioner to conduct a complete census for the Navajos. He allowed himself to fret over the matter for a week and a half before he confronted his superior. He wrote to the commissioner:

It should be remembered that in order to get up such a list accurate enough to be of any service as a means of reference, it would be necessary to confine all of the Indians of this tribe in an open corral for a number of days together while their crops and herds must be left unprotected. It is scarcely necessary to say that they would not submit to such an act of injustice and cruelty.[31]

Although Pyle had difficulty dealing with individual Navajos, he had a strong sense of abstract justice which he was quite willing to voice to his superiors when angry. Nevertheless, he was a loyal public servant, and he promised the commissioner that he would try to act as instructed.[32]

Pyle was also concerned about the continued practice of witchcraft. On July 9, word reached him that the son of Chicquito, the seventh signer of the treaty, had been killed by Mariano's people in retaliation for his father's alleged evil activities. Pyle was gripped by despair for his charges.[33]

The army, on the other hand, energetically tried to keep peace among the Navajos. Captain Bennett left Fort Wingate on July 1 to visit as many Navajo leaders as possible. Whether Bennett's visit was known to Pyle is not clear, but it was obvious that the army was assisting its allies, the chiefs, in any way it could. Bennett remained on assignment until July 30. On the day of his return, Pyle also rode into Fort Wingate. Soon after his arrival, Ganado Mucho, Manuelito, and Mariano rode into the fort with forty others, to hold a council about witchcraft. But when they saw that Pyle was there, their plans were interrupted. In August, Captain W. F. Hegewald and Lieutenant McGunnigle spent seven days on the reservation. At the same time, Pyle learned that the officers at Wingate were taking to heart his feud with them. When Pyle visited the fort in July, he found the officers courteous but unfriendly.[34]

In August, Pyle submitted his annual report to the commissioner of Indian affairs. It was a perceptive document, even though the agent's insights were sometimes clouded by prejudice. Ten years ago, he began, when the Navajos had signed the treaty, they had been a "band of paupers" because of war and exile. Now

they had become "a nation of prosperous, shrewd and (for bar-
barians) intelligent people." Little progress had been made in
getting the Indians to adopt Anglo-American farming methods,
but this was because the Diné had a better understanding of
their soil and environment than their conquerors. During spring
planting, the wind blew away plowed soil; thus, "a Navajo with
a sharp stick and hoe, can get one-third to one-half larger returns
than the white man can from the same ground with the best
improved farm machinery now in use." The Navajos had made
use of all plots of land with available water, with one exception.
Their San Juan River lands had not been utilized for horticulture
because of the Ute danger. Either the removal of the Utes from
southwestern Colorado or the removal of the agency to the San
Juan would enable the Diné to develop these lands. The agent
also urged that the government spend a few hundred dollars to
dig wells and build windmills to allow the Indians to make use
of territory useless for human habitation.[35]

While Pyle saw much progress, he also believed that there
were many problems. The Navajos, first of all, needed more land.
Since the Indians would not give up their desert homes for better
locations, the agent argued that they should be given more desert. He asked:

> Cannot our government afford to be a little magnanimous and give to a
> peaceable and industrious tribe of Indians a few more square miles of
> barren sands? But I suppose it would be worse than folly to ask more
> territory for any tribe, however deserving, from a government that does
> not secure to the Indian the peaceful possession of lands already guar-
> anteed to him by solemn treaty stipulation[36]

This reference to the government's seeming unwillingness to
make the San Juan region safe for the Diné was not politic, but
the development of the area had been a persistent theme of all
the agents who had preceded him except Arny. Yet Pyle did not
see the San Juan territory as a panacea because he believed that
the Navajos would need more land even if it were developed.

Pyle also recommended that rations no longer be issued, except to laborers at the agency and the needy, because the practice was "demoralizing." Instead, he declared that the government should give

> them cattle, sheep, agricultural implements, and seeds, and do more for their education, and by these means they will the sooner become self-supporting. The Navajos are a nation of workers. The drones are very, very few. They are, as a rule, provident. The few thousand sheep given them a few years ago have increased to hundreds of thousands.[37]

Nevertheless, the agent believed that the Navajos would remain peaceful, no matter what the government did. Challenging the army's principal reason for intervening on the reservation, namely, that the tribe might go to war, Pyle thought the Indians had learned their lesson at the Bosque Redondo. The Navajos, with their large herds, simply had too much to lose.[38]

Not everyone agreed with Pyle. To many, the peace on the Navajo frontier seemed precarious. In 1878, there were an estimated 13,000 Navajos, and the estimates were probably low. Half of the tribe lived off the reservation, with no legal title to the land they occupied. The Diné possessed approximately 500,000 sheep, 1,500 head of cattle, and 20,000 horses, but this wealth was not distributed equally. As a result, poor Navajos were still raiding as far away as the Manzano Mountains, near Albuquerque. At the same time, the non-Indian settlement of lands adjacent to the Diné continued. The Mormons, for example, established a new community in September, when Erastus Snow and family, along with Jesse N. Smith and others, settled two miles from Moenkopi, at an important water source for both Navajos and Hopis. This new settlement was named Tuba City.[39]

Also in September, General Sherman visited Fort Defiance. Pyle found out about the impending visit early in the month. He rushed preparations for the general's stopover as much as he could, but there were interruptions. His health forced him to rest, and Manuelito came by to ask for supplies. The agent refused, and they argued. By September 6, Pyle was so tired that he spent the day reading old newspapers and hoped to finish his arrangements for Sherman on Saturday, September 7. As he cleaned house that afternoon, he was surprised by the general at 3:30. Pyle had not had time to dress properly.[40]

Sherman was accompanied by Captain Bennett. According to Pyle's diary, the general was amiable, but when the agent remembered the visit later he charged that Sherman spoke critically of the Interior Department and the Indian Bureau, claiming that the agencies were corrupt and that the men who ran them were unfit for office.[41]

Sherman had come because he had promised the Navajos a visit ten years earlier, at the treaty negotiations. He had been at Fort Wingate since September 5, conferring with the officers. The afternoon after his arrival, Sherman met with Pyle, agency physician Dr. Walter Whitney, William Leonard, and approximately twenty-five headmen, among whom were Muerto de Hambre, Delgadito, Largo, Manuelito, and Ganado Mucho. Pyle stated that Manuelito and Sherman did most of the speaking, but according to Sherman, it was a "full and free talk." Sherman began by carefully explaining to the Indians that he had no authority in Indian affairs; nevertheless, in his capacity as "head soldier," he was interested in their welfare. Although managing reservations was a civilian matter, he let them know that he could help them by encouraging friendship between them and the president. Then the general asked the Navajos to tell him what they felt.[42]

Navajo leaders began by saying that their population and flocks were growing rapidly. They needed a larger reservation to make room for more people and more sheep. They asked for additional land. Not giving the Navajos a forthright answer, Sherman told them that he had no power to renegotiate a treaty, that only the United States Senate had the power to alter treaties. The general knew, but failed to tell them, that land could be added to reservations by executive order. He informed the Navajos that he would help them get the rest of the Canyon de Chelly region because, accidentally, it had not been included in the treaty description of the reservation. He recommended in his report that an executive order be issued to adjust the boundaries to include the entire Chinle Valley. Sherman also wrote an endorsement, which he left with the agent. Pyle sent Sherman's document, along with his own recommendation, to the commissioner of Indian affairs.[43]

Pyle must have used most of the self-control at his disposal to write his terse recommendation, for the rest of the meeting did not go well for him. The general asked the Indians if there was anything else that they would like him to handle. The chiefs declared that they wanted a new agent because Pyle was unresponsive to their needs. Pyle shut himself off from contact with the Navajos. In addition, he often refused to talk with the headmen when they had matters of importance to discuss. Sherman, who was unimpressed by the amount of progress the tribe had made under civilian guidance, was willing to do what he could to help the Diné on this matter. Declaring that the Navajos were one of the most important tribes in the West because of their large population, he wrote to the secretary of war that they should have the agent they desired. Pyle was "a man of infirm health, intelligent, honest, and zealous in the discharge of his duties," but he did not have "the strength or physical energy to fulfil his important office." The commissioner of Indian affairs should transfer him to a less demanding job. The general added that he would not hesitate to recommend Manuelito or Delgadito for the position, but since the politics dictated that a white man should be agent, he could go along with the chiefs' choices, Captain Bennett and Thomas Keam. He believed that Keam would be the best man because the Navajos and the officers at Fort Wingate wanted him and because, as a former member of the California Volunteers, he was a Civil War veteran.[44]

Pyle was furious by the end of the day. In his diary, he claimed that the headmen were self-serving, declaring that they were against him because he did not steal from the tribe like them. He claimed that they were disloyal and ungrateful, as well as easily influenced by evil white men. When Pyle found out in

November that Sherman sided with the chiefs, he wrote a response that he mailed to the commissioner of Indian affairs. According to the agent, Captain Bennett and Thomas Keam had conspired against him. After eating lunch, Sherman had taken a nap. As the general slept, the two conspirators took the Indians to Keam's place nearby and told them what to say.[45]

After accusing Bennett and Keam, Pyle next answered the general's charges. He stated that the chiefs were selfish. Was he to be blamed if he did not wish to speak with men who only wanted more for themselves? He contended that the only time the leaders ever spoke of important matters was when he forced them. The worst one in the group was Manuelito, but Sherman would not hesitate to make him an agent. In Pyle's opinion, Manuelito was a drunkard. Even Captain Bennett was aware of that fact because he had caught the old warrior at home recovering from a three-day binge during the summer.[46]

If Pyle's arguments helped him in Washington, his actions at the agency were not contributing to his credibility. He reported in the middle of September that the Navajos could provide 90 to 95 percent of their own support. By September 30 he was forced to admit that a flood in August had destroyed a large portion of the Navajo wheat and corn crop, but he still believed that there was enough grain available at the agency and stored by Indians to get the tribe through the winter. His optimism, however, proved false, and he was compelled to buy 250,000 pounds of corn by the end of the year.[47]

As October began, Pyle resolved that he would pay little attention to Navajo leaders because all they ever did was ask for more for themselves. It was not long, however, until he found himself in a council with several headmen giving them a temperance lecture. He was surprised when Manuelito refused to listen quietly. The chief asked Pyle why he objected to Indians drinking whiskey, for most white people enjoyed the beverage. He proclaimed that liquor was a good thing; it made the world happier for a short time. Army officers had given him a drink from time to time, and Pyle should do the same.[48] Pyle did not drink; neither did he care to develop close relationships with his charges.

In the army, on the other hand, things were different. The decision to send the Mimbres Apaches back to San Carlos had finally been made in Washington. Captain Bennett was ordered to escort the Indians. He arrived at Ojo Caliente on October 8, with two companies of troops and a number of Navajo scouts. When Bennett explained his orders to Victorio, the Apache leader told the captain that he would never go to San Carlos, and he ran quickly with 80 followers into the nearby mountains, with 17 others following Victorio's example a few days later, and leaving behind 169 of their people. The soldiers and scouts tried to track both groups of fleeing Apaches, but heavy rains obliterated the trails. Bennett loaded the remaining Indians in wagons and took them as far as Fort Apache. Leaving his prisoners with the Apache chief of police, Bennett was back at Fort Wingate on December 1. The scouts who were still under the command of Lieutenant Wright were mustered out of the service ten days later. On December 11, twenty more scouts were enlisted, and they left for Ojo Caliente a week and a half later to chase Victorio.[49]

Pyle, in the meantime, had grown disillusioned as the pressure mounted against him. George G. Smith, a Presbyterian minister in Santa Fe, defended the agent and attacked Thomas Keam as an "outside mischief maker." But Smith's support was not enough to restore Pyle's resolve. He put in a request for a leave of absence on October 21, although he continued on the job until December 1.[50]

Pyle reported at the end of October that the Navajos were at peace with their neighbors and that a teacher, Collin Dixon, had arrived for the school, where, as usual, attendance was low. Encouraging word soon reached the agency that a strip of land twenty miles wide to the west, which included Chinle Valley, had been granted to the Diné by President Hayes, in an executive order dated October 29. There was more good news. The sheep authorized in May, along with fifteen wagons full of annuity goods, arrived at Fort Defiance. In accordance with Irvine's original request, the sheep were to be given only to people who did not have any. Pyle thought this was impossible, but he was determined that the chiefs would not get any sheep. The distribution began on November 11 and took three days. Over nine thousand people were present.[51]

Pyle left for Montana on December 1, leaving Dr. Whitney in charge. He would never return. The chiefs, however, had no knowledge of this. A number of headmen visited Colonel Swaine on December 20. Among the leaders were Manuelito, Narbono, and Mariano. They explained Ganado Mucho's absence from the group by stating that the chief was too old to make the trip in bad weather. Manuelito spoke for the delegation. He wanted Swaine to thank General Sherman for the land to the west. Now, he said, the people on the east side of the reservation also needed land. Swaine told him that Sherman had acquired for them all the territory he could, but the colonel would take down his words and send them to the proper authorities.[52] Manuelito also said:

> From the time, we made the Treaty with General Sherman at Fort Sumner, we have lived as far as possible up to that treaty, but men have been sent to us as agents who have not helped us nor assisted us, nor told us anything when we have requested to have our Great Father written to relative to matters pertaining to us, these agents either lie or do not do it . . .[53]

The chief added that the Navajos wanted Thomas Keam as agent, and Swaine agreed that Keam would be a good man. Once Manuelito's words were translated and written down, the chiefs marked the document as if it were a petition. This act must have done some good, for the Navajos would soon get more land. But they did not get the agent they wanted.[54]

Later that month, Indian Inspector A. L. Earle was sent out by the commissioner to investigate the conditions at Fort Defiance. Earle reported that the Navajos were dissatisfied, but most of this feeling, he concluded, was the result of outside agitation rather than the Indians' true desires.[55] Thomas Keam, one of the alleged instigators, again failed to become agent.

The agent who was leaving was perceptive in many ways about their condition, but he did not understand the complexities of Navajo politics. Nor was he energetic enough to be of much practical help to the poorest of the Diné. Since he was usually not available, they again turned to their most consistent allies, the Hubbell brothers, Thomas Keam, and the army. Charles Hubbell, for instance, had been so willing to help his immediate customers that he risked retaliation from other Navajos. Yet he was adept enough to work with the army and with Navajo leaders to extricate himself. Meanwhile, his brother John Lorenzo managed to be on hand at the conference in the Chuska Mountains, an event that increased his own prestige and enabled his prime benefactor, Ganado Mucho, to distance himself from radical action.

The army had also helped the chiefs by participating in Navajo politics. Pyle understood that these actions interfered with Navajo sovereignty, but he did not comprehend that the army acted to keep Navajo power structures intact. Temporarily, the chiefs enhanced their power. For the long run, their appeal for outside help set up the army (and, by implication, the federal government) as an arbitrator of their affairs, but that was probably inevitable in any case. And for the time being, they had kept their people from needless civil conflict.

The Navajos, who had turned their geographic, economic, and social frustrations inward against each other by practicing witchcraft and retaliating against the practice, had gone through a troublesome time. They had been able to expand their reserve and avoid serious conflict. Yet many people, especially the army, worried that internal anger could easily turn outward.

10

Threat of War

On April 5, the new agent, Galen Eastman, received word of his appointment at his home in Grand Haven, Michigan. In a significant break with Peace Policy practice, Eastman had been recommended for the position by John Lowrie because of influence exerted by Michigan Senator Thomas W. Ferry. Eastman informed his new employers that he would move to Arizona soon. In the meantime, Dr. Walter Whitney served as acting agent, and this was the second time he had done so. A loyal employee of Arny, he had been taken captive when the Navajos seized Fort Defiance. Relieved of authority by Major William Redwood Price, Whitney had served at the Ojo Caliente Agency until it was closed. He then returned to Fort Defiance and had been there for a year.[1]

Eastman arrived at Fort Defiance on April 26. Within a month, he criticized Pyle's budget for being too low, declared the Navajos to be peaceful, arranged to distribute supplies to needy Indians, and disputed Whitney's bookkeeping. When Eastman compared the agency books with the number of items stored in the warehouse, he found large surpluses. Whitney told Eastman that he should simply distribute these undocumented goods without accounting for them, but the agent informed the commissioner of Indian affairs.[2]

The new agent also overturned the recommendation of several agents who had preceded him. Authorization had finally arrived to relocate the agency on the San Juan River. Eastman was against the move. The government plans for the new agency only allowed for five rooms, besides an office and a warehouse. There were more buildings currently at Fort Defiance. In addition, he argued that the lands along the San Juan flooded often and would not be the horticultural bonanza that others promised. The Diné were a "flourishing people" because they were herders, and Eastman, in a break with the Peace Policy, believed that they should continue their pastoral existence. For less money, Eastman concluded, he could repair the agency buildings and construct a boarding school, the only type of educational institution that he believed would work with Native Americans.[3]

When Eastman met with twenty headmen and three hundred of their followers on May 21, the Navajo leaders agreed that the agency should remain at Fort Defiance, accepting Eastman's proposal because a San Juan agency would be farther away for most of them. Beginning in the afternoon and lasting until midnight, the council concerned much more than a new site for the agency. The principal Navajo spokesman, Manuelito, declared that his people needed more land to the east and to the south. Eastman, at first, was against their proposal, but after listening to their arguments, he changed his mind. Happy that their reasoning had convinced their new agent, the Indians were well behaved and pleasant. But they did become angry about Dr. Whitney. They claimed that Whitney had helped Arny steal from them. Eastman asked the Navajos if they would like the physician removed from office. They replied that they were not sure. The next morning, however, Manuelito privately informed the agent that the Indians wanted another doctor. As a result, Eastman put pressure on Whitney, who resigned on May 24. He agreed to stay for the remainder of the year, and attempted to clear his name.[4]

Even though Whitney's pleas for vindication were lost within the Washington bureaucracy, Eastman had gotten off to a good start with his wards by cooperating with the headmen. Nevertheless, he did not maintain these relations long. He cast doubt on his sincerity when he recommended a doctor from his hometown to take Whitney's place. Eastman also hired his son, an inexperienced minor, as agency carpenter and storekeeper. By trying to employ a crony and hiring a relative, he opened himself to criticism. In addition, his resolve to hand out rations to individual Navajos angered the chiefs, who were disappointed that he refused to give them the responsibility of distribution.[5]

The chiefs would turn quickly against Eastman, but it is unlikely that ration distribution had much to do with their discontent. Only one agent, Arny, had freely used the chiefs as disbursing agents, and they had removed him from office. Like Arny and Pyle, Eastman was unable to deal with the Navajos in ways that they understood. He lacked the tact and empathy needed to live among a people who were foreign to him.[6]

Eastman, however, had other qualities. For instance, he would remain a consistent advocate for the material improvement of the Diné. He was also an idealist who believed in the powers of Christianity to rehabilitate the Navajos. Unfortunately for Eastman, the Presbyterians had sent him no missionaries, and he had to concentrate on the children. There were only eleven students in the school, but Eastman saw some progress being made because three pupils were able to read from their McGuffey readers. Taking this limited success as an indication of what could be accomplished, the agent planned work on a boarding school. First making arrangements to use Navajo laborers and pay them with goods rather than cash, Eastman contemplated the use of locally available lumber to accomplish his project inexpensively. The school would remain one of his preoccupations during all of the time he was in office, but in planning only for a maximum of fifty students, he was not overly ambitious.[7]

Eastman's technical activities, however, were not very effective. That summer was dry, and many of the Diné saw the failure of their crops. Apparently, Eastman's practice of distributing rations to individuals proved to be less effective than other methods, for hungry Navajos grew dissatisfied with their condition.[8]

Meanwhile, Navajo scouts continued to participate in the Apache wars. Nine scouts were discharged at Fort Wingate on June 19. Operating out of Fort Bayard, New Mexico, they had seen action along the Mexican border in pursuing outlaw Chiricahua and Mimbres bands and attempting to halt their escape into Mexico. On June 27, ten newly enlisted Navajo scouts returned to Fort Bayard under the command of Lieutenant Robert T. Emmett.[9]

Nineteen other Navajo scouts, commanded by Lieutenant Henry Wright, and fifty-two men of the Ninth Cavalry, under Captain Henry Carroll, were engaged with Apaches at approximately the same time. Chasing Victorio, Carroll's contingent explored the Guadalupe Mountains on the southern New Mexico–Texas border. Then they moved west to the Sacramento Mountains in south-central New Mexico. There, in Dog Canyon, Carroll's troops flushed a group of Mimbres Apaches in August. The Apaches fled. The soldiers fought several skirmishes with the fleeing Indians, killing three Apaches and capturing fourteen horses. As the combatants moved up the canyon, however, Apaches fought a successful rearguard action while the rest of their party managed to take refuge on a ledge some eight hundred feet above the canyon floor. Carroll did not quit his appointed task. With the Apaches firing mercilessly and rolling boulders down on their assailants, the soldiers and the Navajos slowly worked their way up the canyon walls, only to find the Apaches gone when they reached the ledge.[10]

If this engagement seemed to be without triumph, it had the effect of keeping the Mimbres on the run as well as exhausting their resources. With this in mind, several small detachments were ordered to continue the pursuit. Among these were Lieutenants Wright and Emmett and their Navajo scouts. In mid-September, Wright's small patrol joined with others that were under the command of Major Albert P. Morrow. They found Victorio's trail in a canyon in the Mimbres Mountains. Following the trail, the detachments marched straight into a trap. Two Navajo scouts and five soldiers were killed. As soon as Morrow received word of the battle, he dispatched other units to the fight, one of which was Emmett's group of Navajos. Nevertheless, the Apaches escaped. Morrow sent the Navajos to search the Socorro Mountains, but to little avail. Eventually, Morrow's troops were able to chase Victorio out of southwestern New Mexico and into Arizona. Morrow reported at the end of his operation that there were a few renegade Navajos in Victorio's group.[11]

Morrow's report was disturbing, but more frightening news from northwestern Colorado reached the settlers in the San Juan region. In September, the agent to the Northern Utes, Nathan Meeker, attempted to plow traditional grazing lands near the agency and to plant grain. The Utes, already angry at the loss of most of their hunting lands, complained that their horses would be unable to eat and that their movements would be severely restricted in the spring when they needed fresh meat. Meeker, believing that the Indians should settle at a permanent location, refused to consider their objections. The agent, however, understood that his wards were furious, and he sent for troops as a precaution. The Utes concluded that the soldiers were coming to fight. In a state of panic, twenty-five Utes stormed the agency, killed Meeker and eight employees, and took three women and two children hostage. Concurrently, three hundred Utes led by Captain Jack ambushed the approaching soldiers and kept them pinned down for six days before the army could send help.[12]

The women and children were freed, but the "Meeker Massacre" caused an uproar. Settlers in western Colorado worried about a general Indian uprising, and the anxiety spread to northwestern New Mexico. Old rumors of a Navajo-Ute alliance were revived. As Louisa Wetherill, wife of trader John Wetherill, remembered years later, some residents of the area had learned that the Navajos could be trusted not to fight a war. Others, however, reacted in a nearly paranoid manner. For instance, Mora Bueno, a Navajo living south of Farmington, attempted to reassure an Anglo-American woman who lived nearby that the Navajos would remain peaceful. He spoke to her in broken Spanish, a language that she only partially understood. The woman misinterpreted the message and told a neighbor that the Navajos were going to join the Utes in an attempt to annihilate the settlers. The neighbor quickly plotted the formation of a vigilante group to capture Mora Bueno and hold him hostage to keep the Diné in line. Nonetheless, the first man he tried to recruit doubted the story and went to talk with the Indian in person. Having a better understanding of Spanish, he was able to get the story straight. When he informed the would-be kidnapper, he was met with disbelief. This diplomat then went to Mora Bueno's house, brought him to the man's homestead, had the Indian repeat his speech, and translated it for him. Finally, Mora Bueno's message was understood.[13]

The belief in a Navajo-Ute conspiracy was widespread although the Southern Utes did not follow the example of their northern kinsmen and commence hostilities. Yet fear was so prevalent that the army dispatched three companies of Ninth Cavalry with a Gatling gun from Fort Wingate, under the command of Colonel George P. Buell, to investigate the situation along the San Juan River. Although he discovered no evidence that either tribe planned to go to war, Buell found a substantial dispute over land and water between the Diné and the settlers. He learned that the location of the eastern reservation boundary, which ran south from the San Juan, was in dispute. Buell attempted to keep the Navajos and settlers apart and wrote to Eastman requesting information. The agent obtained a statement from the men who had surveyed the reservation in 1869 and wrote that the boundary ran south from a peculiar rock formation named the Hogback.[14]

Eastman sent word to Buell that all Navajos were instructed to live solely upon the reservation. Buell, however, decided to be more lenient, for the situation, although potentially dangerous, had not resulted in much violence. A settler had shot ten sheep belonging to Largo, when the headman's son had driven them to the river, and there was evidence that Navajos were able to buy whiskey. But that was all. The colonel recommended that Navajos be allowed to water their stock on the south side of the river as long as they did not interfere with the settlers. Stating that there were not many settlers south of the San Juan, Buell pointed out that the year had been dry and the Navajos had no other place to water their stock. They had at least as much right to the water as Anglo-American stockmen north of

214

the river, who were restricted to 160 acres by homestead laws but grazed their herds over a larger area. He also suggested that Eastman request an executive order to move the boundary ten miles farther east.[15]

Eastman agreed to allow the Navajos to water their herds at the river. He sent an interpreter to the area to urge the settlers to send a representative to Fort Defiance to discuss their problems. He also repeated his request to the commissioner of Indian affairs that the reservation be expanded to the south and east. While the Diné's request for land made its way through Washington, Anglo-American settlers presented a petition to Buell, who had moved his troops to Animas City, Colorado, to guard against a Ute outbreak. The petition asserted that the Navajos had become a nuisance, driving their herds over the settlers' property. The colonel claimed that his orders did not permit him to leave Colorado unless there was an emergency. He did, however, write to Eastman suggesting that the agent visit the area to investigate.[16]

Frustrated settlers wrote directly to Washington. For example, J. E. Storie, who lived thirty miles east of the reservation, declared that he and his neighbors were "annoyed almost beyond endurance" by Navajos. Grass, he complained, was in short supply due to the drought, and the Indians who grazed on the settlers' lands—even to the point of driving herds right up to their houses—were going to make it impossible to make a profit. The Navajos, he continued, were constantly coming around their homes to beg or to demand trade, thus, making it difficult to leave on errands for fear that the Indians would steal from them. Storie added that the Navajos were so arrogant that if they were asked to leave they would act violently. Another resident, S. H. Conrad, repeated Storie's accusations, adding that the Navajos had even flogged settlers. Complaints were also made that Navajos were living north of the river.[17]

These complaints were referred by the commissioner of Indian affairs to Eastman, who was instructed to keep the Navajos on the reservation. In the meantime, another group of settlers responded to Eastman's invitation and visited Fort Defiance. The agent presented the Navajo point of view and got the delegation to agree to live peacefully with the Diné. Eastman believed that troops in the region had caused much of the hostility, and he hoped that matters would be more peaceful now that Buell was in Colorado.[18]

As Eastman's statement indicated, he was becoming sensitive to military action. Nevertheless, the army at Fort Wingate had the responsibility of policing off-reservation Navajos, and it continued to act accordingly. On August 22, reports reached the fort that Navajos were stealing livestock near McCarty's ranch, east of the reservation. First Lieutenant W. O. Cory was dispatched, with fifteen men from the Ninth Cavalry, to look for stolen stock. Cory's detachment reached McCarty's only to find that Navajo leaders had managed to return the stolen animals.[19]

Eastman considered such actions as interference, and he took pride in acting independently of the army. When he issued annuities in October, 11,400 people appeared at the agency. Ironically for a drought-stricken year, it was raining heavily. The Navajos refused to give him their names, but he did not force them; instead, he took down the names of the chiefs. The agent found the task tiring but satisfying because he had been able to issue goods without relying on the military to control the crowd. Only Captain Bennett witnessed the event, and he informed Eastman that the process had gone well.[20]

The agent continued his concern for educating Navajo youth. Disappointed with the school's low enrollment, Eastman decided to establish a temporary boarding school while the new one was under construction. He requested an additional teacher, a woman, the presence of whom would enable him to open such a facility.[21] Even though Eastman would have preferred to spend more time on school construction, he was distracted by events that fall.

For instance, a squatter named Burgess, who lived on the Little Colorado River, complained that Navajos were crowding the range where he and his brother grazed one hundred head of cattle.

Upon investigation, Eastman discovered that the Indians had moved their flocks south because their sheep faced starvation. Because of the drought and overgrazing, there was no grass left on their own lands. They had established themselves several miles away from Burgess, who would, if he ever bothered to file for the land, be entitled only to 160 acres. Contending that the Navajos had at least as much right to the public domain as squatters, Eastman simply instructed the Indians to avoid contact with Burgess.[22]

The Zunis also complained of Navajo livestock grazing on their land. Although they had a better claim to their property, they were given no more assistance. Left to their own devices, they resorted to magic. At a dance on October 20, the Zunis clubbed a dog to death and, according to missionary Taylor F. Ealy, tore its nose off with their teeth. With this ceremony, called "killing the Navajo," the Zunis attempted to get even with their enemies, but other Navajos visited the pueblo and traded peacefully.[23]

In November, an inspector from the Indian Bureau, J. H. Hammond, visited Fort Defiance. He agreed with Eastman that the agency should remain where it was. Despite the fact that he did not travel to the San Juan River, Hammond declared that relocating the agency to the north would be expensive. He claimed that the agency needed to remain at Fort Defiance to prevent the corrupting influence of Anglo-Americans who lived nearby. Hammond, however, recognized that there were problems with the location of Fort Defiance. The water supply was precarious because adequate dam sites were not available on the current reservation. Stating that there were at least fifty acres which could be irrigated, he recommended that one thousand dollars be appropriated to construct a more suitable dam. Hammond also suggested an extension of the reservation.[24]

Soon after Hammond left the agency, Eastman allegedly offered to make the clerk at George W. Williams's trading post, E. C. Webber, the agency clerk as well as the agency trader if Webber would make the agent's son a partner. Webber revealed this proposition to his employer. Williams, who considered Eastman's son an idiot, was infuriated and informed the commissioner of Indian affairs. He also charged Eastman with storing twelve thousand dollars' worth of supplies for sale to the Indians in Los Angeles and San Francisco. To arrange for unloading the goods through middlemen, Eastman had made a trip to California at government expense, presumably to buy textbooks that could have been ordered through the mail. According to Williams, Eastman's trip cost 387 dollars, more than double the price of the books.[25]

When word of these charges reached Fort Wingate, doubt grew about Eastman's honesty, but the officers there had already begun to fear that he was incompetent. With increasing incidents of Navajo conflict and no apparent lessening of the Indians' discontent, these soldiers worried about the possibility of a war. They had good reason for their concern, for the Navajo frontier would soon acquire a much larger non-Navajo population.

The Atchison, Topeka and Santa Fe Railroad (ATSF) had reached Las Vegas, New Mexico, in July, and the company was rapidly moving toward Albuquerque, a goal it would achieve in April of 1880. The Atlantic and Pacific Railroad, a subsidiary of the ATSF, began surveying a route, roughly along the thirty-fifth parallel, from Albuquerque to the Colorado River. Under the direction of Lewis Kingman and W. A. Drake, survey crews were in and out of the area between Fort Wingate and Flagstaff beginning in the fall of 1879. They found few population centers: the garrison at Wingate, Mexican-American sheepherders near the Puerco River, and Mormons along the Little Colorado. But they did find large numbers of Navajos living on what was supposed to be railroad land. The Diné proved bothersome to the surveyors. Groups of Navajos followed the crews. Although the curious Indians were peaceful, they inspired fear in the surveyors, who, even so, followed company policy and shared food with their visitors. After catching on to this method of adding to their meager rations, the Navajos gathered in increasing numbers. The surveying parties learned that they had to guard their supplies against Navajo theft, and at times, the crews were compelled to evacuate a campsite and attempt to escape close contact.[26]

Despite these troubles, many people understood that the coming of the railroad, with its access to new markets, could bring new vitality to the region's economy as well as wealth to the men who had developed the Navajo trade. One individual who wanted to capitalize on this was John W. Young, the son of Brigham Young. Hoping to corner the northern Arizona wool market, he erected a woolen factory at Tuba City. Completed in November, the factory, suffering from a chronic lack of labor, was never successful, but Young's attempt displayed his faith in the emerging economy.[27]

Like the Diné, however, Young's fellow Mormons were suffering. The Latter Day Saints along the Little Colorado had felt the effects of the drought. Tuba City's crops met reasonable expectations due to the community's reliance on irrigation, but its residents had to accept the routine theft of their cattle by hungry Navajos. The settlers also lived with the almost continual possibility that the Indians would drive their flocks into their fields. Nonetheless, the Mormons intended to stay, and the church planned the settlement of even more land adjacent to the Diné. Mormon leaders were worried that non-Mormon settlement along the San Juan and its tributaries in New Mexico and Colorado would spill over into Utah. Therefore, they dispatched an exploring expedition from Cedar City, Utah, in 1879. Led by Silas S. Smith, the party journeyed first to Moenkopi and Tuba City. Then, traveling northeast, they headed for the portion of the San Juan located in Utah. Smith established a fort at Montezuma Creek, left a few men to guard it, and returned to Cedar City. He reported that a settlement could be maintained in the area. Possessing this intelligence, the church called for two hundred pioneers. In December, these volunteers left Cedar City, taking a more direct route and crossing the Colorado River at Hole in the Rock. The Mormons arrived at Montezuma Creek in April and established the town of Bluff. Unfortunately for the settlers, this community was not immediately successful. The weather proved to be inhospitable and irrigation was difficult, and the Utes and Navajos were so troublesome that half of Bluff's population deserted the town in its first year of existence.[28]

Conflict between the Diné and their neighbors continued elsewhere. Eastman received word in December that some off-reservation Navajos were still causing trouble along the San Juan in New Mexico. Since he had a trip scheduled to meet with Arizona territorial officials in Prescott about controlling the Navajo liquor trade and to visit with leaders of the Mormon Little Colorado settlements, he did not go to the San Juan himself. In his place, Eastman dispatched two delegations of chiefs, one to the river and the other to the tiny community of Bloomfield, New Mexico, southwest of Farmington. The first group told off-reservation Indians to leave the area, and they promised to do so. The agent was not surprised at the peaceful reaction of these Indians because J. H. Benning, who lived at the Hogback had written him that the Navajos were causing no problems. The second delegation of chiefs had less luck. Ordered to inquire about the identity of the troublemakers at the house of J. E. Storie, who had registered a complaint, the chiefs claimed that their horses gave out just before they reached Storie's place, and they had to return to Fort Defiance for fresh mounts. When Eastman returned in January, he sent the chiefs to Bloomfield again. He claimed that a Navajo police force was needed, but maintained that the chiefs did better work than the army.[29]

Eastman had reason to believe that trouble along the San Juan had lessened. Bullock Haines, the postmaster at Bloomfield, wrote the agent that the Navajos were no trouble now that they had removed their flocks from settlers' claims. Other San Juan residents, J. T. Owens and C. T. Synder, also stated that the Diné had stopped bothering homesteaders. Eastman's reliance on the chiefs to restore order in the region seemed to have worked. On January 6, President Hayes signed an executive order expanding the reservation fifteen miles to the east, with the San Juan remaining the northern boundary, and enlarging it six miles to the south, except where railroad land grants took precedence.[30]

Within the next few years, the extension along the San Juan would meet with Anglo-American opposition, be returned to the public domain, and again given to the Navajos. Nevertheless, Eastman's immediate problem had to do with evacuating the non-Navajos who were living on the new lands along the river. Reluctant to use the army, Eastman sent word by courier, and a few days later, Navajos living in the extension forced the settlers to leave. The agent also had to deal with the claims of several individuals living on the lands added to the south. He recommended that Anson Damon, who lived close to Fort Defiance, be allowed a homestead because he was respected by the Indians. Damon agreed to refrain from bringing whiskey on the reservation, and he promised to cooperate with the agent for the good of the Navajos. Eastman did not believe, however, that others should be allowed to stay, even though many of these men were as well respected by the Indians as Damon. The government, he believed, should pay these individuals for their improvements and force them to leave. He mentioned Thomas Keam, George Williams, Charles Hardison, and Pat Bennett as men who deserved such treatment. Although John Lorenzo Hubbell's name was not mentioned by the agent, he was also excluded, and he would fight into the twentieth century for title to his trading post.[31]

The New Mexico territorial legislature protested that one hundred families were being removed from their land, and it claimed that the Navajos had twice as much acreage as they needed. Eastman, however, was unsympathetic. He wanted certain men denied title because he suspected them of conspiring against him as part of a "Santa Fe Ring." He believed that the conspiracy was headed by J. L. Johnston and Company of Santa Fe, a firm that had some Indian contracts. Eastman considerd a number of men as Johnston's representatives in Navajo territory: William Leonard; Fort Wingate post trader and Johnston's nephew, Lambert N. Hopkins; Williams; and Keam. He also accused the military at Fort Wingate of cooperating with them.[32]

In January, it seemed to Eastman as if some agency employees were supporting the ring. Charles Hubbell resigned as Spanish interpreter. Chee Dodge also quit his job. Eastman hired John Navajo, the only other Navajo who could translate directly from Navajo to English, to replace Hubbell and Dodge, but at higher pay. In February, Eastman fired Harry Simpson, the agency clerk, for incompetence. As Simpson's replacement, he employed James R. Sutherland, an acquaintance from his hometown.[33]

In spite of these personnel actions, Eastman went about fixing the reservation's technical problems by preparing to build a new dam for the agency and calling for a complete survey of the reservation's new lands. Eastman, however, was forced to deal with more controversial problems. In early February, Ganado Mucho's son came to Fort Defiance with a disturbing report. He had just made a trip to the Colorado River, where he had a chance to talk with a friend whom he considered trustworthy. Recently, the friend had visited a Paiute lodge, where he observed four mules that had been taken from two murdered white men. Informing the agent that such attacks by Paiutes were frequent, Ganado Mucho's son relayed a concern he had heard from many northern Navajos, namely, that they would be blamed. Eastman promised further investigation.[34]

Before Eastman got around to investigating, he received a letter forwarded to him by the commissioner. H. L. Mitchell, who lived at McElmo Canyon, Utah, complained that Navajos under the leadership of a headman named Hosteen Cah were causing him trouble. Eastman sent a delegation of Navajos to investigate the matter and ordered Hosteen Cah to report to Fort Defiance. The investigators returned with a letter from Mitchell dated February 20. Mitchell wrote that the Navajos were now peaceful, and he thanked Eastman for his efforts, adding, "We have no objections to the Navajos coming among us, but we do not want their herds here." Mitchell also included a statement of citizens in his vicinity who worried about "renegade & lawless white men" infesting the area. Hosteen Cah appeared at the agency on March 11, reporting that he and Mitchell had resolved their dispute. The people in Mitchell's community agreed to keep their livestock north of the San Juan, and the Navajos consented to keep theirs south of the river. The agent assumed that the possibility of conflict was over.[35]

Early in March, an expedition had been dispatched from Fort Wingate, under the command of Captain Bennett, to look into the murders reported by Ganado Mucho's son. On March 20, a letter arrived at Fort Defiance from H. L. Mitchell, making a connection between the Utah trader's troubles and the killings. Mitchell wrote that Indians had killed his son Ernest and a man named James Merrick. Writing on February 27, just two days after his communication to the agent declaring that all was well, Mitchell stated that he had just returned from the burial of his son and Merrick. The bodies were found thirty miles from the reservation, and Mitchell was certain that Navajos had committed the murders, along with renegade Utes and Paiutes, because there were more than one hundred "warriors close to where my son's body lay and Mr. Merrick." Mitchell also declared that the Navajos had killed five additional men whose bodies had not been found.[36] Mitchell wrote:

> Now if you can't take care of these Indians, let us know quick, for if there is not something done, you won't have any Navajos, for there will be in less than 90 days several thousand men here, we can kill just as well as they can, and we do not intend to be run over any longer—the Navajos are terrors, cutthroats, thieves and murderers, we have been always loyal to the Government, the people are the Government and if the officers that we give our money to, cannot protect us from a lot of rubbish, then we can, and you will have to do, what you do, on double quick, for we cannot wait, and the Navajos are off the Reservation all the time, more than half of them now! They say they are going to farm *our* land this year, and if I thought you could not do anything quick, we would commence killing them before . . . they are herding horses on my sons [sic] Ranch whom they have just killed. How do you think we can stand such treatment, we will notify the proper office but we give you a chance to redeam [sic] yourself.[37]

Eastman believed that the murders were committed by Utes or by other nearby Indians. Thinking that the Navajos were "peace-

223

ably inclined," he sent a delegation of chiefs to Mitchell's place to investigate.[38]

Ernest Mitchell and James Merrick were killed, according to Navajo accounts, in Monument Valley, just south of the Utah border. According to gossip in Moenkopi, Bluff, and Mancos, Colorado, Merrick had found silver in Navajo country. He apparently had gone around southwestern Colorado looking for a partner. Martin Rush, a Mancos resident, had been asked. Because he was getting ready for the arrival of his ranching partner, Jack Wade, Rush declined Merrick's invitation, but he claimed to have seen samples of the silver. Merrick eventually arranged for young Mitchell to help him mine the ore. Monument Valley headman Hoskaninni had told his people that Anglo-Americans should never find precious metal in their territory because the land would then be lost, but when Merrick and Mitchell appeared at his hogan with their mules loaded with silver and asked for meat for their return journey, he did not kill them. He gave them mutton. They also asked for the location of water, and Hoskaninni directed them to a spring. The following morning, Merrick and Mitchell were killed by Paiutes who objected to them using their water. When Mitchell's father came to Monument Valley with a party of armed men, Hoskaninni's people directed him to the bodies of the two men.[39]

Not everyone believed that the Navajos were innocent. Word spread that the Navajos had killed Merrick and Mitchell, but it was unlikely since they first reported the murders and cooperated with Mitchell's father. It was possible that Hoskaninni engineered the deaths of the men by directing them to a water hole where he knew the Paiutes would kill them. In any case, no one was punished, although the rumor that the Diné had killed Merrick and Mitchell probably prevented some prospectors from entering Hoskaninni's domain.[40]

Nevertheless, few brave individuals would take the risk. For example, Jack Wade, Louisa Wetherill's father, would look for the legendary silver later in the year. He found no silver, but the story of Hoskaninni's mine remained to draw other treasure hunters to Monument Valley. The *Denver Tribune* helped to spread the legend when it published an article on the Merrick and Mitchell murders on March 17. The article, after speculating on the riches held by Hoskaninni, stated that since the Meeker Massacre renegade Navajos had been meeting with hostile Southern Utes in hopes of establishing an alliance. The newspaper also suggested that the Paiutes had joined in a conspiracy with dissatisfied Navajos, the Utes, and the Mormons, who supplied the Indians with weapons, to drive away the settlers. This sensationalism added to the panic already felt on the San Juan. When Captain Bennett reported, on March 22, that Merrick and Mitchell had been killed by Utes or Paiutes, and not by Navajos, his facts came too late to settle frightened minds.[41]

Eastman, when he received a copy of the *Denver Tribune* article, added another element to the conspiracy. He believed that unscrupulous Anglo-Americans were attempting to undermine him among his wards. He declared that his life was in danger. Either these men would disguise themselves as Indians and kill him or they would influence Navajos to do it, just as Agent Miller had been murdered. Eastman apparently believed gossip perpetrated by Rev. George Smith of Santa Fe to the effect that Thomas Keam had arranged for Navajos to kill Agent Miller.[42]

On April 6, Eastman wrote to the commissioner that four of his employees had left the agency. The other employees, he maintained, were also afraid:

> Since the Meeker murders most white men and women prefer to earn their living inside—I reason with them and state that said Meeker tragedy was almost the first case of the kind occurring at an Agency and that these Indians are peaceful . . . (except a few who have no doubt run with the Utes), but it is *no go*, and the result is the employes [*sic*] do leave.[43]

Although Eastman expected "to rule this people in the future as I have in the past year through persuasive and reasonable arguments and Christian influences," he wanted to purchase ten Winchester repeating rifles with two thousand rounds of ammunition and a double barrel shotgun with five hundred shells.

225

He claimed that the purchase was necessary if he was to retain personnel. Indians had been breaking into storerooms and making stabbing gestures at women employees. The guns that the agency possessed were stored at Fort Wingate. They were rusty, single-shot carbines, and they were useless. But Eastman cast doubt on his sincerity when he requested permission to purchase the weapons in Grand Haven, Michigan.[44]

In spite of his request for arms and ammunition, Eastman still believed that he could handle his charges. He also assumed that he now had the personnel to begin a change among the Navajos. Three teachers and a doctor had arrived at the agency early in the year, and Eastman had been able to establish a temporary boarding school. Even though enrollment was low, the agent hoped for better results. In addition, he was pleasantly surprised when the Presbyterians finally sent him a missionary, A. H. Donaldson.[45]

On April 16, Eastman headed for Albuquerque to make purchases for the agency. He did not stop at Fort Wingate. This bewildered Captain Bennett, who was temporarily in command. He had received reports of trouble at Fort Defiance and was convinced that it was the agent's fault. Nonetheless, Bennett believed that his relations with the agent had been "most friendly." Later in the morning, Mr. Boynton, the recently appointed Hopi agent, appeared at Wingate with his wife and a female employee. He informed Bennett that he had resigned his position. At noon, the captain had four more visitors. The agency physician, J. B. McNett, and the three teachers, Miss Crepe McNett, R. Eleanor Griffin, and Amanda Easterman, had left Fort Defiance because they feared for their lives.[46]

Bennett had recently held councils with the chiefs, and they had told him that many of the Diné harbored ill feelings toward their agent. He heard firsthand that this hatred now included other employees at the agency. For several weeks, the Indians had been breaking into agency buildings to steal government and private property. On April 6, rations had been issued. The crowd was large, and it became disorderly. Eastman attempted to keep people from pushing each other, and several men threw him to the ground, dragging him "for some distance." Rumors spread five days later that a hostile party of Utes was within thirty miles of Fort Defiance. This gossip seemed to spread to peaceful Navajos as well, for the Indians at the agency stayed in their hogans. Shortly thereafter, a man told one of the teachers that he would soon carry her to his home for carnal pleasures. A Navajo woman who spoke broken English informed the women that they should leave, and the children in the school voiced similar opinions. Other Navajos warned that Eastman would be killed soon.[47]

Dr. McNett carried a letter with him from George Williams. He had expressed anxiety over the situation at the agency and asked the trader for advice. In claiming that there would be "serious trouble," Williams offered the example of an influential man who lived near his trading post. Recently, the man had become contentious.[48] He wrote that the man

came to me and asked for a smoke. Being engaged at the time I told him to wait, when he turned on me in a manner to be appreciated one must see and not have described. I never have seen so much devilishness depicted on the countenance of anything that had any pretensions of being human. He told me that they were going to kill me and all the Americans, [the] men . . . above me [the Hubbells] and at the Moquis [the Keams], also those at Defiance. I certainly could have arrested him and taken him to Ft. Defiance as an example to the others, but fearing such action would be misunderstood by the present Agent, I had to take it all.[49]

Williams further stated that the Navajos were "thoroughly conversant with all the particulars of the Ute outbreak." Referring to the fact that the government had not made large-scale reprisals against the Utes, he was certain that hostile Navajos had been encouraged to act in a similar manner. Williams was convinced that it was the wrong time for people like the doctor to be in

Indian country. Paiutes were murdering people, and bands of Navajos and Utes to the northeast were causing trouble. To make matters worse, the agent, by his actions, taught the Navajos that all Anglo-Americans were their enemies.[50]

Williams was afraid, but he had resolved to continue at his post. Like Williams, Bennett believed that Eastman's poor management could provoke a war. Eastman, who believed that the ring and the army were making the Navajos restless, announced that Dr. McNett and the teachers had fled because of "Scare Stories" manufactured by his enemies. James Sutherland, left in charge in Fort Defiance, accused those who had left with disloyalty. On April 18, McNett sent a letter to Sutherland explaining his reasons for going to Fort Wingate, but the clerk believed that it only offered "indisputable evidence of his identification with the opposing influences to the welfare of this agency." Sutherland, meanwhile, rallied the remaining employees to keep the agency operating, especially the school. He made Reverend Donaldson's wife the matron of the school and Nellie Howe, wife of agency farmer J. W. Howe, the teacher. Reverend Donaldson helped out all he could, but he died of pneumonia on April 30. Eastman's hopes of converting the Navajos seemed to die with him. When the agent returned to Fort Defiance on May 1, he ordered the doctor and teachers to return. Miss Easterman obeyed, over Bennett's strong objections. Eastman then tried to fire the others and claimed that conditions at the agency were satisfactory.[51]

In spite of his optimism, events were not running in Eastman's favor. He could not even control Anson Damon. When the agent recommended that Damon be given title to his land, the commissioner had added a stipulation that the trader marry his Navajo wife. Damon refused, stating that the Navajo ceremony was entirely satisfactory. Although Arizona's antimiscegenation law probably would have made it difficult for Damon to obtain a legal marriage, his refusal caused Eastman some embarrassment.[52]

There was considerable restlessness at Fort Defiance, especially among the young men unable to make a living. Drunkenness was common, but this discontent manifested itself more dramatically at other locations. Friendly Navajos warned settlers at Deer Springs in Apache County, Arizona, to leave their settlement because there would be a Navajo uprising. Other Navajos warned trader Joseph W. Thacker, who maintained a post on the Fort Defiance road. Attorney Albert B. Fountain reported that he was attacked by Navajos near Ojo Analla in southern New Mexico. Pinned under a horse and wounded three times, Fountain was able to fight off his attackers until help arrived. Others were not so lucky. Seven Mexican-American herders were killed by Navajos in the Gallinas Mountains, west of Socorro. Navajos killed two Anglo-Americans in early May, approximately fifty miles northwest of Fort Defiance. The Indians took two hundred dollars, a horse, two mules, saddles, and weapons. Not long after this attack, five or six Navajos ambushed a mail carrier near Bluewater, New Mexico, but the Indians, cutting the bags open, did not steal the mail or seriously injure the man.[53]

Eastman was criticized for this Navajo activity. Aware that he might be called to task, he had James Sutherland solicit statements from two agency employees. John Navajo stated that Eastman had the support of the "Chiefs and Indians of my tribe," and Perry Williams, chief herder, who had lived among the Navajos for sixteen years, declared that the Indians thought of Eastman as a just man. But there were enough doubts about the agent's competence that he was called to Washington on May 10.[54]

Sutherland was in charge during Eastman's absence, but the army did not have any confidence in him either. Late in May, William Evan Golden and John Johnson were attacked by Navajos in the Tunicha Mountains. Golden was killed and Johnson seriously wounded. Johnson managed to escape, and his story seemed to verify rumors that the Diné were preparing for war. Rumors continued to circulate about a Navajo-Ute alliance, and New Mexico Chief Justice L. Bradford Prince warned that there would be a war if Eastman was not removed from office.[55]

The army was concerned enough with the possibility of war

that Colonel Buell was ordered on May 26 to take command of Fort Wingate with six companies of soldiers. He arrived on June 5, and three days later, Buell reported that most of the trouble with the Navajos could be attributed to young men who had little property and had their courage fueled by illegal whiskey. According to the colonel, they had taken Victorio's example to heart; the army had not caught the Apache leader, and many young Navajos believed that they too could commit depredations without suffering punishment. Nevertheless, Buell believed that most of the Navajos wanted to live peacefully and that the chiefs, although angry with their present agent, wanted to maintain order.[56]

Buell made three recommendations to keep the Navajos at peace. First, Victorio had to be captured and punished. Second, the Navajo liquor trade had to be stopped. Suggesting that the president suspend constitutional liberties, the colonel argued that the army be allowed to arrest whiskey sellers and try them in special tribunals; New Mexico juries had a tendency to let bootleggers go. Finally, Buell advised that a firm man with good judgment be appointed agent without delay. He was also certain that there was such a man on the scene, Thomas Keam.[57]

Meanwhile, the commissioner of Indian affairs had also investigated charges of Eastman's incompetence by sending Indian Inspector E. B. Townsend to Fort Defiance. Townsend found the Navajos "restless." Trouble had been caused by "drunken renegades," and some Navajos were purchasing modern weapons. Other Indians had warned settlers that violence was about to erupt. Charging that the Indians had been made "bold, insolent and threatening" by "vicious influences," the inspector nevertheless recommended Eastman's removal because his mismanagement of the agency had "created great dissatisfaction." Morale among employees was low, and Eastman had been unable to deliver goods to needy Navajos. Although Townsend was hesitant to advise Keam's appointment, he felt that the chiefs' preference should be given consideration since the Navajos had had bad luck with agents for the past several years.[58]

Another observer, Charles A. Taylor, missionary to the Hopi, felt that Eastman should resign. The agent, he believed, had been betrayed by men he trusted, and so many false rumors had been circulated about him that his rule of the Navajo was ineffective. In addition, Eastman's life was in danger. Dr. Sheldon Jackson of Colorado was also in the area at the time attempting to recruit Navajo children for the Carlisle Indian School in Pennsylvania. Although he too saw Eastman as a victim, Jackson did not believe that Eastman needed to leave. The Utes and Mormons had been inciting the Navajos, but Eastman was competent for his job.[59]

Regardless of whose opinion was correct, the situation among the Navajos was getting worse. On June 9, the day after Buell wrote his initial report, word came to Fort Wingate that young men were not the only Navajos who were disruptive. Manuelito, perhaps frustrated by his attempts to keep his people out of trouble, showed officials that he could still give the appearance of danger. With a wagonload of whiskey, he and several of his followers traveled along the mail route on a drunken spree. Although not actually assaulting anybody, the old chief's band threatened several settlers as far away as San Mateo. Settlers fled from the legendary warrior, and Buell dispatched Captain J. H. Bradford with twelve men in pursuit. After a march of 134 miles, Bradford was able to turn Manuelito around.[60]

The army concluded that it had to take immediate steps to prevent a Navajo war, for its position in the Southwest was precarious. Troop strength was low. Even though some renegade Mescaleros showed signs of wanting to surrender, Victorio and his Mimbres Apaches were tying down large numbers of troops. Reports were made almost daily of Indian scares throughout Arizona. Buell's soldiers had been pulled out of western Colorado, leaving settlers there open to possible Ute attack. Eastman's removal seemed imperative. Not wanting to fight an old battle with the Indian Bureau, the commander of the department of New Mexico, General John Pope, rejected Buell's suggestion that Thomas Keam be made agent. He recommended that Captain Bennett be put in charge of Fort Defiance temporarily.[61]

General Philip Sheridan endorsed Pope's recommendation and forwarded it to Washington.[62] On the following day, June 9, General Sherman wrote to the secretary of war outlining the urgency of the situation:

> I beg to represent that if from any cause whatever the Navajos, numbering 13,000 souls of whom 2,000 are capable of being most dangerous enemies, become hostile we are in no condition to meet them. I have been in person at their Agency at Old Fort Defiance, New Mexico and believe with ordinary prudence they can be held in peace on their small Reservation, and recommend most earnestly that the Hon. Secretary of Interior consent to the removal or transfer of their present Agent, and that Capt. Frank T. Bennett, 9th U. S. Cavalry be placed in charge of the Navajos at least during the present year. It may save us one of the most complicated and difficult Indian Wars of the century.
>
> The Utes on their north are already hostile—the Apaches on their south always have been hostile. In past years we have had two long & bloody wars with these Navajos, and if as too likely, these Indians join with the Utes and Apaches I repeat we are in no condition to fight them successfully, in one of the most difficult . . . regions of this continent.[63]

The War Department urged the secretary of interior to grant Sherman's request, and the secretary quickly complied. Under orders, the commissioner of Indian affairs instructed Eastman, who had returned to New Mexico, to remain in Albuquerque until further instruction. Receiving authority on June 12, Colonel Buell ordered Bennett to assume command at Fort Defiance. Bennett, who was instructed to relieve Sutherland of his temporary duties and take a "correct inventory," occupied the agency on June 13.[64]

The Navajos had again forced an agent from office. This time, however, it was not completely the chiefs' doing. Once the chiefs had put down the witch scare, Navajo tension and aggression had turned against non-Navajos. The chiefs had cooperated with Eastman during the Navajo dispute with H. L. Mitchell and the border conflict along the San Juan. Eastman's refusal to court the chiefs' favor and his failure to use them to control the young Navajos at Fort Defiance might have been his undoing and possibly might have caused potential troublemakers to believe that no one would punish them if they committed other crimes. Holding authority during a time of drought, Eastman probably erred in not leaving some of the distribution of goods and rations to the chiefs; they may have been more efficient at the task, but even if they were not, they would have had to share the blame with the agent when supplies proved to be inadequate. Although he used the chiefs often enough to settle external disputes with settlers, he was reluctant to use them to protect the agency. As a result, agency employees had reason to panic; he lost their support. In addition, Eastman's inability to work with the army hurt him severely. Neither did he help himself when he attempted to remove the likes of John Lorenzo Hubbell and Thomas Keam from lands included on the new addition to the reservation. The chiefs were again put in the position of having to work with conflicting outposts of United States authority, and confusion resulted. Since the Diné had learned to trust the military more than agents, who did not remain long, Eastman put himself at a disadvantage. In short, he was like his predecessor in that he failed to be political with a people who were becoming very political.

11

Bennett and Eastman

When Frank Tracy Bennett took charge at Fort Defiance on June 12, Galen Eastman was ordered to stay away from the agency, but he was not out of the picture. Agency records were not transferred to Bennett's control, and Eastman was not officially notified that he had been "temporarily suspended" until August. Once he understood his status, Eastman began to lobby Michigan Senator T. W. Ferry to restore his position.[1]

In spite of Eastman's intrigues, Bennett began his task with hopes for success, but nature proved troublesome. The summer of 1880 began under dry conditions, and Navajo crops were threatened. The Diné hoped for moisture, but when rain came in late July it fell so heavily that most fields were washed away. To make matters worse, the winter was severe, and many sheep died.[2]

These conditions added to an already unstable situation. According to Indian Bureau Special Agent E. B. Townsend, who visited Fort Defiance in June, the agency was short of supplies. He found employees "demoralized" and the Navajos "bold, insolent, and threatening." Furthermore, James Sutherland, clerk at the agency, worked to undermine Bennett's authority.[3]

Nevertheless, Bennett appeared to be capable of confronting these problems. Realizing that his appointment was temporary, he hurried to consolidate power and reduce tension. He fired Sutherland and defended the teachers who had fled the agency when violence seemed likely. Bennett appointed his nephew, Harry Sinclair, to Sutherland's position.[4] Even though this appointment left the captain open to charges of nepotism, it did not hurt his cause with the Diné.

Although Bennett faced opposition among some off-reservation Navajos because he had tried to remove them from Fort Wingate grazing lands, he did not have to win the cooperation of the chiefs, who knew him well. As a former agent and soldier, he had worked with them for a long time. After his removal as agent in 1871, he had offered to resign his army commission to become agent in 1872.[5] Having spent nine years with the frontier military, he had come to like the Navajos and to trust the political skills of their leaders. And he was fully prepared to help them restore the peace.

Bennett understood that the chiefs were reluctant to assert their authority by violent means. Despite the fact that they had resorted to force in the past, they preferred persuasion. One of the principal elements of social control in Navajo society was its clan structure. As leaders recognized by the government, they could communicate with leading members of each clan and locality and be reasonably sure that order would be maintained because these leaders could appeal to troublemakers, claiming that violence would bring misfortune to their extended families. For years, leaders needing to restrain raiders simply had to mention the Bosque Redondo. As a result, most Navajo depredations had been moderate, and few non-Navajos had been killed. Now, however, they had to reason with young men who had only vague memories of life along the Pecos; they had heard stories of the horrors of exile, but they were not frightened enough to believe that the army would retaliate. As Colonel Buell had commented, these young men may have been influenced by the fact that Victorio had not been apprehended.[6]

Eastman had made it difficult for leaders who were trying to restrain young militants by refusing to ask the army for help. Bennett, on the other hand, advertised that he would use troops. He had met with the chiefs prior to taking charge, and word was sent out that the captain would use soldiers if he was forced. Results were almost immediate. Navajo violence toward their neighbors came to a halt, and talk of a Navajo war faded. By August, Bennett was so pleased that he wrote that "no community of like population will exhibit so small a record of criminal acts of a flagrant character as the Navajos."[7]

Nevertheless, the causes of Navajo discontent had not gone away, and Bennett was forced to deal with difficulties that had become routine for other agents. The young men were still restless. School enrollment was low, and construction of the boarding school had not been completed. Many less-fortunate Navajos were starving, and despite recent additions to the reservation, the Indians did not have enough land to support themselves. Finally, it was difficult to maintain the fragile peace without a police force. Although authorization had been obtained, Bennett was unable to recruit any policemen because the pay was too low.[8]

As 1880 came to an end, however, not all news was discouraging. Victorio was defeated by Mexican troops in Chihuahua. As the railroad moved its way toward Navajo territory, the Diné began to enter the larger American economy. Traders, who were important in moving them away from subsistence, found it easier to bring in merchandise and to ship Navajo products east. The Navajos, with large numbers of weavers, blacksmiths, and silversmiths, seemed well prepared for this change in their economy. In fact, some Navajos—Manuelito, for instance—were able to cash in directly by obtaining wagons and shipping items to and from the railroad. The traders could offer higher prices for wool because of a rise in demand. In addition, the railroad provided wage work for Navajos, putting money into their economy. These items of good news account, in part, for the fact that there were several rich Navajos.[9]

Bennett was successful because he understood the post–Bosque Redondo Navajo environment, but the Navajo frontier was changing as 1881 began. By November the railroad reached Winslow, Arizona, effectively flanking the Diné to the south. Conflict resulted, of course. Settlers who bought land from the railroad dispossessed Navajos from lands they had long inhabited. The Indians soon learned that the settlements along the line made alcohol more available, and some Navajos objected. Others stole

horses and supplies from the crews, and soldiers from Fort Wingate were sent out as guards.[10]

In such a climate, violence was just a matter of time. On
January 4, Hosteen Dil-gnah-ey-Bagah and his father complained
that three Americans had driven them off land forty miles south
of the agency, at a spring close to the Puerco River, where they
had lived for twenty years. Convinced that General Sherman had
granted them the right to settle off the reservation, they protested
to Bennett, who was sympathetic. To his knowledge, they grew
their own crops and did not depend on the government for provisions. He told the two men to return home and try not to
provoke the settlers. The agent, however, was worried that such
incidents would be more common as the railroad sold more
land.[11]

Violence was not restricted to communities along the railroad,
nor was drunkenness confined to Native Americans. On November 28, a Navajo went to Farmington to trade. While he was
in a store, he was insulted by two Anglo-Americans, James Raser
and Frank Meyers, who had been drinking heavily. When this
harassment failed to provoke him, Raser and Meyers left the
store, stole the Navajo's lariat, and turned his horse loose. A
local boy witnessed this mischief and ran down the horse. When
the boy returned with the animal, the Indian was leaving the
store. The boy gave him the horse and identified Raser as the
lariat thief. The Navajo mounted and rode up to Raser to ask
for his property, only to be pulled from his horse and beaten.
When he resisted, Meyers and Raser drew their pistols. Unarmed,
the Navajo climbed on his horse and began to rush out of town
when the two white men fired. One bullet broke his collarbone.
Bleeding severely, he was barely able to cross the San Juan and
get help.[12]

Two days later, twenty-five or thirty Navajos appeared in
Farmington and demanded that Meyers, who had apparently fired
the offending bullet, be arrested. The Farmington citizens present refused, and it looked as if the Navajos would attack. Fortunately for the town, other citizens talked the Indians out of

an attack. When Captain B. H. Rogers from Fort Lewis, Colorado, investigated the incident, he reported that most of the Diné and many residents of the town felt that the attack was unprovoked.[13]

As the authorities began to gain control of the situation in the north, a double murder occurred along the railroad. On April 8, a Navajo entered a grading camp fifteen miles south of the agency near Cook's Ranch, a location recently mentioned by Bennett as a distribution point for illegal liquor. This man had in his possession a burro, which he traded for five dollars with a Mexican-American worker. Shortly, he returned stating that the agreed-upon price was not enough, refunding the cash, and repossessing the animal. The worker, on the other hand, saw the deal differently and showed his objections to the Indian by shooting him in the stomach, inflicting a fatal wound. Not long afterward, the father or father-in-law (Bennett was not sure) came to the camp and shot the Mexican-American worker. Meanwhile, word had gone out among the Diné, and many gathered. Worried that the violence might escalate, Bennett dispatched two chiefs, Francisco and Juanico, to calm the Navajos. He also requested help from Fort Wingate. When a company of soldiers investigated the matter, they were able to restore the peace without making arrests on either side.[14]

In the middle of this conflict, Lieutenant John G. Bourke, army ethnologist and aide to General George Crook, arrived to do fieldwork among the Pueblos and Navajos. In Navajo country, in April, May, and August, he was introduced to the Indians and their culture by several resident non-Navajos: Frank Bennett; Thomas Keam; William Leonard, Fort Defiance trader; John Lorenzo Hubbell; and Dr. Washington Mathews, post surgeon at Fort Wingate and an ethnologist in his own right. Bourke was impressed by the immensity of the land and its rich grass, and he liked the people, whom he considered friendly, attractive, and intelligent. He especially praised Henry Chee Dodge, who helped him make an outline of the Navajo clans, as well as Ganado Mucho, who was in his seventies and still active. Even though Bourke had journeyed to the reservation to learn Navajo customs, he listened as the Indians complained that the government ignored them because they were peaceful. The hostile Utes and Apaches, they charged, received more supplies than the Diné; supplies, in fact, were so limited that many people did not bother to pick them up. Bourke attributed this to mismanagement of Navajo affairs by incompetent and corrupt agents.[15] He described one of the these agents, Galen Eastman, as a "psalm-singing hypocrite whom the Navajos despised and detested and whom they tried to kill."[16]

Eastman, meanwhile, had not been idle. With the help of Senator Ferry, he had returned to Washington to plead his case. The army had lobbied for the appointment of Thomas Keam, but its efforts had proven futile. Instead, Eastman's exertions paid off, and he returned to Fort Defiance on June 30. Bennett, however, claimed that he had received no authorization to hand over the agency, thus forcing Eastman to exchange telegrams with the Interior Department.[17]

Blaming his exile on military meddling, Eastman took to his duties as though he had never left. Nonetheless, he returned to a farming disaster, the result of another dry spell followed by floods. He found that the presence of the railroad was making whiskey and weapons more available. Despite the agent's confidence, the Navajos were not happy with his return. When he met in council with the chiefs, voices were raised against him. On July 9 and 11, Bennett also met with the Navajo leaders who objected to Eastman. To several observers, rebellion of the Diné seemed evident. Colonel L. P. Bradley, commanding officer at Fort Wingate, worried that Eastman's life was in danger, and he was tempted to send troops to the agency. But the agent refused military help. Afraid that Eastman might do something foolish and provoke his wards, Bradley had a conversation with Manuelito. He convinced the warrior to talk with his fellow leaders, "to see that the Agent is not interfered with in any way." As a result, he believed that Eastman was safe for the time being. Nevertheless, Bradley insisted that there was a long-term danger.[18] He wrote:

> This act of sending an unwelcome Agent back to the Navajoes is wrong and a very unwise thing to do, in all accounts.
> Here is a rich and powerful band of Indians, peaceable, industrious and intelligent, in danger of being made hostile and dangerous by a lack of knowledge, or lack of judgement, on the part of some official. . . . [The Navajos] are well behaved and their interests and wishes are entitled to some consideration.[19]

Bradley could have added that agency employees deserved consideration as well, for they had left Fort Defiance in protest.[20]

Eastman ignored Bradley's warnings, claiming that the situation was not serious and that most of his troubles were caused by the army and a ring of traders based in Santa Fe. The struggle, however, was tiring, and he hoped that he and his son could obtain positions somewhere else now that his name had been cleared. While he waited for word from Washington, he continued to battle for what he thought was right. As far as Eastman was concerned, it was a sin to sell alcohol to Indians. Blaming the railroad for the increased supply, he begged for greater civilian enforcement and claimed that the Navajos wanted whiskey to be kept away from them.[21]

In August, however, Eastman was forced to defend himself, for J. M. Haworth, an inspector from the Department of Interior, arrived at the agency. After conferring with agency employees and the chiefs, Haworth concluded that there was little danger of a Navajo uprising, but he added that Eastman's hold on them was tenuous. Haworth also reported that the missionaries at Fort Defiance were dissatisfied with the agent because he had not supported their efforts.[22]

Eastman was quick to reply that progress was being made on the school building. He also cited an example of the Navajos' progress toward Anglo-American civilization because the Diné— inspired perhaps by Manuelito's entry into the freighting business—wanted wagons. He added that the chiefs had promised their support, despite the fact that they would have preferred Bennett or Keam.[23]

Thomas Keam had little support within the Interior Department. The army believed that, for want of a qualified alternative, Eastman would remain in office and endanger the peace. When Colonel Bradley's warning about Eastman worked its way through the chain of command, it ended up on the desk of General Sherman, who added a note recommending the appointment of Manuelito as agent. As far as he was concerned, the chief was entirely capable of doing the job, provided he had clerical help.[24]

Commissioner of Indian Affairs Hiram Price did not take the general's suggestion seriously. Instead, he put his support behind Eastman. It was the agent's honesty, according to Price, that had gotten him into trouble with "interested parties in the neighborhood of the reservation." Specifically mentioned were George M. Williams, who owned a trading post a few miles east of Hubbell's store, and William B. Leonard. According to the commissioner, they had influenced the Navajos. Ganado Mucho, for example, had told Inspector Haworth that most of his opposition to Eastman had been because Williams had given him a "black blanket" in return for his support of Thomas Keam.[25]

While the Keam-Eastman controversy went unresolved, Eastman was forced to deal with the fact that Navajos were living away from their reservation. During the summer, an Apache mystic, Noch-ay-del-Klinne, predicted that all the Anglo-Americans would leave Apache country; then there would be a resurrection of the dead. When he seemed on the verge of uniting the Western Apaches, he was killed by an army guide at Cibecue. As a result, many Chiricahuas bolted for Mexico, with the army in pursuit. Although several Apache families attempted unsuccessfully to flee to safety among the Diné, the Navajos were not involved.[26] Nevertheless, the tribe was affected.

As a consequence of the Apache outbreak, General Sherman ordered that all Indians found off their reservations be considered hostile. Eastman—who obtained a ruling from the commissioner that Navajos could obtain homesteads on the public domain under laws passed in 1875 and 1880—protested, asking that the Navajos be exempted. Sherman wrote that he had not intended to cover peaceful tribes, such as the Navajos, with his directive.

Meanwhile, however, Eastman had felt compelled to move approximately eighty-five Navajos from the Puerco River to the reservation.[27]

As the drought intensified, other Navajos left the lands designated to them by treaty. In October, for example, a number of them ventured north of the San Juan River, into the vicinity of the Mormon settlement of Bluff, Utah. Mormon leaders complained. Eastman ordered his wards to return to the reservation. Nevertheless, when such disputes over land concerned other Native Americans, Navajos were not forced to move. For instance, Navajos, who were allegedly pasturing their horses on Zuni land, became involved in a dispute with ethnologist Frank Hamilton Cushing, who lived among the Zuni. He led a Zuni expedition that shot several Navajo horses. Eastman demanded that the Navajos be allowed to stay where they were and that the Zunis pay one hundred dollars in reparations. In addition, Navajos were getting too close to the Hopi for their comfort, and Eastman had to send Ganado Mucho to restore peace between the two tribes of his ancestry.[28]

Ganado Mucho was busy restoring peace on more than one front. In early November, he brought Eastman news that one of his people had been killed by a drunken Texas cowboy in the new railroad town of Holbrook. Soon, friends of the victim inquired of a white citizen about the identity of the murderer. This bystander pointed him out, and the Indians shot the criminal dead. Upon hearing the chief's story, the agent agreed to go to Holbrook to investigate. Eastman, who took the train with an interpreter, met Ganado Mucho and thirty Navajos at Holbrook, and the situation was resolved. No one in the town blamed the Indians, and all that the Navajos demanded were the dead man's effects, items which were quickly turned over to his wife and brother.[29]

If Eastman could claim success for his negotiations in Holbrook, he could not hold the support of his employees. Two of the teachers, J. D. Perkins and his wife, complained constantly of minor ethical violations by Eastman, and they charged that the agent was taking supplies intended for the Indians and appropriating them for his own use.[30] Mrs. Perkins became so frustrated that she wrote, on November 7, that "Mr. Eastman has no friends here, he is hated by everyone."[31]

Eastman had developed skill in weathering political storms, and it is doubtful that such criticism gave him any pause. But it is also true that he had little time for reflection. On the day of his return from Holbrook, he received news that Narbono and his people had frightened coal miners at Mineral Spring, near Gallup. Fearing violence, he sent Narbono back to the mining camp with an interpreter and a written message explaining that the chief's people had meant no harm. Nonetheless, not all confrontations along the railroad could be labeled as misunderstandings. In early December, Eastman was forced to send a chief to McCarty's Ranch to apprehend a Navajo guilty of a minor crime.[32]

There was no letup in conflict and controversy as 1882 began. The army complained that there were Navajos in the vicinity of Fort Apache; Eastman admitted that he had given his wards permission to be there because food was scarce and they needed to hunt.[33] In addition, the agent had to confront other problems. First, the Diné were arming themselves rapidly, and he had to report that the Indians had five hundred revolvers, one hundred magazine rifles, and three hundred muzzle-loading rifles—a considerable increase from earlier estimates. Secondly, he worried that he might be killed. Convinced that Thomas Keam had been responsible for Agent Miller's murder, Eastman confessed to Senator Ferry that he often thought of the other agents who had died in office.[34]

As January ended, charges came in from the railroad that Navajos were placing obstacles on the tracks to stop the train. Eastman conferred with Tanysusa, the headman along the Puerco River, who denied that his people were guilty. Eastman, however, insisted that such actions not happen again, and the chief promised to catch anyone who tampered with the tracks.[35]

Such misunderstandings were experienced often. Rations and

supplies to the Navajos had been cut, yet whiskey had become more available. As railroad workers, soldiers, and residents of St. Johns took advantage of cheaper and more easily obtained merchandise, the Diné tried to cope with the consequences of alcohol in a society that, until recently, had avoided the drug.[36] Although it may now seem inevitable that Navajo culture would have to adapt to alcohol within its midst, few people in the 1880s believed that any reconciliation could be made among Navajos who wanted to drink, entrepreneurs who wanted to sell to them, and the reformers—both Navajo and non-Navajo—who wanted to bar the substance completely.

The reactions of Anglo-American officials, therefore, were in line with the larger generalizations of nineteenth-century America. Eastman implied that the situation had a great deal to do with the fact that the peaceful Diné were not as well supplied with rations as the hostile Apaches. Despite his economic reasoning, the agent felt that increased police enforcement would contribute to a solution, and he urged that detectives be employed to apprehend bootleggers.[37]

The dilemma of alcohol, however, was intensified by the fact that the new railroad town of Gallup was wide open. Named for railroad paymaster David L. Gallup, the town was little more than a few shacks and saloons catering to railroad workers, soldiers, and Indians. Soon there were so many drunk Navajos that Eastman built a jail at Fort Defiance. In the meantime, residents of Gallup were also concerned about drunks, attacking a saloon owner, and destroying his establishment and stock. Simultaneously, George Williams circulated a rumor that the Diné were ready to wage war to rid the country of new arrivals.[38]

As a result, the army, not trusting Eastman, proposed its own solution. Colonel R. S. Mackenzie, new commander of the district of New Mexico and hero of the Apache wars, proposed that more soldiers be brought to Fort Lewis. Claiming that Mackenzie wanted to start a Navajo war to further his military career, Eastman objected to the colonel's plan.[39]

The Diné complained about new arrivals crossing their territory. In mid-February, Manuelito charged that whites traveling through his territory had committed depredations. One of his camps had been fired into by Anglo-American intruders, and one of his watchdogs was killed. The chief also claimed that prospectors were burning down hogans and bothering people while exploring for minerals.[40]

In Farmington, more serious conflict occurred. A Navajo appeared at Spencer's Store and stole a bolt of calico. The storekeeper fired a warning shot from his revolver as the thief ran out the door. Outside, on the street, stood Tom Nance, a cowboy widely known as a killer; he shot the fleeing man in the back, inflicting serious injury. The news of the wounded Indian circulated across the northern end of Navajo country, and a large crowd marched toward Farmington. At Gallegos Canyon, eight miles south of the San Juan, General Horace Porter's house was burned. It was only through the efforts of Dr. John Brown, a local physician friendly with the Diné, that further trouble was avoided.[41]

Colonel Buell, now in command of Fort Lewis, investigated, criticized Eastman's inaction, and offered an analysis of Farmington that could long be applied to towns bordering the reservation. Local businessmen, he found, did not object to the proximity of the Navajos; in fact, they welcomed it, for the trade in wool and pelts was extremely profitable. The ranchers, on the other hand, who competed with Navajos for grazing land on the public domain, fostered resentment, holding that Indians should have no rights off the reservation. The Navajos understood this resentment and were arming rapidly. Buell added that a Navajo boy had burned Porter's house and that a chief had insisted that the boy's father punish him severely.[42]

Eastman ignored Buell's criticism, but he could not disregard events closer to home. On March 11, several drunks appeared at Fort Defiance on ration day and caused a disturbance. The agent sent to Fort Wingate for help; upon further consideration, however, he withdrew his request. Four days later, Eastman received word that a Navajo had been killed by a train at Navajo

Springs. The deceased's friends were demanding five hundred dollars in compensation; not understanding Navajo custom, railroad officials refused to pay. Nonetheless, Eastman headed off trouble by convincing the company to reconsider. It ultimately gave the dead man's relatives forty dollars' worth of farm equipment, to which the agent added a harness.[43]

Unfortunately, this peace could not be duplicated at the agency. School was closed temporarily because of Navajo drunkenness. Plagued with nonattendance of students and fearing that Eastman had lost all respect from the Indians, teachers openly complained. Eastman recommended that they all be fired.[44] His suggestion was ignored by his superiors, and he had to weather further criticism when an unofficial inspector from the Justice Department, R. S. Martin, appeared in April.

Martin reported that Eastman had no support among the Diné. They considered him a liar, and a war with the Navajos seemed inevitable if the agent was not removed. Upon the recommendations of officers at Fort Wingate and other whites living in the area, the inspector suggested that Thomas Keam be made agent. Eastman flatly denied the charges, suggested that reports of a Navajo uprising were highly exaggerated, and demanded that Martin be fired for drinking gin while visiting the agency.[45]

Martin's charges, however, were not the only accusations leveled at Eastman during the month. Manuelito asked that the government appoint a new agent who could get his people more supplies. Eastman tried to explain that he distributed all that he had been given, but his logic was lost on the chief whom the agent claimed was under the influence of schemers from Fort Wingate and Santa Fe.[46] Soon, Eastman took an opportunity to get even. He wrote the commissioner:

> "Manuelito" is the biggest drunkard in this tribe and because of his large influence . . . is the greatest stumbling block in the way of reform this tribe has to contend with—He promised faithfully two years ago to quit it [whiskey], and he intended to do so, but he now says he knows it is bad for the Navajos to drink it, but as for him, he learned to love it when he was very young, that army officers taught him (Captain B. & others)

and used to give it to him or place it where he could get it *at will*—and he feels that he is now unable & too old to reform etc., he has recently as I learn from his neighbor Indians been off on a drunk and in returning home was thrown from his horse and badly injured.[47]

Despite the fact that Manuelito was temporarily laid up, liquor was involved in another incident.

In late April, Navajos rustled cattle from a ranch three miles east of Gallup; cowboys followed in hot pursuit and took back the animals. When the Indians objected, approximately thirty shots were fired, leaving one dead Navajo and another wounded. Word soon reached Gallup that the Diné were angry and intent on killing the town's population. Panic followed, a train was prepared to evacuate women and children, and help was requested from Fort Wingate. Lieutenant Jesse C. Chance investigated and claimed that alcohol was the cause of the Indians' criminal behavior. But he assumed that the Navajos had exhausted their anger and returned to the fort. Two days later, however, troops had to occupy Gallup because of continued Navajo threats, with the situation not reaching a solution until 250 sheep were given to the family of the dead man.[48]

As the new month began, the chiefs met in council and decided to force Eastman out of office. When they visited Fort Defiance on May 12, they told Eastman that they intended to put him in a wagon and drive him from the reservation, but they did not act because Ganado Mucho urged delay and because the agent promised to resign as soon as someone was appointed to take his place. They did not believe him, so they spoke with Thomas Keam, who wrote to Washington to express their concerns. But no one in the Indian bureaucracy believed that the trader was doing anything more than promoting his own interests.[49]

Eastman's reaction was within character. He stated that he had never been afraid of the Navajos, and he would not resign under pressure, especially from Keam. He also convinced Henry Chee Dodge to write a conditional letter of support, in which the interpreter stated that the Diné were not hostile toward their agent; they just wanted an agent who could get them more supplies.[50]

June permitted Eastman an opportunity to harm Keam's reputation, when Philip Zoeller, a former prospector who had worked as a clerk at Keam's store, appeared at Fort Defiance with a story involving Keam. According to Zoeller, Keam and Smithsonian ethnologist James Stevenson had plotted to mine Monument Valley silver. He claimed that Keam had been involved in the Merrick and Mitchell murders. The prospectors' weapons and pack animals had been brought to Keam and, in the very least, the trader knew who had killed them. Eastman jumped at the opportunity to embarrass his rival and sent Chee Dodge and the agency farmer to Monument Valley with two prospectors, Jonathan P. Williams and William Ross.[51]

As Eastman waited for their report, complaints of Navajo depredations crossed his desk. D. S. Sayer of Mancos, Colorado, complained that Navajos had stolen from him. The agent replied that he would send a delegation to investigate and that if any Navajos were guilty, he would return the property. He was less friendly when two Zunis came to the agency with a letter blaming Navajos for stealing two horses. He gathered the thieves and the Zunis together, listened to both sides, decided in favor of the accusers, and returned the animals. Nonetheless, Eastman continued to press the matter of the horses shot by Cushing. He wrote Cushing, demanding payment. Cushing was not an easy opponent, and the money was not forthcoming.[52]

As the summer progressed, Eastman received more bad news. An inspector for the Department of Interior, C. H. Howard, visited the reservation. Howard took note of large numbers of Navajos living away from their official lands, and he suggested that the reservation be expanded by one hundred miles to the west; then all of the Diné should be forced to live on it, except those who had occupied the public domain for more than two years.[53]

Howard was not so lenient on the agent. The agency at Fort Defiance was ill prepared to deal with the Navajos' many problems because it was poorly funded and the agent could not do his job. He could not control his wards because they did not trust him. In addition, he had not been able to organize a police force. Finally, Eastman had not traveled about the reservation to become acquainted with the people. Therefore, the inspector recommended that Eastman should be replaced by a stronger man.[54]

Howard's report, however, took awhile to work through the Washington bureaucracy. Word reached Eastman in July that Navajos had raided north of the San Juan, robbed a house, and stolen eleven horses. After looking into the matter, he determined what had happened. In May, some Navajos had lost three good horses, which had run north of the reservation boundary. They approached their agent, asking permission to leave the reserve to look for their animals. Eastman agreed to their request and wrote out a pass. When they crossed the San Juan, however, they were intercepted by a company of soldiers under the command of Captain J. W. Beam. The Navajos showed the officer their passes. According to Eastman, the passes were "dishonored." The soldiers seized their weapons and blankets, holding them in custody for twenty-four hours. When the Indians were released, their possessions were returned.[55]

Once these men were free, they continued the search for their lost horses, but they were hungry. Therefore, when they came upon an unoccupied house that afternoon, they stopped to eat. Their meal finished, they confiscated some property from the house and resumed their journey. It was not long until they came across their horses corralled at a ranch. Realizing the purpose of their trip, they confiscated the animals and began their return home. Shortly, however, an opportunity to practice the "old spirit of reprisal" presented itself. At a neighboring ranch, they stole eleven horses.[56]

Upon receipt of this news, Eastman dispatched a Navajo leader, Francisco, to the scene where, after three trips from Fort Defiance, he managed to negotiate a return of the stolen horses. The agent was grateful to the chief, who had followed orders even though the people involved "did not belong to his band." Nonetheless, the only rewards that Eastman was able to bestow upon this loyal man were a few meager supplies, many of which were from Eastman's personal stock. In spite of this discrepancy, when the agent received word in August that Navajos were again grazing their flocks north of the San Juan, the chief dutifully went out to try his skill at convincing his tribesmen to move south. Within a month, Eastman was able to report that Francisco's efforts were successful.[57]

In August, Chee Dodge's delegation returned from its investigation in Monument Valley. From the reports of Dodge, Williams, and Ross, Eastman concluded that good relations had been established with Hoskaninni. As a result, the agent expressed the opinion that the northern chief's followers would not bother any more prospectors in Monument Valley. Ross and Williams returned with stories implicating Thomas Keam in the Merrick and Mitchell murders. Hoskaninni had talked to them, and the old chief said that he had been told by Keam that he would soon be agent. Keam had given him a gun that had belonged to one of the dead prospectors. Zoeller confirmed the stories of Ross and Williams. When he was living in Keams Canyon, he had seen Keam discussing matters with Hoskaninni and the Paiute chief, San-a-pee, who had taken part in the killing of Mitchell and Merrick. Eastman forwarded these reports to his superiors, who refused to do any further investigating.[58]

The failure of Washington officials to go along with Eastman's assessment of Keam's alleged involvement in murder probably had to do with the fact that their confidence in the agent had waned. Howard's report had reached them, and they were no longer willing to trust him. Thus, on September 15, Eastman, responding to Washington's distrust, resigned his position, effective December 31.[59]

Eastman's resignation, however, did not reduce tension on the Navajo frontier. By October, economic conditions were so bad that Eastman allowed several groups of Navajos to hunt north of the reservation. The agent's action led to a reaction from the military. Captain Beam, who had been assigned to the task of moving the Diné back to the reservation, complained that on a single day he had seen forty-six passes signed by Eastman. The captain understood that he had to honor the passes, even though they complicated his job. Nevertheless, he suspected that the agent had allowed so many of his wards off the reservation to extend the Indians' available land. Eastman, however, ordered Navajos grazing their flocks north of the boundary to withdraw to the south.[60]

Eastman's orders were apparently followed, for when soldiers from Fort Lewis investigated the region in November there were no Navajos present. Despite this news, the weather turned bad in predictable fashion, and a Navajo scout on a Gallup drinking spree died of exposure near the railroad in December. As Eastman received this information, there was little he could do except to record it, for on the last day of the month he was relieved of duty.[61] Thus, the Peace Policy among the Navajos ended with little fanfare. Navajos had not changed according to the plans of the reformers or the government, but they had changed to meet new conditions. The chiefs had allied themselves with the military to achieve their purposes, and they achieved some degree of victory. In the fourteen years since the signing of the treaty, they had managed to buy their people some time. Rather than capitulating to their conquerors, the Navajos, as represented by their leaders, had cooperated when their interests were at stake and simultaneously demanded their rights. It had proved to be a useful policy that left Grant's Peace Policy looking naive in conception and corrupt in execution.

12

The Decline
of the Chiefs

G alen Eastman was the last of the Peace Policy agents to
the Navajos. The dream of Protestant missionaries to
isolate Indians from "bad elements" and to ease them
into the mainstream of American life was a failure. Isolation
proved impossible; therefore, a gradual change in the thinking
of reformers took hold. If reservations proved to be ineffective
laboratories for social engineering, it was because they allowed
native cultures to survive. The reformers urged that the Indians
needed to have a sense of property to be truly ready for the
benefits of American civilization. The Dawes Allotment Act,
with the expressed purpose of individualizing Indian landhold-
ings, was passed in 1887 at the urging of reformers. It would be
implemented to break up reservations.[1]

The Navajos were not directly affected by the Dawes Act,
although provisions of the law would eventually be used to expand their territory. Unfortunately for the Diné, territorial officials in Arizona and New Mexico would increase their demands
that Navajo land use be limited to the reservation. But all of that
was in the future. As the new agent, Dennis M. Riordan, took
control in January of 1883, the Navajos were entering a time of
relative prosperity.[2]

Riordan, like Thomas Keam, had come from California. A
politician, he had moved to Arizona Territory for his health.
Although there were numerous testaments to his honesty and
competence, Riordan was not appointed by the Presbyterian board.
His motives for accepting the job in Fort Defiance were not
totally honorable. Rumors had continued to circulate throughout the Southwest that gold and silver could be found in unex-
plored reaches of the Navajo territory. In partnership with Arizona

Governor F. A. Trittle, the new agent wanted the job because it would put him closer to potential mines.[3]

Riordan soon concluded that he did not like Eastman. Calling him an "inert mass of gainlous [sic] obstinacy," he believed that the former agent had stolen from Navajo appropriations. On January 19, Riordan met with the chiefs. Manuelito and Ganado Mucho were the spokesmen, and they reported to the new government representative that they had lost heart under Eastman's rule. In fact, they did not care whether or not they did wrong. According to Riordan, they claimed that Eastman's presence gave them rheumatism; their heads and their legs hurt, and as a result, they had drunk whiskey. Manuelito promised, now that Eastman was gone, he would drink no more. Ganado Mucho added that Eastman had been unfair in distributing goods.[4]

The meeting with the chiefs was hosted by Thomas Keam. Riordan's conference did the trader little good because the agent was not long in condemning Keam for not stocking enough merchandise. In general, he believed that traders tended to stir up trouble.[5] Nevertheless, Keam and other traders continued to be important in Navajo affairs.

Keam expanded his trading post and presented one of his older buildings to the government, joined the Indian Rights Association to advocate reforms that would help the Navajos and Hopis, and did ethnological work until his return to England in 1902. Meanwhile, John Lorenzo Hubbell continued his work at Ganado and opened trading posts in eight other locations within a forty-mile radius of his store. He also became politically active, running successfully in 1882 for Apache County sheriff. Serving two terms, Hubbell put himself in the center of fights between sheepmen and cattle ranchers. At times, his life was in danger, but he survived and continued his work in Indian trading. With his partner, C. N. Cotton, he set out to turn the Navajo trade in blankets into a profitable business—in the process helping the Diné to switch from the production of blankets to that of rugs and standardizing the quality of the Indians' weaving. As a result, he became a rich man. Like Thomas Keam, he sought to improve conditions among the Navajos, becoming almost a fanatic in his campaign against liquor on the reservation and convincing the Presbyterians to build a hospital in Ganado, despite the fact that he was a Catholic. In addition, he became a famous host who entertained political and literary celebrities who visited the area. In 1912, Hubbell made an unsuccessful bid for a United States Senate seat from the new state of Arizona. Nevertheless, he led a long and important life among the Navajos.[6]

Keam and Hubbell were transitional figures who had matured during the Peace Policy years, yet they were able to adapt after it was over. Dennis Riordan, on the other hand, was a new breed of agent. Since the Navajos' return from exile, the Presbyterian and military agents had delegated power to the chiefs. As soon as Riordan arrived, native leaders lost power because he directed Navajo policy from Fort Defiance. Soon discovering that his task was impossible, he became disillusioned.[7] He wrote:

> The labor demanded of an agent here is such to prevent his [the agent] performing any of his duties in a satisfactory manner. The reservation embraces about 10,000 square miles of the most worthless land. . . . An Illinois or Iowa or Kansas farmer would laugh to scorn the assertion that you could raise anything there. However, 17,000 Indians manage to extract their living from it without government aid. If they were not the best Indians on the continent, they would not do it.
>
> No help is given to the indigent and helpless Indians, the agent being compelled to see them suffer . . .[8]

Riordan added that he did not feel that the government would ever keep its promises to the Navajos.[9]

In connection with these complaints, Riordan pushed for increased funding for a police force. After his request, authorization was obtained for such a force—for fifteen men at eight dollars a month. When this sum did not attract candidates, the agent lobbied for more money. Finally, in 1884, a wage of fifteen dollars a month—plus rations, arms, and clothing—was set. Henry Chee

Dodge was made acting chief at a salary of six hundred dollars a year.[10] Unlike the police under Keam and Arny, these men were not chiefs, and they owed their allegiance to the agent.

Riordan, however, had other, more personal considerations. The housing for the agent, for instance, was inadequate. His living quarters were infested with vermin, and snakes crawled out of the walls. Whenever it rained, the floors were flooded. Often he had to tie his children to chairs to keep them from getting wet. "I have seen," he wrote, "my wife, a delicate lady, and who was at that time nursing a baby, walking around with wet feet on the floors of the agent's palatial quarters in a freezing atmosphere, and there wasn't a dry room or a warm room in the house."[11]

With this dissatisfaction in mind, Riordan submitted his resignation in June of 1883; it was not accepted. Instead, two special investigators were sent out in August, and one of them remained for six weeks to help the agent with the work load. Pessimistic about the plight of his wards and convinced that the government was not sincere in its promises, Riordan dutifully carried out his responsibilities until opportunity presented itself. Edward Everett Ayer had established a lumber mill in Flagstaff. Ayer was looking for a man to run the operation when the agent wrote him a letter concerning the purchase of Navajo handicrafts. Ayer was so impressed by the quality of Riordan's communication that he inquired with the Department of Interior concerning the agent's abilities. He was told that Riordan was the best Indian agent in the country. With this in mind, he contacted Riordan, who was in Washington, D.C., and arranged an interview in Chicago. When the two men met, a chemistry was established, and Riordan was offered a position at the Flagstaff mill for ten thousand dollars per year—an eighty-five-hundred-dollar increase in salary—and he accepted.[12]

On April 4, 1884, Riordan submitted his resignation. This time it was granted, effective as soon as a qualified replacement could be found. Nevertheless, the agent was given a leave of absence, beginning April 20. Even though he had curtailed their authority, the chiefs, meeting in council and respecting his honesty, voted to increase his salary by one thousand dollars to get him to stay. Touched by their action, Riordan attempted to withdraw his resignation, but it was too late. Therefore, he moved to his new assignment and was so successful that he was able to buy the lumber mill in 1887. He became a rich man who, like Keam and Hubbell, would speak on behalf of the Diné.[13]

The agents who succeeded Riordan hardly matched his talents and honesty, and none of them remained long enough to get much accomplished—during the next ten years there were five agents. Nonetheless, they were like Riordan in that they relied less on the chiefs and more on the Navajo Police and the army. The first was John Bowman, the former sheriff of Gunnison County, Colorado. He was an energetic man who took to his task willingly. Noticing that there were conflicts between the employees of the agency, he fired several of them and made improvements around Fort Defiance. Unfortunately, Bowman was a womanizer, and this habit provided him with grief. When one of his lovers followed him from Colorado, he installed her as a matron of the school's dorm, an action that angered his wife and gave disgruntled employees a chance to attack his moral character. Forced to resign, he would spend many years in Navajo country.[14]

The next agent, S. S. Patterson, a lawyer from Newton, Iowa, was not as energetic. He believed that the Indians should live exclusively on the reservation, and he blamed the traders for influencing them otherwise. Removed from office for padding the payroll and for his inability to get along with the teachers, he was replaced by Charles E. Vandever, also from Iowa. Vandever had been chief of the Navajo Police and was recommended for his position by the Indian Rights Association. He was removed because he became addicted to morphine. Although the circumstances of his removal were embarrassing to his sponsoring organization, he was able to do a better job in recruiting students for the schools than any of the agents who preceded him.[15]

David L. Shipley, who took charge in December of 1890, was

257

also from Iowa. Like Patterson, he took no pleasure from friendship with his wards. As far as he was concerned, the Diné were a primitive people addicted to gambling and devoted to a religion that was the grossest form of superstition. Even though he condemned Navajo morality, Shipley was accused of graft and nepotism. His downfall, however, had to do with the agency school. He was even better at bringing in students than Vandever. The trademark of his success, however, was the use of force, which led to a negative Navajo reaction. Shipley barely escaped death and later had to face Navajo complaints against conditions in the schools.[16]

When Shipley resigned and left the territory, he was replaced by Lieutenant Edwin H. Plummer, Tenth U.S. Cavalry. His term of office was marked with the efficiency demonstrated by other military agents. Most notable among his accomplishments was bringing a contingent of his wards to the 1893 World's Columbian Exposition in Chicago. Although the lieutenant's stated purpose for the trip was to show the Navajos the benefits of American civilization, it helped to promote a favorable impression of the Diné among people in the East and to educate buyers about the value of Navajo products. Education of another kind also highlighted Plummer's administration, for he used persuasion to fill the school at Fort Defiance, and he built another one at Tohatchi, New Mexico. Nevertheless, Plummer resigned in November of 1894, giving as his reason the burden of too much paperwork.[17]

It came as no surprise that Tohatchi was the first reservation school erected away from the agency, for this community, and the rest of the Chuska Valley, fell within Manuelito's territory. The chief had long favored Anglo-American education, and his followers had requested a school for the area as early as 1876.[18] In the early 1880s, Manuelito revealed his educational philosophy to Henry Chee Dodge. He said:

My grandchild, the whites have many things which we Navajos need. But we cannot get them. It is as though the whites were in a grassy

canyon and there they have wagons, plows, and plenty of food. We Navajos are up on a dry mesa. We can hear them talking but we cannot get
to them. My grandchildren, education is the ladder. Tell our people to
take it.[19]

This statement, along with several of his other accomplishments, would deny the charges of agents who claimed that Manuelito was simply an alcoholic and a beggar; instead, the old
chief had also become a man of vision.

It was not long, however, until Manuelito's convictions were
tested. Sheldon Jackson, superintendent of Presbyterian Missions for the Rocky Mountain West, had been in Navajo country
recruiting students for the Carlisle Indian School in Pennsylvania since 1880. Manuelito agreed to send two sons and a nephew
to the school. Tragically, in 1883, when one of his sons, Manuelito Chow, and the nephew returned during the summer, the
boy was dead of tuberculosis within a week. The chief reacted
violently to the death, saying that he no longer cared what happened to his people, and he demanded that all the boys sent to
Carlisle be brought home at once. Agent Riordan agreed to send
for Manuelito's other son, Manuelito Chiquito, but not the other
students.[20] Quickly, however, another tragedy struck. Riordan
wrote to R. H Pratt, director of the school, in September:

> Am afraid we will have an up-hill pull of it for a while. The deaths of
> Jacks [apparently a student who died at Carlisle] and Manuelito Chow
> created a feeling which was hard to combat; but to add to my embar-
> rassment the boy who accompanied Manuelito Chow home (I forget his
> name) and who the last time I saw him was apparently perfectly well,
> died about a week ago. It is too bad. Really too bad. One can reason till
> the cows come home but he cannot remove the feeling of superstitious
> dread with which these people associate with the cause of education
> when these Carlisle boys are mentioned.[21]

Superstitious or not, the dread continued, for Manuelito's other
son at Carlisle died. Nevertheless, there were still Navajo students there as late as 1885. Even more remarkable, Manuelito

got over his bitterness and again endorsed education in 1891.[22]

Despite Manuelito's support, the new boarding school failed to educate many Navajo children. Between 1881 and 1892, attendance ranged from a low of thirty-three and a high of ninety.[23] Part of this problem had to do with the fact that conditions were poor at the school. Riordan wrote, for example:

> When a blanket Indian came into our school today and took one of our pupils out for the purpose of cleaning him up I could stand it no longer. I felt it a damnable disgrace to me and to the government that such a thing was possible. The Indian was dead right.[24]

Many Navajo students, finding the situation at Fort Defiance intolerable, ran away. In 1884, Agent Bowman relied on the Navajo Police as guards to prevent runaways. The parents also objected, with those in Chinle and Ganado claiming that Fort Defiance was an unhealthy location and demanding schools in their own communities. And all over the reservation, rumors spread that white people were evil and not to be trusted with children.[25]

The agents and the government tried to improve the school. Employees were fired. Reflecting the late nineteenth-century attitude that vocational education was most appropriate for racial minorities, agents made attempts to establish an industrial curriculum. Finally, in 1887, Congress passed a law requiring all Indian parents to send their children to school. This act, along with the growth of off-reservation boarding schools, did little to bring in more pupils. Eventually, force was used as a recruiting method. In 1890, for example, Agent Vandever sent thirty-one Navajo children to the boarding school in Grand Junction, Colorado, without parental consent. Ironically, almost half of them ran away during the first year.[26]

The Navajos received so little consideration regarding their children that it was probably inevitable that a rebellion would break out. David Shipley had the honor of being its cause. Riding with the Navajo Police all over the reservation, he apprehended children, placed them in a buckboard, and carried them off to school. After about a year of enduring such treatment, the Diné were in a contentious mood, and a local leader from Lukachukai, Black Horse, tapped their feelings and preached against the school. By hiding in the Carrizo Mountains, Black Horse had escaped Kit Carson's soldiers. Known as a stubborn traditionalist, he was so charismatic that he could hold the attention of any audience.[27]

In October of 1892, Shipley noticed that no students had been recruited from Black Horse's region of the reservation. With seven policemen, the agency interpreter Frank Walker, Henry Chee Dodge, and the school's industrial teacher, Shipley stopped for the first night in Tsaile. At that spot high in the mountains, Shipley divided his forces the next day. He ordered two police-men to go to Lukachukai to order Black Horse to allow them to collect students; he sent Walker and two policemen to Canyon de Chelly; and he pushed on to Round Rock where Dodge owned a trading post in partnerhsip with Stephen E. Aldrich.[28]

At Round Rock, the Indians had formed two factions, those who were resigned to sending their children to school and those who were not. Left-handed Mexican Clansman remembered that he and his friend, as young boys, were excited about attending school. His grandfather had told him that school was unavoid-able and that he should make the best of it. There also was admiration for Chee Dodge, who had learned the white man's ways and had become rich; maybe a young man who went to school could equal his success. Black Horse, on the other hand, provided the other faction with powerful leadership. He had al-ready arrived on the scene, and with his dynamic personality and some well-defined arguments, he was able to prevail.[29]

Soon after Shipley's arrival, Black Horse rode from his camp up to the trading post with a number of followers. He and Shipley, and several well-armed Navajos, crowded into Dodge's store for a council. Shipley quickly showed his impatience, and perhaps a bit of fear, by threatening Black Horse with harsh punishment if he interfered. The Navajo leader was unimpressed. He com-plained of unhealthy conditions at the school. It was overcrowded, and the children were fed poorly. Many of them got sick. As he lost himself in his arguments, Black Horse showed his radicalism by upping the ante. He demanded that all children presently in school be released immediately and that all traders be forced to leave the reservation. His followers became so angry that they charged Shipley and dragged him and two of his policemen outside, where they beat them. Shipley's nose was broken, and one of the policemen was clubbed. It took the combined efforts of friendly Navajos, Chee Dodge, and his clerk to pull the pathetic representative of civilization free, escort him safely into the store, and bar the door. Dodge loaned his horse to a policeman who was his brother-in-law; thus, Shipley was able to get a message to Lieutenant W. C. Brown, who was camped at Tsaile with a detachment of soldiers. Meanwhile, a thirty-six-hour seige followed at Dodge's trading post, with angry Indians shouting threats from the outside. Some even tried to burn down the store. Fortunately for those inside, it was raining. Finally, Brown arrived with his soldiers and rescued the agent, who retreated to Fort Defiance without any new children for his school.[30]

Shipley wanted to have Black Horse arrested and jailed, but the army was reluctant. When the agent called the chiefs together in council, he tried to get them to discuss the arrest of Black Horse. The chiefs, however, would only complain about conditions in the school. Eventually, Shipley feared for his life and resigned his job.[31] Compulsory education would long be a serious issue, well into the twentieth century.

Potentially more serious clashes came as a result of increased Anglo-American settlement in the area. Although much of this conflict originated with the close contact of culturally dissimilar people, the primary cause was disagreement over land title, and its outcomes were the most violent of the late nineteenth century. The Navajos found themselves more or less successfully defending their frontiers to the north, the east, and the south, while attempting to expand their living space in the west. The Diné fought these battles according to tactics perfected since 1868—by holding or occupying land and only occasionally resorting to violence. The worst upheaval was to the northeast and along the San Juan River, where this once sparsely populated area now had the highest concentration of Navajos and an extremely militant Anglo-American citizenry. To the east and south, conflict was extensive, but the situation, moderated by the profitable Navajo trade along the railroad, eventually developed into a stalemate. Also contributing to this standoff was the fact that the government did not want to provoke a Navajo war and it was unwilling to force the Diné to live exclusively on the reservation.[32]

To the west, conflict was less serious. Navajos had long inhabited lands as far west as the Colorado and Little Colorado rivers in small numbers. As the eastern end of their traditional territory was filled with Anglo-American settlement, however, more of them migrated west, primarily because there was little opposition, with the only settlements of any consequence being the Hopi villages and the Mormon settlements of Moenkopi and Tuba City.[33]

The Navajos and Hopis had lived in close contact since the 1600s, and although their relations had not always been peaceful, they had intermarried and traded for hundreds of years. In the years prior to the Navajo exile along the Pecos, Navajo raids on the Hopi were bothersome; on the other hand, Hopis had played an important role in harassing the Diné who did not surrender to Kit Carson. Nonetheless, the two tribes were able to maintain a suspicious and somewhat hostile truce because their economies were not in direct competition. The Hopis lived on their mesas, high above the surrounding country, and farmed plots of land below in the summer. The Navajos grazed their livestock in the areas surrounding the Hopi mesas during the winter and moved their animals to higher ground in the summer. In some ways the two economies complemented each other. The Diné traded wood, an item not available to the village dwellers, and rabbits, hunted exclusively for the Hopi trade, for corn products.[34]

Disputes between the two people were exacerbated as their economies began to diversify. During the 1870s, the Mormons introduced livestock raising to the Hopi, thus causing clashes over grazing lands around Keams Canyon. Meanwhile, Navajos, partially at the urging of their agents, took to raising corn along Moenkopi Wash, expropriating traditional Hopi farms.[35] Nevertheless, of all the conflicts between the Diné and their neighbors, the dispute with the Hopi was the least serious.

A feeling, however, began to form in the 1880s that some land had to be set aside for the Hopi, regarded as a peaceful people who could easily be victimized by Anglo-Americans and Navajos. In 1882, two proposals were made regarding their future. On July 14, Inspector Howard recommended that the Navajo Reservation be extended one hundred miles west of its current boundary, to include the Hopis and Navajos living there. Howard's solution was not adopted. Instead, Moqui (Hopi) Agent Jesse A. Fleming suggested, on December 4, that a separate reservation be established for the Hopi. On December 16, President Chester A. Arthur signed an executive order creating a reserve for "the use and occupancy of the Moquis Indians, and such Indians as the Secretary of Interior may see fit to settle thereon." Fleming soon resigned, but his recommendation forced the two tribes into a conflict that might have been avoided.[36]

The government estimated that eighteen hundred Hopis and three hundred Navajos were living on the new reservation. As with most estimates, the figure for the Navajos was low because a count was made only of Navajos living near the Hopi villages, and not of all the Diné living on the reserve. The government made attempts to alter the Hopi way of life by trying to convince them to live throughout their reservation. They were urged to build farms and ranches where they conducted their agricultural pursuits. Some Hopis cooperated to the extent of building houses that they occupied during the summer, but they returned to their villages during the winter, only to have the Navajos move in their livestock while they were gone. Unfortunately, the Navajos were under population pressures and not always able to move their herds to higher ground in the traditional manner when the spring came. As a result, conflict increased. In 1884, John Bowman—serving as both Hopi and Navajo agent—complained that young Navajos were careless in herding their animals in the Hopi fields. In 1886, Agent Patterson felt compelled to request troops to stop Navajo depredations on the Hopi. This military expedition was temporarily successful, but Patterson came to the conclusion that the Navajos should be excluded from Hopi land.[37]

Patterson's proposal came close to implementation in 1888, when Herbert Welsh of the Indian Rights Association visited the Hopi. After observing the situation, he accused Navajos, in a letter to the secretary of interior, of committing continual depredations against the Hopi villages. His accusations had political weight, and orders were issued to remove the Navajos from Hopi lands. The army reacted in typical fashion and refused to provoke the Diné. After marching across the territory in question, the military concluded that the situation was more or less peaceful and moved no Navajos.[38] This conclusion was not unfounded, for the records of Hopi-Navajo conflict are small in relation to the conflicts the Diné were experiencing with their other neighbors who, at times, were much more militant.

The Mormons at Tuba City and Moenkopi were a case in point. By 1892, Anglo-American stockmen from all areas bordering on the reservation complained bitterly of Navajos grazing their animals off the reservation, and once again, there was talk of a Navajo war. Strangely, the worst case of violence occurred at Tuba City, where the Mormons had tried to maintain friendly relations with the Indians. When Ganado Mucho had welcomed the Latter Day Saints to the area, he had also warned them not to appropriate the springs. His warning had been ignored. Even though the Mormons wanted to get along with their Native American neighbors—Hopis, Paiutes, and Navajos—their expropriation of water sources made the Indians restless. Of course, the Diné were at the forefront in expressing their concerns by stampeding their animals across Mormon farms and pastures and stealing small numbers of Mormon cattle. Nonetheless, these actions did not seem to bother the settlers, who apparently accepted cattle theft as a kind of ransom.³⁹ The Navajo resentment, however, was deeper than it appeared.

Lot Smith, Mormon leader and businessman, lived in Tuba City. Despite the respect he commanded in northern Arizona, he was known as a highly volatile and violent man, but on June 20, 1892, he met his match. A Navajo named Chach'osh Neez drove a number of sheep onto a pasture claimed by Smith. The Mormon elder proceeded to shoot five of the animals, an act that provoked the Indian into killing five of Smith's cattle. Furious, Smith fired three times at Chach'osh Neez, who returned with five shots of his own, inflicting a mortal wound upon the Mormon. But Smith had enough life left in him to ride home and comment before he died, "That he ought to have quit when they commenced killing his cows, but he thought the Indian wouldn't shoot."⁴⁰

Early versions of the event neglected to point out that Smith had fired first, and there was concern on the part of the Diné and their agent, David Shipley, that Smith's killer would not receive a fair trial. A deputy sheriff was dispatched from Flagstaff to arrest Chach'osh Neez, but a crowd of Navajos gathered and refused to give him up. To avoid further trouble, troops from Fort Wingate were sent to the scene, under the command of Lieutenant R. E. L. Michie. The lieutenant, following an established line of reasoning, did not want to provoke the Navajos. He warned them against further violence, listened to the grievances on both sides of the affair, and returned home without a prisoner. Chach'osh Neez soon surrendered to Shipley, who was reluctant to turn him over to civilian authorities without assurances of a fair trial. While the agent anticipated a reply, the prisoner tired of waiting and turned himself loose. Chach'osh Neez did not stand trial until 1895, when he was acquitted by a Flagstaff jury on the grounds of self-defense. Meanwhile, the Diné continued to contest the Mormon holdings in Tuba City and Moenkopi. Finally in 1900, the government paid the Mormon settlers forty-five thousand dollars for improvements and turned the settlements over to the Indians.[41]

Other problems, such as slavery, defied solution, however, although the frequency and nature of complaints diminished over time. As the decade of the 1880s began, there were still Navajos searching for their kin. In 1881, a headman named Hosteen Tso received permission to look for a sister, niece, and stepson who had been captured by Utes and sold to New Mexican families. Agent Bowman issued passes in 1884 to an unnamed Navajo, to look for his daughter in the Rio Grande Valley, and to a man referred to as De-Nett-tova, to search for relatives at an unspecified location in New Mexico. Finally, Ganado Mucho was granted permission, in 1886, to go to the site of Old Fort Wingate to pick up a girl living with a Mexican-American family. Despite the heartfelt joy that these reunions brought, the fact was that by the 1880s the Diné had located most of the fellow tribesmen who were willing to return to their families. A few were held captive at remote locations, but others chose to remain where they were. A good example of this phenomenon was Deluvina Maxwell, who had been captured by Utes as a child and freed by Lucien Maxwell. She voluntarily stayed on as a servant to Maxwell's widow; her daughter, Paulita, would have an affair with the notorious Billy the Kid.[42]

As agents initiated attempts to free captives held by Navajos, they found the same to be true, except that the frequency of refusals of "freedom" was much higher. Dennis Riordan made the first large-scale effort to free these slaves. In September of 1883, for instance, the agent and an escort of twenty soldiers from Fort Wingate met with a headman at Lukachukai named Na-ki-ten-nai-be-ku-tso-he-yey. After long hours of negotiation, Riordan secured the release of six captive Paiutes. He was frustrated, however, because they ran away from Fort Defiance only days later to return to their master. Riordan's successor, John Bowman, was equally frustrated when he visited Manuelito's home the following year. Demanding that the old chief release his Mexican-American slaves, Bowman was surprised when Manuelito told them that they were free to go and they all chose to remain where they were. Among those refusing liberation was Manuelito's wife, Juanita. Bowman grew philosophical about such events. Captives, he reasoned, had become part of Navajo life and did not resent their masters, who, in any case, did not control them very carefully. As a result of the captives' attitudes, the government gave up trying to free them, and it came as no surprise that Hoskaninni held thirty-two captives as late as 1909.[43]

Hoskaninni remained an influential man in Monument Valley, but he had to survive another controversy before much peace came into his life. Long concerned that prospectors would find minerals in his territory, he did all that he could to keep miners away. When Cass Hite, who claimed to have been a member of Quantrill's Raiders during the Civil War, began prospecting in Monument Valley shortly after the deaths of Mitchell and Merrick, Hoskaninni took a liking to him but would not reveal the site of his supposed silver mine. Nonetheless, Hite kept pressing the chief for the location of minerals; his persistence paid off, for Hoskaninni showed him a site along the Colorado River where he could mine gold dust. Hite lived alone at the site for years in a rock house and made a moderate living.[44] Hoskaninni, however, could not always afford to be so generous.

During the spring of 1884, two prospectors appeared at H. L. Mitchell's trading post at McElmo Canyon, with intentions of looking for precious metals in Monument Valley. Mitchell, who had lost a son in Hoskaninni's territory, could have warned them of danger; whether he did or not has been lost to history. In any case, Samuel Walcott, from Baltimore and advanced in years, and his young partner from Illinois, James McNally, purchased supplies from the trader and began their journey. Word reached Dennis Riordan on April 7 that two men had been killed. Attempting to gather information, the agent sent out two Navajo policemen—Sam Bigodi and "Pete"—on separate fact-finding expeditions.[45]

Pete's report, which relied heavily on the testimony of a man named Dine Tsosie, stated that the events leading to murder began when a number of Navajos approached Walcott and McNally's camp to trade. The prospectors did not appear eager to bargain. Eventually, McNally went in search of the pair's horses. When Walcott still refused to do business, according to Dine Tsosie's story, Hoskaninni's son, Hoskaninni Begay, decided to kill Walcott because "these Americans, they are always mean and have not 'accommodation about them.'" Hoskaninni Begay distracted Walcott by having a boy play with the old man's pistol. When the prospector went to stop the boy, the chief's son hit him over the head with an ax. At that point, an old Navajo named Daghaa Yazzie showed up, expressed his concern about the murder, and asked what Hoskaninni Begay and Dine Tsosie intended to do about the other American. When the two men could not come to a conclusion, Yazzie said, "As long as one is killed, it is better to kill the other one too, for if they are murdered no one will ever know anything about it."[46]

When Hoskaninni Begay and Daghaa Yazzie went after McNally, they had a tough time because the young man fought back, wounding Yazzie before the gunfight was over. Unsuccessful in his task, the chief's son carried his companion home. It was then that Hoskaninni joined his son. They hunted McNally down, and Hoskaninni Begay killed him.[47]

On May 5, Dine Tsosie appeared at Fort Defiance to corroborate Pete's report. Two days later, Hoskaninni and his son reported to the agency, along with a large following and Ganado Mucho. Hoskaninni Begay's story differed from that of Dine Tsosie. According to him, he had struck Walcott to keep Dine Tsosie from being killed by the prospector. His blow had only knocked Walcott out, but after this action Dine Tsosie was so angry that he had used the ax to kill the unconscious man. The solution to the problem of McNally was also decided by Tsosie, who had attempted to kill him. When he was unsuccessful, Hoskaninni Begay had hunted down the white man and killed him.[48]

Acting Agent S. E. Marshall attempted to arrest the chief and his son, but Ganado Mucho would not allow it because it did not seem fair; according to him, H. L. Mitchell had killed Navajos without punishment. Hoskaninni's party left Fort Defiance, but Dine Tsosie surrendered to Marshall on June 18. John Bowman took control of the agency on June 30. Dispatching policemen to Monument Valley, the new agent gave the chief ten days to surrender, and he threatened to use military force. On July 10, Hoskaninni turned himself in, and Daghaa Yazzie gave up the next day. Nonetheless, Hoskaninni Begay did not appear, and it was rumored that he was hiding with renegade Utes who had recently killed two Navajo policemen. In August, Bowman led an expedition of ten policemen, Chee Dodge, and forty soldiers to Monument Valley, with the intention of arresting Hoskaninni Begay. Unable to locate the fugitive, the detachment uncovered the body of Walcott and returned home.[49]

Meanwhile, Hoskaninni, Daghaa Yazzie, and Dine Tsosie were placed under arrest and taken to Fort Wingate. Later, they were transferred to the Apache County jail in St. Johns, Arizona. Hoskaninni secured his release with the equivalent of five hundred dollars in bail. The other two men awaited trial from behind bars. On December 20, however, Dine Tsosie escaped, and Daghaa Yazzi was able to break jail two days later. Tsosie was apprehended by Navajo police, but Yazzie was not recaptured. As the time came for a grand-jury hearing on the Walcott and McNally murders, the sheriff of Apache County arranged for Chee Dodge to testify. Hoskaninni, on the other hand, forfeited his bond—citing severe illness—and failed to report to the hearing. With only one of the accused available for questioning, the grand jury determined that there was not enough evidence to prosecute.[50]

Hoskaninni, who lived longest of the post–Bosque Redondo–era Navajo leaders, remained something of an enigma. This most powerful of the late nineteenth-century local leaders rarely attempted to accommodate the United States government. Under his leadership, Monument Valley Navajos continued to protest the intrusions of prospectors. Nonetheless, he was not opposed to the presence of all Anglo-Americans. During his later years, he developed a strong relationship with Kayenta trader John

Wetherill and his wife, Louisa, with whom his attitude was nearly paternal.[51]

As the Peace Policy came to an end, Ganado Mucho and Manuelito, the two most powerful "national" leaders, seemed to begin the new era with little loss of influence. When Dennis Riordan first met these two aging leaders on January 19, 1883, they made a plea for supplies to distribute among the sick and aged. The agent agreed. His impression of their sincerity was lasting enough that he was willing to help the chiefs with personal favors later in the year. Ganado Mucho's son, Many Horses, was dislocated by settlers from an off-reservation home near a spring, but the agent was able to compensate him and his father by building him an American-style house. In addition, as Manuelito was attempting to develop water supplies within the Chuska Valley, Riordan provided him with irrigation pipe.[52]

Such favors, however, were beginning to be granted infrequently. A year later, the next agent, John Bowman, implied that the two old men were losing their intelligence to senility. Angry that Ganado Mucho had not cooperated in forcing Hoskaninni and his son to surrender, he complained that the chief, at age seventy-five, had "antiquated" ideas and was too feeble to govern. As far as Bowman was concerned, Manuelito was simply a drunken beggar with no influence.[53]

Bowman's conclusions were overstated, but his statements predicted the reactions of his successors. As the decade progressed, the names of these venerable leaders hardly appeared in the communications of the agents. Nevertheless, a shocking anecdote concerning Ganado Mucho does appear in the record. In the winter of 1889, the chief felt deathly ill. Having exhausted all means available to him, he sent word to Fort Defiance asking for treatment by the agency physician. Agent Charles Vandever had some respect for Ganado Mucho, calling him a good influence on other Navajos and a friend of the white man. Nonetheless, when the doctor refused to visit him, Vandever did not force him.[54] Left without medical care, the chief somehow survived his illness, but as a leader he disappeared from the record.

Manuelito, on the other hand, refused such official oblivion, often forcing himself upon officials. In August of 1890, for example, the chief came into the agency to confront Vandever with a problem. He had heard a rumor that a one-hundred-dollar reward had been issued for his capture. Vandever replied that no such sum had been issued, but he added that a reward had been offered for the apprehension of another old man. Why, asked the agent, were the old men setting such poor examples for the restless young men? Manuelito's answer was not recorded. In any case, Vandever mentioned that a rumor was circulating that the chief had been accused of stealing a horse. Angrily denying the crime, Manuelito demanded a pass from the agent, so he could leave the reservation to investigate the charges.[55]

The old warrior, however, could still be cooperative if it suited his vision. As Agent David Shipley began his forceful roundup of children in the summer of 1891, several students were brought in from his community with his apparent support, for Manuelito spoke in favor of Shipley's policies three months later. There seemed to be a determination about him to advocate what experience had taught him. Shipley gathered hostility among the Diné for capturing children and treating them almost like criminals, yet at a council meeting in February of 1892, Manuelito sided with the agent, preaching against hungry Navajos who had left the reservation to kill the settlers' livestock.[56]

Perhaps, Manuelito, who was feared by many, was more selfless than his friend Ganado Mucho, who was known for his diplomacy. His instinctive mixture of intimidation and accommodation, his stubborn clinging to the core of the Navajo ethos while adapting to a new world, symbolized the struggle of the post–Bosque Redondo Navajos.

In 1892, Lieutenant W. C. Brown crisscrossed Navajo lands while doing a water survey. When he entered Manuelito's domain, what he saw surprised him. Between ten and twenty families farmed a large, irrigated parcel of land.[57] Such success had taught Manuelito the value of some Anglo-American ways. Although he had not abandoned his traditional values, he had used them to assimilate other values. Despite the fact that not many of the Diné could duplicate his success, he was admired, for his adaptation was as old as the Navajo people.

In a sense, Manuelito's spirit of mixing traditions killed him. He caught the measles in 1893. Treating himself with traditional Navajo sweat baths and with generous doses of whiskey, he caught pneumonia and died. He was seventy-five. Before he passed on, he spoke with his successor, Henry Chee Dodge, and made him promise to keep the Navajos from destroying themselves by resisting the government. A few weeks later, Ganado Mucho died at age eighty-four.[58]

Conclusion

In January of 1889, a Nevada Paiute named Wovoka, who did farm labor for a living, was sick with a fever of unknown cause. Known to the whites who employed him as Jack Wilson, Wovoka witnessed an eclipse of the sun and went into a trance. When he awoke, he told of a vision; he had been to heaven and seen God as well as all of his people's ancestors, who were happy and contented. God gave Wovoka several songs to control the weather. With this proof of divine contact, he began to preach his revelation. If Indians would be good to each other, put away thoughts of war, and do a dance that Wovoka would teach them (the Ghost Dance), the world would end quickly, and all Indians, living and dead, would live in an earthly paradise.[1]

Messianic revelations were not new to the North American continent. Among native peoples, they date at least as far back as the prophet Deganawidah, who, along with Hiawatha, inspired the Iroquois to create their famous league. Prophets had also been instrumental in provoking pan-Indian movements such as Pontiac's Rebellion and Tecumseh's wars.[2] It may even be argued, with some veracity, that Joseph Smith's visions and the subsequent growth of Mormonism fit into this tradition, which did not seem to be decreasing as the nineteenth century came to a close. In the summer of 1881, for example, a Western Apache mystic preached a dogma similar to Wovoka's, but it was short-lived and did not spread to other peoples.

The Paiute prophet's revelation, however, spread quickly to Native Americans all over the West. When Wovoka's doctrine reached the Sioux, it took on a more militant form, which caused some government officials to panic. Led in part by the venerable medicine man Sitting Bull, the Sioux performed their dances in special "ghost shirts" that would protect them from the bullets of white men. In tragic events that came at the end of 1890, Sitting Bull was killed by Sioux policemen, and at least 150 Sioux were gunned down by soldiers in what has been erroneously called the "Battle" of Wounded Knee.[3]

Navajos did not take up the Ghost Dance. Wovoka's Paiute and Ute apostles brought his doctrines to the Diné, who would have none of it. Why the Ghost Dance did not spread to the Navajos has been a subject of some discussion. Ethnologist James Mooney, who studied the Ghost Dance in detail soon after Wounded Knee, came to the conclusion that the Navajos did not join in the movement because their economy was sound and they had not faced cultural deprivation. W. W. Hill, a researcher in the 1940s, came to the conclusion that the Diné did not like Wovoka's doctrine for the same reason that they refused to live in permanent dwellings at the Bosque: namely, fear of the dead. According to their way of thinking, anyone preaching the resurrection of the dead must either be crazy or a witch.[4] The causes for Navajo rejection of the new religion were many, but it is at least possible to assume that Mooney captured important general truths about Navajo life, while Hill was able to determine an immediate reason.

Mooney's assessment of the Navajo economic situation was correct, at least for the early 1890s, but as the United States entered a depression after the Panic of 1893, Navajos would again face starvation. His contention about Navajo culture, however, needs further study. Navajo culture had certainly changed since the return from the Bosque Redondo. Politically, Navajos relied more on central leadership to mediate differences with their neighbors, and on occasion the chiefs called in outside military authority to settle disputes between internal factions. They had also changed economically, now relying more on traders and manufactured goods. Raiding as a method for gaining wealth was discouraged by the chiefs, but not before the Diné had had a chance to increase greatly their livestock.

Change had long been a part of Navajo culture, but the rapid transformation they faced in the late nineteenth century took its effect. Drunkenness as a method of adaptation was common. Internal tensions developed because the gap between rich and poor grew wider. Poor men who most felt the economic consequences of decreased raiding began to practice witchcraft; at least their rich brethren accused them of it and acted to eliminate evil magic. Undoubtedly, there was resentment when the ricos used the army to force witchcraft underground. Finally, there was the threat that increased immigration into their region would undermine their land title.

Despite the tension faced daily by Navajos, they were not susceptible to the Ghost Dance. Much of the literature concerning Wovoka's prophecy contends that many tribes fell under its influence because people suffered from lack of hope, and the new religion offered hope because old ways seemed to be inoperable. As Mooney pointed out, throughout his study of the Ghost Dance, prophetic religions, under certain circumstances, are normal human reactions to stressful times. The Navajos were under stress, but they did not lack hope.

The years following the Navajo return from the Bosque Redondo had been years of hope. To understand the Navajo feeling of hope, one only has to examine the oral tales concerning the Diné's return from Fort Sumner (presented in chapter 2). They had faced exile and, against the odds, been allowed to return home. At least part of this feeling of hope had to do with their ability to adapt to new circumstances.

Even at the Bosque they had adapted. They tried Euro-American farming techniques, changed their diets, and allowed the chiefs to lead. On the other hand, the Navajos were not willing to give up their cultural core. As a result, they did not send their children to school, convert to Catholicism, or live in permanent dwellings. There was no immediate reward for making these changes, and they did not make them. When the Diné returned home, most Navajos had the same attitude. This would confound the Presbyterians sent to rule them. Missionaries had almost no effect upon the Navajos. Limited numbers of children attended the school at Fort Defiance because parents feared that their children might be exposed to evil—fears that seemed to be dramatically true once Manuelito's sons died at Carlisle. Authorities in the late 1880s and 1890s felt compelled to kidnap children for the schools.

Under the right circumstances, an outside power forcefully taking children for mandatory school attendance would lead a society to believe that it had lost control over one of its most basic functions, the raising of children. Loss of control often leads to the loss of hope. Some Navajos, on the other hand, used this blatant act as an opportunity to display their displeasure.

In late 1892, less than two years after the Sioux seemed to have been robbed of hope at Wounded Knee, Navajos, upset at the kidnapping of children for the school, rebelled against a fourth agent. The chiefs were too old to lead this action, and a younger man, Black Horse, assumed leadership. Agent David Shipley ventured out of Fort Defiance with the new national Navajo leader, Henry Chee Dodge. Black Horse's followers attempted to assault Shipley, but Dodge and a small group of soldiers rescued him. Filled with fear, the agent resigned, and Black Horse was not punished.

Meanwhile, Dodge attempted to show his people that schools could do a great deal to advance the Diné materially, and the old militant, Manuelito, overcame his grief for his sons and promoted education. It was, in fact, in his region of Navajo territory—Tohatchi and the Chuska Valley—where parents first requested that a school be built. Like almost every other complicated society, the Navajos had factions. It appears, however, that neither of these factions was acting out of a loss of hope. Black Horse and his followers demanded that the kidnapping practice be stopped, and Manuelito's followers demanded a school of their own.

The latter group was in the minority, but given the Navajo desire for consensus, their views were influential. This was the kind of contradiction that presented itself in late nineteenth-century Navajo life. There was a dualistic nature in the culture

278

that seemed to embrace paradoxes. For instance, the chiefs could stop raids by appealing to the greater good while, at the same time, working to increase their own wealth and power. Navajos were subject to sharing some of their wealth with fellow clan members, but they could also be highly individualistic in their application of the arts and by taking up new professions such as U.S. Army scout, wage laborer, and freighter. Indeed, each individual seemed bound to preserving his or her culture but also determined to change—a paradox built into the culture and its mythology.

The paradoxes faced daily by the Diné, however, were an advantage to them when dealing with Anglo-Americans. Like every other native culture, the Navajos had their share of detractors, but they were also admired by people in power, who looked mostly at the so-called progressive side of Navajo life with approval. For example, J. H. Beadle, the first travel writer to describe the Diné, could be impressed by their curious, humorous, and hopeful nature, state that they would be quickly civilized, and call them a tribe of "dark Caucasians." American writer Hamlin Garland visited the Navajos in 1895 and was amazed that despite their foreign nature, he found so much in the Navajos to which he could relate: The women wore their hair "like Quaker girls"; they worked hard; they seemed anxious to learn from the white man; and he observed an old man at a trading post who was "almost Scotch-Irish in character." Even agents, who were infuriated by the Navajo refusal to take the school seriously, praised their artistic skills. If these perceptions led to American praise, they did not lead to greater tolerance for Native Americans in general. Military men, for example, who wanted to protect the Navajos from land-hungry Anglo-Americans in the San Juan area, did not care to defend the Utes; and several pioneers, such as Thomas Keam, would argue that Navajos were superior to other Indians.[5]

The army carried this admiration one step further. Even though the Navajos had been defeated easily in 1863–64, they had not been easy for the soldiers at Fort Sumner to rule, and the Navajo confinement at the Bosque Redondo had operated contrary to Carleton's wishes by uniting the Navajos as they never had been before. Once they returned home, army policy gradually became one of keeping the Navajos at peace without forcing them to live solely on the reservation. Acting primarily as moderators, officers at Fort Wingate seemed to accept the Navajos for what they were and to ignore the larger concepts of government policy. General Sherman, who saw himself as a no-nonsense kind of man, outdid the men at Fort Wingate and recommended Manuelito for appointment as agent.

As radical as Sherman's idea was for its time, it demonstrated just how much respect Manuelito had achieved with the military. Paradoxically, many agents hated him. Manuelito seemed cooperative with government aims on one level, but he was a proud and aggressive man who was feared by many. Infamous among whites for his drinking, he was audacious enough to defend himself by stating that his habit helped him to see the world as a better place. Militant enough to go outside of the traditional Navajo leader's role and use force against his own people, he was forceful in defending the Diné's rights and in manipulating the government to grant them more land.

More than any other leader, Manuelito symbolized the baffling nature of the Navajo Nation. The army saw the Navajos as a peaceful group of people, but it worried that it would again turn to war. Agents saw Navajos as amenable to change, but they could not convince them to accept Christianity or to take up full-scale horticulture. The Diné moderated their raids, but they did not stop completely. The chiefs returned stolen property, but they rarely handed over the thieves.

Ganado Mucho had more followers than Manuelito, and his diplomacy provided balance to that of his more militant colleague. Nevertheless, neither one of them represented the Navajos who had not gone to the Bosque. Little is known about the leaders who avoided exile, but these local headmen, who lived mostly to the west and north of the reservation, seemed to cooperate with the chiefs. Barboncito was able to achieve temporary peace between northern Navajo leaders and the Mormons. Hastele, a northern leader, also negotiated a peace with the Latter Day Saints. Still, there is a temptation to regard Hoskaninni as typical of these leaders, and he was much like Manuelito. The Navajos who had not gone to Fort Sumner had faced hardship while their fellow tribesmen had been in exile, and they knew at least indirectly the power of the U.S. military. It was probably for these reasons that a leader like Hoskaninni made efforts to maintain the peace while acting violently to protect his home from prospectors.

The idea of home may indeed have been a dominating factor of late nineteenth-century Navajo life. Losing their homeland and regaining it caused the Diné to value it not only as a sacred region enshrined in their myths, but as a commodity valued by the white man and his institutions. They were given a certain amount of land by treaty, which they knew was not enough. Therefore, they used any excuse—including General Sherman's vague negotiating promise—to settle other lands that were theirs by tradition. Nevertheless, the chiefs understood early after their return that their reservation had to be expanded, and they worked with agents and the army to accomplish their goal.

Meanwhile, there was a widespread suspicion that settlers would demand Navajo land. One of Carleton's stated reasons for exiling the Diné was that their land had too much mineral wealth to leave in the hands of Indians. As a presidential candidate and Sherman's superior, Ulysses S. Grant predicted that the Diné would be pressured by prospectors. At least once, Grant proved to be a good prognosticator. Hoskaninni, through trickery and direct violence, moderated Anglo-American demand. The fates of Mitchell and Merrick, and of Walcott and McNally, made prospectors think twice about entering Navajo lands in search of wealth.

There was an equal demand for the Navajos' agricultural San Juan lands, in part due to the promotion of would-be real estate tycoons, such as Thomas Catron and William F. M. Arny. Once Navajo allies, like John Lorenzo Hubbell and Thomas V. Keam, let the chiefs know that Arny had tricked them into signing away their San Juan territory, their so-called petition to the president was quietly dropped in Washington, D.C., and the Navajos were not long in removing Arny from office.

Two other agents—John Pyle and Galen Eastman—were forced from office by the chiefs in combination with their allies, the traders and the army. Their removal of agents, however, cannot be seen as revolutionary. Time and again, they repeated their demands that the government send them agents who would treat them fairly. They cooperated with most of their agents, and there was never a suggestion that there be no agent at all. They requested Thomas V. Keam on several occasions, but when their wishes were not met, they attempted to cooperate with the new agent. When the new agent was respectful, there was no rebellion.

Navajo leaders liked and trusted Thomas Keam. They saw the Englishman and others like Hubbell as reliable links with an outside world from which they wanted to learn. During his brief term as agent, Keam ironically took more steps to bring the Navajos under government control than his predecessors. With the Indians' trust and a keen political sense, he instituted a police force and put the chiefs in charge. He planned for a more adequate school and hoped to improve the administration of Navajo affairs by establishing a subagency along the San Juan River. Although many of these measures would have improved the Diné's material condition, they also would have brought them more under the agent's power. Nevertheless, the Navajos wanted him in charge because he seemed courteous and concerned about their problems. He was also like the military in that he was practical and more interested in solving immediate problems than in demanding ideological transformations from his wards. He probably would have accomplished a great deal more than the men who followed him, but he was offensive to the Presbyterian leadership because of his Navajo wife and Indian friends.

Keam, therefore, assumed the role of trusted adviser. Many traders of relative honesty also filled this role. The fact that the Diné were willing to learn from outsiders shows that they were anxious to adapt to the greater society, as long as change was not forced upon them. Although government officials other than the military were slow to grasp this concept, the Navajos continued to use it for their own good.

The Diné, in other words, were not the Vanishing Indians of Anglo-American myth. Neither was their reservation a "prison" or an enclave, in which they isolated themselves from the rest of their geographic region. As raiders, diplomats, and traders, they had traveled extensively. Prior to 1882, the chiefs had gone twice to Washington, D.C. Parents had searched through New Mexican villages, looking for captured children. Navajo scouts working for the army had journeyed all over the Southwest in pursuit of renegade Indians. Raiders had done the same to add to their wealth. Navajos had also trekked to Santa Fe and Utah to trade, and during their travels, they had observed the complexity of the society that was surrounding them: pious Mormons, heavy drinking railroad workers, Anglo- and Mexican-American settlers, greedy prospectors, and black soldiers stationed at Fort Wingate with the Ninth Cavalry. The Diné, as a result, had come to understand the plurality of American life better than the Presbyterians who wanted to remake them.

By maintaining a dynamic society, they were able to control events to some extent. This sense of power gave the Navajos hope. Thus, when the Navajos were presented with the doctrines of Wovoka, they did not accept them. W. W. Hill was correct; Navajos did not want to have anything to do with the dead. A highly adaptable people did not want to change their religion, nor did they have any motivation for doing away with a central taboo. Instead, they resisted the prophet as they had rejected missionaries, agents, settlers, and plots to give away their lands. They maintained the peace, but they did not capitulate; they fought off invaders, but they did not start a war. They expanded in the face of expansion. They had changed, but they were still Navajos.

It was as Navajos that they faced the future. The chiefs had established a nation in the years between 1866 and 1882, but the basic self-rule that they established would be endangered as more competent agents used the Navajo Police to exercise control. Nevertheless, rebellious Navajos and Henry Chee Dodge seemed equal to the task, and a more formal government for the Navajos would be established early in the twentieth century, when petroleum was found on the reservation.

The Diné had become a permanent part of southwestern life by 1882. It would not be long until tourists would flock from the East on the new railroad to see colorful Navajos. But the Navajos were more than a sideshow. They had been in the region when the Spanish arrived, and they dominated the scene by the time of Mexican rule. When the Americans arrived, the Navajos waged a long fight against them. When they finally lost to Kit Carson's New Mexico Volunteers and were sent to Carleton's Bosque Redondo, the Diné were difficult to control. In a sense, they became a problem for the army that would not go away. They were sent home because the government did not know that else to do with them. They defeated Grant's Peace Policy in the same manner that they defeated Carleton's utopia. It is indeed difficult to think of a Navajo defeat until the Navajo-Hopi joint-use controversy in the late twentieth century.

The history of Indians in the United States has tended to be written from the perspective of the conquerering white man. As historian Jay Gitlin has observed perceptively about the history of the American West:

> The conquest of the continent, the "winning of the West," figures so prominently in our accout of the formation of the national character that our revolution against the British Empire seems, at times, to be reduced to a quarrel in the family. Indians appear frequently, but usually as straw men. Indians are portrayed either as victims of progress or as hostile opponents who tested the mettle of westering pioneers. Neither portrayal acknowledges Indian people to have played an active, meaningful role in the shaping of the western past.[6]

The Navajos proved this traditional approach to history to be incorrect. In fact, they were also forming their own national character; they were looking for their own "fit" in the larger society without losing what was characteristically theirs, and they succeeded.

Notes

Abbreviations

AP. National Archives, Interior Department, Appointment Papers: New Mexico, Navajo Indian Agency, 1872–82.

FW. National Archives, Returns from U.S. Military Posts, 1800–1916: Fort Wingate, NM, January 1872–December 1882.

IRA. Annual Report, Indian Rights Association.

LB. Selected Letters from the Letter Books of the Navajo Indian Agency (microfilm copy at Northern Arizona University, Special Collections).

LR. National Archives, Record Group 75, Letters Received, Office of Indian Affairs, 1881–1907.

NMIS. National Archives, Record Group 76, Letters Received, New Mexico Indian Superintendency.

OIA. National Archives, Record Group 75, Letters Received, Office of Indian Affairs, New Mexico Superintendency, 1849–80.

RCIA. Annual Report: Commissioner of Indian Affairs.

WD. National Archives, Record Group 98, War Department, Department of NM.

Preface

1. The Navajo origin legend has long been studied by scholars, probably the first account of which was Washington Mathews, *Navajo Legends* (Boston: American Folklore Society, 1897). A complete listing of these accounts here is impossible because of limitations of space. A good idea of the depth and sophistication of Navajo myth, however, can be discovered by reading one of the following: Gladys A. Reichard, *Navaho Religion: A Study in Symbolism* (Princeton, NJ: Princeton University Press, 1977 [repr., 1950 ed.]); Donald F. Sandner, *Navaho Symbols of Healing: A Jungian Exploration of Ritual, Image, and Medicine* (Rochester, VT: Healing Arts Press, 1991 [repr., 1979 ed.]); and Paul G. Zolbrod, *Dine Bahane: The Navajo Creation Story* (Albuquerque: Uni-

versity of New Mexico Press, 1984). The Zolbrod account conveys the myth's religious and poetic majesty best. The account used here, however, is taken from Ethelou Yazzie, ed., *Navajo History*, vol. 1 (Rough Rock, AZ: Navajo Curriculum Center, 1971), pp. 9–10. Ms. Yazzie's book retells the creation story in simplified form for middle and high school students; her account also differs from the versions cited above by contending that there were four worlds in the emergence rather than five. Although Yazzie admits, on p. 4 of her manuscript, that there is a debate among Navajos on the number of previous worlds, Navajo students in the author's English classes at Tohatchi High School, Tohatchi, NM, and Chinle High School, Chinle, AZ, have agreed, when studying this myth, that the number is four. It is out of deference to these students that this account is used.

2. Yazzie, *Navajo History*, pp. 11–12.

3. Ibid., pp. 13–16.

4. Ibid., pp. 17–72.

5. Ruth Underhill, *The Navajos* (Norman: University of Oklahoma Press, 1956), pp. 3–71.

6. Frank McNitt, *Navajo Wars: Military Campaigns, Slave Raids, and Reprisals* (Albuquerque: University of New Mexico Press, 1972), pp. 3–91. For background on the causes of Navajo war, see Jack D. Forbes, *Apache, Navaho, and Spaniard* (Norman: University of Oklahoma Press, 1960).

7. Underhill, *Navajos*, pp. 81–82.

8. Ibid., pp. 85–100; McNitt, *Navajo Wars*, pp. 93–429.

9. For the idea of this version of the "conquest of the West," the author is indebted to Patricia Nelson Limerick, *Legacy of Conquest: The Unbroken Past of the American West* (New York: W. W. Norton, 1987), pp. 322–23. See also: Ray Allen Billington, *America's Frontier Heritage* (Albuquerque: University of New Mexico Press, 1963), pp. 1–22.

10. For a good background in Euro-American ideas concerning the American Indian see Robert F. Berkhofer, *The White Man's Indian* (New York: Vintage Books, 1978); and Bryan W. Dippie, *The Vanishing American: White Attitudes and U.S. Indian Policy* (Middletown, CT: Wesleyan University Press, 1982).

11. Walter Prescott Webb, *The Great Plains* (New York: Ginn and Co., 1931), p. 53.

12. There are, however, a number of individual autobiographies painstakingly recorded and translated into English by anthropologists and others. These stories lack the consistency of tales concerning the Bosque Redondo, but most of them do have one unifying theme: the chiefs and their successor, Henry Chee Dodge, are mentioned in heroic terms. Many of these texts will be cited throughout the manuscript, but a good introductory book that ties together the Bosque Redondo and the years immediately following is Tiana Bighorse, *Bighorse the Warrior*, ed. Noel Bennett (Tucson: University of Arizona Press, 1990).

13. L. G. Moses and Raymond Wilson, eds., *Indian Lives: Essays on Nine-*

teenth- and Twentieth-Century Native American Leaders (Albuquerque: University of New Mexico Press, 1985), pp. 1–14 (quote is from p. 11). See also: Alvin M. Josephy, Jr., The Patriot Chiefs: A Chronicle of American Indian Resistance (New York: Viking Press, 1958), pp. xii–xiv; and R. David Edmunds, Studies in Diversity: American Indian Leaders (Lincoln: University of Nebraska Press, 1980), pp. vii–xiv.

14. Peter Iverson, "Continuity and Change in Navajo Culture: A Review Essay," New Mexico Historical Review 62 (April 1987): 191–200.

15. Lynn R. Bailey, Bosque Redondo: An American Concentration Camp (Pasadena, CA: Socio-Technical Books, 1970); and Gerald Thompson, The Army and the Navajo: The Bosque Redondo Experiment, 1863–1868 (Tucson: University of Arizona Press, 1982).

16. Lawrence C. Kelly, The Navajo Indians and Federal Indian Policy, 1900–1935 (Tucson: University of Arizona Press, 1968); Donald Parman, The Navajos and the New Deal (New Haven, CT: Yale University Press, 1976); and Peter Iverson, The Navajo Nation (Albuquerque: University of New Mexico Press, 1976).

17. Richard Van Valkenburgh, A Short History of the Navajo People (Window Rock, AZ: U.S. Department of Interior, 1938); Underhill, Navajos; Robert W. Young, The Role of the Navajo in the Southwestern Drama (Gallup, NM: The Gallup Independent, 1968).

18. John Upton Terrell, The Navajo: The Past and Present of a Great People (New York: Perennial Library, 1972); and Raymond Friday Locke, The Book of the Navajo (Los Angeles: Mankind Publishing Co., 1976).

19. Edward H. Spicer, Cycles of Conquest: The Impact of Spain, Mexico, and the United States on the Indians of the Southwest, 1533–1960 (Tucson: University of Arizona Press, 1962); David F. Aberle, The Peyote Religion among the Navajo (Chicago: Aldine Publishing Co., 1966); Richard White, The Roots of Dependency: Subsistence, Environment, and Social Change among the Choctaws, Pawnees, and Navajos (Lincoln: University of Nebraska Press, 1983); and Garrick Bailey and Roberta Glenn Bailey, A History of the Navajos: The Reservation Years (Santa Fe: School of American Research Press, 1986).

20. Two examples of Reeve's work are the following: "The Government and the Navaho, 1873–1883," New Mexico Historical Review 14 (July 1941), and "A Navaho Struggle for Land," New Mexico Historical Review 21 (January 1946); Frank McNitt, The Indian Traders (Norman: University of Oklahoma Press, 1962); Lawrence R. Murphy, Frontier Crusader: William F. M. Arny (Tucson: University of Arizona Press, 1972); and David M. Brugge, A History of the Chaco Navajos (Albuquerque: National Park Service, 1980).

21. Robert S. McPherson, The Northern Navajo Frontier, 1860–1900: Expansion Through Adversity (Albuquerque: University of New Mexico Press, 1988); and Norman J. Bender, "New Hope for the Indians": The Grant Peace Policy and the Navajos in the 1870s (Albuquerque: University of New Mexico Press, 1989).

Chapter 1

1. Thompson, *Army and the Navajo*, pp. 8–9; Young, *Role of the Navajo*, p. 39; Charles Avery Amsden, "The Navaho Exile at Bosque Redondo," *New Mexico Historical Review* 8 (January 1933): 36–38; Bailey, *Bosque Redondo*, pp. 16–17 and 20–21; James D. Shinkle, *Fort Sumner and the Bosque Redondo Reservation* (Roswell, NM: Hall-Poorbaugh Press, 1965), pp. 6–8; and Aurora Hunt, *Major General James Henry Carleton, 1814–1873: Western Frontier Dragoon* (Glendale, CA: The Arthur Clark Co., 1958), pp. 274–75.

2. Hunt, *Major General James Henry Carleton*, p. 275; Underhill, *Navajos*, pp. 110–13; Locke, *Book of the Navajo*, pp. 352–53; Thompson, *Army and the Navajo*, p. 10; Young, *The Role of the Navajo*, p. 39; Amsden, "Navaho Exile," pp. 38–39; Ray C. Colton, *The Civil War in the Western Territories: Arizona, Colorado, New Mexico, and Utah* (Norman: University of Oklahoma Press, 1959), pp. 125–27; and Clifford E. Trafzer, *The Kit Carson Campaign: The Last Great Navajo War* (Norman: University of Oklahoma Press, 1982), pp. 58–59.

3. Trafzer, *Kit Carson Campaign*, pp. 59–64; Shinkle, *Fort Sumner*, pp. 20–21; and Colton, *Civil War*, pp. 126–27.

4. Thompson, *Army and the Navajo*, pp. 11–17; Underhill, *Navajos*, pp. 114–15; Young, *The Role of the Navajo*, p. 39; and Trafzer, *Kit Carson Campaign*, pp. 73–75.

5. Trafzer, *Kit Carson Campaign*, pp. 71–80; Colton, *Civil War*, p. 137; Young, *The Role of the Navajo*, p. 240; Shinkle, *Fort Sumner*, p. 29; and William H. Lyon, "Navajo History and Culture" (unpublished manuscript, Northern Arizona University, 1984), p. 270.

6. Lyon, "Navajo History," pp. 270–71; Locke, *Book of the Navajo*, pp. 355–58; Young, *The Role of the Navajo*, pp. 40–41; Hunt, *Major General James Henry Carleton*, pp. 275–78; Amsden, "Navaho Exile," pp. 41–42; Thompson, *Army and the Navajo*, p. 42; and Trafzer, *Kit Carson Campaign*, pp. 80–92, 96–111, and 124–25.

7. Trafzer, *Kit Carson Campaign*, p. 91; Locke, *Book of the Navajo*, pp. 355–58; Underhill, *Navajos*, pp. 114–18. For Navajo oral histories of the campaign, see Frank Mitchell, *Navajo Blessingway Singer*, ed. Charlotte J. Brisbie and David McAllester (Tucson: University of Arizona Press, 1978), pp. 14–16; Crawford R. Buell, "The Navajo 'Long Walk': Recollections by Navajos," in *The Changing Ways of Southwestern Indians*, ed. Albert H. Schroeder (Glorieta, NM: Rio Grande Press, 1973); Ruth Roessel, ed., *Navajo Stories of the Long Walk Period* (Tsaile, AZ: Navajo Community College Press, 1973); and Frances Gillmor and Louisa Wade Wetherill, *Traders to the Navajos: The Story of the Wetherills of Kayenta* (Albuquerque: University of New Mexico Press, 1963 [repr., 1938 ed.]), pp. 143–49. See also: Lynn R. Bailey, *Indian Slave Trade of the Southwest* (Los Angeles: Westernlore Press, 1966), p. 115.

8. Lyon, "Navajo History," pp. 271–72; Thompson, *Army and the Navajo*, pp. 27–28; Underhill, *Navajos*, p. 121; Locke, *Book of the Navajo*, pp. 358–61;

Hunt, *Major General James Henry Carleton*, p. 277; Shinkle, *Fort Sumner*, pp. 29–30; and Trafzer, *Kit Carson Campaign*, pp. 111 and 128–68.

9. Trafzer, *Kit Carson Campaign*, pp. 170–81 and 190–97; Lyon, "Navajo History," p. 272; Thompson, *Army and the Navajo*, p. 30; Underhill, *Navajos*, pp. 124–26; Hunt, *Major General James Henry Carleton*, p. 278; and Locke, *Book of the Navajo*, pp. 361–63. For the hardships of the march to Bosque Redondo, see Ruth Roessel, *Navajo Stories*; and Franc Johnson Newcomb, *Hosteen Klah: Navaho Medicine Man and Sandpainter* (Norman: University of Oklahoma Press, 1964), pp. 52–55.

10. For figures concerning the population of Navajos at the Bosque Redondo, see Thompson, *Army and the Navajo*, pp. 46, 54, 66–67, 80, 100, and 130. See also Locke, *Book of the Navajo*, pp. 364–65; Robert W. Young, *The Navajo Yearbook* (Window Rock, AZ: Navajo Agency, 1957), p. 219; and Shinkle, *Fort Sumner*, p. 30.

11. Carleton's vision of the mission of the Bosque Redondo Reservation is well-outlined in the following: Lyon, "Navajo History," pp. 277–79; Hunt, *Major General James Henry Carleton*, pp. 280–81; Bailey, *Bosque Redondo*, pp. 64–69; Locke, *Book of the Navajo*, pp. 374–48; Paul Horgan, *Lamy of Santa Fe: His Life and Times* (New York: Farrar, Straus & Giroux, 1975), p. 316; and Trafzer, *Kit Carson Campaign*, pp. 53–59 and 182–83. For a more detailed account of the evolution of Carleton's ideas and their practical implementation, see Thompson, *Army and the Navajo*, pp. 12–83.

12. Some of the best brief descriptions of what went wrong at the Bosque Redondo are contained in more general works. Among these are Spicer, *Cycles of Conquest*, pp. 219–20; Francis Paul Prucha, *The Great Father: The United States and American Indians*, vol. 1 (Lincoln: University of Nebraska Press, 1984), pp. 452–56; and Robert M. Utley and Wilcomb E. Washburn, *Indian Wars* (New York: American Heritage, 1985), pp. 201–2. See also Underhill, *Navajos*, pp. 130–32; Bailey, *Bosque Redondo*, pp. 27–29; Locke, *Book of the Navajo*, pp. 364–65; Young, *Navajo Yearbook*, p. 219; Gillmor and Wetherill, *Traders*, p. 150; John L. Kessell, "General Sherman and the Navajo Treaty: A Basic and Expedient Misunderstanding," *The Western Historical Quarterly* 12 (July 1981): 254–56; Shinkle, *Fort Sumner*, pp. 31–32. For a very detailed examination of these failings see: Thompson, *Army and the Navajo*, pp. 11–14 and 28–139. For a discussion of how the Bosque Redondo Reservation came to be chosen see: Frank McNitt, "Fort Sumner: A Study in Origins," *New Mexico Historical Review* 45 (April 1970): 101–15.

13. Thompson, *Army and the Navajo*, pp. 36–40, 43–44, 47, 53, 61, 63, 66–69, 76, 88–89, 101–12, and 135–36; Underhill, *Navajos*, pp. 130–32 and 138–41; Spicer, *Cycles of Conquest*, pp. 219–20; Hunt, *Major General James Henry Carleton*, pp. 285–88; Bailey, *Bosque Redondo*, pp. 118–21; Locke, *Book of the Navajo*, pp. 366–67; Lawrence Kelly, p. 6; and Shinkle, *Fort Sumner*, pp. 34, 42–54, and 62–68.

14. Thompson, *Army and the Navajo*, p. 99; Underhill, *Navajos*, p. 140; and Shinkle, *Fort Sumner*, p. 36.

15. Shinkle, *Fort Sumner*, pp. 41–42; Locke, *Book of the Navajo*, pp. 366–68 and 372; Clyde Kluckhohn and Dorothea Leighton, *The Navaho*, rev. ed. (Garden City, NY: Doubleday, 1962), p. 41; Spicer, *Cycles of Conquest*, p. 220; Thompson, *Army and the Navajo*, pp. 98–99, 128–29, and 133; Bailey, *Bosque Redondo*, pp. 76–77 and 94–95.

16. Not all scholars agree that the Navajos maintained mental health at the Bosque Redondo. For example, Kluckhohn and Leighton, *Navaho*, p. 41, contend that no group of people had ever undergone a greater catastrophe because they suffered the destruction of property and a sudden dependency on a former enemy. Once free, they suffered confinement. These writers add to the idea of psychological defeat by declaring that the Bosque Redondo experience was "a major calamity to the People; its full effects upon their imagination can hardly be conveyed to white readers. Even today it seems impossible for any Navaho of the older generation to talk for more than a few minutes on any subject without speaking of Fort Sumner. Those who were not there themselves heard so many poignant tales from their parents that they speak as if they themselves had experienced all the horror of the 'Long Walk,' the illness, the hunger, the homesickness, the final return to their desolated land. One can no more understand Navaho attitudes—particularly toward white people—without knowing of Fort Sumner than he can comprehend Southern attitudes without knowing of the Civil War." Bailey in *Bosque Redondo*, pp. 2–6, states that the Navajos were subject to stress which "completely wiped away every vestige of tribal organization" (p. 5). For other statements concerning the chastisement of the Navajo that do not necessarily agree with the two above, see Spicer, *Cycles of Conquest*, p. 220; Utley and Washburn, p. 202; William T. Hagan, *American Indians* (Chicago: University of Chicago Press, 1961), p. 106; Amsden, "Navaho Exile," pp. 48–50; Hunt, *Major General James Henry Carleton*, pp. 291–93; Kessell, "General Sherman," p. 270; W. Eugene Hollen, *Frontier Violence: Another Look* (New York: Oxford University Press, 1974), p. 191; and Parman, *Navajos and the New Deal*, p. 8. But many of these authors have not made an extensive study of the Bosque Redondo experience.

17. James F. Downs, *The Navajo* (New York: Holt, Rinehart and Winston, 1972), pp. 15–16; Thompson, *Army and the Navajo*, pp. 162–65; Underhill, *Navajos*, pp. 137–38; Spicer, *Cycles of Conquest*, pp. 219–20; Kluckhohn and Leighton, *Navaho*, pp. 65, 86–87, 92; Kelly, *Navajo Indians*, p. 6; Locke, *Book of the Navajo*, pp. 371–72 and 380; and Bailey, *Bosque Redondo*, pp. 76–77.

18. Bailey, *Bosque Redondo*, pp. 64–69; Underhill, *Navajos*, pp. 135–37; Locke, *Book of the Navajo*, p. 370; Robert L. Wilken, *Anselm Weber, O.F.M.: Missionary to the Navajos, 1898–1921* (Milwaukee: The Bruce Publishing Co., 1955), pp. 14–15; Horgan, *Lamy of Santa Fe*, p. 317; Lyon, "Navajo History," p. 290; Young, *The Role of the Navajo*, pp. 43–44; and Thompson, *Army and the Navajo*, pp. 32–33, 44–45, 56, 60, 71, and 82–83.

19. Thompson, *Army and the Navajo*, pp. 46–47, 64–65, 73, 78, 97, 110, 118–19, 127, 147–48, 156, and 161; Horgan, *Lamy of Santa Fe*, p. 327. The

following items reprinted in J. Lee Correll, ed., *Through White Men's Eyes: A Contribution to Navajo History from the Earliest Times to the Treaty of June 1, 1868*, vol. 5 (Window Rock, AZ: Navajo Heritage Center, 1979); Santa Fe *Weekly New Mexican*, June 22, 1866, pp. 346–47; Carleton to Assistant Adjutant General in Santa Fe, July 23, 1866, p. 354; Lorenzo Labadie to Carleton, October 25, 1866, p. 386. Also see Locke, *Book of the Navajo*, p. 378.

20. Quoted in Correll, *Through White Men's Eyes*, vol. 5, p. 343.

21. Thompson, *Army and the Navajo*, p. 164, contends that at the Bosque Redondo the Navajos first realized that, as a united tribe, they were a force with negotiating power. See also Underhill, *Navajos*, p. 135; and Kluckhohn and Leighton, *Navaho*, pp. 122–23.

22. For a study of the evolution of Navajo leadership, see Richard Van Valkenburgh, "Navajo Common Law I," *Museum Notes: Museum of Northern Arizona* 9 (October 1936): 17–22. See also Kluckhohn and Leighton, *Navaho*, pp. 117–22, 245, 248–49, and 302.

23. Thompson, *Army and the Navajo*, pp. 28–29, 47, 55, and 88–89.

24. See especially Ruth Roessel's foreword to *Navajo Stories* in which she discusses this phenomenon, pp. xi–xiii. See also Mitchell, *Navajo Blessingway Singer*, pp. 19–20; and Lyon, "Navajo History," pp. 240–41 and 296.

25. Lyon, "Navajo History," pp. 240–41; and Virginia Hoffman, *Navajo Biographies*, vol. 1 (Rough Rock, AZ: Rough Rock Demonstration School, 1974), pp. 80–94.

26. Hoffman, *Navajo Biographies*, pp. 95–96; Thompson, *Army and the Navajo*, pp. 41 and 91; Lock, *Book of the Navajo*, pp. 368–70; Gillmor and Wetherill, *Traders*, pp. 143–51; and Buell, "Navajo 'Long Walk,'" p. 183; Trafzer, *Kit Carson Campaign*, pp. 212–23; and Lyon, "Navajo History," p. 241.

27. Lyon, "Navajo History," p. 242; Richard Van Valkenburgh, "Navajo Naat'aani," *The Kiva* 13 (January 1948): 17; Hoffman, pp. 129–32; and Underhill, *Navajos*, p. 108.

28. Underhill, *Navajos*, p. 134; Hoffman, *Navajo Biographies*, pp. 133–39; and Lyon, "Navajo History," p. 242.

29. Lyon, "Navajo History"; Hoffman, *Navajo Biographies*, pp. 106 and 108; Thompson, *Army and the Navajo*, pp. 7 and 88–89; Underhill, *Navajos*, pp. 108 and 133; and Trafzer, *Kit Carson Campaign*, p. 212.

30. Trafzer, *Kit Carson Campaign*; Hoffman, *Navajo Biographies*, p. 109; Lyon, "Navajo History," p. 293; and Underhill, *Navajos*, p. 133.

31. Thompson, *Army and the Navajo*, pp. 89–90. For an account that emphasizes the abuses documented by the Doolittle Commission see: Locke, *Book of the Navajo*, pp. 374–75.

32. Lyon, "Navajo History," p. 293; Shinkle, *Fort Sumner*, pp. 34–36; and Thompson, *Army and the Navajo*, pp. 104–5.

33. Thompson, *Army and the Navajo*, p. 105; and Locke, *Book of the Navajo*, p. 376.

34. Graves was forced to witness New Mexican opposition during his visit

to Santa Fe. See Thompson, *Army and the Navajo*, pp. 105–6. Also, see Shinkle, *Fort Sumner*, pp. 26–27.

35. Shinkle, *Fort Sumner*, pp. 26–27 and 38–41; and Thompson, *Army and the Navajo*, pp. 94–98 and 123.

36. For discussion of the Comanchero trade in relation to the Bosque Redondo, see Shinkle, *Fort Sumner*, pp. 42, 51, 62–68. For specific instances of Comanche problems at the Bosque, see Thompson, *Army and the Navajo*, pp. 88, 93, and 123.

37. Van Valkenburgh, "Navajo Common Law I," p. 19.

38. Thompson, *Army and the Navajo*, pp. 120–21; and Hoffman, *Navajo Biographies*, p. 139.

39. Hoffman, *Navajo Biographies*, pp. 140–41; and Thompson, *Army and the Navajo*, p. 140.

40. Hoffman, *Navajo Biographies*, p. 141.

41. Lorenzo Labadie to Carleton, October 24, 1866, in Correll, *Through White Men's Eyes*, vol. 5, p. 386; and Thompson, *Army and the Navajo*, p. 124.

42. Thompson, *Army and the Navajo*, p. 126.

43. Ibid., pp. 126–27.

44. Ibid., p. 127; Lawrence R. Murphy, *Frontier Crusader: William F. M. Arny* (Tucson: University of Arizona Press, 1972), pp. 127–28.

45. Thompson, *Army and the Navajo*, pp. 128–32.

46. Ibid., pp. 132–33.

47. Ibid., pp. 133–35.

48. Ibid., p. 137. See the following documents in Correll, *Through White Men's Eyes*, vol. 5: Dodd to A. B. Norton, July 10, 1867, p. 455; Report, Board of Officers Convened at Fort Sumner, August 5, 1867, Testimony of Captain E. W. Tarlton, p. 456, and Lieutenant Henry Bragg, p. 457.

49. Report, Testimony of Bragg, p. 457, and Jesus de María, in ibid., p. 459; and Thompson, *Army and the Navajo*, p. 137.

50. Thompson, *Army and the Navajo*, pp. 137–38; and Report, Testimony of Bragg, in Correll, *Through White Men's Eyes*, vol. 5, pp. 457–58.

51. The following all in Correll, *Through White Men's Eyes* vol. 5: Report, Testimony of Tarlton, p. 456, Lieutenant Charles Porter, p. 457, Major James F. Weeds, Assistant Surgeon, p. 458, and Lieutenant P. D. Vernon, p. 458; and Thompson, *Army and the Navajo*, p. 138.

52. Thompson, *Army and the Navajo*, p. 138; the following all in Correll, *Through White Men's Eyes*, vol. 5: Report, Testimony of Porter, p. 457, Weeds, p. 458, Bitter Water, pp. 458–59.

53. Report, Testimony of Tarlton, in Correll, *Through White Men's Eyes*, vol. 5, p. 456; and Thompson, *Army and the Navajo*, p. 138.

54. Thompson, *Army and the Navajo*, pp. 138–39; and Report, Testimony of Tarlton, in Correll, *Through White Men's Eyes*, vol. 5, p. 456.

55. The following all in Correll, *Through White Men's Eyes*, vol. 5: Report, Testimony of Weeds, p. 58, Theodore H. Dodd, p. 457; Letter, Dodd to Norton, July 13, 1867, p. 456.

56. Thompson, *Army and the Navajo*, p. 139.

57. Ibid., pp. 140–41.

58. Ibid., pp 142–43.

59. Ibid.

60. Ibid., pp. 139 and 145; Frank D. Reeve, "The Federal Indian Policy in New Mexico, 1855–1880, Part II," *New Mexico Historical Review* 13 (January 1938): 31.

61. Thompson, *Army and the Navajo*, p. 145.

62. Thompson, *Army and the Navajo*, pp. 145–46; Reeve, "Federal Indian Policy, Part II," p. 31.

63. Van Valkenburgh, "Navajo Common Law I," p. 18.

64. Reeve, "Federal Policy II," pp. 30–31 and 38; and Santa Fe *Weekly New Mexican*, April 21, 1868.

65. Reeve, "Federal Indian Policy, Part II," p. 32; and Thompson, *Army and the Navajo*, pp. 147–50.

66. Thompson, *Army and the Navajo*, pp. 147–50.

67. Ibid., pp. 150–52.

68. Ibid., p. 151.

69. Robert G. Athearn, *William Tecumseh Sherman and the Settlement of the West* (Norman: University of Oklahoma Press, 1956), p. 190; and Kessell, "General Sherman," pp. 251, 253, and 257.

70. Kessell, "General Sherman," p. 251; Bailey, *Bosque Redondo*, p. 145; and Reeve, "Federal Indian Policy, Part II," p. 33.

71. Reeve, "Federal Indian Policy, Part II," p. 33; Athearn, *William Tecumseh Sherman*, pp. 80 and 205–6; and Kessell, "General Sherman," pp. 256–57.

72. Kessell, "General Sherman," p. 258; and Athearn, *William Tecumseh Sherman*, p. 203.

73. Thompson, *Army and the Navajo*, p. 152; Ruth Roessel, *Navajo Stories*, pp. 212, 238, and 244; and Hoffman, *Navajo Biographies*, pp. 113–33.

74. Quoted in Reeve, "Federal Indian Policy, Part II," pp. 34–35.

75. Quoted in Kessell, "General Sherman," pp. 285–59; and Thompson, *Army and the Navajo*, pp. 151–52.

76. Thompson, *Army and the Navajo*, p. 152; and Kessell, "General Sherman," p. 259.

77. Kessell, "General Sherman," p. 259.

78. Ibid., p. 261; and Athearn, *William Tecumseh Sherman*, p. 203.

79. Proceedings of Council, May 28, 1868, in Correll, *Through White Men's Eyes*, vol. 6, pp. 103–31; and Hoffman, *Navajo Biographies*, p. 109.

80. Hoffman, *Navajo Biographies*, p. 109; and Proceedings, May 28, 1868, in Correll, *Through White Men's Eyes*, vol. 6, pp. 131–32.

81. Proceedings, May 28, 1868, in Correll, *Through White Men's Eyes*, vol. 6, pp. 131–32; and Hoffman, *Navajo Biographies*, pp. 109–10.

82. *Hoffman, Navajo Biographies*, pp. 110–13; and Proceedings, May 28, 1868, in Correll, *Through White Men's Eyes*, vol. 6, p. 132.

83. Proceedings, May 28, 1868, in Correll, *Through White Men's Eyes*, vol. 6, p. 132; and Hoffman, *Navajo Biographies*, p. 113.

84. Proceedings, May 28, 1868, in Correll, *Through White Men's Eyes*, vol. 6, pp. 133–34; Thompson, *Army and the Navajo*, p. 154; Kessell, "General Sherman," pp. 260–61; and Athearn, *William Tecumseh Sherman*, p. 203.

85. Athearn, *William Tecumseh Sherman*, pp. 203–4; Thompson, *Army and the Navajo*, p. 155; Hoffman, *Navajo Biographies*, p. 118; and Kessell, "General Sherman," p. 260.

86. Kessell, "General Sherman," p. 261; Shinkle, *Fort Sumner*, p. 70.

87. Proceedings of Council, May 29, 1868, in Correll, *Through White Men's Eyes*, vol. 6, p. 136. Also quoted in Kessell, "General Sherman," p. 262.

88. Kessell, "General Sherman," pp. 262 and 266; and Proceedings, May 29, 1868, in Correll, *Through White Men's Eyes*, vol. 6, pp. 136–37.

89. Accounts of the southwestern slave trade can be found in Bailey, *Indian Slave Trade*. For a detailed discussion of slavery in the Southwest, see David M. Brugge, *Navajos in the Catholic Church Records of New Mexico: 1694–1875* (Window Rock, AZ: Navajo Parks and Recreation Dept., 1968), pp. 99–134.

90. McNitt, *Navajo Traders*, p. 34; Anselm Weber, "Navajo Indians," *The Catholic Encyclopedia*, vol. 10 (New York: Robert Appleton Co., 1911), p. 720; and Bailey, *Indian Slave Trade*, pp. 86–88, 105–8, 114–15, and 119–25.

91. Proceedings, May 29, 1868, in Correll, *Through White Men's Eyes*, vol. 6, pp. 136–37; Bailey, *Indian Slave Trade*, pp. 126–30; Thompson, *Army and the Navajo*, p. 155; and Kessell, "General Sherman," p. 262.

92. Kessell, "General Sherman," p. 262.

93. Quoted in ibid., p. 263; and Proceedings of Council, May 30, 1868, in Correll, *Through White Men's Eyes*, vol. 6, p. 139.

94. Kessell, "General Sherman," pp. 263–65.

95. Quoted in ibid., p. 267.

96. Ibid., p. 267.

97. Ibid., pp. 268–69; Locke, *Book of the Navajo*, p. 385; and Reeve, "Federal Indian Policy, Part II," pp. 36–37.

98. Reeve, "Federal Indian Policy, Part II," p. 36; Locke, *Book of the Navajo*, pp. 385–86; Underhill, *Navajos*, p. 196; Thompson, *Army and the Navajo*, p. 155.

99. Kessell, "General Sherman," pp. 269–70.

100. Ibid., pp. 270–71.

101. Thompson, *Army and the Navajo*, pp. 155–56.

102. Ibid., p. 156.

103. Ibid.

Chapter 2

1. *RCIA*, 1868, p. 165; Underhill, *Navajos*, pp. 146–47; Irving Telling, "New Mexican Frontiers: A Social History of the Gallup Area, 1881–1901" (master's thesis, Harvard University, 1952), pp. 24–25; Roscal Mangiante, "History of Fort Defiance: 1851–1900" (master's thesis, University of Arizona, 1950), p.

59; and Brugge, *History of the Chaco Navajos*, pp. 49–50. The figures for Navajo livestock are official estimates. The only actual count taken in 1868 was made by Santiago Hubbell on his toll bridge across the Rio Puerco. He counted 464 horses and 4,190 sheep. His count of sheep may have included goats. See Bailey and Bailey, *History of the Navajos*, p. 38.

2. Mitchell, *Navajo Blessingway Singer*, p. 19.

3. Newcomb, *Hosteen Klah*, pp. xviii–xix.

4. Santa Fe *Daily New Mexican*, August 11, 1868; and Buell, "Navajo 'Long Walk,'" p. 183.

5. Buell, "Navajo 'Long Walk,'" pp. 171–72.

6. Ibid., pp. 183–84; Locke, *Book of the Navajo*, p. 387.

7. Reeve, "Federal Indian Policy, Part II," p. 31; Underhill, *Navajos*, p. 147; *RCIA*, 1868, p. 159; H. R. Clum, Acting Commissioner of Indian Affairs to Nathaniel Pope, New Mexico Superintendent of Indian Affairs, August 16, 1871, *NMIS*; and Santa Fe *Daily New Mexican*, July 7, 1868.

8. Robert W. Frazier, *Forts of the West: Military Forts and Presidios and Posts Commonly Called Forts West of the Mississippi River to 1898* (Norman: University of Oklahoma Press, 1965), p. 108; Telling, "New Mexico Frontiers," p. 25; Ralph Emerson Twitchell, *The Leading Facts of New Mexican History*, vol. 3 (Cedar Rapids, IA: The Torch Press, 1917), p. 372; McNitt, *Indian Traders*, p. 109; Gary Tietjen, "Encounter with the Frontier" (unpublished manuscript: Los Alamos, NM, 1969 [copy in the Gallup Public Library, Gallup, NM]), p. 109; and Young, *The Role of the Navajo*, p. 43.

9. Locke, *Book of the Navajo*, p. 392; Mangiante, "History of Fort Defiance," p. 59; Underhill, *Navajos*, p. 150; Brugge, *History of the Chaco Navajos*, p. 51; and Bailey and Bailey, *History of the Navajos*, p. 49.

10. Frank Waters, *Masked Gods: Navajo and Pueblo Ceremonialism* (Chicago: Swallow Press, 1950), pp. 167–73; Kluckhohn and Leighton, *Navaho*, pp. 45–51; and James M. Goodman, *Navajo Atlas: Environments, Resources, People, and History of the Dine Bikeyah* (Norman: University of Oklahoma Press, 1982), p. 11.

11. Locke, *Book of the Navajo*, p. 392; and Norman M. Littell, Attorney for the Navajo Tribe, *Proposed Findings of Fact in Behalf of the Navajo Tribe of Indians in the Area of the Overall Navajo Claim Before the Indian Claims Commission*, vol. 2 (Window Rock, AZ: Navajo Tribal Printing Section, 1967), pp. 462–71, 515–18; vol. 5, pp. 1053–1178.

12. Lawrence Kelly, *Navajo Indians*, pp. 4–5; Telling, "New Mexico Frontiers," p. 30; Littell, *Proposed Findings*, p. 515; Brugge, *History of the Chaco Navajos*, p. 50; and Bailey and Bailey, *History of the Navajos*, p. 74.

13. Underhill, *Navajos*, pp. 152–53; Locke, *Book of the Navajo*, pp. 391–94. See also the statement of Comiarrah, a Navajo woman, to Jacob Hamblin in James A. Little, *Jacob Hamblin: A Narrative of His Personal Experience, Missionary to the Indians and Explorer* (Freeport, NY: Books for Libraries Press, 1971 [repr., 1881 ed.]), p. 108. For an account of help given by Navajos who did not go to the Bosque, see Gillmor and Wetherill, *Traders*, pp. 153–54. See

also Terrell, *Navajo*, pp. 227–28; and Young, *The Role of the Navajo*, p. 45.

14. *RCIA*, 1868, p. 164; Thompson, *Army and the Navajo*, p. 72; Lawrence R. Murphy, ed., *Indian Agent in New Mexico: The Journal of Special Agent W. F. M. Arny, 1870* (Santa Fe: Stagecoach Press, 1967), p. 38; and Spicer, *Cycles of Conquest*, p. 219.

15. Young, *The Role of the Navajo*, pp. 40, 42–43; J. Lee Correll, "The Killing of Lott Smith, Noted Mormon, at Tuba City," *Navajo Times*, March 3, 1966; Agnes Morely Cleaveland, *No Life for a Lady* (Boston: Houghton Mifflin Co., 1941), pp. 300–301; Van Valkenburgh, "Navajo Common Law I," p. 19; Donald L. Parman, "The 'Big Stick' in Indian Affairs: The Bai-a-lil-le Incident in 1909," *Arizona and the West* 20 (Winter 1978): 343–44; J. Lee Correll, "Navajo Frontiers in Utah and Troublous Times in Monument Valley," *Utah Historical Quarterly* 39 (Spring 1971): 149–51; Charles Kelly, "Hoskaninni," *Desert Magazine* 4 (July 1941): 6–9, and "Chief Hoskaninni," *Utah Historical Quarterly* 21 (July 1953): 220–22; Byron Cummings, *Indians I Have Known* (Tucson: Arizona Silhouettes, 1952), pp. 2–4; and Richard E. Klink, *Land Enough and Time Enough* (Albuquerque: University of New Mexico Press, 1958), p. 25.

16. *RCIA*, 1868, pp. 164–65.

17. Ibid., p. 164; Reeve, "Federal Indian Policy, Part II," p. 39; Young, *Navajo Yearbook*, p. 222; McNitt, *Indian Traders*, p. 109; and Mangiante, "History of Fort Defiance," pp. 59–60.

18. Newcomb, *Hosteen Klah*, p. xxi; Navajo Agent William F. M. Arny to Colonel L. Edwin Dudley, New Mexico Superintendent of Indian Affairs, April 16, 1874, *NMIS*; Twitchell, *Leading Facts*, p. 373; Brugge, *History of the Chaco Navajos*, p. 51; Aberle, *Peyote Religion*, p. 37; Cleaveland, *No Life for a Lady*, pp. 97–98; Frank McNitt, *Richard Wetherill: Anasazi*, rev. ed. (Albuquerque: University of New Mexico Press, 1966), pp. 48–49; and Marc Simmons, *New Mexico: A Bicentennial History* (New York: W. W. Norton, 1977), pp. 157–58.

19. McNitt, *Indian Traders*, pp. 304–5. The following items from Correll, *Through White Men's Eyes*, vol. 5: Santa Fe *Weekly New Mexican*, June 22, 1866, p. 346; Captain Edmond Butler, Fort Wingate, to Carleton, July 12, 1866, p. 350; and Carleton to Assistant Adjutant General in Santa Fe, July 23, 1866, p. 354. *RCIA*, 1868, pp. 165, 167, and 196; and Murphy, *Frontier Crusader*, pp. 144–45.

20. *RCIA*, 1868, p. 165.

21. Underhill, *Navajos*, p. 150; Terrell, *Navajo*, p. 230; Reeve, "Federal Indian Policy, Part II," p. 39; and Major J. Carry French to J. M. Gallegos, New Mexico Superintendent of Indian Affairs, February 20, 1869, *NMIS*.

22. Van Valkenburgh, "Navajo Naat'aani," p. 14; and Young, *The Role of the Navajo*, p. 43.

23. French to Gallegos, February 20, 1869, *NMIS*; and Santa Fe *Daily New Mexican*, March 23, 1869.

24. French to Gallegos, March 26, 1869, *NMIS*; and Reeve, "Federal Indian Policy, Part II," pp. 43–44.

25. Reeve, "Federal Indian Policy, Part II," p. 44; French to Gallegos, March

26, 1869, *NMIS;* Underhill, *Navajos,* p. 161; Locke, *Book of the Navajo,* p. 395; Terrell, *Navajo,* p. 232; and Hoffman, *Navajo Biographies,* p. 244.

26. French to Gallegos, March 26, 1869, *NMIS.* For a brief history of the Southern Utes see: Frank D. Reeve, "The Federal Indian Policy in New Mexico: 1858–1880, Part III," *New Mexico Historical Review* 13 (April 1938): 146–58.

27. McNitt, *Indian Traders,* p. 48; Navajo Agent Frank T. Bennett to New Mexico Superintendent of Indian Affairs Major William Clinton, October 7 and 26, 1869, *NMIS.*

28. The following letters are all in *NMIS:* Bennett to Clinton, October 7 and 26, December 8, 1869, and August 19, 1870; and Navajo Agent James Miller to New Mexico Superintendent of Indian Affairs Nathaniel Pope, March 14 and May 18, 1872.

29. *RCIA,* 1869, p. 238; Brugge, *History of the Chaco Navajos,* p. 52; and French to Gallegos, June 18, 1869, *NMIS.*

30. J. Francisco Chavez to Clinton, August 14, 1869, and E. D. Franz to General A. V. Kautz, Commander Fort Craig, NM, July 24, 1869, *NMIS.*

31. Reeve, "Federal Indian Policy, Part II," p. 45; Gallegos to Major General George W. Getty, Commander, District of New Mexico, July 13, 1869, *NMIS;* and Santa Fe *Daily New Mexican,* July 13, 1869.

32. Santa Fe *Daily New Mexican,* July 13, 1869; and Major William A. Kobbe, AAA General, District of New Mexico, July 14, 1869, *NMIS.*

33. *RCIA,* 1869, pp. 437–38.

34. W. T. Stracham, Albuquerque, to Commanding Officer, Fort Craig, NM, July 24, 1869; and Santa Fe *Daily New Mexican,* July 31 and August 4, 1869.

35. Reeve, "Federal Indian Policy, Part II," p. 45.

36. Major A. W. Evans, Commander, Fort Wingate, NM to the AAA General, District of New Mexico, August 8, 1869, *NMIS;* Brugge, *History of the Chaco Navajos,* p. 52; *RCIA,* 1870, p. 151; and Charles H. Lange and Carroll L. Riley, eds., *The Southwestern Journals of Adolph Bandelier* (Albuquerque: University of New Mexico Press, 1966), p. 297n.

37. Young, *The Role of the Navajo,* p. 42; Kessell, "General Sherman," p. 267; Spicer, *Cycles of Conquest,* p. 219; Certificate, Narciso Pino, Justice of the Peace, Cubero, NM, September 5, 1869, *NMIS;* and Santa Fe *Daily New Mexican,* June 22, 1869.

38. Bennett to Clinton, September 9, 1869, and Evans to AAA General, District of New Mexico, October 20, 1869, *NMIS.* See also Pino certificate, September 9, 1869, *NMIS.*

39. Evans to AAA General, August 8 and October 20, 1869, *NMIS.*

40. Evans to AAA General, August 8, 1869, *NMIS.*

41. Ibid.; Bennett to Clinton, August 26, 1869, *NMIS;* and Brugge, *History of the Chaco Navajos,* p. 54.

42. Athearn, *William Tecumseh Sherman,* p. 205.

43. Kessell, "General Sherman," p. 267; E. D. Townsend, Adjutant General, to Major General J. M. Schofield, Department of Missouri, Fort Leavenworth,

Kansas, August 20, 1869, and Bennett to Clinton, August 26, 1869, *NMIS*; and Reeve, "Federal Indian Policy, Part II," p. 45.

44. The following in *NMIS:* Brevet Major Charles McClure, Headquarters, District of New Mexico, to Clinton, September 4, 1869; Kobbe to Commanding Officer, Fort Wingate, NM, September 29, 1869; and Sherman to Getty, November 26, 1869.

Chapter 3

1. Francis B. Heitman, ed., *Historical Register and Dictionary of the United States Army, From Its Organization, September 29, 1789, to March 2, 1903* (Washington, D.C.: GPO, 1903), vol. 1, p. 211.

2. Underhill, *Navajos*, pp. 151 and 154; Locke, *Book of the Navajo*, pp. 392 and 394; Bailey and Bailey, *History of the Navajos*, p. 29; and *RCIA*, 1869, pp. 237–38 and 1870, p. 159; Bennett to Clinton, August 26, 1869, *NMIS*; McNitt, *Indian Traders*, p. 126; and Terrell, *Navajo*, pp. 236–37.

3. For a good description of American rejection of the idea of limited resources in the American West and the story of a man who fought against it, see Wallace Stegner, *Beyond the Hundredth Meridian: John Wesley Powell and the Second Opening of the West* (Lincoln: University of Nebraska Press, 1953). A description of traditional Navajo farming methods can be found in Mitchell, *Navajo Blessingway Singer*, p. 41.

4. Van Valkenburgh, *Short History*, p. 42; and Bailey and Bailey, *History of the Navajos*, pp. 36–37, 51, and 56.

5. *RCIA*, 1869, p. 240; Report, Bennett to Commissioner of Indian Affairs, September 29, 1869, *NMIS*; Locke, *Book of the Navajo*, p. 394; and Terrell, *Navajo*, p. 231.

6. Bennett to Clinton, September 9, 16, and 25, 1869, *NMIS*; and *RCIA*, 1870, p. 151.

7. Bennett to Clinton, September 25, 1869, and Report, Bennett to Commissioner of Indian Affairs, September 29, 1869, *NMIS*.

8. *RCIA*, 1869, pp. 237–38.

9. Bennett to Clinton, October 3 and 16, 1869, and Antonio José Sedillo to Clinton, October 16, 1869, *NMIS*.

10. Van Valkenburgh, *Short History*, p. 44; Underhill, *Navajos*, pp. 155–56; Bailey and Bailey, *History of the Navajos*, p. 38; Jules Luh, *Lords of the Earth: A History of the Navajo Indians* (New York: Crowell-Collier Press, 1971), p. 135; Tietjen, "Encounter with the Frontier," p. 121; Terrell, *Navajo*, p. 229; Locke, *Book of the Navajo*, p. 395; and Reeve, "Federal Indian Policy, Part II," p. 42.

11. Bennett to Clinton, November 11, 1869, *NMIS*. The livestock was claimed in December by José Pedro Gallegos. See Bennett to Clinton, December 8, 1869, *NMIS*.

12. Bennett to Clinton, November 16, 1869, *NMIS*; McNitt, *Indian Traders*, p. 127; and Bennett to Clinton, November 16, 1869, *NMIS*.

13. Santa Fe *Daily New Mexican*, November 17 and 23, 1869.

14. Bennett to Clinton, December 8, 1869, *NMIS*.

15. Bennett to Clinton, December 1, 1869, *NMIS.*

16. Bailey and Bailey, *History of the Navajos,* p. 30; and Brugge, *History of the Chaco Navajos,* p. 56.

17. *RCIA,* 1870, p. 151; and Simon Bibo, Cebolleta, NM, to Clinton, May 11, 1870, *NMIS.*

18. Bennett to Clinton, January 3 and February 1, 1870, *NMIS;* and Bender, "*New Hope for the Indians,*" pp. 33–34.

19. McNitt, *Indian Traders,* pp. 124–26.

20. Bennett to Clinton, February 1, 1870, *NMIS;* and *RCIA,* 1870, pp. 151–52.

21. Bennett to Clinton, February 1, 1870, *NMIS.*

22. Bennett to Clinton, January 3, 1870, and Manuel Antonio Jaramillo to Clinton, January 17, 1870, *NMIS.*

23. Bennett to Evans, February 9, 1870, and Evans to Lieutenant Cooper, Pueblo Agent, February 10, 1870, *NMIS.*

24. Evans to Cooper, February 10, 1870, and Evans to Bennett, February 10, 1870, *NMIS.*

25. Evans to Bennett, February 10, 1870, *NMIS.*

26. Ibid.; Evans to Cooper, February 10, 1870, *NMIS.*

27. Bennett to Evans, February 14, 1870, and Bennett to Clinton, March 1 and 2, 1870, *NMIS.*

28. Bailey and Bailey, *History of the Navajos,* pp. 38–39.

29. Bennett to Clinton, March 2, May 2, and June 1, 1870, Kobbe to Clinton, March 1, 1870, Brevet Major Charles McClure to Clinton, March 18, 1870, *NMIS;* and Brugge, *History of the Chaco Navajos,* pp. 52–53 and 57–58.

30. Bennett to Clinton, March 2 and May 2, 1870, and Governor William A. Pile to Secretary of State Hamilton Fish, May 29, 1870, *NMIS.* See also Brugge, *History of the Chaco Navajos,* p. 56.

31. Brugge, *History of the Chaco Navajos,* p. 56; Bennett to Clinton, May 11, June 1, and October 1, 1870, and Kobbe to Getty, March 31, 1870, *NMIS;* James H. McClintock, *Mormon Settlement in Arizona* (Tucson: University of Arizona Press, 1985 [repr., 1921 ed.]), pp. 177–78; Byrd H. Granger, rev. *Will C. Barnes' Arizona Place Names* (Tucson: University of Arizona Press, 1960), p. 21; Edward H. Peplow, Jr., *History of Arizona,* vol. 2 (New York: Lewis Historical Publishing Co., 1958), p. 149; and Thomas Edwin Farish, *History of Arizona* (Phoenix: privately printed, 1918), vol. 5, pp. 320–21 and vol. 6, p. 276.

32. Brugge, *History of the Chaco Navajos,* p. 56; and Bennett to Clinton, May 11, June 1, and October 1, 1870, *NMIS.*

33. Bennett to Clinton, June 1, 1870, *NMIS;* Brugge, *History of the Chaco Navajos,* p. 57; and Bailey and Bailey, *History of the Navajos,* p. 45.

34. *RCIA,* 1870, pp. 151–52; and Bennett to Clinton, July 1, 1870, *NMIS.*

35. Price to Kobbe, June 11, 1870, *NMIS.*

36. Ibid.

37. Murphy, *Indian Agent,* p. 35; and Bennett to Clinton, August 7 and 8, Kobbe to New Mexico Superintendent of Indian Affairs, August 3, 1870, *NMIS.*

38. Captain S. B. W. Young to Lieutenant John W. Pullman, Post Adjutant, Fort Wingate, August 26, 1870, *NMIS*.

39. Ibid.

40. Ibid.

41. Bailey and Bailey, *History of the Navajos*, p. 30, point out that Manuelito and Narbono resorted to force in August to recover stolen stock from raiders. They contend that this was the first time that Navajo leaders had resorted to force to control their people in light of white authority. Actually, this is not true, for Manuelito had arrested Navajo rustlers at the Bosque Redondo. Labadi to Carleton, October 24, 1864, in Correll, *Through White Men's Eyes*, vol. 5, p. 386. The action by Manuelito and Narbono, however, was the first such action since the Navajos' return home.

42. Price to Kobbe, August 27, and Price to Bennett, August 26, 1870, *NMIS*; and Bender, "New Hope for the Indians," p. 35.

43. Bender, "New Hope for the Indians," p. 35.

44. Arny to Dudley, April 16, 1874, and Bennett to Clinton, October 1, 1870, *NMIS*; and Murphy, *Indian Agent*, p. 53.

45. George Warton James, *Indians of the Painted Desert* (Boston: Brown, Little, Brown and Co., 1919), p. 135; Brugge, *History of the Chaco Navajos*, p. 57.

46. Charles S. Peterson, *Take Up Your Mission: Mormon Colonizing Along the Little Colorado River, 1870–1900* (Tucson: University of Arizona Press, 1973), pp. 4–6 and 193; W. L. Rusho and C. Gregory Crampton, *Desert River Crossing: Historic Lee's Ferry on the Colorado* (Santa Barbara, CA: Peregrine Smith, Inc., 1981), p. 14; and Winn Whiting Smiley, "Ammon M. Tenney: Mormon Missionary to the Indians," *Journal of Arizona History* 13 (Summer 1972): 851.

47. Peterson, *Take Up Your Mission*, pp. 2–3 and 193; McNitt, *Indian Traders*, p. 92; McClintock, *Mormon Settlement*, pp. 59–61; Stegner, *Beyond the Hundredth Meridian*, p. 132; and Smiley, "Ammon M. Tenney," p. 85.

48. Rusho and Crampton, *Desert River Crossing*, pp. 14–18; Peterson, *Take Up Your Mission*, p. 3; Smiley, "Ammon M. Tenney," pp. 86–91; Little, *Jacob Hamblin*, pp. 58, 66, 77–79, and 81–95; Littell, *Proposed Findings*, p. 54; Peter Gottfredson, *History of Indian Depredations in Utah* (Salt Lake City: Skelton Publishing Co., 1919), p. 290; C. Gregory Crampton and David E. Miller, "Journal of Two Campaigns by the Utah Territorial Militia Against the Navajo Indians, 1869," *Utah Historical Quarterly* 29 (April 1961): 149–76; and Andrew Carl Larson, *Erastus Snow: The Life of a Missionary Pioneer for the Early Mormon Church* (Salt Lake City: Skelton Publishing Co., 1971), pp. 395–61, 387–92, 397, 401, 417, and 424–27.

49. Larson, *Erastus Snow*, p. 425; and Bennett to Clinton, January 6, 1870, *NMIS*.

50. Larson, *Erastus Snow*, pp. 438 and 440; and Evans to Cooper, February 11, 1870, *NMIS*.

51. Peterson, *Take Up Your Mission*, pp. 159 and 211–13; and Little, *Jacob Hamblin*, p. 95.

52. Little, *Jacob Hamblin*, p. 95.

53. Ibid.

54. Ibid., pp. 95–98; Stegner, *Beyond the Hundredth Meridian*, pp. 128–34; McNitt, *Indian Traders*, pp. 92–93; McClintock, *Mormon Settlement*, pp. 76–78; C. Gregory Crampton, *Land of Living Rock* (New York: Alfred A. Knopf, 1972), pp. 128–29; Peterson, *Take Up Your Mission*, p. 4; and Smiley, "Ammon M. Tenney," pp. 91–92.

55. Smiley, "Ammon M. Tenney," pp. 92–93; McClintock, *Mormon Settlement*, pp. 76–79; Stegner, *Beyond the Hundredth Meridian*, p. 135; and Paul Bailey, *Jacob Hamblin: Buckskin Apostle* (Los Angeles: Westernlore Press, 1948), pp. 314 and 318.

56. Bailey, *Jacob Hamblin*, pp. 319–20; Stegner, *Beyond the Hundredth Meridian*, p. 135; and McClintock, *Mormon Settlement*, pp. 96–97.

57. Quoted in ibid., p. 77; and, in part, in Smiley, "Ammon M. Tenney," p. 93. A full account of Hamblin's words can be found in Bailey, *Jacob Hamblin*, pp. 320–21.

58. Bailey, *Jacob Hamblin*, pp. 322–23; and McClintock, *Mormon Settlement*, p. 77.

59. McClintock, *Mormon Settlement*, pp. 77–79; Smiley, "Ammon M. Tenney," p. 93; and Little, *Jacob Hamblin*, pp. 101–2.

60. Little, *Jacob Hamblin*, pp. 102–3 and 108–9; McClintock, *Mormon Settlement*, p. 78; Larson, *Erastus Snow*, pp. 440–41; and Hoffman, *Navajo Biographies*, pp. 124–26.

61. Brugge, *History of the Chaco Navajos*, p. 58; and Bennett to Pope, January 1, 1871, *NMIS*.

62. William Werner to Clinton, December 28, 1870, Bennett to Clinton, January 1, 1871, Commissioner of Indian Affairs E. S. Parker to New Mexico Superintendent of Indian Affairs, January 28 and May 26, 1871, *NMIS*.

63. Bender, "*New Hope for the Indians*," p. 36; and Bennett to Pope, February 1, 1871, *NMIS*.

Chapter 4

1. For full accounts of what happened at Camp Grant, see Dan L. Thrapp, *The Conquest of Apacheria* (Norman: University of Oklahoma Press, 1967), pp. 79–94; and James R. Hastings, "The Tragedy of Camp Grant in 1871," *Arizona and the West* 1 (Summer 1959): 146–60. See also Odie B. Faulk, *Arizona: A Short History* (Norman: University of Oklahoma Press, 1970), pp. 132–34; and Douglas D. Martin, *An Arizona Chronology* (Tucson: University of Arizona Press, 1963), April 10, 1871. (This book contains no page numbers. It is arranged by dates.)

2. Thrapp, *Conquest*, pp. 86–94; Faulk, *Arizona*, p. 134; and Martin, April 10, 1871.

3. Violence in Arizona during the 1870s is starkly and simply portrayed under the appropriate dates in Martin. For examples of New Mexican violence, see Robert W. Larson, *New Mexico's Quest for Statehood: 1846–1912* (Albuquerque: University of New Mexico Press, 1968), pp. 137–40; and Simmons,

New Mexico, pp. 168–72. For a good summary of predominant western attitudes toward Native Americans and how they contrasted with eastern views see: Dippie, *Vanishing American*, pp. 132–38.

4. Dippie, *Vanishing American*, pp. 132–38; and Berkhofer, p. 92. For examples of western newspapers committed to militancy see the 1870s issues of the Santa Fe *Daily New Mexican* and the *Arizona Weekly Miner* (Prescott).

5. Prucha, *Great Father*, vol. 1, pp. 479–83 and 496–500.

6. Ibid., pp. 485–86; and Robert M. Utley, *The Indian Frontier of the American West: 1846–1890* (Albuquerque: University of New Mexico Press, 1984), p. 129.

7. Utley, *Indian Frontier*, pp. 129–34; and Prucha, *Great Father*, vol. 1, pp. 503–8.

8. Prucha, *Great Father*, vol. 1, pp. 509–12; Francis Paul Prucha, *American Indian Policy in Crisis: Christian Reformers and the Indians, 1865–1900* (Norman: University of Oklahoma Press, 1964), pp. 30–32; Utley, *Indian Frontier*, pp. 132–34; and Robert H. Keller, Jr., *American Protestantism and United States Indian Policy* (Lincoln: University of Nebraska Press, 1983), pp. 150–51.

9. Prucha, *Great Father*, vol. 1, pp. 520–27; and Utley, *Indian Frontier*, pp. 151–55.

10. Farish, *History of Arizona*, vol. 6, pp. 293–94.

11. Prucha, *Great Father*, vol. 1, pp. 517–19; and Norman J. Bender, ed., *Missionaires, Outlaws, and Indians: Taylor F. Ealy at Lincoln and Zuni* (Albuquerque: University of New Mexico Press, 1984), pp. xiv–xv.

12. Bailey and Bailey, *History of the Navajos*, p. 63; Michael J. Warner, "The Fertile Ground: The Beginnings of Protestant Missionary Work with the Navajo, 1852–1890," in *The Changing Ways of Southwestern Indians*, ed. Albert H. Schroeder (Glorieta, NM: Rio Grande Press, 1973), p. 195; and Bender, "*New Hope for the Indians*," pp. 14–20 and 24.

13. Bender, "*New Hope for the Indians*," p. 20; Warner, "Fertile Ground," pp. 195–96; Underhill, *Navajos*, p. 199; Terrell, *Navajo*, pp. 246–47; Locke, *Book of the Navajo*, pp. 407–8; Steve Pavlik, "A Short History of Navajo Education, Part I," *Journal of Navajo Education* 2 (Winter 1985): 26; Thomas Jesse Jones, *The Navajo Indian Problem* (New York: Phelps-Stokes Fund, 1939), p. 52; *RCIA*, 1870, p. 150; and Charity Gaston to Bennett, August 23, 1870, *NMIS*.

14. Mary Shepardson, *Navajo Ways in Government* (Menasha, WI: American Anthropological Association, 1963), p. 13; Gaston to Bennett, August 23, 1870, *NMIS*; *RCIA*, 1870, p. 150; Warner, "Fertile Ground," p. 196; Terrell, *Navajo*, pp. 246–47; Locke, *Book of the Navajo*, p. 408; and Bender, "*New Hope for the Indians*," p. 22.

15. Bender, "*New Hope for the Indians*," pp. 30–31.

16. Ibid., pp. 39–40; and Underhill, *Navajos*, pp. 198–99.

17. Locke, *Book of the Navajo*, p. 396; McNitt, *Indian Traders*, p. 126; and Bender, "*New Hope for the Indians*," p. 39.

18. Bender, "*New Hope for the Indians*," pp. 47–48; McNitt, *Indian Traders*,

p. 126; and the following, all *NMIS:* Miller to Pope, February 6, 11, 17, and 22, 1871, and Miller to Price, February 24, 1871.

19. Brugge, *History of the Chaco Navajos,* p. 58; and Price to Miller, February 23, 1871, and Miller to Price, February 24, 1871, *NMIS.*

20. Telling, "New Mexico Frontiers," p. 72; McNitt, *Indian Traders,* pp. 151–52; Peterson, *Take Up Your Mission,* pp. 4, 24, and 47; Van Valkenburgh, *Short History,* p. 44; Rusho and Crampton, *Desert River Crossing,* pp. 31–32; and McClintock, *Mormon Settlement,* p. 82.

21. Miller to Pope, March 6 and April 5, 1871, *NMIS;* and Brugge, *History of the Chaco Navajos,* pp. 58–59.

22. Ibid., p. 59; and Miller to Pope, March 8 and 31, 1871, *NMIS.*

23. Brugge, *History of the Chaco Navajos,* pp. 58–59; Miller to Pope, March 17 and 31, *NMIS;* and McNitt, *Indian Traders,* p. 126n.

24. McNitt, *Indian Traders,* p. 126n; and Brugge, *History of the Chaco Navajos,* p. 59.

25. Brugge, *History of the Chaco Navajos,* p. 59; Bailey and Bailey, *History of the Navajos,* p. 67; and Miller to Pope, April 5, 1871, *NMIS.*

26. Brugge, *History of the Chaco Navajos,* p. 59; and McNitt, *Indian Traders,* p. 127.

27. Miller to Pope, May 18 and 31, 1871, *NMIS.*

28. Miller to Pope, June 2, 1871, *NMIS.*

29. Miller to Pope, June 23 and 30, 1871, *NMIS;* and Bailey and Bailey, *History of the Navajos,* p. 30.

30. Brugge, *History of the Chaco Navajos,* pp. 59–60.

31. Quoted in ibid., p. 60.

32. Ibid.; and McNitt, *Indian Traders,* p. 128.

33. Bailey and Bailey, *History of the Navajo,* p. 40; and Brugge, *History of the Chaco Navajos,* p. 60.

34. Miller to Pope, August 5 and 22, 1871, and Miller's annual report to the Commissioner of Indian Affairs, August 17, 1871, *NMIS.* See also: Young, *The Role of the Navajo,* pp. 45–46.

35. Miller's annual report to the Commissioner of Indian Affairs, August 17, 1871, and Miller to Pope, September 11, 1871, *NMIS;* and Larson, *Erastus Snow,* pp. 442–43.

36. Rusho and Crampton, *Desert River Crossing,* p. 24.

37. McNitt, *Indian Traders,* pp. 128–29.

38. Miller to Pope, November 1, 1871, *NMIS.*

39. Miller to Pope, November 30 and December 29, 1871, and January 1, 1872, *NMIS.*

40. The following, all *NMIS:* Miller to Pope, January 1, 12, 22, and 27, 1872; February 1, 5, 21, and 27, 1872; and Pope to Commanding Officer, District of New Mexico, March 6, 1872.

41. Miller to Pope, March 21, 1872, *NMIS.*

42. Miller to Pope, March 14, 1872, *NMIS;* and McNitt, *Indian Traders,* pp. 130–31.

43. J. S. Armstrong to Miller, May 18, 1872, *NMIS.*

44. McNitt, *Indian Traders*, pp. 131–32.

45. Ibid., pp. 100–101.

46. Hugh McBride and Other Concerned Citizens of Los Lunas, NM, to Captain Kaufman, Fort Wingate, NM, May 14, 1872, *NMIS*.

47. Miller to Pope, May 23, 1872, *NMIS*.

48. Miller to Pope, May 28, 1872, *NMIS*.

49. J. H. Beadle, *The Undeveloped West; or Five Years in the Territories* (Philadelphia: National Publishing Co., 1873), pp. 511–20. Portions of Beadle's book are quoted in Young, *The Role of the Navajo*, pp. 46–47; and Young, *Navajo Yearbook*, pp. 220–35.

50. Beadle, pp. 522–23.

51. Ibid., pp. 523–24.

52. Ibid., p. 517.

53. Ibid., pp. 526–27; Young, *The Role of the Navajo*, p. 46; McNitt, *Indian Traders*, p. 133; and Keam to Pope, September 9, 1872, *NMIS*. See also Aberle, *Peyote Religion*, p. 39; Brugge, *History of the Chaco Navajos*, p. 61; Locke, *Book of the Navajo*, p. 396; and Terrell, *Navajo*, pp. 237–38.

54. Beadle, p. 527.

Chapter 5

1. McNitt, *Indian Traders*, p. 124; and Pope to Commissioner of Indian Affairs, July 25, 1872, *AP*.

2. Murphy, *Frontier Crusader*, pp. 209–10.

3. Richard Van Valkenburgh, "Thomas Keam" (unpublished manuscript), Richard Van Valkenburgh Collection, Arizona Room, Arizona State University, Tempe.

4. David M. Brugge, *History of the Chaco Navajos*, p. 61; Keam to Pope, July 6, 1872, *NMIS*; Bender, "New Hope for the Indians," p. 84; and Bailey and Bailey, *History of the Navajos*, p. 40.

5. Keam to Pope, July 6, 1872, *NMIS*.

6. Ibid.

7. Keam to Pope, July 27, 1872, *NMIS*.

8. McNitt, *Indian Traders*, p. 134; and Captain A. B. Kauffman, Commander, Fort Wingate, NM, to Pope, July 27, 1872, *NMIS*.

9. Oliver O. Howard, *My Experiences Among Our Hostile Indians: A Record of Personal Observations, Adventures, and Campaigns Among the Indians of the Great West with Some Accounts of Their Life, Habits, Traits, Religion, Ceremonies, Dress, Savage Instincts, and Customs in Peace and War* (New York: Da Capo Press, 1972 [repr., 1909 ed.]), pp. 179–81, and *Famous Indian Chiefs I Have Known* (Lincoln: University of Nebraska Press, 1989 [repr., 1908 ed.]), pp. 137–48; Bender, "New Hope for the Indians," p. 81; McNitt, *Indian Traders*, p. 135; Brugge, *History of the Chaco Navajos*, p. 61; and *Weekly Arizona Miner* (Prescott), January 18, 1873.

10. Brugge, *History of the Chaco Navajos*, p. 61; Locke, *Book of the Navajo*,

p. 404; Terrell, *Navajo*, p. 245; and Keam to Pope, September 8 and 9, 1872, *NMIS*.

11. the following are all in *NMIS:* Bennett to Clinton, August 19, 1870; Miller to Pope, August 17, 1871; and Keam to Pope, August 21, September 7 and 9, 1872. Howard, *My Experiences*, pp. 181–82. See also McNitt, *Indian Traders*, pp. 136–37; Mitchell, *Navajo Blessingway Singer*, p. 118n; Bailey and Bailey, *History of the Navajos*, p. 30; Tietjen, "Encounter with the Frontier," p. 121; Underhill, *Navajos*, p. 162; Van Valkenburgh, *Short History*, p. 40; Young, *The Role of the Navajo*, p. 47; Terrell, *Navajo*, p. 240; and Bender, "*New Hope for the Indians*," pp. 81–82.

12. Bender, "*New Hope for the Indians*," p. 82; Keam to Pope, August 15, 1872, *NMIS*; and McNitt, *Indian Traders*, pp. 135–36.

13. Ibid., p. 136; and Keam to Pope, August 15, 1872, *NMIS*.

14. Keam to Pope, August 15, 1872, *NMIS*.

15. Benjamin M. Thomas to Pope, August 28, 1872, *NMIS*.

16. McNitt, *Indian Traders*, p. 138; D. Irving, Secretary of the Presbyterian Foreign Mission Board, to C. Delano, Commissioner of Indian Affairs, July 6, 1872, and Joseph Casey, Clerk of U.S. Court of Claims, to Delano, April 23, 1872, *AP*; and Report, W. F. Hall to Commissioner of Indian Affairs, September 9, 1872, in Robert A. Roessel, *Pictorial History of the Navajo: From 1860–1910* (Rough Rock, AZ: Navajo Curriculum Center, 1980), p. 139.

17. Roessel, *Pictorial History*, p. 139; and E. D. Peck, Perrysburg, Ohio, to Secretary of Interior, July 12, 1872, and Henry Bennett (Frank Bennett's father), Toledo, Ohio, to Secretary of Interior, July 18, 1872, *AP*.

18. Report, Pope to Commissioner of Indian Affairs, 1872, in Robert Roessel, *Pictoral History*, pp. 138–39; and Hall to Pope, September 9, 1872, and Keam to Pope, September 1 and 9, 1872, *NMIS*.

19. Keam to Pope, September 1 and 7, 1872, *NMIS*.

20. Henry J. Perkinson, *The Imperfect Panacea: American Faith in Education, 1865–1965* (New York: Random House, 1968), pp. 15–16, 18–21, 23–25, 30, 43, 49–51, and 68–69; Henry Allen Bullock, *A History of Negro Education in the South: From 1619 to the Present* (Cambridge: Harvard University Press, 1967), pp. 60, 74, 79–83, and 99–100; and John D. Pulliam, *History of Education in America*, 3rd ed. (Columbus, OH: Charles E. Merrill Publishing Co., 1982), pp. 91–120.

21. Keam to Pope, September 9, 1872, *NMIS*; and McNitt, *Indian Traders*, p. 138.

22. For a good, short biography of Dodge, see David M. Brugge, "Henry Chee Dodge: From Long Walk to Self-Determination," in *Indian Lives: Essays on Nineteenth- and Twentieth-Century Native American Leaders*, ed. L. G. Moses and Raymond Wilson (Albuquerque: University of New Mexico Press, 1985), pp. 91–112.

23. McNitt, *Indian Traders*, pp. 138–41.

24. Price to AAA General, District of New Mexico, September 7, 1872, *NMIS*.

25. Report, Pope to Commissioner of Indian Affairs, 1872, in Robert Roessel, p. 138; and Bailey and Bailey, *History of the Navajos*, p. 41.

26. *Weekly Arizona Miner*, December 14, 1872.

27. Peterson, *Take Up Your Mission*, pp. 6–7.

28. *Weekly Arizona Miner*, December 14, 1872; and Warner, "Fertile Ground," p. 196.

29. Ibid., pp. 195–96; Shepardson, "Navajo Ways in Government," pp. 13–14; Underhill, *Navajos*, p. 199; and Bender, "*New Hope for the Indians*," p. 95.

30. McNitt, *Indian Traders*, p. 136.

31. Bailey and Bailey, *History of the Navajos*, pp. 56–57.

32. Van Valkenburgh, *Short History*, p. 44; and McNitt, *Indian Traders*, p. 102.

33. McNitt, *Indian Traders*, pp. 61–62; Walter Dyk, ed., *Son of Old Man Hat: A Navajo Autobiography* (Lincoln: University of Nebraska Press, 1938), p. 299; and Underhill, *The Navajos*, pp. 184–85. For a brief analysis of the historical importance of the trader see: Iverson, *Navajo Nation*, p. 12.

34. Bailey and Bailey, *History of the Navajos*, pp. 58–59.

35. McNitt, *Indian Traders*, p. 70; and Underhill, *Navajos*, pp. 182–83.

36. Underhill, *Navajos*, pp. 183–84; Le Charles G. Eckel, "History of Ganado, Arizona," *Museum Notes: Museum of Northern Arizona* 6 (April 1934): 48; Van Valkenburgh, *Short History*, p. 46; and Frank C. Lockwood, *Pioneer Portraits: Selected Vignettes* (Tucson: University of Arizona Press, 1968), p. 129.

37. Lockwood, *Pioneer Portraits*, pp. 129–32; Eckel, "History of Ganado," p. 48; Underhill, *Navajos*, pp. 183–84; Van Valkenburgh, *Short History*, p. 46; and McNitt, *Indian Traders*, pp. 142–44.

38. McNitt, *Indian Traders*, p. 142; Eckel, "History of Ganado," pp. 48–49; and Lockwood, *Pioneer Portraits*, p. 132.

39. McNitt, *Indian Traders*, p. 142; Van Valkenburgh, *Short History*, pp. 44–46; Underhill, *Navajos*, p. 183; Erna Fergusson, *Our Southwest* (New York: Alfred A. Knopf, 1940), p. 216; Telling, "New Mexico Frontiers," pp. 27–28; and Murphy, *Frontier Crusader*, pp. 205–6.

40. Bender, "*New Hope for the Indians*," p. 94.

41. Later in the year, some Utes reported that they had killed Miller's murderers who were allegedly members of a Ute band that associated with Paiutes. See McPherson, *Northern Navajo Frontier*, p. 16. See also Hall to Dudley, January 1, February 24 and 25, and June 7, 1873, *NMIS*.

42. Lowrie to Secretary of Interior, April 22, 1873, *AP*.

43. Ibid.

44. Warner, "Fertile Ground," p. 196; McNitt, *Indian Traders*, pp. 137–38n and 140–41n; Brugge, *History of the Chaco Navajos*, p. 62; and Lowrie to Secretary of Interior, June 12, 1873, *AP*.

Chapter 6

1. Arny to Smith, August 13, 1873, *NMIS*.

2. Hall to Dudley, August 14, 1873, *NMIS*.

3. Murphy, *Frontier Crusader*, pp. 3–19, 28–37, 40, 42, 54–55, and 62.

4. Ibid., pp. 102–53, 157, and 183–85.

5. Ibid., pp. 127–28, 166, and 191. A brief account of Lamy's side of the controversy with Arny can be found in Horgan, *Lamy of Santa Fe*, pp. 369–72.

6. Murphy, *Frontier Crusader*, pp. 111 and 159.

7. Murphy, *Frontier Crusader*, p. 204; Underhill, *Navajos*, p. 199; and Terrell, *Navajo*, p. 244.

6. For Arny's objections to the Bosque Redondo see: Murphy, *Frontier Crusader*, pp. 127–28.

9. Arny to Smith, September 6, 1873, and Arny to Rev. John Lowrie, September 23, 1873, *NMIS*. Accounts of Arny's disputes with these employees can also be found in the following: Tietjen, "Encounter with the Frontier," p. 122; McNitt, *Indian Traders*, p. 145; Bender, "New Hope for the Indians," p. 102; and Murphy, *Frontier Crusader*, pp. 205–6.

10. Murphy, *Frontier Crusader*, pp. 209–10; Bender, "New Hope for the Indians," p. 102; and Arny to Smith, September 6, 1873, and Arny to Lowrie, September 23, 1873, *NMIS*.

11. Arny to Smith, September 13, 1873, *NMIS*; McNitt, *Indian Traders*, p. 145; and Murphy, *Frontier Crusader*, p. 210.

12. Brugge, *History of the Chaco Navajos*, p. 62.

13. Gould to Dudley, August 31, 1873, *NMIS*.

14. McNitt, *Indian Traders*, pp. 138–44; Murphy, *Arny*, p. 151; and Arny to Smith, September 6, 1873, *NMIS*.

15. Arny to Dudley, September 25 and 27, 1873, *NMIS*.

16. Arny to Smith, September 5, 1875, *NMIS*; and Murphy, *Frontier Crusader*, p. 213.

17. Murphy, *Frontier Crusader*, pp. 207–8 and 210; Gould to Dudley, two letters written on September 29, 1873, and Arny to Dudley, two letters written on October 13, 1873, *NMIS*; and Locke, *Book of the Navajo*, p. 398.

18. Arny to Dudley, October 2, 1873, Arny to Gould, October 4, 1873, and Arny to Smith, November 1, 1873, *NMIS*; and Murphy, *Frontier Crusader*, p. 214.

19. Kluckhohn and Leighton, *Navaho*, p. 38; and Arny to Smith, November 4, 1873, *NMIS*.

20. Arny to Smith, November 4, 1873, *NMIS*.

21. Ibid. Also see: Littell, *Proposed Findings*, vol. 2, p. 465.

22. Arny to Smith, November 4, 1873, *NMIS*.

23. Ibid.

24. Arny to Dudley, November 20 and December 1, 1873, *NMIS*.

25. Ibid.; and Arny to Dudley, January 2, 1874, *NMIS*.

26. Arny to Dudley, January 2 and 31, 1874, *NMIS*; Young, *The Role of the Navajo*, p. 47; and Murphy, *Frontier Crusader*, p. 214.

27. Murphy, *Frontier Crusader*, p. 213; and Arny to Dudley, January 31, 1874, *NMIS*.

28. John Wesley Powell, *The Exploration of the Colorado and Its Canyons*

(New York: Dover Publications, 1961 [repr., 1895 ed., entitled *Canyons of the Colorado*]), p. 84; Newcomb, *Hosteen Klah*, p. 91; and Murphy, *Frontier Crusader*, pp. 219–20.

29. Murphy, *Frontier Crusader*, pp. 219–20; and Arny to Dudley, January 31, 1874, *NMIS*.

30. McClintock, *Mormon Settlement*, p. 84; Bailey, *Jacob Hamblin*, p. 350; and McNitt, *Indian Traders*, p. 147. See also Peterson, *Take Up Your Mission*, p. 201; Smiley, "Ammon M. Tenney," p. 92; McPherson, *Northern Navajo Frontier*, p. 31; and Murphy, *Frontier Crusader*, p. 320.

31. Gottfredson, *History*, pp. 330–31; and Rusho and Crampton, *Desert River Crossing*, p. 39.

32. McNitt, *Indian Traders*, pp. 146–47; McPherson, *Northern Navajo Frontier*, p. 31; and Arny to Dudley, January 31, 1874, *NMIS*.

33. Arny to Dudley, January 31, 1874; Little, *Jacob Hamblin*, p. 115; Tietjen, "Encounter with the Frontier," p. 123; and Murphy, *Frontier Crusader*, p. 220.

34. Arny to Dudley, February 16, 1874, *NMIS*.

35. Ibid.; Arny to Dudley, February 28, 1874, *NMIS*; Murphy, *Frontier Crusader*, pp. 156–57, 159–62, and 225–26; Dane and Mary Roberts Coolidge, *The Navajo Indians* (Boston: Houghton Mifflin Co., 1930), p. 267; Locke, *Book of the Navajo*, p. 400; and McNitt, *Indian Traders*, p. 150.

36. Gottfredson, *History*, p. 331.

37. Little, *Jacob Hamblin*, p. 120; Harry C. James, *Pages from Hopi History* (Tucson: University of Arizona Press, 1974), p. 94; Bailey, *Jacob Hamblin*, p. 350; Shuichi Nagata, *Modern Transformation of Moenkopi Pueblo* (Urbana: University of Illinois Press, 1970), p. 32; and Rusho and Crampton, *Desert River Crossing*, p. 40.

38. Rusho and Crampton, *Desert River Crossing*, p. 40; and Santa Fe *Daily New Mexican*, May 18 and 20, 1874.

39. Rusho and Crampton, *Desert River Crossing*, p. 40; Bailey, *Jacob Hamblin*, p. 351; McNitt, *Indian Traders*, p. 147; Tietjen, "Encounter with the Frontier," p. 122; McClintock, *Mormon Settlement*, p. 84; and Little, *Jacob Hamblin*, p. 111.

40. Little, *Jacob Hamblin*, p. 112.

41. Ibid.; and Rusho and Crampton, *Desert River Crossing*, p. 40.

42. Rusho and Crampton, *Desert River Crossing*, p. 40; McClintock, *Mormon Settlement*, p. 84; Bailey, *Jacob Hamblin*, pp. 351–54; and Little, *Jacob Hamblin*, pp. 112–13 and 121–22.

43. Little, *Jacob Hamblin*, pp. 114–18 and 122–27; and Rusho and Crampton, *Desert River Crossing*, pp. 40–41.

44. Little, *Jacob Hamblin*, p. 119.

45. Ibid., pp. 125–27; and Rusho and Crampton, *Desert River Crossing*, pp. 40–41.

46. Little, *Jacob Hamblin*, pp. 127–28.

47. Ibid., pp. 128–29.

48. Hamblin to Navajo Indian Agent, March 7, 1874, *NMIS*; and McPherson, *Northern Navajo Frontier*, p. 31.

49. McPherson, *Northern Navajo Frontier*, p. 31; and Arny to Hamblin, March 28, 1874, *NMIS*.

50. Arny to Hamblin, March 28, 1874, and Arny to Dudley, March 28, 1874, *NMIS*; McNitt, *Indian Traders*, p. 148; McPherson, *Northern Navajo Frontier*, pp. 31–32; and Murphy, *Frontier Crusader*, p. 221.

51. Murphy, *Frontier Crusader*, p. 222; Rusho and Crampton, *Desert River Crossing*, p. 41; McClintock, *Mormon Settlement*, p. 86; Peterson, *Take Up Your Mission*, p. 201n; and Smiley, "Ammon M. Tenney," p. 94.

52. McNitt, *Indian Traders*, pp. 148–49; and Murphy, *Frontier Crusader*, p. 222.

53. Rusho and Crampton, *Desert River Crossing*, p. 42.

54. Brugge, *History of the Chaco Navajos*, p. 63; and Santa Fe *Daily New Mexican*, May 20, 1874.

55. Santa Fe *Daily New Mexican*, May 20 and 23, 1874.

56. Ibid., May 20, 1874.

57. Ibid.

58. Ibid.

59. McNitt, *Indian Traders*, pp. 150–51.

60. Rusho and Crampton, *Desert River Crossing*, pp. 41–42.

61. Murphy, *Frontier Crusader*, p. 222; and McNitt, *Indian Traders*, p. 149.

62. McNitt, *Indian Traders*, pp. 146–48.

63. Ibid.

64. Ibid., pp. 130–31.

65. Ibid., p. 131.

66. Ibid., pp. 131–32.

67. Ibid.; McClintock, *Mormon Settlement*, p. 86; and Smiley, "Ammon M. Tenney," pp. 95–96.

Chapter 7

1. Arny to M. A. Otero, May 12, 1874, *NMIS*; Murphy, *Frontier Crusader*, p. 218; and Brugge, *History of the Chaco Navajos*, pp. 63–64.

2. Arny to Dudley, January 31 and February 16, 1874, and Arny to Dudley, May 12, 1874, *NMIS*; Santa Fe *Daily New Mexican*, May 23, 1874; and Murphy, *Frontier Crusader*, p. 218.

3. Murphy, *Frontier Crusader*, pp. 218–19; and Otero to Arny, May 25, 1874, *NMIS*.

4. Otero to Arny, May 25, 1874, *NMIS*; and Murphy, *Frontier Crusader*, pp. 218–19.

5. Murphy, *Frontier Crusader*, pp. 214–17; Arny to Dudley, February 12 and April 3, 1874, *NMIS*; and Bailey and Bailey, *History of the Navajos*, pp. 29–30.

6. Bailey and Bailey, *History of the Navajos*, p. 31; Murphy, *Frontier Crusader*, p. 213; Young, *The Role of the Navajo*, p. 47; and *RCIA*, 1874, pp. 306–7.

7. August 1874, *FW*; and Brugge, *History of the Chaco Navajos*, p. 63. Not

all observers, however, believed that the Navajos were good scouts. Many felt that they were reluctant to fight Apaches. See: Thomas W. Dunley, *Wolves for the Blue Soldiers: Indian Scouts and Auxiliaries with the United States Army, 1860–90* (Lincoln: University of Nebraska Press, 1982), p. 65.

8. Dunley, *Wolves*, p. 65; Murphy, *Frontier Crusader*, p. 222–23; Young, *The Role of the Navajo*, p. 47; Bender, "New Hope for the Indians," pp. 112–13; and *RCIA*, 1874, p. 307.

9. *RCIA*, 1874, p. 307; Murphy, *Frontier Crusader*, p. 223; and Bender, "New Hope for the Indians," p. 113.

10. *RCIA*, 1874, pp. 307–8.

11. Ibid., p. 307.

12. Arny to B. M. Thomas, Agent for the Southern Apaches, June 18, 1874, *NMIS*; and Mary Ellen Jenkins, "Navajo Activities Affecting the Acoma-Laguna Area," in *Navajo Indians, II: American Indian Ethnohistory of the Southwest*, ed. David Agee Horr (New York: Garland Publishing Co., 1974), p. 216.

13. Bender, "New Hope for the Indians," pp. 119–20; and Murphy, *Frontier Crusader*, p. 226.

14. Murphy, *Frontier Crusader*, pp. 226–27; Bender, "New Hope for the Indians," pp. 120–21; and McNitt, *Indian Traders*, pp. 150–51.

15. McNitt, *Indian Traders*, p. 151; *RCIA*, p. 307; and Murphy, *Frontier Crusader*, p. 225. See also Aberle, *Peyote Religion*, p. 39; and Roessel, *Pictorial History*, p. 84.

16. Roessel, p. 85; Buell, "Navajo 'Long Walk,'" p. 173; Bender, "New Hope for the Indians," pp. 116 and 121; Santa Fe *Daily New Mexican*, November 20, 1874; and Murphy, *Frontier Crusader*, pp. 228–29.

17. Murphy, *Frontier Crusader*, pp. 228–29; Bender, "New Hope for the Indians," pp. 121–24; and Santa Fe *Daily New Mexican*, December 4, 1874.

18. McNitt, *Indian Traders*, p. 151.

19. Murphy, *Frontier Crusader*, p. 230.

20. Murphy, *Frontier Crusader*, pp. 230–31; Affidavit, William F. M. Arny, September 13, 1875, *AP*; Bender, "New Hope for the Indians," p. 124; and McNitt, *Indian Traders*, pp. 152–53.

21. Santa Fe *Daily New Mexican*, January 6, 1875; Locke, *Book of the Navajo*, p. 399; and Murphy, *Frontier Crusader*, pp. 230–31.

22. Chris Emmett, *Fort Union and the Winning of the Southwest* (Norman: University of Oklahoma Press, 1965), pp. 363–64.

23. Emmett, *Fort Union*, p. 364; and Murphy, *Frontier Crusader*, p. 231.

24. Santa Fe *Daily New Mexican*, February 6, 1875.

25. Ibid.; Murphy, *Frontier Crusader*, pp. 231–32; Affidavit, William F. M. Arny, September 13, 1875, *AP*; and *RCIA*, 1875, p. 331.

26. Santa Fe *Daily New Mexican*, February 9, 1875; Murphy, *Frontier Crusader*, p. 232; and McNitt, *Indian Traders*, p. 154.

27. McNitt, *Indian Traders*, pp. 154–55; and Murphy, *Frontier Crusader*, p. 232.

28. Murphy, *Frontier Crusader*, p. 232.

29. Ibid.; and *RCIA*, 1875, p. 332.

30. McNitt, *Indian Traders*, pp. 155–56.

31. *RCIA*, 1875, p. 331.

32. Beadle, p. 547, provides an example of this admiration of Navajo women. He wrote that they were "the only Indian girls I ever saw who even approximate to the [James Fenimore] Cooper ideal. Their dress is picturesque, consisting of separate waist and shirt; the former leaves the arms bare, and is made loose above and neat at the waist; the latter is of flowered calico, with a leaning to red and black, and terminates just below the knee in black border or frills. Neat moccasins complete the costume, the limbs being left bare generally in the summer. They are very shapely and graceful, and their strength is prodigious. How these mountaineers, on the thin food they have, manage to produce such specimens of perfect physical womanhood, is a mystery to me." For additional praise of nineteenth- and early twentieth-century Navajo women, see Hilda Faunce, *Desert Wife* (Lincoln: University of Nebraska Press, 1981 [repr., 1928 ed.]), p. 158; Franc Johnson Newcomb, *Navaho Neighbors* (Norman: University of Oklahoma Press, 1966), pp. 5–6 and 9; Francis E. Leupp, *The Indian and His Problem* (New York: Charles Scribners Sons, 1910), p. 15; McNitt, *Richard Wetherill*, pp. 94 and 181–82; and Joseph Schmedding, *Cowboy and Indian Trader* (Albuquerque: University of New Mexico Press, 1974 [repr., 1951 ed.]), p. 17.

33. *RCIA*, 1875, p. 331.

34. A brief account of the lives of average enlisted men on the frontier can be found in Joseph A. Stout, Jr., *Apache Lightning: The Last Great Battles of the Ojo Calientes* (New York: Oxford University Press, 1974), pp. 51–59. For the beginnings of Navajo prostitution, see Thompson, *Army and the Navajo*, pp. 3, 9, 48, and 81. See also Telling, "New Mexico Frontiers," p. 91.

35. *RCIA*, 1875, pp. 331–32; and Mangiante, "History of Fort Defiance," p. 69; Terrell, *Navajo*, p. 244; Murphy, *Frontier Crusader*, pp. 233–34; and Bender, "New Hope for the Indians," p. 125.

36. Bender, "New Hope for the Indians," p. 125; and Murphy, *Frontier Crusader*, p. 233.

37. Murphy, *Frontier Crusader*, p. 234; and United States Attorney Thomas B. Catron to Smith, July 12, 1875, *AP*. The brothel story appears to have originated with agency farmer William Traux who filed a complaint with Rev. Lowrie. See: Bender, "New Hope for the Indians," p. 133.

38. Murphy, *Frontier Crusader*, pp. 232–33; and McNitt, *Indian Traders*, pp. 156–58.

39. Lowrie to Smith, June 18, 1875, *AP*; Murphy, *Frontier Crusader*, p. 234; and Bender, "New Hope for the Indians," p. 139.

40. Victor Westphall, *Thomas B. Catron and His Era* (Tucson: University of Arizona Press, 1973), p. 27; and Catron to Smith, July 12, 1875, *AP*.

41. Catron to Smith, July 12, 1875, *AP*.

42. Catron to Smith, July 12, 1875, and G. A. Smith to Commissioner Smith, July 13, 1875, *AP*; and Murphy, *Frontier Crusader*, pp. 234–35.

43. Chilson to Acting Assistant Adjutant General, District of New Mexico, July 17, 1875, *AP*.

44. Murphy, *Frontier Crusader*, p. 235; McNitt, *Indian Traders*, p. 156; Bender, "*New Hope for the Indians*," p. 140; and Petition, Navajo Chiefs, July 15, 1875, *AP*.

45. Petition, Navajo Chiefs, July 15, 1875, *AP*; and Affidavit, Captain George Chilson, July 15, 1875, *AP*; and Murphy, *Frontier Crusader*, pp. 235–36.

46. Murphy, *Frontier Crusader*, p. 235; and Arny to Delano, July 22, 1875, and Lowrie to Delano, August 11, 1875, *AP*.

47. Murphy, *Frontier Crusader*, p. 236.

48. Ibid.; *RCIA*, 1875, p. 330; Bender, "*New Hope for the Indians*," p. 142; and McNitt, *Indian Traders*, p. 159.

49. McNitt, *Indian Traders*, pp. 159–60.

50. Emmett, *Fort Union*, pp. 366–68.

51. Ibid., pp. 367–68; Santa Fe *Daily New Mexican*, October 4, 1875; and Murphy, *Frontier Crusader*, p. 237.

52. Gregg to Headquarters, Department of Missouri, August 25, 1875, *AP*.

53. Sherman to Secretary of War, August 26, 1875, *AP*.

54. Acting Chief Clerk for the Secretary of War to Secretary of Interior, August 27, 1875, *AP*; Murphy, *Frontier Crusader*, p. 237; McNitt, *Indian Traders*, p. 161; and *FW*, September 1875.

55. *FW*, September 1875; and Gregg to Pope, n.d., *AP*.

56. Gregg to Pope, n.d., *AP*; *FW*, September 1875; and McNitt, *Indian Traders*, p. 161.

57. McNitt, *Indian Traders*, p. 161; Gregg to Pope, n.d., *AP*; *FW*, September 1875; and Emmett, *Fort Union*, p. 368.

58. Bender, "*New Hope for the Indians*," p. 143; and McNitt, *Indian Traders*, pp. 161–62.

59. Quoted in McNitt, *Indian Traders*, p. 162.

60. Ibid.; and Murphy, *Frontier Crusader*, pp. 238–39.

61. *RCIA*, pp. 332–33.

62. Brugge, *History of the Chaco Navajos*, p. 66.

63. Quoted in ibid.

64. Murphy, *Frontier Crusader*, p. 238.

65. Ibid.; Affidavit, D. H. Davis, March 22, 1875, *AP*; *RCIA*, 1875, pp. 330–32; Bender, "*New Hope for the Indians*," p. 143; and McNitt, *Indian Traders*, p. 161–65.

66. Brugge, *History of the Chaco Navajos*, p. 66.

Chapter 8

1. Santa Fe *Daily New Mexican*, September 21 and October 18, 1875; and Irvine to Price, November 11 and 18, 1875, *OIA*.

2. Price to Acting Assistant Adjutant General, District of New Mexico, Lieutenant Thomas P. Blain, November 25, 1875, and W. L. Riggs to Price, n.d., *OIA*; Bailey and Bailey, *History of the Navajos*, pp. 44–45.

3. Brugge, *History of the Chaco Navajos*, p. 66; F. Stanley, *The Jicarilla Apaches of New Mexico: 1540–1967* (Pampa, TX: Pampa Print Shop, 1967), p.

151; and Veronica E. Velarde Tiller, *The Jicarilla Apache Tribe: A History, 1846–1970* (Lincoln: University of Nebraska Press, 1983), p. 80. For information about the Jicarillas losing their land, see ibid., pp. 70–81; and Gertrude B. Van Roekel, *Jicarilla Apaches* (San Antonio, TX: The Naylor Co., 1971), pp. 9–10.

4. For information concerning the Ute loss of territory, see Leroy R. Hafen, "Historical Survey of the Ute Indians and the San Juan Mining Region," in Horr, *Ute Indians II*, pp. 317–24.

5. Brugge, *History of the Chaco Navajos*, p. 67; and Hartaill Lloyd Clark, "History of San Juan County, New Mexico" (master's thesis, University of Tulsa, 1963), pp. 40–42.

6. Nagata, *Modern Transformations*, p. 32; Warner, "Fertile Ground," p. 197; Peterson, *Take Up Your Mission*, pp. 15–16; Little, *Jacob Hamblin*, p. 134; and McClintock, *Mormon Settlement*, p. 157.

7. McClintock, *Mormon Settlement*, p. 93; Thompson, *Army and the Navajo*, pp. 10–11, 94, 126, and 151; Prucha, *Great Father*, vol. 1, pp. 452–53; Kessell, "General Sherman," pp. 256–57; Bailey, *Bosque Redondo*, p. 30; Young, *The Role of the Navajo*, pp. 39–40; Beadle, pp. 521 and 541–42; Martin, July 30, 1872; and Correll, "Navajo Frontiers," p. 151

8. J. Frank Dobie, *Apache Gold and Yaqui Silver* (Albuquerque: University of New Mexico Press, 1971 [repr., 1928 ed.]), pp. 3–31, 57–59, 85–87, 89–100, 103–4, 110–12, 117–18, 131–32, and 141–45.

9. Murphy, *Indian Agent*, pp. 15, 27, and 30; *Weekly Arizona Miner* (Prescott), December 14, 1872; Rusho and Crampton, *Desert River Crossing*, pp. 32–33; Little, *Jacob Hamblin*, pp. 95–134; Billie Williams Yost, *Bread upon the Sands* (Caldwell, ID: The Caxton Printers, 1958), p. 19.

10. Cummings, *Indians I Have Known*, p. 7; and Faunce, *Desert Wife*, pp. 260–63.

11. Blain to Price, November 30, 1875, and Commissioner of Indian Affairs to Secretary of Interior, December 30, 1875, *AP*; December 1875, *FW*; and Price to Blain, December 9, 1875, *OIA*.

12. Price to Blain, December 9, 1875, and Price to Blain, December 30, 1875, *OIA*.

13. *RCIA*;, 1875, pp. 106–10; Irvine to Commissioner of Indian Affairs, November 9, 1877, *OIA*; Bender, "*New Hope for the Indians*," p. 154.

14. Irvine to Commissioner, March 1 and April 6, 1876, *OIA*.

15. Irvine to Commissioner, April 6, 1876, *OIA*; Bender, "*New Hope for the Indians*," pp. 159–60.

16. Bender, "*New Hope for the Indians*," p. 160; *RCIA*, 1876, p. 109; Brugge, *History of the Chaco Navajos*, pp. 68–69; January 1876, *FW*; and Irvine to Commissioner, March 1, 1876, *OIA*.

17. Irvine to Commissioner, March 1, 1876, *OIA*.

18. Ibid.

19. Descriptions of the Little Colorado River can be found in the following: Yost, *Bread upon the Sands*, p. 141; Martha Summerhayes, *Vanished Arizona* (Lincoln: University of Nebraska Press, 1979 [repr., 1911 ed.]), p. 113; Mc-

Clintock, *Mormon Settlement*, pp. 141–42; John G. Bourke, *Snake Dance of the Moquis* (Tucson: University of Arizona Press, 1984 [repr., 1884 ed.]), p. 346; and Peterson, *Take Up Your Mission*, p. 177.

20. Peterson, *Take Up Your Mission*, pp. 202–3; and White, *Roots of Dependency*, pp. 244–45.

21. McClintock, *Mormon Settlement*, pp. 138–48; Peterson, *Take Up Your Mission*, pp. 16–20 and 202; and James S. Brown, *Life of a Pioneer: Being the Autobiography of James S. Brown* (Salt Lake City: George O. Cannon and Sons, 1900), pp. 457–67. Brief accounts of Mormon settlement west and south of the Navajo Reservation can be found in Telling, "New Mexico Frontiers," pp. 167–68; Correll, "Killing of Lot Smith"; Howard F. Daniels, "Mormon Colonization in Northern Arizona" (master's thesis, University of Arizona, 1960), pp. 94–97 and 106–8; Terrell, *Navajo*, p. 276; and Platt Cline, *They Came to the Mountain: The Story of Flagstaff's Beginnings* (Flagstaff, AZ: Northland Press, 1976), pp. 58–61.

22. Cline, *They Came to the Mountain*, pp. 63–65; and Peterson, *Take Up Your Mission*, pp. 166–68.

23. Irvine to Commissioner of Indian Affairs J. Q. Smith, April 13, 1876, *OIA*; Bender, "New Hope for the Indians," p. 156; and *RCIA*, 1876, p. 110. Two writers have mistakenly concluded that the Navajos did not learn about the railroad's land grant until 1876. See the following: Van Valkenburgh, *Short History*, p. 41; and Young, *Navajo Yearbook*, p. 236.

24. Irvine to Smith, April 13, 1876, *OIA*.

25. Irvine to Smith, June 6, 1876, *OIA*; McNitt, *Indian Traders*, p. 164; and *RCIA*, 1876, p. 110.

26. *RCIA*, 1876, p. 110; Thompson, *Army and the Navajo*, p. 101; McNitt, *Indian Traders*, p. 292; Bender, "New Hope for the Indians," p. 157; and Clark, "History," p. 41.

27. *RCIA*, 1876, p. 110.

28. Brugge, *History of the Chaco Navajos*, p. 67; Clark, "History," pp. 41–42; McNitt, *Indian Traders*, p. x; and Agnes Miller Furnham, *Tohta: An Early Day History of Farmington and San Juan County, New Mexico, 1875–1900* (Wichita, TX: Nortex Press, 1977), pp. 21 and 62.

29. Cline, *They Came to the Mountain*, pp. 65–96; Federal Writers Project, *Arizona: A State Guide* (New York: Hastings House, 1940), p. 189; and McClintock, *Mormon Settlement*, pp. 149–51.

30. McClintock, *Mormon Settlement*, pp. 161–67, 177–80, and 188–89; Peterson, *Take Up Your Mission*, pp. 23–24, 30–34, and 204–27; Young, *The Role of the Navajo*, p. 43; and Farish, *History of Arizona*, vol. 6, p. 288.

31. *RCIA*, 1876, pp. 109–10; Bender, "New Hope for the Indians," pp. 154 and 160. Irvine's fears that the Latter Day Saints were converting Navajos were not entirely inaccurate. The Mormons, in fact, were making conversions. For instance, Christian L. Christensen, a Mormon missionary, reported the baptizing of ninety Navajos between November 3, 1879, and August 8, 1882. See McPherson, *Northern Navajo Frontier*, p. 28.

32. McPherson, *Northern Navajo Frontier*, p. 109; Bender, "New Hope for

the Indians," p. 159; Bailey and Bailey, *History of the Navajos,* pp. 41–42; Terrell, *Navajo,* p. 245; and Young, *The Role of the Navajo,* p. 47.

33. January 1877, *FW;* and *RCIA,* 1877, pp. 158–59.

34. *RCIA,* 1877, p. 159; and Kluckhohn and Leighton, *Navaho,* pp. 114–17.

35. Irvine to Smith, July 26, 1877, *OIA;* and *RCIA,* 1877, p. 159.

36. Irvine to Smith, March 28, 1877, *OIA.*

37. Ibid.

38. Irvine to Smith, April 19, 1878, *OIA;* Bender, *"New Hope for the Indians,"* p. 168; and *RCIA,* 1877, p. 159.

39. *RCIA,* 1877, p. 159; and Prucha, *Great Father,* vol. 1, p. 585.

40. *RCIA,* 1877, p. 159; Irvine to Smith, April 21 and May 15, 1877, *OIA;* Bender, *"New Hope for the Indians,"* p. 170; and Irvine to Smith, July 1, 1877, *AP.*

41. Keam to John Lowrie, May 4, 1877, Keam to President Rutherford B. Hayes, May 1, 1877, Keam to Edward Hatch, August 12, 1877, and W. H. Davis to Secretary of Interior Carl Schurz, September 28, 1877, *AP;* and the following endorsements are all in *AP:* Alexander Irvine, September 20, 1877; Frank Tracy Bennett, May 1, 1877; F. V. Lauderdale, Assistant Surgeon, Fort Wingate, May 1, 1877; John Menaul, May 9, 1877; and Ninety-eight Residents, September 1877. See also Frank D. Reeve, "The Government and the Navaho: 1878–1883," *New Mexico Historical Review* 16 (July 1941): 276–77.

42. Reeve, "Government and the Navaho, 1878–1883," p. 277; and the following are all in *AP:* Catron to D. B. Elkins, Washington, D.C., September 27, 1877; E. Haight to Commissioner, September 27, 1877; Affidavit, Thomas Keam, September 17, 1877; Keam to Schurz, December 12, 1877; and Keam to Assistant Secretary of Interior A. Bell, January 29, 1878.

43. Brugge, *History of the Chaco Navajos,* pp. 70–71; and William H. Leckie, *The Buffalo Soldiers: A Narrative of the Negro Cavalry of the West* (Norman: University of Oklahoma Press, 1967), pp. 178–79.

44. Ralph Hedrick Ogle, *Federal Control of the Western Apaches: 1848–1886* (Albuquerque: University of New Mexico Press, 1970), p. 183; and Thrapp, *Conquest,* pp. 172–77.

45. Thrapp, *Conquest,* pp. 177–78; Ogle, *Federal Control,* pp. 183–84; and Dan L. Thrapp, *Victorio and the Mimbres Apaches* (Norman: University of Oklahoma Press, 1974), pp. 200–202.

46. Thrapp, *Victorio,* pp. 201–3; and Ogle, *Federal Control,* p. 184. The Mimbres Apaches were returned to San Carlos in October of 1878 under the escort of two companies of Ninth Cavalry commanded by Captain Frank Tracy Bennett. See Thrapp, *Conquest,* p. 179; and Stout, *Apache Lightning,* p. 85.

47. Brown, *Life of a Pioneer,* pp. 471–75. Brown referred to Ganado Mucho by his Navajo name, Totsohnii Hastiin, which he spelled "Totoso-ne-Huste" but also mentioned his Spanish name as being "Garanu Namunche." For information on his name, see Hoffman, *Navajo Biographies,* p. 129.

48. Brown, *Life of a Pioneer,* p. 473.

49. Ibid., pp. 473–74.

50. Ibid., pp. 474–76.

51. Brugge, *History of the Chaco Navajos*, p. 170.
52. Clark, "History," pp. 43–44.
53. Ibid., p. 44; and Furnham, *Tohta*, pp. 70–72; and Brugge, *History of the Chaco Navajos*, p. 71.
54. Furnham, *Tohta*, pp. 63–64.
55. Ibid., p. 65.
56. Frank Plounteaux to Commissioner, July 30, 1877, *OIA*; and *RCIA*, 1877, p. 159.
57. *RCIA*, 1877, p. 159; and Irvine to Smith, September 3, 1877, *OIA*.
58. Irvine to Commissioner, October 14 and 23, and November 26, 1877, *OIA*.
59. *RCIA*, 1877, p. 158. See also: Bender *"New Hope for the Indians,"* p. 168.
60. Irvine to Commissioner, November 12, 1877, *OIA*.
61. Brugge, *History of the Chaco Navajos*, p. 71.
62. Irvine to Commissioner, January 2 and 4, and February 25 and 28, 1878, *OIA*.
63. Brugge, *History of the Chaco Navajos*, p. 72.
64. Ibid.; and Irvine to Commissioner of Indian Affairs E. A. Hayt, March 7, 1878, *OIA*.
65. March 1878, *FW*; and Brugge, *History of the Chaco Navajos*, pp. 72–73.
66. Brugge, *History of the Chaco Navajos*, p. 73; and Irvine to Hayt, March 28, 1878, *OIA*.
67. Reeve, "Government and Navaho, 1878–1883," p. 284.
68. Secretary of War John Sherman to Schurz, April 19, 1878, *OIA*.

Chapter 9

1. John Lowrie to Secretary of Interior Carl Schurz, July 21, 1874, *AP*; Pyle to Commissioner of Indian Affairs, March 8, 1878, two letters, *OIA*; Bender, *"New Hope for the Indians,"* pp. 172–73 and 182; and John Erasmus Pyle, "Diary, January 1–November 27, 1878: Kept As Navaho Indian Agent, Fort Defiance" (unpublished manuscript, Bancroft Library, University of California, Berkeley), February 10–21, March 20, 26–31 , and April 23–31.
2. Pyle, "Diary," March 31–April 6, May 2, and September 3, 1878; and Reeve, "Government and Navaho, 1878–1883," p. 278.
3. Pyle, "Diary," April 25–26, 1878; and Pyle to Commissioner, April 15, 1878, *OIA*.
4. Pyle to Commissioner, April 13, 1878, and May 20, 1878, *OIA*.
5. Circular, Fort Wingate, May 15, 1878, and Secretary of War to Secretary of Interior, June 8, 1878, *OIA*; Reeve, "Government and Navaho, 1878–1883," p. 278; and Brugge, *History of the Chaco Navajos*, p. 73.
6. For brief descriptions of the causes of nineteenth-century Navajo witchcraft see: Van Valkenburgh, "Navajo Common Law II: Navajo Law and Justice," *Museum Notes: Museum of Northern Arizona 9* (April 1937): 51–52; Clyde Kluckhohn, *Navaho Witchcraft* (Boston: Beacon Press, 1967), pp. 114–20.

7. Kluckhoh, *Navaho Witchcraft*, pp. 81–82, 88–91, 94–99, 104, 107–13, and 119–20; Irvine to Commissioner, February 28, 1878, *OIA*; Kluckhohn and Leighton, *Navaho*, pp. 122, 240, and 247–52; and Martha Blue, *The Witch Purge of 1878: Oral and Documentary History in the Early Navajo Reservation Years* (Tsaile, AZ: Navajo Community College Press, 1988), pp. 12 and 29–30.

8. Blue, *Witch Purge*, pp. 3 and 4; General William Tecumseh Sherman to Secretary of War, September 9, 1878, *OIA*; and Van Valkenburgh, "Navajo Naa'taani," p. 17.

9. Blue, *Witch Purge*, pp. 3–4 and 7–9; Lieutenant G. K. McGunnigle to Post Adjutant, Fort Wingate, June 17, 1878, 3074, and Charles Hubbell to W. B. Leonard, May 31, 1878, 3069, *WD*.

10. Charles Hubbell to W. B. Leonard, May 31, 1878, 3069, *WD*; and Blue, *Witch Purge*, pp. 5–6 and 9–11.

11. C. Hubbell to Leonard, May 31, 1878, 3070, *WD*.

12. Ibid.; and Blue, *Witch Purge*, p. 6.

13. C. Hubbell to Leonard, May 31, 1878, 3071, *WD*; and Lockwood, *Pioneer Portraits*, pp. 136–37.

14. May and June 1878, *FW*; Swaine to Pyle, June 1, 1883, Pyle to Commissioner, August 17, 1878, and Endorsement, P. T. Swaine, June 27, 1878, *OIA*; and Swaine to Assistant Adjutant General, Department of New Mexico, June 3, 1878, 3068, *WD*.

15. McGunnigle to Post Adjutant, June 17, 1878, 3074, *WD*; and Pyle, "Diary," June 2, 1878.

16. Pyle, "Diary," June 3, 1878; McGunnigle to Post Adjutant, June 17, 1878, 3074, *WD*.

17. McGunnigle to Post Adjutant, June 17, 1878, 3074, *WD*.

18. Blue, *Witch Purge*, p. 15.

19. Pyle to Commissioner, August 17, 1878, *OIA*; Pyle, "Diary," June 3, 1878; and McGunnigle to Post Adjutant, June 17, 1878, 3074, *WD*.

20. McGunnigle to Post Adjutant, June 17, 1878, 3074, *WD*; Pyle, "Diary," June 4 and 5, 1878; McPherson, *Northern Navajo Frontier*, p. 40; and Pyle to Commissioner, August 17, 1878, *OIA*.

21. McGunnigle to Post Adjutant, June 17, 1878, 3074, and John L. Hubbell to Commanding Officer, Fort Wingate, June 10, 1878, 3078, *WD*; Blue, *Witch Purge*, pp. 18–20; Endorsement, Swaine, June 27, 1878, *OIA*; and June 1878, *FW*.

22. June 1878, *FW*; the following account of the army's meeting with the Navajos concerning witchcraft is from D. D. Mitchell to Post Adjutant, Fort Wingate, June 18, 1878, 3075, *WD*.

23. For accounts that use traditional Navajo figures for the number of people killed, see Van Valkenburgh, *Short History*, p. 47; and Hoffman, *Navajo Biographies*, p. 148. Many writers have dealt superficially with the role of Ganado Mucho and Manuelito in the witchcraft scare of 1878. See Underhill, *Navajos*, p. 160; Kluckhohn and Leighton, *Navaho*, p. 249; Kluckhohn, *Navaho Witchcraft*, pp. 114–16; Terrell, *Navajo*, pp. 242–43; Locke, *Book of the Navajo*, p. 403; Robert W. Young and William Morgan, eds., *The Trouble at Round*

Rock by Left-Handed Mexican Clansman with Related Anecdotes by Howard Gorman and the Nephew of Former Big Man (Phoenix: U.S. Indian Service, 1952), p. 7; Berard Haile, *Soul Concepts of the Navajo* (Rome: Vatican Polygot Press, 1943), p. 91; McNitt, *Indian Traders*, p. 203; and Reeve, "Government and the Navaho, 1878–1883," pp. 279–80. Most of the writers cited above assume that the chiefs, being powerful, used the accusation of witchcraft as a ploy to get rid of Navajos who were raiding, an assumption that does not seem to agree with documentary facts. Recently, other writers have advocated the other extreme, maintaining that Ganado Mucho and Manuelito appealed to the army out of weakness. This opinion is defensible, but it probably ignores the very real power possessed by the chiefs prior to military intervention. See Blue, *Witch Purge*; and Bailey and Bailey, *History of the Navajos*, pp. 33–34.

24. Swaine to Headquarters, District of New Mexico, June 19, 1878, 3075, *WD*.

25. Pyle to Commissioner, June 21, 1878, *OIA*; and Blue, *Witch Purge*, p. 17.

26. Endorsement, Swaine, June 27, 1878, Pyle to Swaine, June 31, 1878, and Pyle to Commissioner, August 17, 1878, *OIA*.

27. Gladfield Richardson, "Mystery Cave," *Arizona Days and Ways* (December 3, 1967), pp. 48 and 50; Gladfield Richardson, *Two Guns, Arizona* (Santa Fe: Bluefeather Press, 1968), pp. 8–9; and Philip Johnston, "The Bravest Man I Ever Knew" (unpublished manuscript, n.d. [copy in Northern Arizona Library, Special Collections]), p. 2.

28. Clyde Bennally, with Andrew O. Wiget, John R. Alley, and Barry Blake, *A Utah Navajo History* (Monticello, UT: San Juan School District, 1982), p. 151.

29. Leckie, *Buffalo Soldiers*, p. 19; and Brugge, *History of the Chaco Navajos*, p. 73.

30. Pyle, "Diary," June 30, 1878.

31. Pyle to Commissioner, July 10, 1878, *OIA*.

32. Ibid.

33. Pyle, "Diary," July 9, 1878.

34. Ibid., July 3, 7, and 30, 1878; Blue, *Witch Purge*, p. 25; and July–August 1878, *FW*.

35. *RCIA*, 1878, pp. 108–9.

36. Ibid., p. 108.

37. Ibid., p. 109.

38. Ibid.

39. Ibid.; Van Valkenburgh, *Short History*, p. 42; Fergusson, *Our Southwest*, p. 218; Bailey and Bailey, *History of the Navajos*, pp. 41 and 299; Sherman to Secretary of War, September 9, 1878, *OIA*; McClintock, *Mormon Settlement*, p. 158; Larson, *Erastus Snow*, p. 362; Klink, p. 51; Peterson, *Take Up Your Mission*, pp. 22–23; and Nagata, *Modern Transformations*, pp. 1 and 32.

40. Pyle, "Diary," September 2–6, 1878.

41. Ibid., September 7 and 11, 1878; Pyle to Commissioner, November 8, 1878, *OIA*; and September 1878, *FW*.

42. September 1878, *FW*; and Pyle to Commissioner, November 8, 1878, and Sherman to Secretary of War, September 9, 1878, *OIA*.

43. Sherman to Secretary of War, September 9, 1878; Endorsement, Sherman, September 8, 1878, and Pyle to Commissioner, September 9, 1878, *OIA*; Brugge, *History of the Chaco Navajos*, pp. 73–74; Kessell, "General Sherman," p. 269; and Bender, "*New Hope for the Indians*," p. 183.

44. Bender, "*New Hope for the Indians*," p. 183; and Sherman to Secretary of War, September 9, 1878, *OIA*.

45. Pyle, "Diary," September 9–10, November 8, 1878; Bender, "*New Hope for the Indians*," p. 183; and Pyle to Commissioner, November 8, 1878, *OIA*.

46. Pyle to Commissioner, November 8, 1878, *OIA*.

47. Pyle to Commissioner, September 18 and 30, 1878, *OIA*; and Brugge, *History of the Chaco Navajos*, p. 73.

48. Pyle, "Diary," October 1 and 3–4, 1878.

49. December 1878, *FW*; Thrapp, *Conquest*, pp. 179–80; Ogle, *Federal Control*, pp. 193–94; and Stout, *Apache Lightning*, pp. 85–86.

50. Reeve, "Government and the Navaho, 1878–1883," pp. 280–81; and Pyle, "Diary," October 21, 1878.

51. Pyle, "Diary," November 4–5 and 8–13, 1878; Pyle to Commissioner, October 31 and November 14, 1878, *OIA*; Bailey and Bailey, *History of the Navajos*, pp. 79–80; Goodman, *Navajo Atlas*, pp. 56–57; Iverson, *Navajo Nation*, pp. 14–15; Lawrence Kelly, *Navajo Indians*, pp. 17–19; Underhill, *Navajos*, pp. 148–49; and Reeve, "Government and the Navaho, 1878–1883," p. 285.

52. Reeve, "Government and the Navaho, 1878–1883," p. 285; Bender, "*New Hope for the Indians*," p. 183; and Swaine to Adjutant General, District of New Mexico, December 20, 1878, *OIA*.

53. Swaine to Adjutant General, District of New Mexico, December 20, 1878, *OIA*.

54. Ibid.

55. Reeve, "Government and the Navaho, 1878–1883," p. 281.

Chapter 10

1. Pyle to Commissioner of Indian Affairs, April 5, 1879, and Eastman to Commissioner, April 8, 1879, *OIA*; Reeve, "Government and the Navaho, 1878–1883," p. 282; Murphy, *Frontier Crusader*, pp. 236–38; Thrapp, *Victorio*, pp. 201–7; and Bender, "*New Hope for the Indians*," p. 184.

2. Eastman to Commissioner, April 28 and 30, May 1 and 10, 1879, *OIA*.

3. Eastman to Commissioner, May 1 and 23, 1879, *OIA*; and Reeve, "Government and the Navaho, 1878–1883," p. 382.

4. Reeve, "Government and the Navaho, 1878–1883," p. 382; and Eastman to Commissioner, May 22, 23, and 24, 1879, and J. M. Whitney (Whitney's brother) to Commissioner, June 20, 1879, *OIA*.

5. Eastman to Commissioner, April 30 and May 22, 1879, *OIA*; and Reeve, "Government and the Navaho, 1878–1883," pp. 298–99.

6. Reeve, "Government and the Navaho, 1878–1883," p. 297; and Bailey and Bailey, *History of the Navajos*, p. 31.

7. Reeve, "Government and the Navaho, 1878–1883," pp. 297–98; Shepardson, *Navajo Ways*, p. 13; Eastman to Commissioner, May 23, 27, and September 1, 1879, *OIA*; and *RCIA*, 1879, pp. 116–18.

8. *RCIA*, 1880, p. 131; Locke, *Book of the Navajo*, p. 420; and Reeve, "Government and the Navaho, 1878–1883," pp. 295–96.

9. June 1879, *FW*; Brugge, *History of the Chaco Navajos*, p. 74; Leckie, *Buffalo Soldiers*, p. 192.

10. Leckie, *Buffalo Soldiers*, p. 191.

11. Brugge, *History of the Chaco Navajos*, p. 74; and Thrapp, *Victorio*, pp. 239–51.

12. For a popularized account of the Ute uprising of 1879, see Robert Emmitt, *The Last War Trail: The Utes and the Settlement of Colorado* (Norman: University of Oklahoma Press, 1954). See also Wilson Rockwell, *The Utes: A Forgotten People* (Denver: Sage Books, 1956), pp. 133–37; and James Jefferson, Robert W. Delany, and Gregory C. Thompson, *The Southern Utes: A Tribal History*, ed. Floyd A. O'Neil (Ignacio, CO: Southern Ute Tribe, 1972), p. 33.

13. Jefferson et al., *Southern Utes*, p. 33; Gillmore and Wetherill, *Traders*, pp. 21, 46, and 93; and Furnham, *Tohta*, pp. 107–8; and Rockwell, *Utes*, p. 138.

14. Rockwell, *Utes*, p. 138; Furnham, *Tohta*, p. 108; Eastman to Commissioner, October 20, 1879, and Statement, Oliver A. Whitney, Charles Hunt, and Archie Angell, Surveyors, October 30, 1879, *OIA*; Frank D. Reeve, "A Navaho Struggle for Land," *New Mexico Historical Review* 21 (January 1946): 4; and Brugge, *History of the Chaco Navajos*, p. 74.

15. Brugge, *History of the Chaco Navajos*, pp. 74–75.

16. Ibid., pp. 75–76; and Reeve, "Navaho Struggle," p. 4.

17. Reeve, "Navaho Struggle," pp. 4–5; and Brugge, *History of the Chaco Navajos*, p. 76.

18. Brugge, *History of the Chaco Navajos*, p. 77.

19. August and September 1879, *FW*.

20. Eastman to Commissioner, October 18, 1879, *OIA*.

21. Eastman to Commissioner, October 3, 1879, *OIA*.

22. Eastman to Commissioner, January 5, 1880, *OIA*.

23. Bender, *Missionaries*, pp. 92, 107, 119, and 125–26; Jesse Green, ed., *Zuni: Selected Writings of Frank Hamilton Cushing* (Lincoln: University of Nebraska Press, 1979), p. 71; and Young and Morgan, *Trouble at Round Rock*, p. 7.

24. Brugge, *History of the Chaco Navajos*, p. 76; and Reeve, "Government and the Navaho, 1878–1883," p. 283.

25. Reeve, "Government and the Navhao, 1878–1883," pp. 298 and 300.

26. Keith L. Bryant, Jr., *History of the Atchison, Topeka and Santa Fe Railway* (Lincoln: University of Nebraska Press, 1974), pp. 61–62 and 66; and L. L. Waters, *Steel Trails to Santa Fe* (Lawrence: University of Kansas Press, 1950), pp. 67–68. See also Telling, "New Mexico Frontiers," p. 19; and Bender, *Missionaries*, pp. 124–25.

27. McClintock, *Mormon Settlement*, p. 159; and Peterson, *Take Up Your Mission*, pp. 127–28.

28. Peterson, *Take Up Your Mission*, pp. 127–28 and 202–3; and Klink, *Land Enough*, pp. 51–53.

29. Eastman to Commissioner, January 5 and 30, 1880, *OIA*.

30. Bullock Haines to Eastman, January 19, 1880, and J. T. Owens and C. T. Snyder to Eastman, January 20, 1880, *OIA*. Mention of the executive order of January 6, 1880, can be found in the following: Van Valkenburgh, *Short History*, p. 47; Reeve, "Navaho Struggle," p. 5; Underhill, *Navajos*, p. 149; Kelly, *Navajo Indians*, pp. 17–19; Goodman, *Navajo Atlas*, pp. 56–57; Bailey and Bailey, *History of the Navajos*, p. 80; Iverson, *Navajo Nation*, pp. 14–15.

31. Iverson, *Navajo Nation*, pp. 14–15; Goodman, *Navajo Atlas*, pp. 56–57; Lawrence Kelly, *Navajo Indians*, pp. 18–19; Reeve, "Navaho Struggle," pp. 5–6; Brugge, *History of the Chaco Navajos*, pp. 90–91; Eastman to Commissioner, January 29 and February 12, 1880, Keam to Eastman, February 12, 1880, and Mathias Ebert, Farmington, NM, to Secretary of Interior Carl Schurz, April 2, 1880, *OIA*; and McNitt, *Indian Traders*, p. 219.

32. Telling, "New Mexico Frontiers," p. 107 and Reeve, "Government and the Navaho, 1878–1883," pp. 286–87.

33. Reeve, "Government and the Navaho, 1878–1883," p. 298; and Eastman to Commissioner, January 15, 1880, *OIA*.

34. Eastman to Commissioner, January 26 (two letters) and February 6, 1880, *OIA*.

35. Eastman to Commissioner, March 20, 1880, *OIA*.

36. McPherson, *Northern Navajo Frontier*, pp. 42–43; and Eastman to Commissioner, March 8 and 20, 1880, and H. L. Mitchell to Eastman, February 27, 1880, *OIA*.

37. H. L. Mitchell to Eastman, February 27, 1880, *OIA*.

38. Eastman to Commissioner, March 20, 1880, *OIA*; and McPherson, *Northern Navajo Frontier*, p. 43.

39. Gillmor and Wetherill, *Traders*, pp. 12–18 and 95–96; Bennally et al., *Utah Navajo History*, pp. 153–55; McNitt, *Indian Traders*, pp. 177–78; Correll, "Navajo Frontiers," p. 151; Kelly, "Chief Hoskaninni," p. 223; and Klink, *Land Enough*, pp. 28–33.

40. Some writers assume Navajo guilt. See Klink, *Land Enough*, pp. 28–31; Cummings, *Indians I Have Known*, pp. 7–8; and Jack Breed, "Flaming Cliffs of Monument Valley," *National Geographic* 88 (October 1945): 461–62. For brief mention of the Merrick and Mitchell murders, see Locke, *Book of the Navajo*, p. 105; Neil M. Judd, *Men Met Along the Trail* (Norman: University of Oklahoma Press, 1968), p. 29. See also McNitt, *Indian Traders*, pp. 178–80; Tietjen, "Encounter with the Frontier," p. 123; and Gillmor and Wetherill, *Traders*, p. 15.

41. Gillmor and Wetherill, *Traders*, pp. 17–18; and Bailey and Bailey, *History of the Navajos*, p. 81. A copy of the *Denver Tribune* article is attached to Eastman's letter to the Commissioner, March 23, 1880, *OIA*.

42. Eastman to Commissioner, March 23, 1880, *OIA*; and Reeve, "Government and the Navaho, 1878–1883," p. 299n.

43. Eastman to Commissioner, April 6, 1880, *OIA*.

44. Ibid.; Bailey and Bailey, *History of the Navajo*, p. 81; and Reeve, "Government and the Navaho, 1878–1883," p. 300.

45. Telling, "New Mexico Frontiers," p. 155; Warner, "Fertile Ground," p. 197; and *RCIA*, 1880, p. 133.

46. Bennett to Acting Assistant Adjutant General, District of New Mexico, April 16, 1880, *AP*.

47. Ibid.; Bender *"New Hope for the Indians,"* p. 185; Statement, J. B. McNett, Crepe McNett, R. Eleanor Griffin, and Amanda Easterman, April 18, 1880, *AP*; and Bennett to Commissioner, June 20, 1880, *OIA*.

48. Williams to McNett, April 11, 1880, *AP*.

49. Ibid.

50. Ibid.

51. Sutherland to Eastman, May 1, 1880, Eastman to Commissioner, May 2, 1880, and Bennett to Commissioner, June 20, 1880, *OIA*; and Reeve, "Government and the Navaho, 1878–1883," pp. 300–301. A brief description of Dr. McNett and the teachers leaving can also be found in Bailey and Bailey, *History of the Navajos*, p. 81. See also Warner, "Fertile Ground," p. 197; and *RCIA*, 1880, p. 132.

52. Eastman to Commissioner, May 4, 1880, *OIA*; Roger D. Hardeway, "Unlawful Love: A History of Arizona's Miscegenation Law," *Journal of Arizona History* 27 (Winter 1986): 377–90; and Reeve, "Government and the Navaho, 1878–1883," p. 286.

53. Reeve, "Government and the Navaho, 1878–1883," pp. 300–301; *RCIA*, 1880, p. 133; William A. Keleher, *The Fabulous Frontier: Twelve New Mexico Items*, rev. ed. (Albuquerque: University of New Mexico Press, 1962), pp. 235–36; and Bailey and Bailey, *History of the Navajos*, p. 81.

54. John Navajo to Eastman, May 6, 1880, and Perry Williams to Eastman, May 7, 1880, *OIA*; and Reeve, "Government and the Navaho, 1878–1883," p. 301.

55. Reeve, "Government and the Navaho, 1878–1883," pp. 301–2; and Bailey and Bailey, *History of the Navajos*, pp. 81–82.

56. Buell to Assistant Adjutant General, Department of New Mexico, June 8, 1880, *AP*; and Reeve, "Government and the Navaho, 1878–1883," p. 302.

57. Reeve, "Government and the Navaho, 1878–1883," p. 302; and Buell to AA General, June 8, 1880, *AP*.

58. E. B. Townsend to Commissioner, June 8, 1880, *AP*; and Reeve, "Government and the Navaho, 1878–1883," pp. 302–4.

59. Reeve, "Government and the Navaho, 1878–1883," pp. 301n and 304; and Acting Commissioner of Indian Affairs E. J. Brooks to Secretary of Interior, June 5, 1880, *AP*.

60. Telling, "New Mexico Frontiers," p. 118; and June 1880, *FW*.

61. General John Pope to Colonel W. D. Whipple, Assistant Adjutant General, Chicago, June 9, 1880, *AP*; Reeve, "Government and the Navaho, 1878–

1883," pp. 302–3; and Will C. Barnes, *Apaches and Longhorns: The Reminiscences of Will C. Barnes*, ed. Frank C. Lockwood (Los Angeles: The War Ritchie Press, 1941), p. 37.

62. General Philip Sheriden to General E. D. Townsend, Washington, D.C., June 8, 1880, *AP.*

63. General William T. Sherman to Secretary of War, A. Ramsey, June 9, 1880, *AP.*

64. Chief Clerk, War Department, to Secretary of Interior, June 10, 1880, *AP*; Reeve, "Government and the Navaho, 1878–1883," p. 303; and Buell to Bennett, June 12, 1880, *OIA.*

Chapter 11

1. Bender, "*New Hope for the Indians*," pp. 184–85; E. J. Brooks, Acting Commissioner of Indian Affairs, to Secretary of War, August 14, 1880, *AP*; and Reeve, "Government and the Navaho, 1878–1883," p. 303.

2. Reeve, "Government and the Navaho, 1878–1883," p. 296; *RCIA*, 1880, p. 131; Brugge, *History of the Chaco Navajos*, p. 92; Van Valkenburgh, *Short History*, p. 48; and Alban W. Hoopes, "The Indian Rights Association and the Navaho, 1890–1895," *New Mexico Historical Review* 21 (January 1946): 26.

3. Reeve, "Government and the Navaho, 1878–1883," p. 302.

4. Ibid., p. 305; and Bennett to Commissioner of Indian Affairs, June 20, 1880, *OIA.*

5. Brugge, *History of the Chaco Navajos*, p. 91; Bennett to New Mexico Superintendent of Indian Affairs Nathaniel Pope, February 1, 1872, *NMIS*; and Henry Bennett (Frank Bennett's father), Toledo, OH, to Secretary of Interior, July 18, 1872, *AP.*

6. Buell to Assistant Adjutant General, Department of New Mexico, June 8, 1880, *AP*; and Reeve, "Government and the Navaho, 1878–1883," p. 302.

7. Reeve, "Government and the Navaho, 1878–1883," p. 291; *RCIA*, 1880, p. 132; and Bailey and Bailey, *History of the Navajos*, p. 82. Also see Telling, "New Mexico Frontiers," p. 68; and Coolidge, *Navajo Indians*, p. 256.

8. Reeve, "Government and the Navaho, 1878–1883," pp. 292–93; Brugge, *History of the Chaco Navajos*, p. 92; Bennett to Commissioner of Indian Affairs, October 1 and 14, 1880, *LB*; *RCIA*, 1880, pp. 132–33; Aberle, *Peyote Religion*, p. 35; and Bailey and Bailey, *History of the Navajos*, p. 35.

9. Bailey and Bailey, *History of the Navajos*, pp. 54, 55, and 78; Bryant, *History*, pp. 89–90; Hoopes, "Indian Rights Association," p. 24; Thrapp, *Conquest*, pp. 208–10; and Telling, "New Mexico Frontiers," p. 39.

10. Telling, "New Mexico Frontiers," pp. 38–41, 61–62, 68, and 93; David F. Myrick, *Arizona Pioneer Railroads* (Golden, CO: Colorado Railroad Museum, 1968), p. 12; J. M. Erskine, "The First Settlement of Flagstaff," *The Coconino Sun* (Flagstaff), July 20, 1901; Terrell, *Navajo*, p. 273; Littell, *Proposed Findings*, vol. 2, p. 466; Bennett to Commissioner, January 7, 1881, *LB*; and Bryant, *History*, pp. 85–90. For specific complaints about liquor sales, see

Bennett to Post Adjutant, Fort Wingate, May 19, 1881, and Bennett to AAA General, District of New Mexico, June 18, 1881, *LB*.

11. Bennett to Commissioner, January 7, 1881, *LB*.

12. Ibid.; Brugge, *History of the Chaco Navajos*, p. 93; Young, *The Role of the Navajo*, p. 49. For a Farmington oral history of this event, see Furnham, *Tohta*, p. 109. This account, however, combines the event with another incident at a Farmington store in March of 1882. See McNitt, *Indian Traders*, p. 173n.

13. Bennett to Post Adjutant, Fort Wingate, April 9, 1881, and Bennett to Commissioner, May 2, 1881, *LB*.

14. Accounts of Bourke's visit can be found in the following: McNitt, *Indian Traders*, pp. 79–80, 168–71; Joseph C. Porter, "John G. Bourke," in Paul Andrew Hutton, *Soldiers West: Biographies from the Military Frontier* (Lincoln: University of Nebraska Press, 1897), p. 148; Joseph C. Porter, *Paper Medicine Man: John Gregory Bourke and His American West* (Norman: University of Oklahoma Press, 1986), pp. 95–111; and Bourke, *Snake Dance*.

15. Bourke, *Snake Dance*, pp. 55, 60–66, 69–72, 81, 88–89, and 343–44; Porter, *Paper Medicine Man*, pp. 96–97; and McNitt, *Indian Traders*, p. 168.

16. Quoted in McNitt, *Indian Traders*, p. 168; and Porter, *Paper Medicine Man*, p. 96.

17. Bender, "New Hope for the Indians," p. 185; General Edward Hatch, Commander, Department of New Mexico, to Secretary of Interior, March 14, 1881, *AP*; McNitt, *Indian Traders*, pp. 167–68; Telling, "New Mexico Frontiers," p. 108; Eastman to Commissioner, August 20, 1881, *LB*; Reeve, "Government and the Navaho, 1878–1883," pp. 303–7; and *RCIA*, 1881, p. 137.

18. *RCIA*, 1881, p. 137; Eastman to Commissioner, August 20, 1881, *LB*.

19. Bender, "New Hope for the Indians," p. 185; Reeve, "Government and the Navaho, 1878–1883," p. 307; and L. P. Bradley to Hatch, July 28, 1881, *AP*.

20. L. P. Bradley to Hatch, July 28, 1881, *AP*.

21. Ibid.; and Reeve, "Government and the Navaho, 1878–1883," p. 307.

22. Ibid.; and Eastman to Commissioner, August 20, 1881, *LB*.

23. Bender, "New Hope for the Indians," pp. 185–86.

24. Eastman to Commissioner, August 20 and 31, 1881, *LB*.

25. Commissioner of Indian Affairs Hiram Price to Secretary of Interior, September 3, 1881, and Endorsement, AAA General, Headquarters of the Army, C. McKeaver, September 24, 1881, *AP*.

26. McNitt, *Indian Traders*, p. 169; and Price to Secretary of Interior, September 3, 1881, and Secretary of War Robert Lincoln to Secretary of Interior, December 1, 1881, *AP*.

27. Porter, *Paper Medicine Man*, pp. 144–46; and Thrapp, *Conquest*, pp. 217–36.

28. Bailey and Bailey, *History of the Navajos*, p. 90; Brugge, *History of the Chaco Navajos*, p. 94; and Reeve, "Government and the Navaho, 1878–1883," p. 289.

29. Reeve, "Government and the Navaho, 1878–1883," p. 290; Eastman to

Commissioner, October 31, 1881, and Eastman to Moqui Agent, December 10, 1881, *LB*; and Green, *Zuni*, p. 10.

30. Eastman to Commissioner, November 9, 1881, *LB*.

31. Bender, *"New Hope for the Indians,"* pp. 186–87.

32. Quoted in ibid., p. 187.

33. Eastman to F. W. Smith, Superintendent of the Atlantic and Pacific Railroad, Albuquerque, NM, November 9 and December 2, 1881, *LB*.

34. Eastman to Bradley, January 12, 1882, *LB*; and McNitt, *Indian Traders*, p. 172. Actually, the Navajos also visited Fort Apache to trade. Although the Navajo Nation had represented a northern boundary to Apache operations for years, the two peoples did trade with each other occasionally. See John M. Carroll, ed., *The Black Military Experience in the American West*, Short ed. (New York: Liveright, 1973), pp. 159–60.

35. Eastman to Commissioner, January 28, 1882, *LB*; and Reeve, "Government and the Navaho, 1878–1883," p. 309.

36. Eastman to A and P Section Boss, January 31, 1882, *LB*.

37. Eastman to Commissioner, February 8, 1882, *LB*.

38. Ibid.; and Eastman to Commissioner, February 13 and 28, 1882, and Eastman to U.S. Attorney S. M. Barnes, February 13, 1882, *LB*.

39. Telling, "New Mexico Frontiers," pp. 42–43; Eastman to Smith, March 20, 1882, *LB*; and Reeve, "Government and the Navhao, 1878–1883," pp. 293–94.

40. Reeve, "Government and the Navaho, 1878–1883," p. 309; J'Nell L. Pate, "Ronald S. Mackenzie," in Hutton, *Soldiers West*, p. 187; McNitt, *Indian Traders*, p. 172; and Eastman to Commissioner, February 22, 1882, *LB*.

41. Notices to citizens of San Juan Region from Eastman, February 17 and 20, 1882, and Eastman to Dargar Sikie, March 13, 1882, *LB*.

42. McNitt, *Indian Traders*, p. 173; and Brugge, *History of the Chaco Navajos*, pp. 99–100.

43. Brugge, *History of the Chaco Navajos*, pp. 99–100; and McNitt, *Indian Traders*, p. 173.

44. Smith to Eastman, May 15, 1882, *LB*; and Reeve, "Government and the Navaho, 1878–1883," pp. 287–88.

45. Reeve, "Government and the Navaho, 1878–1883," p. 311n; and Bailey and Bailey, *History of the Navajos*, p. 65.

46. McNitt, *Indian Traders*, pp. 173–74.

47. Reeve, "Government and the Navaho, 1878–1883," pp. 310–11.

48. Eastman to Commissioner, April 11, 1882, *LB*.

49. Telling, "New Mexico Frontiers," pp. 119–20.

50. McNitt, *Indian Traders*, pp. 175–76; and Reeve, "Government and the Navaho, 1878–1883," p. 311.

51. Reeve, "Government and the Navaho, 1878–1883," p. 311.

52. McNitt, *Indian Traders*, pp. 178–79; and Reeve, "Government and the Navaho, 1878–1883," p. 312.

53. Eastman to Sayer, June 7, 1882, Eastman to Bentley, June 21 and July 20, 1882, and Eastman to Cushing, July 20, 1882, *LB*.

54. Littell, *Proposed Findings*, p. 516; Bailey and Bailey, *History of the Navajos*, p. 90; and Brugge, *History of the Chaco Navajos*, p. 100.

55. Bender, *"New Hope for the Indians,"* p. 187; and Reeve, "Government and the Navaho, 1878–1883," p. 312.

56. Brugge, *History of the Chaco Navajos*, p. 100; and Eastman to Commissioner, August 14, 1882, *LB*.

57. Eastman to Commissioner, August 14, 1882, *LB*.

58. Ibid.; and Eastman to Mackenzie, September 8, 1882, and Pass for Francisco Capitan, August 14, 1882, *LB*.

59. McNitt, *Indian Traders*, p. 180.

60. Ibid.; Bender, *"New Hope for the Indians,"* pp. 187 and 235n.

61. Eastman to Commissioner, October 14 and 31, 1882, *LB*; Bailey and Bailey, *History of the Navajos*, p. 48; and Brugge, *History of the Chaco Navajos*, p. 102.

Chapter 12

1. Prucha, *Great Father*, vol. 1, pp. 611–63.

2. Frank D. Reeve, "The Government and the Navaho, 1883–1888," *New Mexico Historical Review* 18 (January 1943): 33 and 37n.

3. Reeve, "Government and the Navaho, 1883–1888," p. 17; and Bender, *"New Hope for the Indians,"* p. 187.

4. Reeve, "Government and the Navaho, 1883–1888," pp. 18–20; and McNitt, *Indian Traders*, p. 60.

5. McNitt, *Indian Traders*, pp. 60–61; and Reeve, "Government and the Navaho, 1883–1888," pp. 26–28.

6. Reeve, "Government and the Navaho, 1883–1888," pp. 38 and 43; McNitt, *Indian Traders*, pp. 186–99 and 203–24; Robert A. Trennert, "Fairs, Expositions, and the Changing Image of Southwestern Indians, 1876–1904," *New Mexico Historical Review* 62 (April 1987): 138–39; Lockwood, *Pioneer Portraits*, pp. 146, 147, 149–51, and 157–59; Farish, *History of Arizona*, vol. 6, pp. 281–83; Nicholas Roosevelt, *Theodore Roosevelt: The Man As I Knew Him* (New York: Dodd, Mead and Co., 1967), pp. 118–19 and 121–22; Lawrence Clark Powell, *Southwest Classics* (Tucson: University of Arizona Press, 1974), pp. 74, 220, and 309; and William T. Hagan, *The Indian Rights Association: The Herbert Welsh Years, 1882–1904* (Tucson: University of Arizona Press, 1985), p. 30.

7. General statements about Riordan's superior abilities and his disillusionment can be found in the following: Coolidge, *Navajo Indians*, pp. 252–53; Underhill, *Navajos*, pp. 171–72; Telling, "New Mexico Frontiers," pp. 109–10; Locke, *Book of the Navajo*, pp. 410–11; and Terrell, *Navajo*, pp. 274–75.

8. *RCIA*, 1883, pp. 119–20. Also quoted in Underhill, *Navajos*, pp. 171–72.

9. Underhill, *Navajos*, pp. 171–72; and Reeve, "Government and the Navaho, 1883–1888," pp. 19 and 29.

10. Reeve, "Government and the Navaho, 1883–1888," p. 23; Bailey and

Bailey, *History of the Navajos*, p. 35; and Aberle, *Peyote Religion*, pp. 34–35.

11. Underhill, *Navajos*, p. 172; and Reeve, "Government and the Navaho, 1883–1888," p. 29.

12. Reeve, "Government and the Navaho, 1883–1888," pp. 28–30; Cline, *They Came to the Mountain*, pp. 194–96; and Frank C. Lockwood, *Arizona Characters* (Los Angeles: Times-Mirror Press, 1928), pp. 170–72.

13. Lockwood, *Arizona Characters*, pp. 170–72; Reeve, "Government and the Navaho, 1883–1888," pp. 30–31; Cline, *They Came to the Mountain*, pp. 162 and 197.

14. Underhill, *Navajos*, p. 172; Telling, "New Mexico Frontiers," p. 110; and Reeve, "Government and the Navaho, 1883–1888," pp. 31 and 44.

15. Reeve, "Government and the Navaho, 1883–1888," pp. 44 and 48–49; McNitt, *Indian Traders*, p. 50; Underhill, *Navajos*, pp. 172–73; Hagan, *Indian Rights Association*, p. 114; and Telling, "New Mexico Frontiers," pp. 111–12.

16. Telling, "New Mexico Frontiers," pp. 112–13; McNitt, *Indian Traders*, pp. 277–78; and Young, *The Role of the Navajo*, pp. 51–52.

17. Telling, "New Mexico Frontiers," p. 113; Underhill, *Navajos*, p. 210; Van Valkenburgh, *Short History*, p. 51; Wilken, *Anselm Weber*, p. 76; Newcomb, *Hosteen Klah*, pp. 113–14; "A Plan for Advancement of Education Among the Navajos," *IRA*, pp. 17–19; "The Navajo Indians," *IRA*, 1894, pp. 14 and 17–18; Young and Morgan, *Trouble at Round Rock*, p. 19; Aberle, *Peyote Religion*, p. 90; Hoopes, "Indian Rights Association," pp. 29–30; and Trennert, "Fairs, Expositions," pp. 133–40.

18. Irvine to Commissioner, April 6, 1876, *OIA*.

19. Manuelito's statement was remembered and repeated in translation by Henry Chee Dodge. See Locke, *Book of the Navajo*, p. 409; and Pavlik, "Short History," p. 27.

20. The story of Manuelito's sons at Carlisle is told in a number of sources. See Pavlik, "Short History," p. 28; Bender, *"New Hope for the Indians,"* p. 200; Underhill, *Navajos*, p. 207; Bailey and Bailey, *History of the Navajos*, p. 65; Hoffman, *Navajo Biographies*, pp. 101–2; Locke, *Book of the Navajo*, p. 409; and Warner, "Fertile Ground," p. 199. See also Riordan to Captain R. H. Pratt, Carlisle, PA, August 13, 1883, *LB*.

21. Riordan to Pratt, September 27, 1883, *LB*.

22. Underhill, *Navajos*, pp. 207–8; Warner, "Fertile Ground," p. 199; Bailey and Bailey, *History of the Navajos*, p. 65; Hoffman, *Navajo Biographies*, pp. 101–2; Shipley to Commissioner, September 19, 1819, *LB*; and *RCIA*, 1889, p. 259.

23. Attendance figures for the schools are available in the following: *RCIA*, 1883, p. 122, 1886, p. lxxix, and 1889, pp. 258–59; Bailey and Bailey, *History of the Navajos*, p. 65; Young, *The Role of the Navajo*, p. 50; Mitchell, p. 74n; and Shepardson, *Navajo Ways*, p. 14.

24. Quoted in Mangiante, "History of Fort Defiance," p. 75.

25. *RCIA*, 1884, p. 135, 1887, p. 173, and 1889, pp. 258–59; Bailey and Bailey, *History of the Navajos*, p. 65; and Young, *Role of the Navajo*, p. 50.

26. Young, *Role of the Navajo*, p. 58; Bailey and Bailey, *History of the Navajos*, p. 65; Mangiante, "History of Fort Defiance," pp. 75–76; *RCIA*, 1887, p. 173 and 1889, pp. 258–59; and *IRA*, 1889, p. 7.

27. Van Valkenburgh, "Navajo Naa'taani," p. 18; and McNitt, *Indian Traders*, pp. 277–79.

28. McNitt, *Indian Traders*, p. 279; Brugge, "Henry Chee Dodge," p. 96; and Shipley to Commissioner, November 2, 1892, *LR*.

29. Young and Morgan, *Trouble at Round Rock*, pp. 24–26.

30. Ibid., pp. 9–10 and 26–35; McNitt, *Indian Traders*, pp. 280–81; Wilken, *Anselm Weber*, pp. 100–102; Brugge, "Henry Chee Dodge," p. 96; and Shipley to Commissioner, November 2, 1892, *LR*.

31. Shipley to Commissioner, November 2, 1892, *LR*; and Young and Morgan, *Trouble at Round Rock*, pp. 11–12.

32. The Letter Books of the Navajo Agency and the newspapers in Gallup and Farmington, NM, as well as the annual commissioners' reports are full of examples of this border conflict. They are, however, too extensive to cite here but will undoubtedly be cited as an extensive study of this period of Navajo history is written. Some secondary works mention this conflict but only superficially. The most extensive studies are those which deal with problems to the north and east. See Brugge, *History of the Chaco Navajos*, pp. 104–50; and McPherson, *Northern Navajo Frontier*, pp. 21–95.

33. White, *Roots of Dependency*, pp. 244–45; and David F. Aberle, "Statement for Submission to the Senate Committee on Indian and Insular Affairs, July 24, 1974," in *Navajo-Hopi Land Dispute: Hearing Before the Committee on Interior and Insular Affairs, United States Senate 2nd Session on HR10337, S.3230, S.2424 and S.3724* (Washington, D.C.: GPO, 1974), pp. 4–8.

34. Aberle, "Statement," pp. 4–8; Mitchell, *Navajo Blessingway Singer*, pp 38–40; and Charles H. Stephens, "The Origin and History of the Hopi-Navajo Boundary Dispute in Northern Arizona" (master's thesis, Brigham Young University, 1961), p. 68.

35. Nagata, *Modern Transformations*, pp. 31–33; and Littell, *Proposed Findings*, vol. 5, pp. 1063–64.

36. Littell, *Proposed Findings*, vol. 5, p. 1064; John J. Wood, Walter M. Vanette, and Michael J. Andrews, *A Sociocultural Assessment of the Livestock Reduction Program in the Navajo-Hopi Joint Use Area* (Flagstaff: Department of Anthropology, Northern Arizona University, 1979), p. 21; James, *Pages from Hopi History*, p. 101; Frank Waters, *Book of the Hopi* (New York: Penguin Books, 1963), pp. 287–89; and Stephens, "Origin and History," pp. 67–74.

37. Stephens, "Origin and History," pp. 81–82; Aberle, "Statement," p. 9; and Wood et al., *Sociocultural Assessment*, p. 22.

38. Stephens, "Origin and History," pp. 82–84; Coolidge, *Navajo Indians*, p. 257; and Hagan, *Indian Rights Association*, p. 68.

39. Hoopes, "Indian Rights Association," pp. 27–28; McPherson, *Northern Navajo Frontier*, pp. 33–36; Peterson, *Take Up Your Mission*, pp. 202–3; and Correll, "Killing of Lot Smith."

40. Correll, "Killing of Lot Smith"; McPherson, *Northern Navajo Frontier*, p. 36; and Lieutenant R. E. L. Michie to Assistant Adjutant General, Department of Arizona, *LR*. For statements concerning Smith's character, see Peterson, *Take Up Your Mission*, p. 16; McClintock, *Mormon Settlement*, p. 160; and Earle R. Forrest, *Arizona's Dark and Bloody Ground* (Tucson: University of Arizona Press, 1984 [repr., 1950 ed.]), pp. 328–29n. For brief mention of Smith's murder, see Van Valkenburgh, *Short History*, p. 52; and Young and Morgan, *Trouble at Round Rock*, p. 8.

41. McPherson, *Northern Navajo Frontier*, p. 36; Correll, "Killing of Lot Smith"; Michie to AA General, July 13, 1892, and Shipley to Commissioner, August 30, 1892, *LR*; and the following are all in *LB:* Shipley to Commissioner, July 1, August 30, and November 11, 1892, Shipley to Dennis M. Riordan, Flagstaff, August 30, 1892, and Shipley to A. D. Ross, Flagstaff, August 30, 1892.

42. Bowman to Whom It May Concern, October 6, 1884, and Patterson to Colonel Crofton, Fort Wingate, September 23, 1886, *LB*; Robert M. Utley, *Billy the Kid: A Short and Violent Life* (Lincoln: University of Nebraska Press, 1989), pp. 160–61; and Bailey, *Indian Slave Trade*, pp. 133–34.

43. Bailey, *Indian Slave Trade*, pp. 134–36; *RCIA*, 1884, p. 136; Hoffman, *Navajo Biographies*, pp. 101–2; and Gillmore and Wetherill, *Traders*, p. 180.

44. Klink, *Land Enough*, p. 33; and Kelly, "Hoskaninni," p. 223.

45. Bennally et al., *Utah Navajo History*, p. 150; and Correll, "Navajo Frontiers," pp. 151–52.

46. Correll, "Navajo Frontiers," pp. 153–54. See also, J. Lee Correll, "Chief Hashkeneinii and the Monument Valley Murders," *Navajo Times*, May 5 and 12, 1966.

47. McNitt, *Indian Traders*, pp. 181–82; and Correll, "Navajo Frontiers," p. 154.

48. Correll, "Navajo Frontiers," p. 155; and Richard Van Valkenburgh, "Blood Revenge of the Navajo," *Desert Magazine* 6 (October 1943): 22–23.

49. Correll, "Navajo Frontiers," pp. 155–60; and Bowman to Commissioner, July 3, 11, 12, and August 5 and 25, 1884, and Bowman to Post Commander, Fort Wingate, December 18, 1884, *LB*.

50. Bowman to Commissioner, January 30 and February 2, 1885, *LB*.

51. For a sympathetic portrayal of Hoskininni as an old man see: Gillmor and Wetherill, *Traders*, pp. 135, 152–54, 157–59, and 172–81.

52. Riordan to Commissioner, July 11, 1883, *LB*; and Reeve, "Government and the Navaho, 1883–1888," pp. 20 and 39.

53. Bowman to Commissioner, July 24 and September 30, 1884, *LB*; and Aberle, *Peyote Religion*, p. 35.

54. Vandever to Commissioner, February 26, 1889, *LB*.

55. Vandever to Commissioner, September 2, 1890, *LB*.

56. Shipley to Commissioner, June 1 and September 19, 1891, and March 4, 1894, *LB*.

57. McNitt, *Indian Traders*, p. 203n.

58. Ibid.; Aberle, *Peyote Religion*, p. 36; Locke, *Book of the Navajo*, p. 420; Wilken, *Anselm Weber*, p. 175; and *McKinley County Republican* (Gallup), December 16, 1905.

Conclusion

1. James Mooney, *The Ghost Dance Religion and Wounded Knee* (New York: Dover Publications, 1973 [repr., 1896 ed., "The Ghost Dance Religion and the Sioux Outbreak of 1890"]), pp. 763–64. See also: Utley, *Indian Frontier*, pp. 251–52; and L. G. Moses, *The Indian Man: A Biography of James Mooney* (Urbana: University of Illinois Press, 1984), pp. 67–68.

2. Josephy, pp. 17–23; and Mooney, pp. 662–745.

3. Utley, *Indian Frontier*, pp. 255–59.

4. Mooney, pp. 809–11; Moses, *Indian Man*, pp. 94–95; and W. W. Hill, "The Navaho Indians and the Ghost Dance of 1890," *American Anthropologist* 46 (1944): 523–24.

5. Lonnie E. Underhill and Daniel F. Littlefield, Jr., "Hamlin Garland and the Navajos," *Journal of Arizona History* 13 (Winter 1972): 275–85; and McNitt, *Indian Traders*, p. 193.

6. "On the Boundaries of Empire: Connecting the West to Its Imperial Past," in *Under an Open Sky: Rethinking America's Western Past*, ed. William Cronon, George Miles, and Jay Gitlin (New York: W. W. Norton and Co., 1992), p. 73.

Bibliography

Public Documents

Aberle, David F. "Statement for Submission to the Senate Committee on Indian and Insular Affairs, July 24, 1974," in *Navajo-Hopi Land Dispute: Hearing Before the Committee on Interior and Insular Affairs, United States Senate 2nd Session on HR10337, S.3230, S.2424 and S.3724*. Washington, D.C.: GPO, 1974.

Commissioner of Indian Affairs. *Annual Report*, 1864–1880.

Correll, J. Lee, ed. *Through White Men's Eyes: A Contribution to Navajo History, A Chronological Record of the Navajo People from Earliest Times to the Treaty of June 1, 1868*, 6 vols. Window Rock, AZ: Navajo Heritage Center, 1979.

National Archives. *Interior Department, Appointment Papers: New Mexico, Navajo Indian Agency, 1872–1902*.

National Archives. *Record Group 75, Letters Received, Office of Indian Affairs, 1881–1907*.

National Archives. *Record Group 75, Letters Received, New Mexico Indian Superintendency*.

National Archives. *Record Group 75, Letters Received, Office of Indian Affairs, New Mexico Superintendency, 1849–1880*.

National Archives. *Record Group 98, War Department, Department of New Mexico*.

National Archives. *Returns from U.S. Military Posts, 1800–1916: Fort Wingate, NM, January 1872–December 1882*.

Selected Letters from the Letter Books of the Navajo Indian Agency (microfilm copy at Northern Arizona University, Special Collections).

Unpublished Works

Clark, Hartaill Lloyd. "History of San Juan County, New Mexico." Master's thesis, University of Tulsa, 1963.

Daniels, Howard F. "Mormon Colonization in Northern Arizona." Master's thesis, University of Arizona, 1960.

Johnson, Philip. "The Bravest Man I Ever Knew," n.d. Copy in Northern Arizona Library, Special Collections.

Lyon, William H. "Navajo History and Culture." Northern Arizona University, 1984.

Mangiante, Roscal. "History of Fort Defiance: 1851–1900." Master's thesis, University of Arizona, 1950.

Pyle, John Erasmus. "Diary, January 1–November 27, 1878: Kept as Navajo Indian Agent, Fort Defiance." Bancroft Library, University of California, Berkeley.

Stephens, Charles H. "The Origin and History of the Hopi-Navajo Boundary Dispute in Northern Arizona." Master's thesis, Brigham Young University, 1961.

Telling, Irving. "New Mexico Frontiers: A Social History of the Gallup Area, 1881–1901." Master's thesis, Harvard University, 1952.

Tietjen, Gary. "Encounters with the Frontier." Los Alamos, NM, 1969 (copy in Gallup Public Library, Gallup, NM).

Newspapers

Arizona Weekly Miner (Prescott).
McKinley County Republican (Gallup, NM).
Navajo Times (Window Rock, AZ).
Santa Fe Daily New Mexican.

Books

Aberle, David F. *The Peyote Religion Among the Navajo.* Chicago: Aldine Publishing Co., 1966.

Atheran, Robert G. *William Tecumseh Sherman and the Settlement of the West.* Norman: University of Oklahoma Press, 1956.

Bailey, Garrick and Roberta Glenn Bailey. *A History of the Navajos: The Reservation Years.* Santa Fe: School of American Research Press, 1986.

Bailey, Lynn R. *Bosque Redondo: An American Concentration Camp.* Pasadena, CA: Socio-Technical Books, 1970.

———. *Indian Slave Trade in the Southwest.* Los Angeles: Westernlore Press, 1966.

Bailey, Paul. *Jacob Hamblin: Buckskin Apostle.* Los Angeles: Westernlore Press, 1948.

Ball, Larry D. *United States Marshalls of New Mexico and Arizona.* Albuquerque: University of New Mexico Press, 1978.

Beadle, J. H. *The Undeveloped West; or Five Years in the Territories.* Philadelphia: National Publishing Co., 1873.

Bennally, Clyde with Andrew O. Wiget, John R. Alley, and Garry Blake. *A Utah Navajo History.* Monticello, UT: San Juan School District, 1982.

Bender, Norman J., ed. *Missionaries, Outlaws, and Indians: Taylor F. Ealy at Lincoln and Zuni, 1878–1881.* Albuquerque: University of New Mexico Press, 1984.

———. *"New Hope for the Indians": The Grant Peace Policy and the Navajos in the 1870s.* Albuquerque: University of New Mexico Press, 1989.

BIBLIOGRAPHY

Berkhoffer, Robert F. *The White Man's Indian*. NY: Vintage Books, 1978.

Bighorse, Tiana. *Bighorse the Warrior*. ed. Noel Bennett. Tucson: University of Arizona Press, 1990.

Billington, Ray Allen. *America's Frontier Heritage*. Albuquerque: University of New Mexico Press, 1974.

Blue, Martha. *The Witch Purge of 1878: Oral and Documentary History in the Early Navajo Reservation Years*. Tsaile, AZ: Navajo Community College Press, 1988.

Bourke, John G. *Snake Dance of the Moquis*. Tucson: University of Arizona Press, 1984 (reprint of 1884 ed.).

Brown, James S. *Life of a Pioneer: Being the Autobiography of James S. Brown*. Salt Lake City: George O. Cannon and Sons, 1900.

Brugge, David M. *A History of the Chaco Navajos*. Albuquerque: National Park Service, 1980.

————. *Navajos in the Catholic Church Records of New Mexico: 1690–1875*. Window Rock, AZ: The Navajo Tribe, 1968.

Bryant, Keith L., Jr. *History of the Atchison, Topeka and Santa Fe Railway*. Lincoln: University of Nebraska Press, 1974.

Bullock, Henry Allen. *A History of Negro Education in the South: From 1619 to the Present*. Cambridge: Harvard University Press, 1967.

Carroll, John M., ed. *The Black Military Experience in the American West*, short ed. NY: Liveright, 1973.

Cleaveland, Agnes Morely. *No Life for a Lady*. Boston: Houghton Mifflin Co., 1941.

Cline, Platt. *They Came to the Mountain: The Story of Flagstaff's Beginnings*. Flagstaff, AZ: Northland Press, 1976.

Colton, Ray C. *The Civil War in the Western Territories: Arizona, Colorado, New Mexico, and Utah*. Norman: University of Oklahoma Press, 1959.

Coolidge, Dane and Mary Roberts Coolidge. *The Navajo*. Boston: Houghton Mifflin Co., 1930.

Crampton, C. Gregory. *Land of Living Rock*. NY: Alfred A. Knopf, 1972.

Cronon, William, George Miles, and Jay Gitlin. *Under an Open Sky: Rethinking America's Western Past*. NY: W. W. Norton, 1992.

Cummings, Byron. *Indians I Have Known*. Tucson: Arizona Silhouettes, 1952.

Dippie, Bryan W. *The Vanishing American: White Attitudes and U.S. Indian Policy*. Middletown, CT: Wesleyan University Press, 1982.

Dobie, J. Frank. *Apache Gold and Yaqui Silver*. Albuquerque: University of New Mexico Press, 1971 (reprint of 1928 ed.).

Downs, James F. *The Navajo*. NY: Holt, Rinehart and Winston, 1972.

Dunley, Thomas W. *Wolves for the Blue Soldiers: Indian Scouts and Auxiliaries with the United States Army, 1860–90*. Lincoln: University of Nebraska Press, 1982.

Dyk, Walter, ed. *Old Mexican: A Navaho Biography*. NY: Johnson Reprint Corp., 1967 (reprint of 1947 ed.).

————. *Son of Old Man Hat: A Navajo Autobiography*. Lincoln: University of Nebraska Press, 1938.

BIBLIOGRAPHY

Edmunds, R. David. *Studies in Diversity: American Indian Leaders.* Lincoln: University of Nebraska Press, 1980.

Emmett, Chris. *Fort Union and the Winning of the Southwest.* Norman: University of Oklahoma Press, 1965.

Emmitt, Robert. *The Last War Trail: The Utes and the Settlement of Colorado.* Norman: University of Oklahoma Press, 1954.

Farish, Thomas Edwin. *History of Arizona,* 8 vols. Phoenix: Thomas Edwin Farish, 1918.

Faulk, Odie B. *Arizona: A Short History.* Norman: University of Oklahoma Press, 1970.

Faunce, Hilda. *Desert Wife.* Lincoln: University of Nebraska Press, 1981 (reprint of 1928 ed.).

Federal Writers Project. *Arizona: A State Guide.* NY: Hastings House, 1940.

Fergusson, Erna. *Our Southwest.* NY: Alfred E. Knopf, 1940.

Forbes, Jack D. *Apache, Navaho, and Spaniard.* Norman: University of Oklahoma Press, 1960.

Forrest, Earle R. *Arizona's Dark and Bloody Ground.* Tucson: University of Arizona Press, 1984 (reprint of 1950 ed.).

Frazier, Robert W. *Forts of the West: Military Forts and Presidios and Posts Commonly Called Forts West of the Mississippi River to 1898.* Norman: University of Oklahoma Press, 1965.

Furnham, Agnes Miller. *Tohta: An Early History of Farmington and San Juan County, New Mexico, 1875–1900.* Wichita, TX: Nortex Press, 1977.

Gillmor, Frances and Louisa Wade Wetherill. *Traders to the Navajos: The Story of the Wetherills of Kayenta.* Albuquerque: University of New Mexico Press, 1953.

Goodman, James M. *The Navajo Atlas: Environment, Resources, People, and History of the Dine Bikeyah.* Norman: University of Oklahoma Press, 1982.

Gottfredson, Peter. *History of Indian Depredations in Utah.* Salt Lake City: Skelton Publishing Co., 1919.

Granger, Byrd H., rev. *Will C. Barnes' Arizona Place Names.* Tucson: University of Arizona Press, 1960.

Green, Jesse, ed. *Zuni: Selected Writings of Frank Hamilton Cushing.* Lincoln: University of Nebraska Press, 1979.

Hagan, William T. *American Indians.* Chicago: University of Chicago Press, 1961.

———. *The Indian Rights Associations: The Herbert Welsh Years, 1882–1907.* Tucson: University of Arizona Press, 1985.

Haile, Berard. *Soul Concepts of the Navajo.* Rome: Vatican Polygot Press, 1943.

Heitman, Francis B., ed. *Historical Register and Dictionary of the United States Army, from Its Organization, September 29, 1789, to March 2, 1903,* vol. 1. Washington, D.C.: GPO, 1903.

Hoffman, Virginia. *Navajo Biographies,* vol. I. Rough Rock, AZ: Rough Rock Demonstration School, 1974.

Hollen, W. Eugene. *Frontier Violence: Another Look.* NY: Oxford University Press, 1974.

Horgan, Paul. *Lamy of Santa Fe: His Life and Times.* NY: Farrar, Straus and Giroux, 1975.

Horr, David Agee, ed. *Navajo Indians II: American Indian Ethnohistory of the Southwest.* NY: Garland Publishing Co., 1974.

———, ed. *Ute Indians II: American Indian Ethnohistory of the Southwest.* NY: Garland Publishing Co., 1974.

Howard, O. O. *Famous Indian Chiefs I Have Known.* Lincoln: University of Nebraska Press, 1989 (reprint of 1908 ed.).

———. *My Experience Among Our Hostile Indians: A Record of Personal Observations, Adventures, and Campaigns Among the Indians of the Great West with Some Accounts of Their Life, Habits, Traits, Religion, Ceremonies, Dress, Savage Instincts, and Customs in Peace and War.* NY: Da Capo Press, 1972 (reprint of 1909 ed.).

Hunt, Aurora. *Major General James Henry Carleton, 1814–1873: Western Frontier Dragoon.* Glendale, CA: The Arthur Clark Co., 1958.

Hutton, Paul Andrew. *Soldiers West: Biographies from the Military Frontier.* Lincoln: University of Nebraska Press, 1987.

Iverson, Peter. *The Navajo Nation.* Albuquerque: University of New Mexico Press, 1981.

James, George W. *Indians of the Painted Desert.* Boston: Brown, Little, Brown and Co., 1919.

James, Harry C. *Pages from Hopi History.* Tucson: University of Arizona Press, 1974.

Jefferson, James, Robert W. Delany, and Gregory C. Thompson. *The Southern Utes: A Tribal History,* ed. Floyd A. O'Neil. Ignacio, CO: Southern Ute Tribe, 1972.

Jones, Thomas Jesse. *The Navajo Indian Problem.* NY: Phelps-Stokes Fund, 1939.

Josephy, Alvin M., Jr. *The Patriot Chiefs: A Chronicle of American Indian Resistance.* NY: The Viking Press, 1958.

Judd, Neil M. *Men Met Along the Trail.* Norman: University of Oklahoma Press, 1968.

Keleher, William A. *The Fabulous Frontier: Twelve New Mexico Items,* rev. ed. Albuquerque: University of New Mexico Press, 1962.

Keller, Robert H., Jr. *American Protestantism and United States Indian Policy.* Lincoln: University of Nebraska Press, 1983.

Kelly, Lawrence C. *The Navajo Indians and Federal Indian Policy.* Tucson: University of Arizona Press, 1968.

Klink, Richard E. *Land of Room Enough and Time Enough.* Albuquerque: University of New Mexico Press, 1973.

Kluckhohn, Clyde. *Navajo Witchcraft.* Boston: Beacon Press, 1967.

Kluckhohn, Clyde and Dorothea Leighton. *The Navaho,* rev. ed. Garden City, NY: Doubleday, 1962.

337

Lange, Charles H. and Carroll L. Riley, eds. *The Southwestern Journals of Adolf F. Bandelier*. Albuquerque: University of New Mexico Press, 1966.

Larson, Andrew Karl. *Erastus Snow: The Life of a Missionary Pioneer for the Early Mormon Church*. Salt Lake City: University of Utah Press, 1971.

Larson, Robert W. *New Mexico's Quest for Statehood: 1846–1970*. Albuquerque: University of New Mexico Press, 1968.

Laut, Agnes C. *Through Our Unknown Southwest: The Wonderland of the United States—Little Known and Unappreciated—The Home of the Cliff Dweller and the Hopi, the Forest Ranger and the Navajo—The Lure of the Painted Desert*. NY: Robert M. McBride and Co., 1913.

Leckie, William H. *The Buffalo Soldiers: A Narrative of the Negro Cavalry in the West*. Norman: University of Oklahoma Press, 1967.

Leupp, Francis E. *The Indian and His Problem*. NY: Charles Scribners Sons, 1910.

Limerick, Patricia Nelson. *The Legacy of Conquest: The Unbroken Past of the American West*. NY: W. W. Norton, 1987.

Littell, Norman M. *Proposed Findings of Fact in Behalf of the Navajo Tribe of Indians in the Area of the Overall Claim (Dockett 229) Before the Indian Claims Commission*. Window Rock, AZ: Navajo Tribal Printing Section, 1967.

Little, James A. *Jacob Hamblin: A Narrative of His Personal Experience, Missionary to the Indians and Explorer*. Freeport, NY: Books For Libraries Press, 1971 (reprint of 1881 ed.).

Locke, Raymond Friday. *The Book of the Navajo*. Los Angeles: Mankind Publishing Co., 1976.

Lockwood, Frank C., ed. *Apaches and Longhorns: The Reminiscences of Will C. Barnes*. Los Angeles: The Ward Ritchie Press, 1941.

———. *Arizona Characters*. Los Angeles: Times-Mirror Press, 1928.

———. *Pioneer Portraits: Selected Vignettes*. Tucson: University of Arizona Press, 1968.

Luh, Jules. *Lords of the Earth: A History of the Navajo Indians*. NY: Crowell-Collier Press, 1971.

McClintock, James H. *Mormon Settlement in Arizona*. Tucson: University of Arizona Press, 1985 (reprint of 1921 ed.).

McNitt, Frank. *The Indian Traders*. Norman: University of Oklahoma Press, 1962.

———. *Navajo Wars: Military Campaigns, Slave Raids, and Reprisals*. Albuquerque: University of New Mexico Press, 1972.

———. *Richard Wetherill: Anasazi, Pioneer Explorer of Southwestern Ruins*, rev. ed. Albuquerque: University of New Mexico Press, 1966.

McPherson, Robert S. *The Northern Navajo Frontier, 1860–1900: Expansion Through Adversity*. Albuquerque: University of New Mexico Press, 1988.

Martin, Douglas D. *An Arizona Chronology: The Territorial Years, 1846–1912*. Tucson: University of Arizona Press, 1963.

Mathews, Washington. *Navajo Legends*. Boston: American Folklore Society, 1897.

Mitchell, Frank. *Navajo Blessingway Singer*, ed. Charlotte J. Frisbie and David McAllester. Tucson: University of Arizona Press, 1978.

Mooney, James. *The Ghost Dance Religion and Wounded Knee*. NY: Dover Publications, 1973 (reprint of 1896 ed., "The Ghost Dance Religion and the Sioux Outbreak of 1890").

Moses, L. G. and Raymond Wilson, eds. *Indian Lives: Essays on Nineteenth- and Twentieth-Century Native American Leaders*. Albuquerque: University of New Mexico Press, 1985.

Moses, L. G. *The Indian Man: A Biography of James Mooney*. Urbana: University of Illinois Press, 1984.

Murphy, Lawrence R. *Frontier Crusader: William F. M. Arny*. Tucson: University of Arizona Press, 1972.

————, ed. *Indian Agent in New Mexico: The Journal of Special Agent W. F. M. Arny, 1870*. Santa Fe: Stage Coach Press, 1976.

Myrick, David F. *Arizona Pioneer Railroads*. Golden, CO: Colorado Railroad Museum, 1968.

Nagata, Shuichi. *Modern Transformations at MoenKopi Pueblo*. Urbana: University of Illinois Press, 1970.

Newcomb, Franc Johnson. *Hosteen Klah: Navaho Medicine Man and Sand Painter*. Norman: University of Oklahoma Press, 1964.

————. *Navaho Neighbors*. Norman: University of Oklahoma Press, 1966.

Ogle, Ralph Hedrick. *Federal Control of the Western Apaches: 1848–1886*. Albuquerque: University of New Mexico Press, 1970.

Parman, Donald L. *The Navajos and the New Deal*. New Haven: Yale University Press, 1976.

Pearce, T. M. *New Mexico Place Names: A Geographical Dictionary*. Albuquerque: University of New Mexico Press, 1965.

Peplow, Edward H., Jr. *History of Arizona*, vol. 2. NY: Lewis Historical Publishing Co., 1958.

Perkinson, Henry J. *The Imperfect Panacea: American Faith in Education, 1865–1965*. NY: Random House, 1968.

Peterson, Charles S. *Take Up Your Mission: Mormon Colonizing Along the Little Colorado River, 1870–1900*. Tucson: University of Arizona Press, 1973.

Porter, Joseph C. *Paper Medicine Man: John Gregory Bourke and His American West*. Norman: University of Oklahoma Press, 1986.

Powell, John Wesley. *The Exploration of the Colorado River and Its Canyons*. NY: Dover Publications, 1961 (reprint of 1895 ed., *Canyons of the Colorado*).

Powell, Lawrence Clark. *Southwest Classics*. Tucson: University of Arizona Press, 1974.

Prucha, Francis Paul. *American Indian Policy in Crisis: Christian Reformers and the Indian, 1865–1900*. Norman: University of Oklahoma Press, 1964.

————. *The Great Father: The United States Government and the American Indians*, 2 vols. Lincoln: University of Nebraska Press, 1984.

Pulliam, John D. *History of Education in America*, 3rd ed. Columbus, OH: Charles E. Merrill Publishing Co., 1982.

Reichard, Gladys. *Navaho Religion: A Study of Symbolism.* Princeton, NJ: Princeton University Press, 1977 (reprint of 1950 ed.).

Richardson, Gladfield. *Two Guns, Arizona.* Santa Fe: Bluefeather Press, 1968.

Rockwell, Wilson. *The Utes: A Forgotten People.* Denver: Sage Books, 1956.

Roessel, Robert A., Jr. *A Pictorial History of the Navajo from 1860 to 1910.* Rough Rock, AZ: Navajo Curriculum Center, 1980.

Roessel, Ruth, ed. *Navajo Stories of the Long Walk Period.* Tsaile, AZ: Navajo Community College Press, 1973.

Roosevelt, Nicholas. *Theodore Roosevelt: The Man As I Knew Him.* NY: Dodd, Mead and Co., 1967.

Rusho, W. L. and C. Gregory Crampton. *Desert River Crossing.* Santa Barbara, CA: Peregrine Smith, Inc., 1981.

Sandner, Donald. *Navaho Symbols of Healing: A Jungian Exploration of Ritual, Image, and Medicine.* Rochester, VT: Healing Arts Press, 1991 (reprint of 1979 ed.).

Schmedding, Joseph. *Cowboy and Indian Trader.* Albuquerque: University of New Mexico Press, 1974 (reprint of 1951 ed.).

Schroeder, Albert H., ed. *The Changing Ways of Southwestern Indians.* Glorieta, NM: Rio Grande Press, 1973.

Shepardson, Mary. *Navajo Ways in Government.* Menasha, WI: American Anthropological Association, 1963.

Shinkle, James D. *Fort Sumner and the Bosque Redondo Reservation.* Roswell, NM: Hall-Poorbaugh Press, 1965.

Simmons, Marc. *New Mexico: A Bicentennial History.* NY: W. W. Norton, 1977.

Spicer, Edward H. *Cycles of Conquest: The Impact of Spain, Mexico, and the United States on the Indians of the Southwest, 1533–1960.* Tucson: University of Arizona Press, 1962.

Stanley, F. *The Jicarilla Apaches of New Mexico: 1540–1967.* Pampa, TX: Pampa Print Shop, 1967.

Stegner, Wallace. *Beyond the Hundredth Meridian: John Wesley Powell and the Second Opening of the West.* Lincoln: University of Nebraska Press, 1953.

Stout, Joseph A. *Apache Lightning: The Last Great Battles of the Ojo Calientes.* NY: Oxford University Press, 1974.

Summerhayes, Martha. *Vanished Arizona.* Lincoln: University of Nebraska Press, 1979 (reprint of 1911 ed.).

Terrell, John Upton. *The Navajos: The Past and Present of a Great People.* NY: Perennial Library, 1972.

Thompson, Gerald. *The Army and the Navajo: The Bosque Redondo Reservation Experiment, 1863–1868.* Tucson: University of Arizona Press, 1976.

Thrapp, Dan L. *The Conquest of Apacheria.* Norman: University of Oklahoma Press, 1967.

———. *Victorio and the Mimbres Apaches.* Norman: University of Oklahoma Press, 1974.

Tiller, Veronica E. Velarde. *The Jicarilla Apache Tribe: A History, 1846–1970.* Lincoln: University of Nebraska Press, 1983.

Trafzer, Clifford E. *The Kit Carson Campaign: The Last Great Navajo War.* Norman: University of Oklahoma Press, 1982.

Twitchell, Ralph Emerson. *The Leading Facts of New Mexican History,* 5 vols. Cedar Rapids, IA: The Torch Press, 1911–1912.

Underhill, Ruth M. *Here Come the Navajo!* Lawrence, KS: U.S. Indian Service, 1953.

——. *The Navajos.* Norman: University of Oklahoma Press, 1956.

Utley, Robert M. *Billy the Kid: A Short and Violent Life.* Lincoln: University of Nebraska Press, 1989.

——. *The Indian Frontier of the American West: 1846–1890.* Albuquerque: University of New Mexico Press, 1984.

Utley, Robert M. and Wilcomb E. Washburn. *Indian Wars.* NY: American Heritage, 1985.

Van Roekel, Gertrude B. *Jicarilla Apaches.* San Antonio, TX: The Naylor Co., 1971.

Van Valkenburgh, Richard. *A Short History of the Navajo People.* Window Rock, AZ: U.S. Department of Interior, 1938.

Waters, Frank. *Book of the Hopi.* NY: Penguin Books, 1963.

——. *Masked Gods: Navajo and Pueblo Ceremonialism.* Chicago: Swallow Press, 1950.

Waters, L. L. *Steel Trails to Santa Fe.* Lawrence: University of Kansas Press, 1950.

Webb, Walter Prescott. *The Great Plains.* NY: Ginn and Co., 1931.

Westphall, Victor. *Thomas B. Catron and His Era.* Tucson: University of Arizona Press, 1973.

White, Richard. *The Roots of Dependency: Subsistence, Environment, and Social Change Among the Choctaws, Pawnees, and Navajos.* Lincoln: University of Nebraska Press, 1983.

Wilken, Robert L. *Anselm Weber, O.F.M.: Missionary to the Navaho, 1898–1921.* Milwaukee: The Bruce Publishing Co., 1955.

Wood, John J., Walter M. Vanette, and Michael J. Andrews. *A Sociocultural Assessment of the Livestock Reduction Program in the Navajo-Hopi Joint Use Area.* Flagstaff: Department of Anthropology, Northern Arizona University, 1979.

Yazzie, Ethelou. *Navajo History,* vol. 1. Rough Rock, AZ: Navajo Curriculum Center, 1971.

Yost, Billie Williams. *Bread upon the Sands.* Caldwell, ID: The Caxton Printers, 1958.

Young, Robert W. *The Navajo Yearbook.* Window Rock, AZ: Navajo Agency, 1957.

——. *The Role of the Navajo in the Southwestern Drama.* Gallup, NM: The Gallup Independent, 1968.

Young, Robert W. and William Morgan, eds. *The Trouble at Round Rock with Anecdotes by Howard Gorman and The Nephew of Former Big Man.* Phoenix: U.S. Indian Service, 1952.

Zolbrod, Paul G. *Diné Bahane': The Navajo Creation Story.* Albuquerque: University of New Mexico Press, 1984.

Articles

Amsden, Charles Avery. "The Navaho Exile at Bosque Redondo," *New Mexico Historical Review* 8 (January 1933): 31–50.

Breed, Jack. "Flaming Cliffs of Monument Valley." *National Geographic* 22 (October 1945): 462–71.

Brugge, David M. "Henry Chee Dodge: From Long Walk to Self-Determination," in *Indian Lives: Essays on Nineteenth- and Twentieth-Century Native American Leaders,* ed. L. G. Moses and Raymond Wilson. Albuquerque: University of New Mexico Press, 1985.

Buell, Crawford R. "The Navajo 'Long Walk': Recollections by Navajos," in *The Changing Ways of Southwestern Indians,* ed. Albert H. Schroeder. Glorieta, NM: Rio Grande Press, 1973.

Correll, J. Lee. "Chief Hashkeneinii and the Monument Valley Murders," *Navajo Times,* May 5 and 12, 1966.

———. "The Killing of Lot Smith, Noted Mormon, at Tuba City—1892," *Navajo Times,* March 3, 1966.

———. "Navajo Frontiers in Utah and Troublous Times in Monument Valley," *Utah Historical Quarterly* 34 (Spring 1971): 145–61.

Crampton, C. Gregory and David E. Miller, eds. "Journal of Two Campaigns by the Utah Territorial Militia Against the Navajo Indians, 1869," *Utah Historical Quarterly* 29 (April 1961): 149–76.

Eckel, Le Charles G. "History of Ganado, Arizona," *Museum Notes: Museum of Northern Arizona* 6 (April 1934): 47–50.

Erskine, J. M. "The First Settlement of Flagstaff," *The Coconino Sun* (Flagstaff), July 20, 1901.

Gitlin, Jay. "On the Boundaries of Empire: Connecting the West to Its Imperial Past," in *Under an Open Sky: Rethinking America's Western Past,* ed. William Cronon, George Miles, and Jay Gitlin. NY: W. W. Norton, 1992.

Hafen, Leroy R. "Historical Survey of the Ute Indians and the San Juan Mining Region," in *Ute Indians II: American Indian Ethnohistory of the Southwest,* ed. David Agee Horr. NY: Garland Publishing Co., 1974.

Hardeway, Roger D. "Unlawful Love: A History of Arizona's Miscegenation Law," *Journal of Arizona History* 27 (Winter 1986): 377–90.

Hastings, James R. "The Tragedy of Camp Grant in 1871," *Arizona and the West* 1 (Summer 1959): 146–60.

Hill, W. W. "The Navaho Indians and the Ghost Dance of 1890," *American Anthropologist* 46 (1944): 523–27.

Hoopes, Alban W. "The Indian Rights Association and the Navajo, 1890–1895," *New Mexico Historical Review* 21 (January 1946): 22–46.

342

BIBLIOGRAPHY

Jenkins, Mary Ellen. "Navajo Activities Affecting the Acoma-Laguna Area," in *Navajo Indians II: American Indian Ethnohistory of the Southwest*, ed. David Agee Horr. NY: Garland Publishing Co., 1974.

Kelly, Charles. "Chief Hoskaninni," *Utah Historical Quarterly* 21 (July 1953): 219–26.

Kessell, John L. "General Sherman and the Navajo Treaty of 1868: A Basic and Expedient Misunderstanding," *Western Historical Quarterly* 22 (July 1981): 251–72.

McNitt, Frank. "Fort Sumner: A Study in Origins," *New Mexico Historical Review* 45 (April 1970): 101–15.

Osburn, Katherine Marie Birmingham. "The Navajo at the Bosque Redondo: Cooperation, Resistance, and Initiative, 1864–1868," *New Mexico Historical Review* 60 (October 1985): 399–413.

Pate, J'Nell L. "Ronald S. Mackenzie," in *Soldiers West: Biographies from the Military Frontier*, ed. Paul Andrew Hutton. Lincoln: University of Nebraska Press, 1987.

Pavlik, Steve. "A Short History of Navajo Education, Part I," *Journal of Navajo Education* 2 (Winter 1985): 25–34.

Porter, Joseph C. "John G. Bourke," in *Soldiers West: Biographies from the Military Frontier*, ed. Paul Andrew Hutton. Lincoln: University of Nebraska Press, 1987.

Reeve, Frank D. "The Federal Indian Policy in New Mexico, 1855–1880, Part II," *New Mexico Historical Review* 13 (January 1938): 14–62.

————. "The Federal Indian Policy in New Mexico: 1858–1880 III," *New Mexico Historical Review* 13 (April 1938): 146–58.

————. "The Government and the Navaho, 1873–1883," *New Mexico Historical Review* 14 (July 1941): 275–312.

————. "The Government and the Navaho, 1883–1888," *New Mexico Historical Review* 18 (January 1943): 17–51.

————. "A Navaho Struggle for Land," *New Mexico Historical Review* 21 (January 1946): 1–21.

Richardson, Gladfield. "Mystery Cave." *Arizona Days and Ways* (December 3, 1967): 48–51.

Smiley, Winn Whiting. "Ammon M. Tenney: Mormon Missionary to the Indians," *Journal of Arizona History* 13 (Summer 1972): 82–108.

Trennert, Robert A. "Fairs, Expositions, and the Changing Image of Southwestern Indians, 1876–1904," *New Mexico Historical Review* 62 (April 1987): 127–50.

Underhill, Lonnie E. and Daniel F. Littlefield, Jr., "Hamlin Garland and the Navajos," *Journal of Arizona History* 13 (Winter 1972): 275–85.

Van Valkenburgh, Richard. "Blood Revenge of the Navajo," *Desert Magazine* 6 (October 1943): 19–23.

————. "Navajo Common Law I," *Museum Notes: Museum of Northern Arizona* 9 (October 1936): 17–22.

————. "Navajo Common Law II," *Museum Notes: Museum of Northern Arizona* 9 (April 1937): 51–54.

———. "Navajo Naa'taani." *The Kiva* 13 (January 1948): 14–21.

Warner, Michael J. "The Fertile Ground: The Beginnings of Protestant Missionary Work with the Navajos, 1852–1890," in *The Changing Ways of Southwestern Indians*, ed. Albert H. Schroeder. Glorieta, NM: Rio Grande Press, 1973.

Weber, Anselm. "Navajo Indians," *The Catholic Encyclopedia* 10. NY: Robert Appleton Co., 1911, p. 720.

Wilson, James Q. "The Rise of the Bureaucratic State," in *Public Administration: Concepts and Cases*, 3rd ed., ed. Richard J. Stillman II. Boston: Houghton Mifflin Co., 1984.

Index